Social Trends & Indicators USA

Volume 1:
Work & Leisure

Social Trends & Indicators USA

Volume 1: Work & Leisure

Arsen J. Darnay, Managing Editor

Monique D. Magee, Editor

Helen S. Fisher, Robert Lazich,
Joyce Piwowarski, and Linda Schmittroth,
Assistant Editors

GALE®

THOMSON
★
GALE

Detroit • New York • San Diego • San Francisco • Cleveland • New Haven, Conn. • Waterville, Maine • London • Munich

Social Trends & Indicators USA
Work & Leisure

Monique D. Magee, Editor

Project Editor
Amanda C. Quick

Editorial
Arsen J. Darnay, Helen S. Fisher, Robert Lazich,
Joyce Piwowarski, Linda Schmittroth

Product Design
Pamela A. E. Galbreath

Manufacturing
NeKita McKee

ISBN 0-7876-5906-1 (set)
ISBN 0-7876-5907-X (v.1)
ISBN 0-7876-5908-8 (v.2)
ISBN 0-7876-5909-6 (v.3)
ISBN 0-7876-5910-X (v.4)
Library of Congress Control Number: 2002117074

Printed in the United States of America
10 9 8 7 6 5 4 3 2 1

TABLE OF CONTENTS

Introduction

Upon this gifted age, in its dark hour,
Rains from the sky a meteoric shower
Of facts ... they lie unquestioned, uncombined.
Wisdom enough to leech us of our ill
Is daily spun; but there exists no loom
To weave it into fabric.
Edna St. Vincent Millay

Social Trends & Indicators – The Concept

The idea for this series, *Social Trends & Indicators USA*, arose because we are inundated by statistics, but the meaning of the numbers is often elusive. We are getting outrageously obese, for instance, yet we are living longer. Layoffs are devastating sectors, yet the economy seems to be booming. We are the most educated society on earth, yet Johnny can't read. The crime rate is dropping, but we do not feel safe. The workweek is shrinking, yet we never have time.

The Federal Government's many statistical agencies produce a great wealth of superb data. We are undoubtedly the best documented and most measured society that has ever existed. Newspapers attractively box factoids to amaze or to alarm us. Competing interests marshal their data to make their cases, often omitting numbers that do not bolster the argument. Statistics become catch-phrases. The rich fabric of our national experience is thinned by the speed and noise of the mass media attempting to "infotain" us.

But statistics out of context — and without historical background — are often less than informative. They can be confusing and lead to wrong conclusions. Whereas a properly developed presentation on an issue, using what numbers are available, is often very revealing, at times sobering, and frequently reassuring. A balanced presentation of facts within context can serve the public by illuminating hidden facets of an issue and, as often happens, show that beneath the hoopla and the hype is a deeper-lying demographic movement.

This series was born from such considerations, and from our long experience in dealing with, and publishing, statistics. The idea, simply, was to present statistics in context, with as much historical background as possible, in order to answer questions and to pinpoint trends.

Organization of the Series

Work & Leisure, the current volume in the series, deals with the whole economic realm — work, productivity, employment, unemployment, income, and fringe benefits — and with how we organize our leisure time. *Community & Education* covers who we are, where we live, all kinds of family structures, race and ethnicity, politics, religion, and the vast subject of education and the many issues it encompasses. *Crime & Justice* attempts to shine a statistical light into the darker woods of our nature — victimization, crime, law enforcement, the drug war, terrorism, the justice system, and how all these matters affect us. *Health & Sickness* takes on the body and the mind and what can go wrong with us — our state of health and illness, old and emerging diseases, risky behaviors, prevention and treatment, our preoccupation with drugs, disability, sexuality, and the people and institutions that deal with us when we are ailing.

Each volume, of course, is divided into chapters. In their totality, the chapters present a fairly complete picture of the subject in each volume. But the objective is not to create a compendium on health and sickness, for instance, but to deal with issues of current concern. Dealing with the issues of today, of course, often causes us to look backwards — all the way back to the 19th century sometimes. But the focus is on current trends and on indicators of what is likely to happen tomorrow.

Each chapter is divided into several so-called "panels" (see below). Panels tend to come in two flavors: those that provide background information on a subject, including general trends, and those aimed specifically at answering a question: "Is government really growing? Which parts? Why?" "Will future jobs all require an advanced degree? No? Why not?" "Why are today's children suddenly so frequently 'learning disabled'?"

The Mode of Presentation: The Panel and the Tables

Each volume in the series presents statistical information in two forms. In Part I of the book, data are presented in graphic format followed by explanations and commentaries.

The principal unit of presentation in Part I is thus a "panel" — one topic, one main graphic, and a commentary of usually no more than two pages. Panels sometimes also feature additional graphics and statistics laid out in tabular format. The text is a discussion of the topic. It may feature footnotes for additional comment. A source note concludes each panel citing the sources used. In most instances, web addresses are provided pointing to sites where the user can obtain additional information.

Sometimes a single panel is not sufficient to develop a subject. In that case, the discussion continues with another panel, with its own graphic. Groups of panels form chapters, and each chapter has a brief introduction.

Users of such works as *Social Trends & Indicators USA* find graphics a vivid way to show data, but they want to see the actual numbers as well. For this reason, *Work & Leisure* produces all of the data graphed in Part II, the Data Presentation. Here, statistical data are presented in tabular format. Frequently only the data used to create the graphics are shown. Sometimes, however, additional time series are provided as well for a more comprehensive documentation of the subject. Tables in Part II are organized by chapters for rapid access. These chapters are organized to correspond to panels in Part I. The tables are also fully indexed.

Accessing Information

Each volume of *Social Trends & Indicators USA* provides a Table of Contents and an Index. The Table of Contents will guide the user to appropriate chapters. The Index lists important concepts, names, institutions, and issues. Page numbers cited refer to the pages where text or data can be found under the topic listed.

Sources of Information

Data presented in *Work & Leisure*, and in the other volumes, come predominantly, but not exclusively, from Federal or State statistical agencies. Data from not-for-profit organizations and from commercial sources are also sometimes shown. Sources of data are always referenced in footnotes or source notes. Where such data are copyrighted, the copyright notice is provided.

An important feature of this series is that data from different sources are analytically combined and presented together. A typical example might be to show birth data in combination with population data on women of child-bearing age. Another might be to show a flow of expenditures but rendered in constant dollars (for comparability year to year) — for which purpose index data from the Consumer Price Index (or the Gross Domestic Product deflator) may have been used to transform the dollar quantities. Data on alcohol, tobacco, and illegal drug consumption — derived from three sources — might be shown together.

Data were obtained using the Internet or from print sources. Web-based data are "sourced" showing the web site from which they were obtained. The links shown, however, are not guaranteed to be functioning at some later date. Most will be accessible because they are predominantly governmental sites. Historical data were obtained from the *Historical Statistics of the United States, Colonial Times to 1970*, published by the Bureau of the Census.

Authorship and Presentation

Work & Leisure was prepared by five individuals (three women, two men), each responsible for chapter-length segments of the book. The authors are all skilled statistical analysts but none is an expert on the subject presented. All members of the editorial group reviewed and discussed every panel contained in this work. Changes, revisions, and augmentation of the material took place as a consequence of these reviews. Finally, all materials were reviewed and edited by the senior editor in charge. However, no attempts were made — or thought to be desirable — to conform the presentational style of the authors to produce a uniform (and possibly bureaucratic-sounding) voice.

Our aim is to present often complicated and difficult subjects — as these are seen by the educated layperson — the view of the proverbial "man on the street." To the extent that expert opinion was required, it was obtained from the literature and is quoted in the panels. We made a serious effort to present as balanced a view as possible, resisting both the temptation to be politically correct and the temptation to range far off the reservation. No doubt people of all persuasions will find fault with something in these panels, all will find something to applaud.

How to Use this Book

Although *Work & Leisure* is, above all, a reference work, it is best approached by actually *reading* a chapter. Within a chapter, the different panels are closely related to develop the subject. The panels are relatively short. It is not difficult to peruse a chapter from beginning to end.

Use of a panel should begin with a close study of the graphic presented (only very few panels lack a graphic). Each graphic has a title. The meaning of the curves and bars is indicated in legends (or shown in the graph itself). Sometimes both the left and the right scale of the graphic is used to measure data sets that would not otherwise be visible. Please note that some of the graphics are in logarithmic scale. The log scale is used when the lowest value charted would be all but invisible — or in cases where the slope of curves is important to show how one set of data is growing more or less than the other. Some graphics are quite "busy," but a little study will well repay the effort. The general message is usually contained in the chart, although, in a few instances, the graphic is just a way of enticing the user to read the text.

Once the graphic is understood, the text will be more accessible. The objective of the text is to make clear what is depicted and then to add other information to put the subject into perspective. Sometimes parts of the information charted are also shown in tabular form in the text itself. This is done in those cases where the numerical values — not merely the pattern that they form — is of great importance. Sometimes additional, smaller graphics are shown to highlight additional aspects of the data or to present new information.

The user who wishes to look at the numbers charted can immediately refer to Part II, which presents data in tabular format.

The source note at the end of the panel may list one or more web sites for more information. The user might wish to be "distracted" into checking out those web sites — or continue on to the next panel until the entire subject is fully developed.

Introduction to this Volume – *Work & Leisure*

Work & Leisure attempts to identify and to explain major trends that impact on our daily round of work, our 9-to-5, our 7-to-4, our night-shift, or our work-at-home. It also tries to address the influences that shape our evenings and our weekends.

Somewhat more than half of the book explores work — or lack of work. In line with our general concept, we focus on the major trends. In summary, they are:

- The services economy. Are we really turning into a society where we make our living taking in each other's laundry? Or, in modern terms, designing each other's Web pages?

- Women in the work force. The big increase in female workforce participation is probably *the* work force issue of the late 20th century. But we also cover the prospects of Generation X, the role played by minorities, and by illegal labor.

- How many jobs does it take to make a living? Have you been outsourced, brother? Is every unemployed person a home-based business? Are we preparing for the right jobs?

- The chapter titled *People and Their Money* reports on the view from the peak of "dot com" mountain — before things suddenly changed. Very significant shifts in income show that the rich are getting much richer, but the poor are also taking part. In future volumes we shall look at the aftermath.

- Increases in income are to a large extent the result of productivity gains. This complex subject gets a reasonably understandable treatment. Who makes the money? Is it people or machines? Or some new-fangled android?

- Women in the work force, again, have made huge changes in the nature and kinds of fringe benefits we all enjoy. We track the trends here. Women have cares that extend beyond the workplace, and the workplace is straining to respond, although it is asking employees to help pay more of a share than heretofore.

- Issues in the workplace center around discrimination — sex, race, and age. It's a lot safer in the workplace, but more litigious. New laws have been causing one tidal wave after the other.

The middle of *Work & Leisure* illuminates leisure in all of its aspects using statistical spotlights. We look, first of all, at *time* and *money*. How much free time do we have? And how much money do we spend on it? There is some reason to think that the family vacation might join the snail darter on the endangered species list. But short vacations are very much "in." Much of leisure used to be devoted to sport. One easy way to enjoy it is to look at other people huff and puff — spectator sports. What are the trends? We try to discern the trends. Then we look at the sports we pursue in our own sweats, and what our children do. Not all the indicators are positive. No wonder we're all growing fatter.

Some of our leisure time is spent doing something for our community. We take a chapter to look at leisure time in our community. Interesting patterns emerge in volunteering and in our church activities. We check the pulse of our libraries. And check in at the community college.

Last but not least, in this wired age, we look at time spent on-line — and at who is hunkered over that keyboard staring at the screen. At first it was young, "nerdish," or wealthy men. Not any more. The profile of the Internet population is looking — surprise! — exactly like the profile of America. And the amazing things we now do in cyberspace...

Comments and Suggestions

Those of us who have labored on *Work & Leisure* — and those who have suffered us while we did so — welcome your comments and suggestions. We have made every effort to be accurate, fair, and complete. No doubt we succeeded only in trying. Should errors have occurred, despite best efforts, they will be corrected in future editions. We shall be pleased to incorporate users' suggestions to the extent possible. To reach authors directly, please call Editorial Code and Data, Inc. at (248) 356-6990.

Please address other communications to:

Editor
Social Trends & Indicators USA
Work & Leisure
Gale
27500 Drake Road
Farmington Hills, MI 48331-3535
248-699-GALE
BusinessProducts@gale.com

Chapter 1

Employment Trends

This chapter highlights trends in employment. We try to answer the question, Where do people work? And, under what institutional arrangements? The first question is a focus on "sectors" of the economy, rather than physical location of jobs. The second examines such things as the subdivisions of the sectors — private and public, profit-making and not-for-profit, unionized and non-union.

The general argument, presented in eight panels, might be framed like this:

- There has been a great deal of change in the way the U.S. economy's sectors are aligned. We were once farmers, later producers of physical goods. Now we are becoming predominantly a services society.

The first two panels present the sectoral changes, first over the span of a century, then over the last 20 years.

- The Services Producing sector has become by far the most dominant employer of people.

We explore some of the reasons why in the third panel. There we focus closely on the fastest growing element of the Services Producing sector, namely "services" as more narrowly defined. A good deal more on this subject is provided in Chapter 5, Productivity and Training, where some of the underlying reasons for this shift are further analyzed.

- Government is said to be growing. Is this borne out by the facts? The Educational Establishment is largely a governmental function in the United States and much in the news for its splendid achievements or dismal failures — all depending on the speakers and the issues. What do the numbers show?

The fourth panel looks at general trends in government employment. We note that federal employment has declined, state government employment grown only slightly, and that most of the growth has been at the local level. This leads to a look at where the growth has been. The answer is, in Education. The fifth panel takes a closer look at this subject. In the sixth panel, we focus more closely on the Federal Government as an employer, and note that defense employment is down, U.S. Postal Service employment is up — the Federal Government's two largest sectors.

- Unions are said to be "in trouble" or "making a comeback." What are the facts here? What are trends in unionized labor in the age of services and of the Internet?

The last two panels in this chapter present interesting information on trends over the last 40 years, with a look back at the beginnings of organized labor. The benefits of working under union contracts are highlighted in the final panel. Changes underlying shifts in union participation are touched upon.

The Sectors – A Century of Change

1900

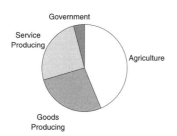

2000

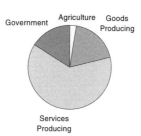

People work in various sectors of the economy. One way to divide the "place" of work is to divide the economy into Agriculture, Goods Producing Activities (mining, construction, manufacturing), Services Producing Activities (transportation, wholesale and retail trade, utilities, finance and its related branches, and "services" narrowly viewed), and finally into Government. Education is *largely* in the Government sector but some of it is private and falls into Services. We shall have more to say about Education later under this topic.

Another way is to look at "public" and "private" sectors and to further divide the private sector into a "profit-making" and a "not-for-profit" segment. Data to illuminate that perspective come later.

The pie charts above are based on employment in 1900 and in 2000; the sectors are shown as percent of total employment. In 1900 total employment was a little shy of 26.9 million, in 2000 just shy of 136.5 million; the second pie represents a lot more people.

We were once an agricultural nation. Now we are a nation of service providers. Agriculture and Goods Producers are the losers, Services and Government the gainers in this process. Agriculture and Goods Producers benefited from tremendous improvements in productivity (which has its own chapter in this volume). Services, in a way, have had to "absorb" the employment freed by technology and automation primarily in mining and manufacturing.

An interesting thing to note is that today it takes proportionally far fewer people to provide the "basics," the first level of production — food, fibers, timber, minerals, and the products and the structures that are made of them. In 1900, 43 people out of every hundred labored to produce grains, vegetables, fruits, and meat. In 2000, two people — helped by a part-timer who worked two days a week — got the job done. But they were indirectly helped by people who made tractors, mined fuels and distilled them, and provided scientifically perfected seed, fertilizers, and pesticides.

Sources: U.S. Bureau of the Census. *Historical Statistics of the United States, 1975.* Washington, DC: U.S. Government Printing Office, 1975 (for 1900 data). U.S. Bureau of the Census for data on the 2000 structure of employment.

The Sectors – The Last 20 Years

Major Sectors over 20 Years
(Values in thousands of employees)

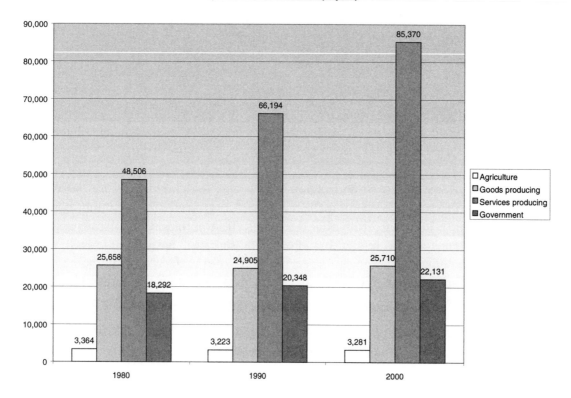

The growth in the services producing sector is the striking feature of this graph, showing the sectors of the U.S. economy for three decades in thousands of employees. The services producing sector nearly doubled in the 1980 to 2000 period, employing 48.5 million people in 1980 and 85.4 million in 2000 — essentially absorbing all of the growth in employment in this 20-year period. Total employment grew by 40.7 million, services employment by 36.9 million, thus the latter accounted for just under 91% of all new jobs.

The services producing sector is made up of transportation, utilities; finance, insurance, and real estate; wholesale and retail trade; and the services sector more narrowly construed. This latter portion includes everything from doctors and nurses to museum curators, from lawyers to filling-station attendants, from consultants to pet groomers. In a panel in this series, we shall look a little closer at these components.

Note that agricultural employment has declined and that the goods producing sector has remained essentially flat. The goods producing sector consists of mining, construction, and manufacturing. Yet population in this period increased by 49.8 million, from 226.3 million in 1980 to 276.1 million in 2000. This means that roughly the same number of people are now providing essentials — food, shelter, and products — as they did 20 years before — to a population that has increased by the addition of more people than live in Spain and Denmark combined. This ignores import-export dynamics and globalization, but it was, in good part, possible only because of tremendous improvements in productivity, which has a chapter of its own later in this book.

The governmental sector has increased in total employment by 3.8 million people (about 21%). This increase directly reflects the growth of the educational establishment, which is geared to population growth. Population increased 22% in the same period. We shall present more detail on the government sector later.

The following table shows the shares of total employment held by each of the sectors. The sectors are also divided into Private Sector and Government and into Profit-making and Not-for-profit segments.

Percent of Total Employment and Change

	1980	1990	2000	Change 80-00	Change 90-00
Private Sector	80.9	82.3	83.8	2.9	1.5
Agriculture	3.5	2.8	2.4	-1.1	-0.4
Goods producing	26.8	21.7	18.8	-7.9	-2.9
Services producing	50.6	57.7	62.5	11.9	4.8
Government	19.1	17.7	16.2	-2.9	-1.5
Federal civilian	3.0	2.7	2.0	-1.0	-0.7
Federal military	2.1	1.8	1.1	-1.1	-0.7
State government	3.8	3.8	3.5	-0.3	-0.2
Local government	10.2	9.5	9.6	-0.6	0.1
Profit-making		64.2	69.6		5.4
Not-for-profit		35.8	30.4		-5.4
Government	19.1	17.7	16.2		-1.5
Private tax-exempt		18.1	14.2		-3.9

We are growing more *private* and more *profit-making*. This pattern may change after the terrorist attacks of September 11, 2001, but this was the pattern evolving until that time. Within the private sector, gains in share have been posted by the services producing segment, mostly at the expense of goods producing activities. In the government sector, all elements have lost share except local government. Its minute gain is due to elementary and secondary education. Losses by the not-for-profit sector are greatest in the privately managed portion; losses in share by the government have been less.

Sources: U.S. Bureau of Labor Statistics. "Employees on nonfarm payrolls by major industry, 1950 to date." Online. Available: http://www.bls.gov/ces/home.htm. January 2002. U.S. Bureau of the Census. *Statistical Abstract of the United States, 2000*. Table 672, p. 420, for data on agricultural employment. Government totals include data obtained from the U.S. Department of Defense, and published in *Statistical Abstract, 2000*, Table 579, p. 168. The military on active duty for the year 2000, included but not shown, was estimated from 1998 data by the editors.

Services - Where More and More People Work

The Services Producing Sector's Component Elements
(In % of Total Sectoral Employment)

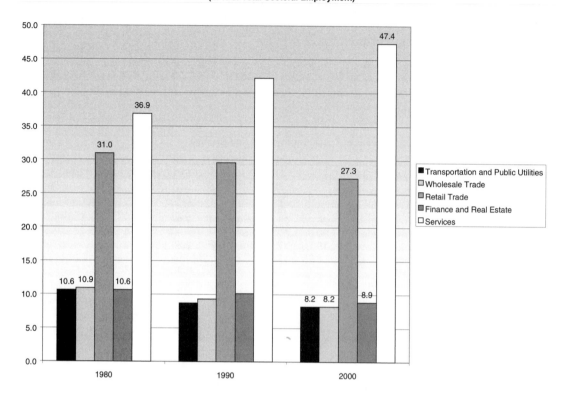

This graphic shows the component elements of the fastest growing economic sector in the U.S. — the Services Producing Sector. Each component industry is shown as a percent of the total Services Producing Sector's employment. In each of the years shown, "services" is the dominant component, rapidly gaining relative share of employment in the Services Producing Sector, reaching nearly 50% by 2000. The elements that make up "services" are discussed in this panel further below. The growth rates of these components, measured in employment, are shown below. The values are annual, compounded growth rates in employment.

Sector Component	Growth 1980-1990	Growth 1990-2000
Transportation and Public Utilities	1.2	2.0
Wholesale Trade	1.6	1.3
Retail Trade	2.7	1.7
Finance, Insurance, and Real Estate	2.7	1.2
Services	4.6	3.8

In the first decade of this period, Services led in annual growth of employment, followed by Retail Trade and Finance, Insurance, and Real Estate (F.I.R.E.), growing at equal rates. In the second, most recent decade, Services has continued its strong advance, followed by Retail. The F.I.R.E. component's growth rate had dropped behind that of both Transportation and Wholesale Trade.

The 1980s saw many and significant innovations in mass merchandising; it was also the era when large parts of the public became involved in the stock market, through mutual funds and 401k retirement plans; Financial Services flourished. In the 1990 to 2000 period, the Transportation and Public Utilities industry shows strong growth; this is at least in part explained by the popularity of just-in-time inventory programs, which stimulated transportation early in this period; later in the period came Internet-related delivery activities. In that connection it might be noted that postal employment also increased strongly, although the postal service is classified as government.

Services, the most rapidly growing component, requires disaggregation. It is too diverse for general explanation. The following table shows the industries that make up this component in two years of the Economic Census, 1992 and 1997. Growth rates are annual, compounded rates.

Employment (in thousands) and Growth (in % and Rank)

Industries in Services	1992	1997	Annual Growth - %	Growth Rank
Hotels and lodging	1,489	1,686	2.5	8
Personal services	1,218	1,303	1.4	10
Business services	**5,542**	**8,652**	**9.3**	**1**
Automotive repair	864	1,094	4.8	6
Miscellaneous repair	428	419	-0.4	12
Amusement	**1,382**	**1,810**	**5.5**	**3**
Health care - for profit	4,453	5,520	4.4	7
Legal services	924	956	0.7	11
Social Services - for profit	**505**	**662**	**5.6**	**2**
Engineering services	2,271	2,932	5.2	4
Museums, zoological gardens	66	84	4.9	5
Health care - not-for-profit	5,565	5,759	0.7	11
Social services, not-for-profit	1,407	1,586	2.4	9
Membership organizations	511	172	-19.6	13
Total	28,617	34,632	3.9	

The table shows the leading industries within the services aggregation; they are shown in bold type. All the industries are ranked by growth. The growth of the leader, Business Services, and the 4th ranked, Engineering Services, is in part explained by the popularity of "outsourcing," whereby activities that once were *inside* manufacturing or other industries, as part of the overhead (and classified *as* manufacturing, transportation, etc.) are now performed as services.

The other rapidly growing services are genuine "social indicators" rather than "business indicators." For-profit social services also reflect an outsourcing effect. Privately operated prisons come to mind. Amusement includes professional sports, fitness facilities (serving the Baby Boom as it grows a little thicker in the middle), and theatrical and music producers and production services, stimulated by the growth in cable TV, a voracious consumer of product for a proliferating number of channels.

In the last panel we observed that we are getting more "profit-making." Within the services category, health care for profit ranks 7th, health care not-for-profit 11th in employment growth. Similarly, social services for profit rank second, not-for-profits 9th. It is somewhat troubling that, at least in the five-year period shown, membership organizations have seen a most dramatic decline in compounded annual growth in employment, nearly 20% a year. This category includes some 22,000 associations of all kinds. Are we growing less social, less community-minded?

Sources: U.S. Bureau of Labor Statistics. "Employees on nonfarm payrolls by major industry, 1950 to date." Online. Available: http://www.bls.gov/ces/home.htm. January 2002. Data for the breakdown of services is from the Economic Census, 1992 and 1997. U.S. Bureau of the Census. *Statistical Abstract of the United States, 2000*. Table 1299. p. 770.

Trends in Government Employment

Government Employment, by Level of Government
(In thousands of employees)

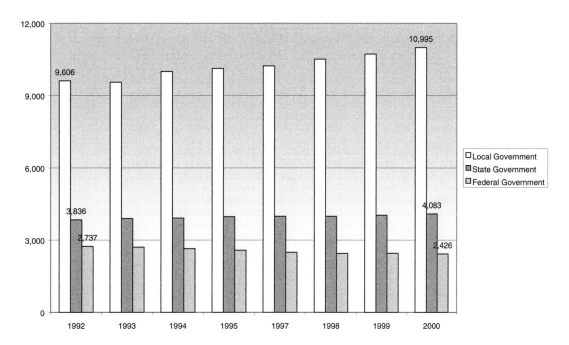

Government employs 13 out of every 100 people. In this and the next two panels, let's look more closely at government as an employer.

This chart shows how that employment, around 17.5 million people in 2000[1], breaks down into three major divisions: local, state, and federal. The largest of these, local government, includes municipal government at all sizes, counties, as well as special districts — school districts, above all, as well as water districts, sewage districts, port authorities, transportation districts, and the like. This largest sector has also had the most rapid growth in the last eight years, 1.7% a year on a compounded basis. The population grew at a rate of just shy of 1% (0.995) in the same period[2]; local government employment has thus outpaced population increase.

---

[1] Data from the Bureau of the Census' Census of Government. Data used in earlier panels, taken from the Bureau of Labor Statistics, augmented by data from the U.S. Department of Defense for military forces, are higher (22.1 million). If that number is used, Government accounts of 16.2% of employment. The difference is accounted for in part by the inclusion of military forces and temporary employees, which are only partially reflected in the data used by us here. Other differences are due to different data acquisition methods.

[2] Rate includes immigration. Natural increase, through births, is lower.

State government is smaller and had lower growth — 0.78% a year. There is one employee for every 2.69 people at the local level. Much as elementary and secondary education represents the bulk of local government employment, so employment by public colleges and universities represents the bulk of state government employment.

The federal government is the smallest government sector. There are six people employed at the state and local government level for each federal employee. Uniformed military forces are excluded here. Federal employment in this period has been going down, declining 1.5% a year. The two largest components of the federal government are civilian defense employees and the Postal Service.

Frustrated with taxes, especially in early Spring, bombarded by controversies in the media, Americans sometimes ask: Is government getting too big? Based on overall employment, government is 12.8% of employment, as noted above. The true size of the actual administrative apparatus, however, is revealed only when the educational establishment is first set apart. This is shown explicitly in the following table:

Analysis of Government and Public Education Employment

(Data in thousands and in %)

	Total employ- ment	Govern- ment employ- ment	Employ- ment in Public Education	Government employment without Pub- lic Education	Govt. as % of total employ- ment	Gov. with- out educa- tion as % of total
1992	110,408	16,178	6,021	10,158	14.7	9.2
1995	118,709	16,671	6,681	9,990	14.0	8.4
2000	136,492	17,504	7,375	10,128	12.8	7.4

These data show that government, without the inclusion of public education functions, is actually shrinking, down from 9.2% of total employment in 1992 to 7.4% in 2000. The educational component of government has increased by 1.35 million; government exclusive of education has essentially remained unchanged.

We continue to examine the larger components of government in the next panel.

Sources: U.S. Bureau of the Census. Public Employment and Payroll. Online. Available: http://www.census.gov/govs/www/apes.html. December 21, 2001. Total employment: U.S. Bureau of Labor Statistics, augmented by data from U.S. Department of Defense, published in *Statistical Abstract of the United State, 2000*. Table 579, p. 368; military employment data estimated from 1998 data by the editors.

Growth in Government = Education

Elementary and High School Education
(Staff and enrollment in thousands and student-to-staff ratio)

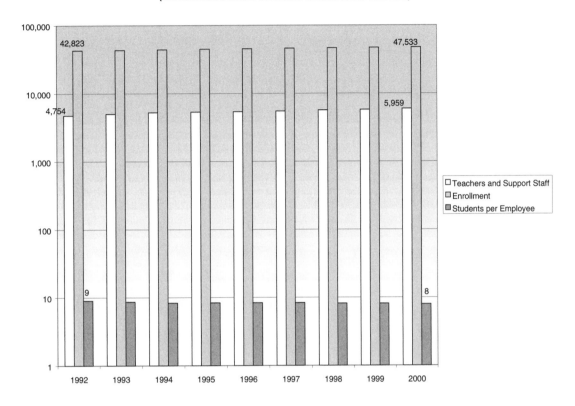

Fairly rapid growth in employment in public elementary and secondary education (K-12) has outstripped the increase in students enrolled in the 1992 to 2000 period. Teachers and staff increased at an annual, compounded rate of 2.9%. Student enrollments have increased at 1.3%. The data above are shown in log scale so that growth patterns can be easily compared despite differences in scale.

This increase in employment at the K-12 end of public education is the single most important factor in increasing overall "government" employment. Public school staff is classified as "government" in all of the federal reporting systems. School employment at the local level increased 6.5 times as much as all other employment at the local government level. And local government, the largest employer in the government sector, experienced the strongest growth in employment. Federal employment actually declined from 2.7 million in 1992 to 2.4 million in 2000.

Interestingly, the growth in "government" can thus be led back to parents' desire for smaller class size. In this period (1992-2000), public elementary and secondary ratios, pupils to all staff, not just teachers, declined from 9 per staff member to 8.

Lest this be thought an exaggeration, consider the following. Between 1992 and 2000, the government sector increased by 1.3 million jobs (using the more conservative U.S. Census data). Public Elementary and High School Education accounted for 91% (1.2 million jobs) of that change. If gains in higher education are added (which are concentrated at the state level), Public Education accounted for *all* gains in the Government Sector.

The following table provides the numerical picture for both K-12 and higher publicly funded education:

Analysis of Growth Trends in Public Education

	Growth in Employment (% per year, 1992-00)	Growth in Enrollment (% per year, 1992-00)	Ratio, students to staff, 1992	Ratio, students to staff, 2000
Elementary and High	2.87	1.31	9.0	8.0
Colleges and Universities	1.40	0.40	8.9	8.3

Sources: U.S. Bureau of the Census. Public Employment and Payroll. Online. Available: http://www.census.gov/govs/www/apes.html. December 21, 2001. Values for 1996 are extrapolated. School enrollment data: National Center for Education Statistics, published in *Statistical Abstract of the United States, 2000* Table 239, p. 151.

Federal Employment: Defense Yields to the Courier

Defense and Postal Service as Elements of Federal Employment
(In thousands of employees)

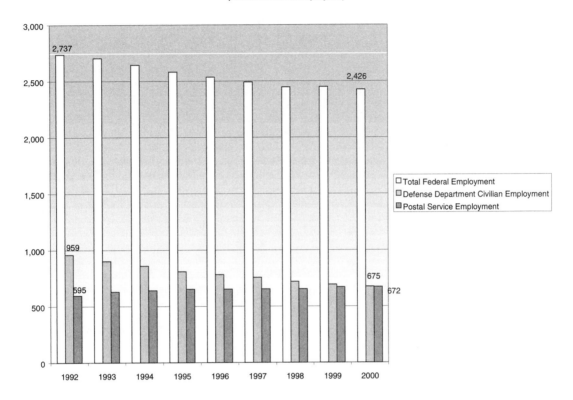

In the last eight years (1992-2000), federal employment declined by more than 310,000. More than 90% of this decline was accounted for by the shrinkage of civilian employment in the Department of Defense, down 284,000. Uniformed military forces on active duty also shrank some 350,000 in this period — but they are not included in the chart above. We didn't know that something was coming on September 11, 2001.

The two largest components of federal employment are the civilians in the Department of Defense and the employees of the U.S. Postal Service. Together these two activities accounted for more than 50% of federal jobs, 56.8% in 1992 and 55.5% in 2000.

The rate of employment in the Postal Service grew annually by 1.5%, reflecting an expanding volume of mail. Despite the rise in communications by e-mail, the avalanche of letters handled by the Postal Service did not show signs of diminishing until after 9/11. During this time the Post Office also participated in the Internet boom, when it began to sell its goods and services online. Total federal employment declined annually by the same percentage. Defense shrank at the rate of 4.3% a year

Sources: U.S. Bureau of the Census. Public Employment and Payroll. Online. Available: http://www.census.gov/govs/www/apes.html. December 21, 2001. Values for 1996 are extrapolated.

Unionized Sector —Trend Is Down...

Union Membership and Coverage

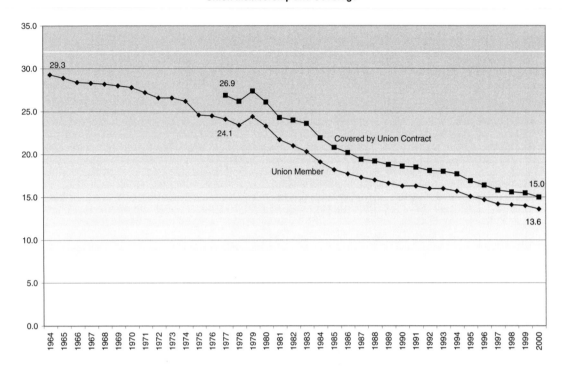

Unionized labor has been declining over the last 40 years, both as a percentage of the total workforce and in absolute terms. In percentile terms, 29.3% of the employed workforce (non-agricultural sectors) had union membership in 1964, 24.1% in 1977. This percentage had declined to 13.6% by 2000.

Those covered by union contracts — they need not necessarily belong to unions — were 26.9% of the employed workforce in 1977. This rate had declined to 15% by 2000.

Union membership, in absolute numbers, appears to have peaked in the late 1970s at just over 21.7 million. The number had dropped to just shy of 16.5 million by 1999. Those covered by union contracts (union members and others), stood at around 20.8 million in 1983 and had declined to around 18.4 million by 1999.

The labor union movement had its first measurement in the 19th century. In 1897, the Bureau of Labor Statistics reported 440,000 people as members of labor unions. Ten years later the number had risen to 2 million, by 1941 to 10.5 million, and topped 20 million in 1968.

Union members, as a percent of non-agricultural employees, reached a peak in 1945 at 35.5% — corresponding to the lower of the curves above. The rate remained at or very near 30% between 1943 through 1962 and then began a slow decline, most of which is shown on the chart above. Historical data in numerical format are presented in Part II of this volume for further reference.

The character of unionized labor is changing; private sector unionized workers are dropping in number, public sector union membership is growing — even as the total union employment is declining. Unionized jobs, and jobs under union contracts, continue to pay higher median wages today as in the past. These subjects, and some discussion of the reasons for declining unionization, are presented in the following panel.

Sources: Trend data from: Barry T. Hirsch, David A. Macpherson, and Wayne G. Vroman, "Estimates of union density by state," Monthly Labor Review, July 2001. Data on union membership from: *Historical Statistics of the United States*, Part I, p. 178-179, and from *Statistical Abstract of the United States*, 1980, 1991, 1995, 1996, and 2000 under Labor Organizations, Membership, in each volume.

... But Union Labor is Ahead of the Rest

Median Weekly Pay, Selected Years, Unionized, Covered by Union Contract, and All Workers (2000 Constant Dollars)

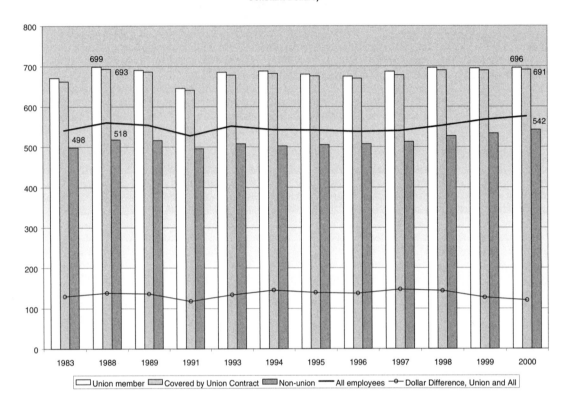

Union membership is down, as shown in the last panel, but this chart shows that union members, and those who work under union contracts, outpace other workers by a substantial margin a week — about $135 a week on average in the selected years shown here. Again, on average, union members earn just shy of 25% more than those not covered by union contracts at all.

Data are expressed in deflated year 2000 dollars so that trends can be clearly seen. In this period — 1983 through 2000 — no *strong* trends are discernible. Income growth has been strongest in the non-unionized segment (0.5% a year) and slowest in the union member category (0.22%) a year; those working under union contracts have increased earnings more than union members (0.25%). Growth, in other words, has been inversely proportional to the level of the pay received.

The decline in the unionized work force appears to be due in part to the substantial median wage differential between unionized and non-union workers. Employers appear intent on reducing this differential by various means — including the export of high-paying jobs to low-wage countries, decertification efforts, and other means.

Other forces at work are the substantial growth in the services sector — large portions of which are not unionized, the growing productivity of industrial labor, which ultimately erodes highly skilled jobs, and the consequent efforts, by labor organizations, to recruit members from public sector organizations, which tend to be lower paid and more heavily skewed toward the clerical. The following table shows the shift of union membership from private to public sector organizations:

Share of Sectors and Growth Rates

	1983	2000	1983-2000 growth or decline
Union membership (000)	17,717	16,268	-8.0
Covered by unions (000)	20,532	17,944	-12.6
Private sector membership share - %	67.6	56.2	-11.4
Public sector membership share - %	32.4	43.7	11.3
Private sector coverage share - %	65.4	55.6	-9.8
Public sector coverage share - %	34.6	44.4	9.8

Overall, both union membership and the number of those covered by unions are down over this 17-year period. The only gains shown are in the public sector's share of unionized jobs.

Sources: *Statistical Abstract of the United States*, 1980-2001, United States Department of Commerce. Charted data have been normalized to 2000 dollars using the Bureau of Labor Statistics' Consumer Price Index, All Items series.

Chapter 2

The Workforce

This chapter discusses the changing workforce. The workforce is continuing to grow older and become more ethnically diverse and women are increasing their share of the workforce.

In the next 20 years, 76 million Baby Boomers will be retiring. At the same time, growth is expected to add a little over 22 million jobs to the economy in just the first 10 years alone. Will succeeding generations be able to fill the jobs? The next four panels answer this question both in general terms and for specific occupations.

Over the past 50 years, more women have been entering and staying in the workforce. Women's share of the workforce is expected to increase at least until 2015. Does this mean that women will surpass men in the workforce? Two panels discuss the effects the increased workforce participation rate of women has on the overall workforce, and in various job categories. A third panel discusses how periodic recessions and recoveries affect men and women in the workforce.

As the general population becomes more ethnically and racially diverse, so does the workforce. Immigration, birth rates, the aging Baby Boomers, education levels, and workforce participation rates all affect the changing composition of the workforce. Four panels discuss all of these factors and how they affect the white, black, Hispanic-American, and Asian-American workforce populations.

A discussion of the workforce in America would not be complete without discussing the subject of illegal labor. An estimated 5.4 million people were working illegally in the United States in 2000. Four panels discuss the enforcement of illegal labor laws in this country.

The Aging Workforce and Its Effects on the Future Job Market

Percentage of Workers per Occupational Category, by Age, March 2000

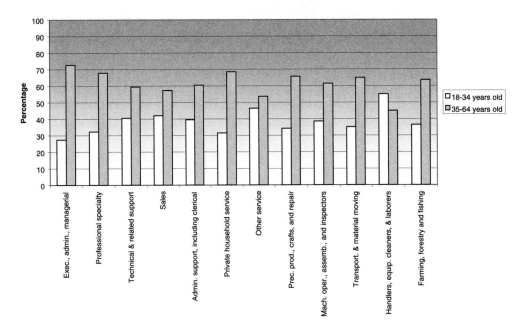

The chart shows occupations by two age groups and the percentage that each represents of the U.S. workforce. For most categories, those aged 35-64 are in the majority. The exception is "Handlers, equipment cleaners, and laborers," people who do work probably easier on younger workers.

By 2020, many of those 35 and older will be retired or nearing retirement age. In most categories, the younger workers are not numerous enough to replace those likely to leave. Shortages by category may diminish or increase depending on those now aged 18 to 24. Some of these people will switch occupations as they complete their education, others will stay on.

A closer look at the 18 to 34 age group further emphasizes the problems of a workforce skewed toward the older age groups. In 2000, the workforce aged 18 to 24 was 17.1 million people, those aged 25 to 34 were 30.6 million strong. As the workforce ages, a much smaller younger group will have to fill the jobs of their elders.

The youngest age group, of course, is disproportionately employed in the lower skilled or less desirable occupations. As these people age, improve their skills, and get degrees, they will find themselves in a buyer's market for labor — employers looking to fill 13.4 million jobs in the 25-34 cohort — for which there are no people presently in the pipeline. The younger people will therefore undoubtedly gravitate toward the better paid jobs and — as will be shown in other panels to follow — are now preparing for such jobs academically.

As the 21st century advances, problems are therefore likely to appear (they are already tangibly with us) in areas such as sales, services, administrative and support, certain stressful occupations (teaching and healthcare), and low-skilled materials handling occupations.

As the Baby Boom comes of retirement age, and the 25 to 34 age group advances to replace a larger 35 to 40 age group, the problem will intensify. To pursue this matter further, we shall look at the impact of Baby Boom retirement on the work force in selected occupational categories.

Sources: Graph and cohort data: U.S. Census Bureau. "Table 6. Educational Attainment of Employed Civilians 18 to 64 Years, by Occupation, Age, Sex, Race, and Hispanic Origin: March 2000." December 19, 2000. Retrieved December 12, 2001 from http://www.census.gov/population/socdemo/education/p20-536/tab06.txt. Labor force participation rates: Howard N. Fullerton, Jr. "Labor force participation: 75 years of change, 1950-98 and 1998-2025." *Monthly Labor Review,* December 1999. Population data: U.S. Census Bureau. Population Projections Program. Population Division. *(NP-D1-A) Projections of the Resident Population by Age, Sex, Race, and Hispanic Origin: 1999 to 2100 (Middle Series).* January 13, 2000. Job growth data: Daniel E. Hecker "Occupational employment projections to 2010." *Monthly Labor Review,* November 2001.

Baby-Boomer Retirement Effects

Retirement and Job Openings - 2000-10

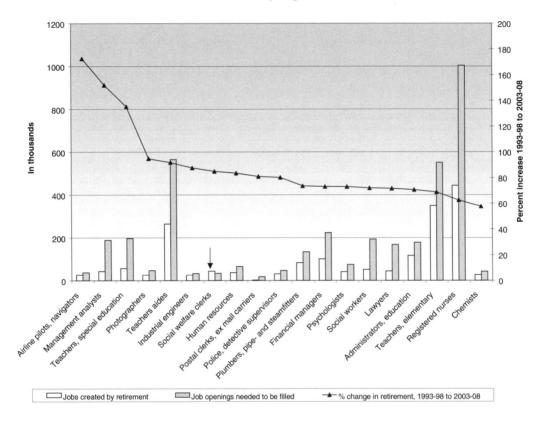

Jobs created by retirement | Job openings needed to be filled | ▲ % change in retirement, 1993-98 to 2003-08

The chart shows the occupations with the largest increases in worker retirement from 1993-1998 to 2003–2008 (the curve), the number of jobs created by retirement in the 2000-2010 period, and the total new job openings in the same period.

To understand the curve, consider the following. In the 1993-1998 period, 5,000 airline pilots and navigators retired. In the 2003-08 period, 14,000 will retire, a 180% increase between the two periods[1]. High rates of growth in retirement are due to many factors — the retirement programs offered as incentives to highly skilled individuals or in occupations where age reduces performance (as in piloting craft), pension plans, the wealth of the group as a whole, and, sometimes, the stress factor inherent in the job.

Those retiring have to be replaced — and sometimes not. In one of these occupations, Social Welfare Eligibility Clerks, those retiring will exceed those needed — indicating a shrinking occupation (see arrow). In all other cases, some, but not all of the jobs, will be created by the need to replace those retiring.

---

[1] The actual increase was 172.7% because the value was calculated using unrounded numbers.

These occupations, all with high retirement rates, are not equally affected by the Baby Boom's withdrawal from the work force. Industrial Engineers, Airline Pilots/Navigators, and Supervisors of Police and Detectives will generate the largest demand for people by retirement; 79%, 71%, and 67% of jobs, respectively, will be created by retirement.

By contrast, Postal Clerks, Management Analysts, Social Workers, and Lawyers are predicted, by the Bureau of Labor Statistics, to have the most intense growth in this group of occupations marked by a high rate of retirement growth. Only 1%, 23%, 26.8% and 26.9% of openings in these occupations will be created by retirement, the rest by growth.

The occupations with the most openings in this group will be Registered Nurses, Elementary School Teachers, and Teacher's Aides — all occupations that require human contact with sometimes difficult clienteles.

Job growth, therefore, is a factor in the percentage of job openings that are due to retirement. The least growth is associated with those occupations where the replacement of retirees creates the most new jobs. The Baby Boomer generation's retirement will thus have varied effects depending on occupation.

In the next panel we look at the College Degree and Job Need disconnect. Are people getting degrees to qualify for occupations that won't need quite so many people?

Sources: Dohm, Arlene. "Gauging the labor force effects of retiring baby-boomers." *Monthly Labor Review,* July 2000. Daniel E. Hecker. "Occupational employment projections to 2010." *Monthly Labor Review*, November 2001.

Will College Graduates Be Able to Fill Future Job Openings?

Job Openings and Number of Degrees Conferred, by Occupation

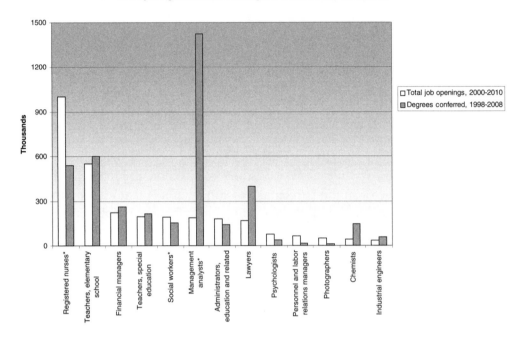

The chart above shows the projected number of job openings from 2000 to 2010 and the projected number of degrees conferred to students from 1998 to 2008.[2] The occupations listed were selected from the previous panel. Only those occupations requiring a college degree were chosen. Degrees conferred under the occupation "Registered nurses" include all nursing degrees. Degrees conferred under the occupation "Management analyst" include all business administration and management degrees. Degrees conferred under "Social workers" include only Master's degrees and higher. The standard requirement for a job in social work is a Master's degree.

Those who received their degrees from the mid-1980s to the late 1990s will be replacing the retiring Baby Boomers. They will have been working in their jobs for years and gaining the experience necessary to replace the retirees. The younger and less experienced workers will take over the jobs left by those workers replacing the Baby Boomers. These workers will also fill many new jobs created due to growth in an occupation.

If we assume that for each degree conferred there is one qualified employee ready to take a job in that field of study, then in some occupations there will be a shortfall of workers, in others a glut. The following list shows the shortfall or oversupply of workers by occupation.

---

[2] Projections are based on data from 1993 to 1998. Over this 5-year period, the number of degrees conferred has remained steady.

Projected Shortfall or Oversupply of Workers by Occupation, 2000-2010

Registered nurses[3]	-466,000
Teachers, elementary school	51,000
Financial managers	39,000
Teachers, special education	17,000
Social workers	-41,000
Management analysts[4]	1,233,000
Administrators, education and related	-38,000
Lawyers	230,000
Psychologists	-37,000
Personnel and labor relations managers	-50,000
Photographers	-38,000
Chemists	103,000
Industrial engineers	23,000

The biggest shortfall will be in the nursing field. At the current graduation rate, there will be nearly a half million shortfall. The biggest glut of qualified workers will be in business administration and management. The number of jobs open will be a fraction of the number of qualified workers. In that case, most will have to find jobs in other occupations. This will also be the case for lawyers. Many may go into private practice, but the need for lawyers will determine if most stay in the profession.

Despite predictions of a shortfall of workers in teaching, if graduation rates remain steady, the pool of qualified elementary and special education teachers will actually exceed the number of jobs available. The shortfall comes when those with teaching certificates would rather take jobs in other professions. This could be due to monetary concerns and possibly poor working conditions in the districts with the most need.

If the data in the chart are to be believed, those needing photographers will find the pickings slim — but this outcome is likely only if the employer seeks a photographer with a college degree. Many skilled photographers learn their business on the job. Those workers aren't tracked. It is therefore difficult to project whether the occupation will actually see a shortfall.

Personnel and labor relations managers are expected to see the second biggest shortfall of qualified workers. In 1998, fewer students graduated with a management degree in this field than in 1993. The decline in the popularity of unions may be fueling the decline in the popularity of this course of study. The need for human resources managers, however, is growing; employees in this specialization have a wide-ranging function in modern corporations entangled with managing health and retirement plans, discrimination, and many other issues.

---

[3] Number of degrees conferred includes all nursing degrees.

[4] Number of degrees conferred includes all business administration and management degrees.

The potential surpluses and shortfalls in occupations requiring specialized training continue this presentation.

Sources: Chart data: National Center for Education Statistics. U.S. Department of Education. *Digest of Education Statistics.* 1997-2000 editions. Labor relations manager description: Bureau of Labor Statistics. U.S. Department of Labor. *Occupational Outlook Handbook 2002-03 Edition*, Washington D.C., 2001.

Will Supply Meet Demand in Occupations Requiring Specialized Training?

Job Openings (2000-2010) as Percentage of Total 2010 Employment in Occupation

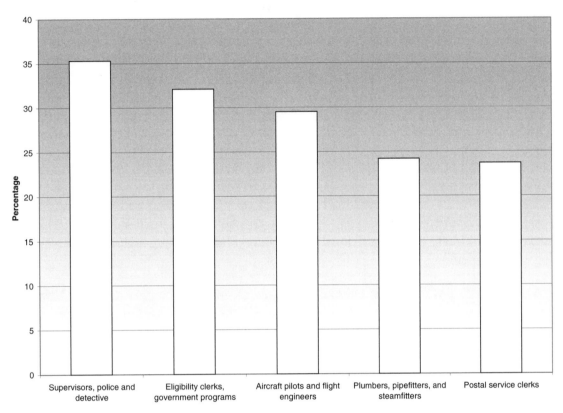

The graph shows the projected job openings for the decade 2000-2010 as a percentage of employment in 2010. The occupations listed are from "Baby Boomer Retirement Effects" not discussed in the previous panel. In the following discussion, the term "newly hired" means those hired during the 2000-2010 period.

Newly hired police and detective supervisors are expected to make up 35.3% of the workforce in this field by 2010. Because police and detective supervisors are taken from the ranks of the police force itself, there should be a surplus of qualified candidates. In the year 2000, there were 713,000 non-supervisory police officers and detectives. The expected number of job openings during the next decade is projected to be 48,000. Also, many more people are entering the law enforcement field than are needed because of high pay and good benefits. Therefore, there is likely to be a surplus of replacements for those who enter supervisory positions.

Newly hired government program eligibility clerks are expected to make up 21.7% of the employment in the field by 2010, even though projected job openings as a percentage of employment is 32.1%. The demand for eligibility clerks is expected to decline; 34,000 people will retire or leave their jobs for other reasons, but only 23,000 jobs will have to be filled. Improvements in systems are reducing the need for clerks. New systems, employing computer forms, allow each clerk to service more people in less time. The demand for clerks increases in a recession as more people seek assistance. But, overall, the field will experience a job decline over the next decade. The pool of qualified workers should outpace demand, with highly skilled applicants, especially those with backgrounds in customer service, taking the available jobs. But there are no data that project either a short supply or an oversupply of workers applying for these jobs.

Newly hired aircraft pilots and flight engineers will make up slightly less than 30% of the workforce in these fields by 2010. The supply of airline pilots and flight engineers is expected to outpace demand. Many more potential workers are expected to become pilots because of the high pay, prestige, and benefits. Those with military experience who have logged the most hours flying highly sophisticated aircraft, and those with multiple FAA licenses are preferred when hiring.

Newly hired plumbers, pipefitters and steamfitters will make up 24.2% of the workforce in these fields if the demand is met. Demand is expected to outpace supply. The training involves 4 –5 years on the job with 144 hours of classroom instruction in such subjects as mathematics, applied physics, and chemistry. Those with computer and drafting skills are preferred. Many jobs also require industry-specific knowledge. Hence there is an anticipated problem.

The demand for postal service clerks is expected to grow in the next decade. New hires are expected to make up 23.7% of the workforce in 2010. Automation has cut many jobs; but window service clerks are expected to increase in response to an emphasis on customer service at the U.S. Postal Service. Postal workers must wait one or two years after passing the civil service exam to gain the necessary experience to become postal clerks. Because there were 613,000 non-clerk postal employees in 2000, and there will be a demand for only 18,000 new clerks in the next decade, the number of qualified candidates for postal clerk will exceed the demand. The number of postal service applicants to replace those that transfer to clerk positions is expected to exceed the demand as well.

In conclusion, in those fields offering high pay and good benefits, the supply of potential workers is expected to outpace demand. In jobs that offer high pay for highly skilled labor, but also demand strenuous work, there will be a shortage of qualified applicants.

Sources: Bureau of Labor Statistics. U.S. Department of Labor. *Occupational Outlook Handbook 2002-03 Edition,* Washington D.C., 2001. Daniel E. Hecker. "Occupational employment projections to 2010." *Monthly Labor Review,* November 2001.

Will Women Outnumber Men?

Percentage of Labor Force by Gender and Participation Rates, 1950-2025

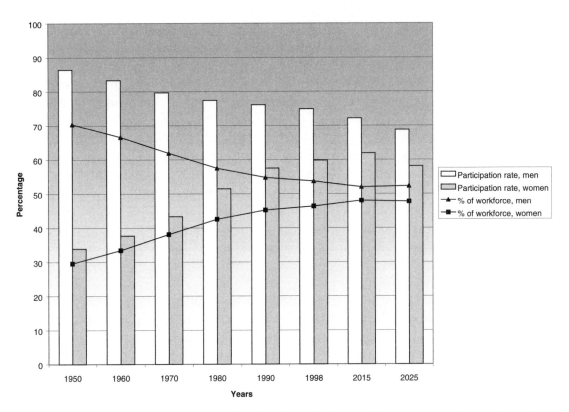

The chart above shows the percent distribution of the workforce by gender. Also shown is the labor force participation rates by gender for 1950 to 2025. Until 2015, the participation rates and, consequently, the share of the workforce has increased for women. In the same time period, the participation rates and share of the workforce for men have dipped. After 2015, the men's participation rate is expected to continue to decrease. The women's participation rate is also expected to decrease, but at a slightly faster rate than the men's. As a result, the men's share of the workforce is projected to increase and the women's share is projected to decrease, thereby reversing the trend of the past 65 years.

The decrease in men's participation rates can be partially attributed to the aging of the population. The availability of Social Security benefits made it possible for more men to retire after age 65. During the 1970s, Social Security payments were relatively high due to over-adjusting for inflation. As a result, even more men over age 65 retired during this period than in the 1960s. When those aged 62 and older became eligible for Social Security, more men retired from the workforce. By 1994, only half the men 62 years and older were in the workforce; in 1970 the ratio was 75 percent.

The change in the Social Security Act of 1960 made those under age 50 eligible for disability payments. This has been attributed to the decrease by 4.3% in the labor force participation rate of men aged 25 to 34 during the years 1960 to 1998. A greater availability of pensions also contributed to the reduction of men's participation in the workforce.

The increase in women's participation rates coincided with the modern Women's Rights Movement. More women entered the workforce at younger ages and stayed in the workforce after their children were born. From 1980 to 2000, the participation rate for those women with children under 18 increased by 16.3%. Those with children under age 6 increased their participation rate by 18.5%.

More women are now heads of household and sole support of their families. In 1995, nearly 28% of all households were headed by women, 16.3% of which were headed by single women — a striking difference from 1950. In that year, the total percentage of households headed by singles was 9.3%, with only a fraction of that headed by women.

After 2015, the participation rate for women is expected to decline. This has to do with the increasing diversity of the workforce and the different participation rates of each race and ethnic group. Hispanics are expected to have the highest growth rate in the working-age population, but the participation rates for Hispanic women are the lowest among the top ethnic groups. Meanwhile, the white, non-Hispanic working-age population is expected to have the biggest decrease, but this group has the highest female participation rate. Therefore, the aggregate labor force participation rate for women is projected to decrease.

During this time period, the men's aggregate participation rate is also expected to decrease, but at a slower rate than the women's: Hispanic men have a high rate. This helps to offset the decrease in the participation rates of white, non-Hispanic men. As a result, the men's share of the workforce starts trending upward, while the women's share starts trending downward.

The next panel discusses gender differences in employment during the past 25 years.

Sources: Fullerton, Jr., Howard N., "Labor force participation: 75 years of change, 1950-98 and 1998-2025", *Monthly Labor Review*, December 1999. Bureau of Labor Statistics. U.S. Department of Labor. "Table 6. Labor force participation rates of women by presence and age of children, March 1980-2000", *Report on the American Workforce 2001*. Washington D.C.: U.S. Government Printing Office, 2001. U.S. Census Bureau. "Table 1. Projections of Households by Type: 1995 to 2010, Series 1, 2, and 3" Retrieved December 5, 2001 from http://www.census.gov/population/projections/nation/hh-fam/table1n.txt. U.S. Census Bureau. "Historical Census of Housing Tables – Living Alone." Retrieved December 5, 2001 from: http://www.census.gov/hhes/www/housing/census/historic/liv-alone.html.

Where Do Women Surpass Men?

Women as Percentage of Total Workforce by Occupation, 1975, 1995, 2000

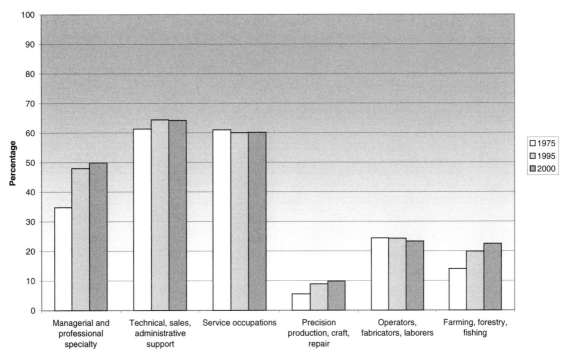

The chart shows the percentage of women employed in the various occupational categories for 1975, 1995, and 2000. All data are for workers 16 years old and over. Women consistently have made up the majority of workers in the Technical, Sales, Administrative Support and Service Occupations categories. In the year 2000, the numbers of women and men employed in the Managerial and Professional fields were nearly equal. This represents a 15.1% jump in employment of women in these fields since 1975.

Women have not yet surpassed men in the other three occupational categories shown, though more women are working in each of the occupations in the Precision Production, Craft, and Repair fields. This includes jobs as mechanics and jobs in the construction trades More women are also working in Farming, Forestry and Fishing occupations.

Fewer women are working as Operators, Fabricators and Laborers. This is a trend not only for women, but also for men. Automation and foreign competition have reduced the jobs for machine operators, assemblers and inspectors in the last five years. These jobs make up most of the employment in this job category.

Service occupations also saw a decrease in women employed. Although most service jobs saw an increase in women employed, the private household services and protective services saw decreases. Also, more men than women are employed in protective service occupations and in cleaning and building service. Women still hold most of the service jobs, but more men are being hired, thereby slowly closing the employment gap in this sector.

The following list shows the occupations in which fewer women were employed in the year 2000 than in the recent past. The asterisk next to the occupation means fewer men are also employed in these jobs. This could be due to automation, as with machine and computer equipment operators, or to a decline in the occupation over all.

Managerial and professional specialty
    Engineers
    Lawyers and judges*
Technical, sales, and administrative support
    Technicians, except health, engineering, and science
    Sales supervisors and proprietors
    Sales workers, retail and personal services*
    Computer equipment operators*
    Secretaries, stenographers, and typists*
    Mail and message distributing
Service occupations
    Private household services*
    Protective services*
Operators, fabricators, and laborers
    Machine operators, assemblers, and inspectors*

Women are increasing their presence in many occupations, including those that were considered traditionally male domains — such as mechanical trades and construction. They continue to maintain a majority of the workforce in the traditionally female occupations — teaching and clerical work. Women have increased their presence in the managerial and professional fields in the past 25 years. If this trend continues, the percentage of women in these fields will surpass that of men in the near future.

The next panel discusses the gender differences in employment during times of economic downturn and recovery.

Sources: Wooten, Barbara H., "Gender differences in occupational employment", *Monthly Labor Review*, April 1997, p. 17. Bureau of Labor Statistics. U.S. Department of Labor. "9. Employed persons by occupation, sex and age", *Current Population Survey*. Washington D.C.: U.S. Government Printing Office, 2001. U.S. Census Bureau. Special Populations Branch. Population Division. "Table 11. Major Occupation Group of the Employed Civilian Population 16 Years and Over by Sex: March 2000", *Current Population Survey*. Washington D.C.: U.S. Government Printing Office, 2001.

Are Women Better Able to Weather Economic Storms?

Percentage of Job Losses and Gains by Gender During Periods of Decline and Recovery in Employment, 1970-1993

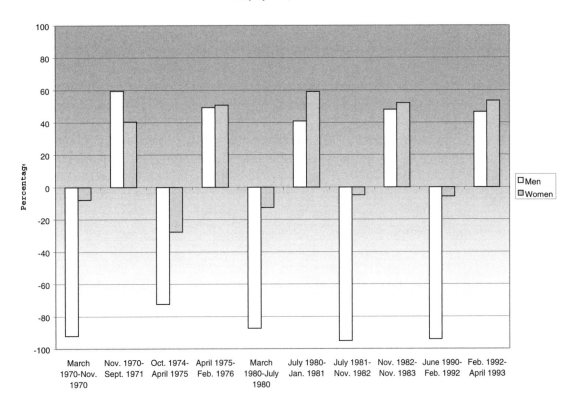

The chart above shows the percentage of job losses and gains by gender and by periods of employment decline and recovery from 1970 to 1993. The data used to create the chart include only non-farm employment. They do not include self-employment.

In every economic recovery since September 1971, women have gained a larger percentage of the newly created jobs than men have, even though men have consistently lost most of the jobs during times of economic downturn.

Most of the jobs lost during the economic downturns have been in industries that are easily affected by the ups and downs of the economy, such as construction and manufacturing. Men, traditionally, have held most of these jobs. On the other hand, many of the jobs that are traditionally held by women continued to grow during the last economic downturn and gained even more during the economic recovery. These jobs include health care occupations, social services, and public school occupations. The following table shows the percentage of men and women in the various industries.

Approximate Percentage of Employment by Gender, 1993

Industry	Men (%)	Women (%)
Construction	90	10
Manufacturing	67	33
Health care	18	82
Social services	22	78
Local public schools	30	70

In an economic downturn, the goods-producing sector and those industries that deal with that sector, such as retail trade, are the ones that lose the most jobs. Even when there was a recovery, the manufacturing industry still continued to lose jobs. This was due to automation, foreign competition, and cutbacks in government and commercial contracts.

While people are less likely to buy goods during an economic slowdown, there is always a need for health care, social services, and schools. The aging of the population, the increased priority people put on health care, and the added jobs when new treatments are developed all contribute to the increase in health care and social service jobs. During the last recovery, the number of jobs in state and local government also expanded, with much of that growth in the school system.

In conclusion, overall, women are more likely to keep and gain jobs during economic cycles than men due to the types of industries that employ the majority of women. More men are employed in goods-producing industries, which are affected more by economic slowdowns, automation, and foreign competition. More women are employed in service industries and state and local government. These industries do not lose as many jobs during economic downturns and, in recent years, tend to expand the number of jobs both in downturns and recoveries.

Source: Goodman, William. "Women and jobs in recoveries: 1970-1993." *Monthly Labor Review*, July 1994.

Share of the Workforce Population by Race, 1988-2008

Percentage Distribution of the Labor Force, 16 years old and older, 1988-2008

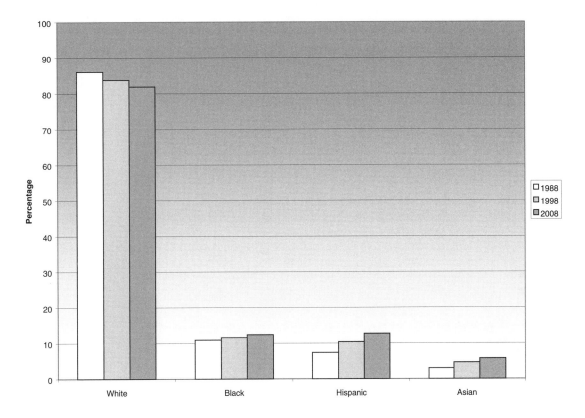

The graph shows the percent distribution of the workforce, by race, at decade intervals from 1988 to 2008. Whites, as expected, hold the largest share of jobs; this share is trending down, however, as minority shares rise to take up the slack. Hispanics share of the workforce will grow most in this period. The black and Asian populations, in combination, will gain 4.2%, the same percentages lost by whites. The table below shows the change in numbers.

Percentage Change in Workforce Share, 1988-2008

	Change (%)
White	-4.2
Black	+1.5
Hispanic	+5.3
Asian	+2.7

The whites' share is declining for three reasons: large numbers of older workers are leaving the workforce; whites have a low fertility rate and therefore provide fewer new workers, relatively; they are also receiving a decreasing share of immigrants from Europe.

The increase in the share of blacks is due to a younger age structure; more blacks, reaching retirement age, choose to remain at work for reasons to be discussed later. Blacks have a higher fertility rate than whites; more black women are and will be entering the workforce; black educational attainment is improving and leads to greater employability. The reasons for Hispanic gains parallel those for blacks; in addition, Hispanics also have a high immigration rate.

Asians have fewer workers of retirement age, display higher fertility than whites, have high educational attainment, are increasing their female presence in the work force, and also immigrate at high rates.

A closer look at the reasons behind the changing workforce follows.

Source: Fullerton, Jr., Howard N., "Labor force projections to 2008: steady growth and changing composition." *Monthly Labor Review*, November 1999.

Who's Entering and Who's Leaving?

Percentage of Labor Force by Race, Entrants and Leavers, 1988-1998

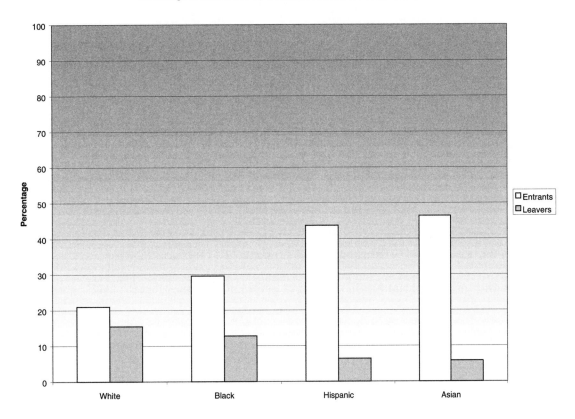

The graph shows the percentage of workers, within four racial/ethnic groups, that entered and left the workforce between the years 1988 and 1998. A greater proportion of whites left the workforce than any other group; Asians showed the highest rate of new entrants.

The whites' exodus foreshadows a Baby Boom phenomenon expected to loom even larger later unless other factors (war, tumbling markets) change the situation. During the late 1990s and early 2000s, the Baby-Boomer generation was entering its 40s and 50s. Boomers are now enjoying their highest career earnings. Many have also worked for the same company for many years and have accumulated sizeable retirement accounts. These factors contribute to the incentive to retire early. Over the years, the average retirement age has continued to decline from 68.3 in 1950 to a projected age of 61.5 in 2005. This could be a sign that pension and retirement plans are providing more post-retirement income; many people do not have to wait for Social Security entitlements (at age 65) in order to retire.

Blacks and Hispanics are leaving the workforce at lower levels for two reasons. Fewer blacks and Hispanics are at or near the retirement age. Many are working beyond age 65: they earn less and fewer have private pension and retirement plans. They have less incentive for early retirement, must wait for Social Security entitlement, and many must continue to work even after age 65 until forced out by poor health. The following table shows the median family net worth for 1992, 1995, and 1998. For all three years reported, median family net worth for blacks and Hispanics remained considerably below that of whites. Therefore, with little financial security, more blacks and Hispanics are staying in the workforce.

Median Family Net Worth, 1992-1998

	1992	1995	1998
Hispanic	$4,300	$5,300	$3,000
Non-Hispanic White	$71,300	$65,200	$81,700
Non-Hispanic Black	$12,000	$7,900	$10,000

Like blacks and Hispanics, Asians have a lower percentage of workers at retirement age. But, unlike blacks and Hispanics, Asians do not face quite the same financial uncertainty in retirement that forces others to stay in the workforce. Asians as a group are better educated and therefore earn more than all other ethnic and racial groups. According to the Social Security Administration, the median income of Asian-Americans in 1996 was $20,000. This is $1,000 more than the working-age population as a whole. A sizeable 40.3% of working age Asian and Pacific Islanders make $45,000 and more. Those earning within the $15,000-$44,999 range make up nearly as much, at 39.8%.

A discussion of the potential future workforce population comes next.

Sources: Chart data: Fullerton, Jr., Howard N., "Labor force projections to 2008: steady growth and changing composition." *Monthly Labor Review,* November 1999. Retirement data: Murray Gendell and Jacob S. Siegel, "Trends in the retirement age by sex, 1950-2005." *Monthly Labor Review,* July 1992. Social Security Administration. "Social Security...a foundation for building a secure retirement." Social Security *Retirement Planner.* Retrieved October 25, 2001 from http://www.ssa.gov/retire2/index.htm. Income data: Social Security Administration. "Fact Sheet: Social Security is Important to Asian Americans," March 2001. Retrieved October 25, 2001 from http://www.ssa.gov/pressoffice/asian-fact.htm. Net worth data: Amy Friedrich and Eric Rodriguez, "Financial Insecurity Amid Growing Wealth: Why Healthier Savings is Essential to Latino Prosperity." *NCLR Issue Brief,* August 2001.

The Potential Future Workforce

High School Completion Rates by Race, 1980-2000

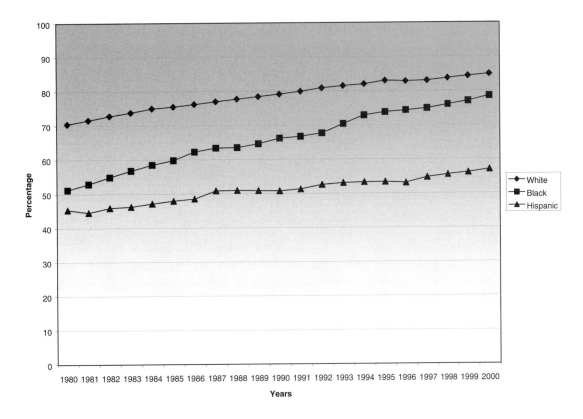

The graph above shows the high school completion rates for those 25 years old and older for 1980-2000. There were no high school data available for the Asian population, but we can assume that the high school completion rates are high if we look at college completion rates. Asian-Americans, in 1996, had the highest college completion levels, 50.2%. This exceeded all other races by 7.5 percentage points or more.

As the graph illustrates, over time high school completion rates have been going up for all races reported. Whites have consistently had the highest high school completion rates. Blacks are second, and steadily gaining on the whites. Hispanics trail blacks by a large margin, but that population also has been increasing its high school completion rate. Blacks' completion rates are lower than whites, but blacks have gained the most in the past decade. In the year 2000, 12.3% more blacks graduated than they did in 1980. This is quite a bit more than the 5.8% increase for whites, and the 6.2% increase for Hispanics.

With education comes increased employability; more of the population enters the workforce. It might be concluded, therefore, that since blacks have increased their graduation rates the most, they have the highest percentage of workers ready to enter the workforce. But, as shown on an earlier graph, Hispanics and Asians have a greater percentage of entrants to the workforce.

The fertility rates of the various races must be looked at in conjunction with the educational attainment rates to get a better understanding of this issue. The table below shows fertility rates by race. Blacks, Hispanics, and Asians all have higher fertility rates than whites. This partially explains why the whites' workforce population share is decreasing and the minority share is increasing, even though employability is high for whites. Hispanics have consistently the highest fertility rate at over 100 births per 1,000 women. That is at least 30 births more per 1,000 women than the rate for blacks and Asians, and at least 50 more births per 1,000 women than shown for whites. The rates are based on the total number of births per 1,000 women aged 15-44. A dash (-) means that data were unavailable.

Fertility Rate by Race, 1995-1997 and 1999-2000

	1995	1996	1997	1999	2000
White	57.6	57.3	57.0	57.8	58.7
Black	74.5	72.5	72.4	70.1	71.4
Hispanic	105.0	104.9	102.8	102.0	106.9
Asian	-	-	-	65.6	70.7

Although higher education levels and higher fertility levels do help to increase the number of people in the workforce, immigration also influences the number of people entering the workforce. A closer look at immigration's role in the diversification of the workforce follows.

Sources: Educational Attainment data: U. S. Census Bureau. "Table A-2. Percent of People 25 Years Old and Over Who Have Completed High School or College, by Race, Hispanic Origin and Sex: Selected Years 1940 to 2000," December 19, 2000. Kim Mahoney. "UCLA Study Finds Number of College Students Successfully Earning Bachelor's Degrees is Declining," UCLA Higher Education Research Institute, October 1, 1996. Retrieved December 10, 2001 from http://www.gseis.ucla.edu/heri/press_darcu.htm. Fertility rate data: Centers for Disease Control and Prevention. U.S. Department of Health and Human Services. "Table 1-4. Birth Rates by Live-Birth Order and Hispanic Origin of Mother and by Race for Mothers of Non-Hispanic Origin: United States, 1990-97." *Vital Statistics of the United States, 1997, Volume I, Natality*, Washington D.C.: U.S. Government Printing Office, August 2000. Centers for Disease Control and Prevention. U.S. Department of Health and Human Services. "Table 1. Births and birth rates by age, race, and Hispanic origin of the mother: United States final 1999 and preliminary 2000." *National Vital Statistics Report*, Vol. 49, No. 5, July 24, 2001.

Immigration's Diversifying Effect on the Workforce

Percent of Foreign-Born Population, 2000

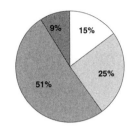

The pie charts show the percentage of the foreign-born population according to country of origin for the years 1960 and 2000. There has been a considerable increase in those coming from Latin America and from Asia and a substantial decrease in those coming from Europe. Those coming from other countries also had an overall decrease. Among the foreign-born, whites are now the minority and Hispanics are the majority.

The increase in Latin American and Asian immigration has led to more Hispanic and Asian workers entering the workforce. The increase is so dramatic, that, coupled with the high of these groups and their increasing employability due to higher educational attainment, the number of entrants to the workforce is much greater than in the white or the black population.

Percent of Foreign-Born Population, 1960

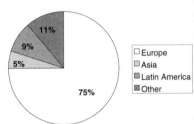

☐ Europe
☐ Asia
☐ Latin America
☐ Other

Hispanic immigrants are generally younger and of an age ready to enter the workforce. Many also bring their families and continue to have children after arriving. Therefore, not only do the parents enter the workforce shortly after arrival, but the children they bring and those born later ensure that there will be large numbers of Hispanics entering the workforce in the future.

Asian immigrants are also generally younger and of an age ready to enter the workforce. By 2008, Asians are expected to make up 5.7% of the workforce, up from 3.0% in 1988. During the 1980s, the immigration rate from Asia increased 77.5% from the 1970s, with 1,057,000 more Asians entering during the 1980s than during the 1970s. This rate has slowed somewhat during the 1990s, but 405,000 more Asians entered than in the previous decade. Overall, nearly 3 million Asians entered the United States during the 1990s, up from 1.3 million during the 1970s.

Black immigrants make up the smallest number of the foreign-born population compared with whites, Hispanics, and Asians. In 1990, blacks made up 7.4% of the foreign-born population. In 1997, foreign-born blacks were just 6% of the total black population. Therefore, immigrants are not adding significant numbers to the black workforce population.

Immigration from Europe has declined substantially in the past 40 years. White immigration provides fewer people to the white labor force than immigrants from Latin America and Asia.

Sources: Chart data: U.S. Census Bureau. "Table 2. Region of Birth of the Foreign-Born Population: 1860 to 1930 and 1960 to 1990," March 9, 1999. Retrieved March 26, 2002 from http://www.census.gov; U.S. Census Bureau. "Table 3.1 Foreign-Born Population by Sex, Age, and World Region of Birth: March 2000," January 3, 2001. Retrieved March 26, 2002 from http://www.census.gov.Bureau of Labor Statistics. U.S. Department of Labor. *Report on the American Workforce 2001*. Washington D.C.: U.S. Government Printing Office, 2000. "Foreign Born by Group, 1997." Retrieved October 31, 2001 from http://icg.fas.harvard.edu/~sa54/lectures/02_14_01_Lecture.pdf. U.S. Census Bureau. *We the American...Foreign Born*. Washington D.C.: U.S. Government Printing Office, September 1993.

Illegal Teenage Labor in the United States

15- to 17-Year Olds Working Illegally as a Percentage of Total Youth Labor Force: 1971-1997

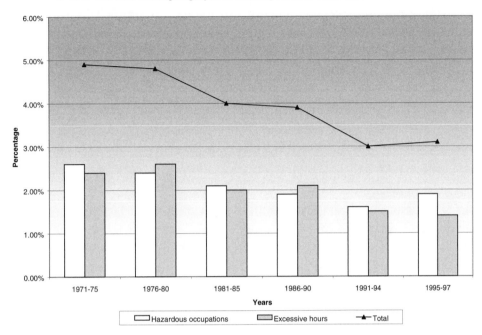

The chart above shows the percentage of workers aged 15-17 who worked illegally during the years 1971 to 1997. The chart shows that the prevalence of child labor is declining within this age group. This decline goes contrary to the number of child labor law violations found during the 1983-1991 time period; they nearly tripled. The high number of violations, which does not appear in the data, could be due to violations involving workers younger than age 15 — or in unreported places of work such as sweatshops.

Except for the years 1976-1980 and 1985-1990, most of the labor violations related to teenagers working in hazardous occupations. According to the Fair Labor Standards Act (FLSA), workers under 18 who work in non-agricultural jobs cannot work in hazardous occupations.

The table below shows the percentage of illegal child workers in the some of the occupations considered most hazardous. Teenagers working in hazardous occupations have a greater chance of sustaining injuries, including those that are permanently disabling or life-threatening.

Percentage of Illegal Child Workers, by Age and Occupation

Occupation	% of Illegal Workers	
	Age 15	Age 16-17
Precision production, craft, repair; Operators, fabricators, laborers; Helpers and laborers; Transportation, material moving	48.3%	88.9%

The FLSA also sets guidelines on the number of hours those under age 16 may work. During a school week, 14 and 15 year olds may work 18 hours a week. During a week when school isn't in session, 14 and 15 year olds may work no more than 40 hours a week. Using these guidelines, if a child works the maximum number of hours allowable by law, he/she will average 23 hours per week over the course of a year.

The table below shows the percentage of legally and illegally working 15-year olds and the hours worked per week. On average, 15-year olds employed illegally worked 11.9 hours more per week than those working legally, with a majority, 80.4%, working slightly less or over the average maximum allowable hours per week.

Percentage of 15-year Old Workers, by Hours Worked, 1995-1997

Usual weekly hours	Legally working (%)	Illegally working (%)
1-18	78.4	19.7
19-25	11.2	49.6
26-40+	10.4	30.8

When teenagers work more hours than allowable by law, they have less time for school-work and other activities. In most cases, their grades suffer. In many cases, those working the most hours drop out of school. Most of these workers are in low-paying or labor-intensive jobs. Without an education, they will not be able to move up to a higher paying job that will allow them to earn a comfortable living. Also, they will not have the skills necessary to move to jobs that are less labor intensive as they get older and can no longer do such strenuous work.

In the next panel, we turn to the detection of illegal child labor and child labor violations.

Sources: Kruse, Douglas and Douglas Mahony, "Illegal Child Labor in the United States: Prevalence and Characteristics." Cambridge, MA: National Bureau of Economic Research, March 1998. Employment Standards Administration. Wage and Hour Division. U.S. Department of Labor. *Child Labor Provisions of the Fair Labor Standards Act (FLSA) For Nonagricultural Occupations.* Retrieved November 29, 2001 from http://www.dol.gov/dol/esa/public/regs/compliance/whd/whdfs43.htm.

Government Enforcement of Child Labor Laws

Detected Illegal Employment of Minors: 1990-2000

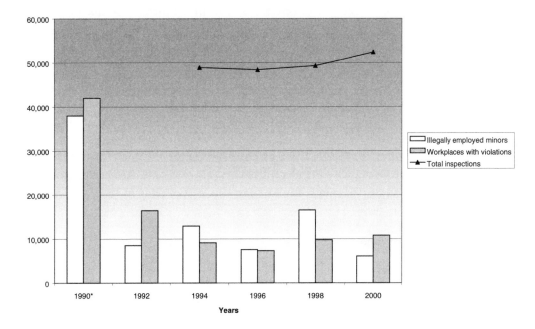

The chart shows the number of workplaces with child labor violations and the detected number of illegally employed minors for the years 1990-2000. It also shows the total number of inspections performed for the years 1994-2000.

During the early 1990s, the Department of Labor instituted a series of investigations called "Operation Child Watch" that specifically targeted employers of youth. For 1990, the chart shows the number of violations found rather than the number of workplaces with violations. As a result of this targeted crackdown, the government in 1990 detected the most violations and the most illegally working minors than in any year since.

During the years 1992-2000, the number of states detecting child labor violations has been fairly consistent at 28 or 29 states, except in 1998, when the number of states jumped to 33. This could partially explain why the number of illegally working minors detected was considerably higher during this year. Another factor could be the increased number of compliance officers whose sole responsibility is child labor law enforcement. There was an average of 8.5 officers covering 46 states in 1996 — and 22 covering 42 states in 1998. This increased hiring of officers may have signaled a push to target child labor violators. This could have been in response to a highly publicized 1997 Associated Press study that targeted child labor in the United States. The increased hiring has continued into the year 2000.

In both 1994 and 2000, an average of 40 officers worked in the field. Although inspections were up during 2000, and consequently child labor violations were up, the number of detected illegally working minors was down by about half from 1994. It could be that the number of illegally working minors in the industries that currently undergo inspection is down, as partially seen in an earlier panel.

Unfortunately, the numbers of detected illegal minor workers do not tell a complete story. The inspections mentioned above only account for a minimal number of inspections in the agriculture sector where an estimated 800,000 children work as migrant and seasonal workers. In fact, in 1996, only 7 states conducted inspections where child labor in agriculture was targeted, and only 3 of those states conducted a significant number of inspections in that same year. Of those three, 31 employers were found to be in violation, with a total of 91 minors employed illegally.

The table below shows the estimated number of illegally working minors in 1996 by industry. Although many children work in the agricultural sector — they are subject to more lenient labor laws than non-agricultural child workers — the estimated number of illegal child workers in this sector is much lower than those working in non-agricultural industries.

Estimated Illegal Child Workers in the United States, 1996

Total	290,200
Non-agricultural industries	285,300
Agricultural industries	4,900

The illegal adult labor force is discussed in the next panel.

Sources: Child Labor Coalition. "Overview on Enforcement", *Child Labor in the US*. Retrieved November 30, 2001 http://www.stop childlabor.org/USchildlabor/enforce-mentoverview.htm Child Labor Coalition. "State Survey Chart on Child Labor", *Child Labor in the US*. Retrieved November 30, 2001 from http://www.stopchildlabor.org/ USchildlabor/kidchart.htm. Child Labor Coalition. "Children in the Fields Fact Sheet", *Consumer Campaigns, Legislation, and Best Practice Solutions*. Retrieved November 30, 2001 from: http://www.stopchildlabor.org/USchildlabor/ fields.htm. Child Labor Coalition. "Highlights of the Child Labor Coalition's 1997 Child Labor State Survey", *Child Labor in the US*. Retrieved November 30, 2001 from http://www.stopchildlabor.org/Archives/ 97statesurv.html.

Estimated Illegal Workforce Population

Estimated Illegal Workforce Population for Top 10 Countries of Origin, 1996

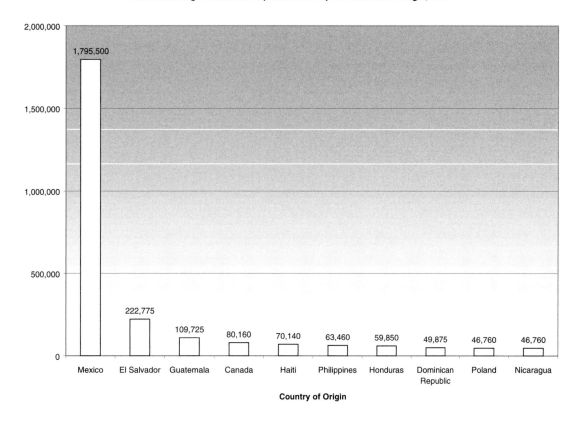

The chart above shows the estimated number of illegal workers in the United States by country of origin for 1996. Only the top 10 countries are shown. The data are based both on the labor force participation rates in 1996 and the estimated illegal immigrant population in that year. The participation rate used for the Mexican, Central American, and South American population is the rate for those of Hispanic origin. The participation rate used for all others is the rate for all workers 16 years and older in 1996.

According to the U.S. Immigration and Naturalization Service, there were an estimated 5 million illegal immigrants in this country in 1996. By 2000, that number had grown to 8 million. Based on the total labor force participation rate in those years, the estimated number of illegal workers was 3,340,000 in 1996 and 5,376,000 in 2000. As the chart above shows, most of the illegal workers come from Mexico, making up 54% of the illegal worker population.

Forty-one percent of the illegal immigrant population are nonimmigrant overstays. Nonimmigrant overstays are those who came here legally on a temporary basis but who failed to leave when their temporary visas expired. Even though most of the illegal population is Mexican, only 16% are nonimmigrant overstays. Twenty-six percent of those from Central America are nonimmigrant overstays, and 91% of illegal immigrants from

---

all other countries are classified in this category. This means that most of the illegal worker population came here illegally.

A discussion of illegal labor law enforcement follows.

Sources: U.S. Immigration and Naturalization Service. "Illegal Migration." *The Triennial Comprehensive Report on Immigration,* Washington D.C.: U.S. Government Printing Office, October 1996. U.S. Department of Labor. Bureau of Labor Statistics. "Table 5. Civilian labor force participation rates for selected demographic groups, annual averages, 1948-2000." Retrieved December 3, 2001 from http://www.bls.gov/opub/rtaw/pdf/table05.pdf. Camarota, Steven A., "Census Bureau: Eight Million Illegal Aliens in 2000", *Center for Immigration Studies,* October 24, 2001. Retrieved December 4, 2001 from http://www.cis.org/articles/2001/census-release1001.html.

Illegal Labor Law Enforcement

Percentage of Total Illegal Workers Arrested by the U.S. Immigration and Naturalization Service, 1994-1999

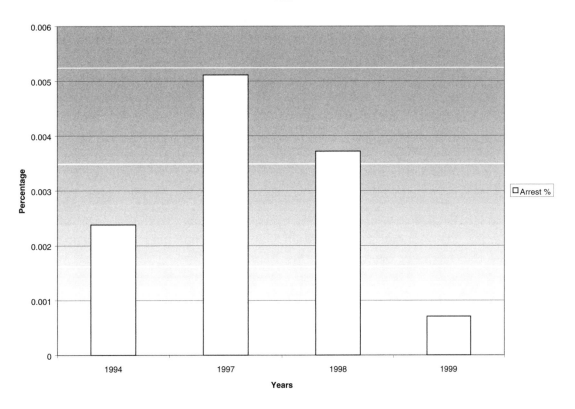

The chart above shows the percentage of the estimated total illegal worker population arrested during the years 1994 to 1999. Illegal labor law is minimally enforced. Even in 1997, when arrests reached the highest among the four years shown, there were only 17,552 arrests out of an estimated total illegal working population of nearly 3.5 million.

The lack of illegal labor law enforcement can be attributed to two factors. One is the focus in the past five years on the Border Patrol. In the five years prior to 2000, the number of agents had doubled and probably will continue to increase due to terrorist concerns as of September 11, 2001. This increased funding and manpower has also increased the number of illegal immigrants who are apprehended at the border. As the following table shows, apprehensions of those trying to enter the country illegally have gone up.

Apprehensions of Illegal Aliens by Border Patrol, 1997-1999

Year	Apprehensions
1997	1,536,520
1998	1,679,439
1999	1,714,035

Despite the growing number of people being stopped at the border, between 300,000 and 500,000 illegal immigrants enter each year. There are only 300 full-time Immigration and Naturalization Service (INS) agents nationwide whose responsibility is to enforce the ban on hiring illegal workers. With millions of places of business throughout the United States, and only 300 agents on patrol, once the illegal immigrants are here, there's a good chance that they will never be found by the INS.

Another factor in the low illegal labor law enforcement numbers is opposition by political leaders. In Austin, Texas, for example, where many of Texas's estimated 700,000 illegal workers live and work, the City Council passed a resolution in 1997 forbidding city agencies from asking a person's immigration status. The Austin Police Department also enacted the same policy that year. In 1998, INS raided a farm in Georgia looking for illegal workers. After the raid, Congress sent a letter to U.S. Attorney General Janet Reno criticizing INS for its "lack of regard for farmers" (Krikorian). In recent years, the INS has switched from raids to audits. The INS makes an appointment with a business to audit employees' work documents. Advance warning will tend to clear the decks, one presumes. Yet this technique has caused opposition from the Social Security Administration. It refused to give INS access to its records because of privacy concerns.

In 2000, Robert Bach, then a top INS official, admitted that the illegal labor laws were not being enforced. With political opposition to its efforts and inadequate manpower and funding, the INS has since been focusing its attention on finding illegal aliens who have committed crimes. As a result, the number of criminal aliens who have been deported has risen from 51,000 in 1997 to 69,000 in 1999.

Sources: Krikorian, Mark, "Controlling Illegal Immigration: There are Ways, But Little Will", *Investor's Business Daily*, March 21, 2001. Retrieved December 4, 2001 from http://www.cis.org/articles/2001/msk03-21-01.html. Steven A. Camarota. "Census Bureau: Eight Million Illegal Aliens in 2000." Center for Immigration Studies, October 24, 2001. Retrieved December 4, 2001 from http://ww.cis.org/articles/2001/census-release1001.html. Office of Policy and Planning. U.S. Immigration and Naturalization Service. Robert Warren. "Annual Estimate of the Unauthorized Immigrant Population Residing in the United States and Components of Change 1987 to 1997," September 2000. David Harmon, "Illegal labor fuels hot Austin economy*", Austin American-Statesman*, December 5, 1999. U.S. Immigration and Naturalization Service. *Statistical Yearbook of the Immigration and Naturalization Service*. 1997-1999 Editions. Washington D.C.: U.S. Government Printing Office, annual.

Chapter 3

Trends in Occupations

Our society is changing. The types of jobs of the future are changing as well. Advances in technology have fueled a tremendous increase in the need for computer professionals. The population of those 65 years old and older is expected to double from 35 million in 2000 to 70.3 million in 2030[1]. As the population ages and more and more elderly are staying in their homes, there will be a greater need for home health services. The shortages of doctors and nurses will create a demand for assistants. With more people taking advantage of the health care system, insurance paperwork will increase. The first panel discusses the 20 fastest growing occupations.

Technology will create many new jobs, but will also eliminate many jobs. Many jobs that were once performed by one person in a company have now been integrated into the job responsibilities of others in the organization. The second panel will discuss the top 20 declining occupations.

Many of the new jobs created will require at least some college education, with most requiring a degree. Will we be able to keep up with the increasing need for a highly educated workforce? The next three panels present a surprising answer.

Over 8 million people worked two or more jobs in 1997. The fourth panel provides answers to why we need (or want) to work more than one job. The fifth panel discusses those that work full-time, but do so by working part-time jobs.

The number of independent contractors has increased since the mid-1990s, totaling nearly 8.6 million in 2001. The next three panels present a picture of who they are, where they work, and whether they can earn a living working in this non-traditional work arrangement.

Home-based businesses have been growing in number, but home-based businesses as a percentage of all small businesses have been declining. The last panel in the chapter attempts to explain this phenomenon and shows that with technological advances and the Internet, home-based businesses may increase their percentage of the small business market.

---

[1] Administration on Aging. "Future Growth." *A Profile of Older Americans: 2001,* December 21, 2001 downloaded January 24, 2002 from http://www.aoa.dhhs.gov/.

Fastest Growing Occupations

Top 20 Fastest Growing Occupations, 2000-2010

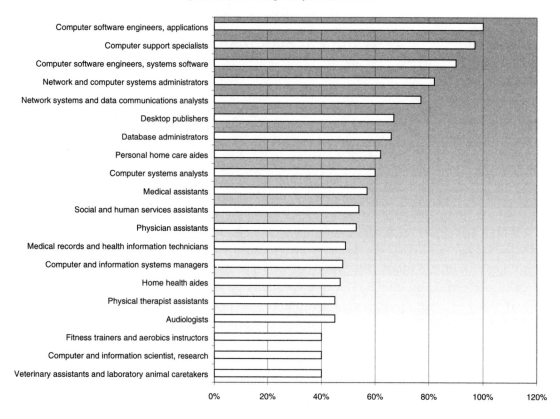

The chart above shows the occupations likely to grow most rapidly in the 2000 to 2010 period. Growth is shown in percentages. The fastest growing occupations reflect our changing society. Most of the occupations involve computers or health care. In looking at such projections, it is well to remember that they are made by knowledgeable people peering ahead at the unknowable future — and reflect perceptions of trends at the time the projections are made. Events — such as those of September 11, 2001 — could clearly cause changes in these perceptions and in occupational outcomes ten years out.

The worldwide web is, technologically, the dominant phenomenon of the early 21st century. Computers touch nearly every facet of our lives. As businesses expand and new ones develop, the need to improve and develop new systems and software arises. As a result, the need for more computer professionals — especially software engineers, networking experts, database administrators, and systems managers — is predicted.

Medical advances and an emphasis on preventive care and healthy living have caused people to live longer and healthier lives. As a result, there will be an increased need for workers in the health and wellness fields. The rise in popularity of health clubs and fitness centers has created a high demand for fitness trainers and aerobics instructors.

Aging Baby Boomers are creating an increase in the elderly population. Certain surgical advances have created an increased need for physical and occupational therapy aides and assistants. The increased risk of suffering a debilitating stroke has created a greater need for physical and occupational therapy in this population. All this creates an even higher demand for physical and occupational therapy assistants.

More families are choosing to take care of elderly relatives in their homes. This demand is increasing the call for home care aides.

The demand for physicians' assistants is also high, stimulated by the shortage of physicians (medical school applications are down 26% over the last 5 years[2]). Because physicians' assistants examine, diagnose, and treat patients under the supervision of the physician, patients with less serious illnesses may be treated by physicians' assistants, so that the physicians have the time to spend with patients who have more serious health problems.

More patients and increased paperwork from insurance companies are creating a high demand for medical assistants and medical records and health information technicians. In doctors' offices with many patients, there may be multiple medical assistants to take care of all the clerical tasks so that the office runs smoothly. Medical assistants may also handle tasks that once were performed by nurses. They administer lab tests, draw blood, remove sutures and change dressings. As the shortage of nurses grows, the demand for medical assistants to do some of the simpler tasks nurses used to do will increase.

The next panel examines the 20 occupations that will decline most in the next decade.

Source: Chart data: Hecker, Daniel E. "Occupational employment projections to 2010." *Monthly Labor Review*, November 2001. Physician assistant and medical assistant data: U.S. Bureau of Labor. Bureau of Labor Statistics. *Occupational Outlook Handbook 2002-03 Edition.* Barbara Martinez. "Some Doctors Say They May Stop Seeing Medicare Patients After Cuts." *Wall Street Journal,* January 15, 2002.

---

[2] According to the Association of Medical Colleges. *Wall Street Journal*, January 15, 2002

Most Rapidly Declining Occupations

Top 20 Occupations With the Largest Job Decline, 2000-2010

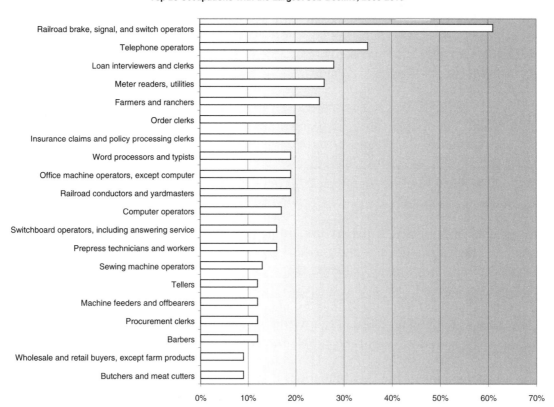

Some occupations will increase, others will decline. The occupations predicted to be declining most rapidly by the Bureau of Labor Statistics are shown. Declines are in percentages for the 2000 to 2010 period.

The driving force behind the decline in most of these occupations is automation — but there are some exceptions. Two of these are barbers and butchers and meat cutters.

The decline in barbers is said to be caused by the rise in salons where, in unisex settings, all types of hair treatments — along with manicures, pedicures, and massages — are administered to people in large establishments — and the traditional barbershop is therefore in decline, "hairdressers" doing the job for all genders. No haircutting robots seem poised to take over the job.

The decline in the number of butchers and meat cutters has more to do with structural realignments — the growth in the centralized processing of meat and poultry — than with automation per se. Demand for meat, poultry, and fish continues to be high, but more and more of the cutting and processing is done at slaughterhouses and meatpacking plants by lower paid slaughterers and meatpackers

Automation has the potential of totally eliminating the job of utility meter reader. New automated meter reading (AMR) systems monitor meters and bill customers from a centralized location. Because all meters have not been converted to this new system yet, there will still be a need for meter readers, but available jobs will be those freed by retirements or by people quitting rather than growth.

Automation has also nearly eliminated the need for ordering and procurement clerks. Business-to-business electronic commerce, and automated phone systems have made it possible for managers or selected employees to order stock directly from the suppliers. Electronic data interchange allows computers to communicate with each other to place orders; the need for human interaction in routine ordering is diminishing.

Automation and the lessening reliance on passenger railroads will make the need for railroad brake, signal, and switch operators decline the most in the next decade. But, even though passenger railroad transportation is declining, the need for railroad conductors and yardmasters is not declining as fast as brake, signal, and switch operators. As long as there are railroads, there will be a need for conductors and yardmasters. Those jobs cannot be fully automated.

Certain jobs, such as word processors and typists, computer operators, and office machine operators have generally been incorporated into other jobs. With the increased user-friendliness of office machines, including computers with built-in word processing programs, word processing is done as a routine part of other jobs.

In most cases, automation won't eliminate an occupation entirely, but certain occupations will "fade away" as the functions they used to fulfill are assumed by other occupations in whole or part.

Employees in fifteen out of the top 20 growing occupations need a post-secondary vocational award or higher. Employees in 18 out of the top 20 declining occupations need only on-the-job work experience. Will the educational attainment level of the workforce population keep up with the increasing demand for more intensely-educated workers? We will take a closer look at this issue in the next panel.

Sources: Hecker, Daniel E. "Occupational employment projections to 2010." *Monthly Labor Review,* November 2001. Bureau of Labor Statistics. U.S. Department of Labor. *Occupational Outlook Handbook 2002-03 Edition.* National Center for Education Statistics. U.S. Department of Education. *Digest of Education Statistics, 2000.* U.S. Census Bureau. Population Projections Program. *(NP-D1-A) Projections of the Resident Population by Age, Sex, Race, and Hispanic Origin: 1999 to 2100,* January 13, 2000. Retrieved January 7, 2002 from http://www.census.gov.

Are We Too Educated for the Future Job Market?

Educational Attainment of the Civilian Labor Force, 16 years and over, 1993-2000

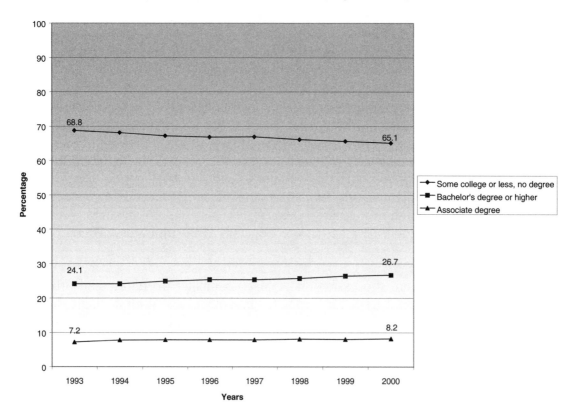

The graph shows the percentage of the civilian workforce population, 16 years and older, that has attained various levels of education. A demand for a workforce that must have an associate degree or higher has been matched by an increase in people with degrees. But the number of people in the workforce who have a degree is greater than the number of jobs that call for a degree.

The following table shows the match-up between people in the civilian workforce, grouped by educational attainment and the jobs available for them. Data are for 2000. If all available jobs were filled, many who had degrees did not find work in fields requiring a degree. The table also shows that there was (and is) a shortage of workers overall. Even if all of the surplus workers with degrees took jobs not requiring a degree, there would have been a shortfall of 5.14 million workers in 2000. The shortfall becomes greater if unemployment is taken into account.[3]

---

[3] Worker shortages and surpluses are also discussed in the chapter entitled "The Workforce."

Jobs and Workforce Population, by Educational Level, 2000

Education & Training Level	Number of Jobs	Civilian Workforce Population	Shortfall or Surplus of Workers
Work experience, high school, post-secondary vocational award	110,438,000	91,416,000[4]	-19,022,000
Associate degree or higher	35,155,000	49,037,000	13,882,000

If we look at the issue over time, it appears that the problem of underemployment of college graduates is growing. The percentage of underemployed college graduates during the 1991 to 2005 is expected to jump considerably from earlier years. During 1991-2005, there is expected to be 50,000 fewer jobs annually for college graduates than during the 1984-1990 period. In addition, the number of college graduates is expected to increase by 132,000 annually.

Percentage of College Graduates in Jobs Not Requiring a College Degree or Unemployed

Year	Employed in jobs not requiring a degree or unemployed (%)
1967	11.7
1970	11.3
1975	16.7
1980	18.6
1985	19.2
1990	19.9
1991-2005	30.8[5]

Does this mean that there is an abundance of qualified workers to fill job openings in those occupations that require a college degree? Not necessarily. The next panel presents data on the shortfalls and surpluses in occupations requiring a college degree.

Sources: U.S. Census Bureau. *Current Population Survey,* annual. Job data: Daniel E. Hecker. "Occupational employment projections to 2010." *Monthly Labor Review*, November 2001. Underemployment data: Kristina J. Shelley. "The future of jobs for college graduates." *Monthly Labor Review*, July 1992. John Tyler, et. al. "Are more college graduates really taking 'high school' jobs?" *Monthly Labor Review*, December 1995.

---

[4] Those with some college education or less, but without a degree.

[5] Annual percentage. Kristina J. Shelley. "The future of jobs for college graduates." *Monthly Labor Review*, July 1992.

Are We Undereducated for the Real World?

Job Openings and Degrees Conferred, 1998-2008

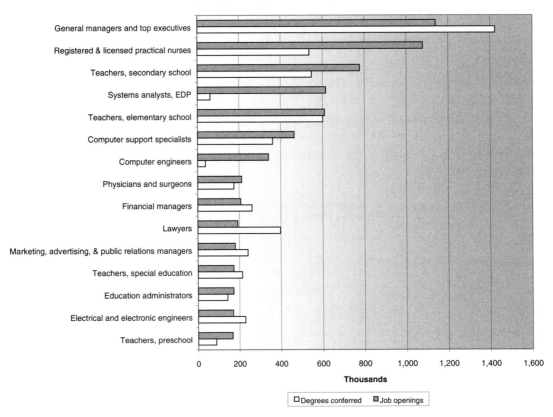

Thousands

☐ Degrees conferred ■ Job openings

The chart shows job openings for occupations that call for a degree (dark bar) and the number of degrees conferred in the specialty (light bar). Data are for the years 1998 to 2008[6,7]. The degrees conferred for "general managers and top executives" include all degrees in business administration and management.

The previous panel showed that, overall, there are more college graduates than job openings requiring a degree. This would seem to suggest that all jobs requiring a degree would be filled by qualified applicants. Not so. As the chart shows, many of the occupations

---

[6] Two occupations were left out of the list due to lack of data on degrees conferred. Those were accountants and auditors, which will have 288,900 openings during 1998-2008; and engineering, mathematical and natural science managers, which will have 198,900 openings.

[7] Projections were based on data from 1993-1998 in the *Digest of Education Statistics,* editions 1997 to 2000. Degrees conferred for systems analysts, EDP include all degrees for information science and systems and computer systems analysis. EDP stands for electronic data processing. Degrees conferred for computer support specialists include all degrees in computer and information science, even though many with these degrees are overqualified for the job.

with the highest number of job openings are not the most popular among college students seeking a degree. Business administration degrees remain popular. All management occupations, with the exception of education administrators, will experience surpluses in qualified workers. Lawyers, engineers, and special education teachers will also experience a surplus of workers.

The remaining 9 out of 15 occupations, however, will experience shortfalls in qualified workers. The following table lists these shortfalls.

Worker Shortfalls, 1998-2008

Systems analyst, data processing	-555,000
Registered and licensed practical nurses	-540,400
Computer engineers	-303,700
Teachers, secondary school	-228,600
Computer support specialists	-104,300
Teachers, preschool	-79,500
Physicians and surgeons	-38,300
Education administrators	-30,000
Teachers, elementary	-8,900

With this projected shortfall of qualified workers, what are organizations doing to meet their employment needs? They are looking outside the United States for qualified workers — a controversial process especially in times when recession may or may not be a fact and layoffs are daily announced. During the first and second quarters of the 2001 fiscal year (October 2000-March 2001), 172,126 petitions for H-1B visas[8] were approved. In fiscal year 2000 (October 1999-September 2000), a total of 257,000 H-1B visas were approved.

Does this mean that those with degrees in fields of shortage are guaranteed a job? Do companies only look for qualified foreign workers when no domestic workers apply for a position? Not necessarily. Cisco Systems Inc., a high-tech firm, had the third highest number of H-1B petitions approved: 398 foreign workers were granted legal working status between October 1999 and February 2000. At the same time, the company admitted in 2000 to being inundated with 20,000 resumes per month, but only hiring 5% of those applicants. Microsoft Corporation had the sixth highest number of H-1B workers (362) and yet admitted to only hiring 2% of the thousands of applicants that apply.

In some cases, companies save money by hiring foreign workers. According to Norman Matloff of the *Washington Post,* CEOs from womenConnect.com and Ecutel testified before Congress in favor of a bill to increase the H-1B quota[9]. A Freedom of Information

---

[8] Work visas given to foreign, nonimmigrant skilled workers working in many different occupational categories.

[9] The bill, known as American Competitiveness in the Twenty-First Century Act of 2000, was passed in October 2000. It raised the annual cap of H-1B workers to 195,000 a year. It also eliminated quotas in some occupational categories and allowed visa holders to extend their status beyond 6 years under certain circumstances.

Act inquiry on the companies found that they paid their H-1B status programmers $10,000 less per year than the national average for new computer science graduates.

Where do college-educated workers find jobs if they can't find them in their field of study? If an estimated 30.8% of college graduates face underemployment or unemployment, is a college education worth the trouble and expense? We shall attempt to answer this question next.

Sources: Chart data: "Occupations with the Most Openings Requiring a Bachelor's Degree or Higher." *America's Career Infonet.* Retrieved January 31, 2002 from http://www.acinet.org; "Occupations with the Most Openings Requiring Post-Secondary Training or an Associate's Degree." *America's Career InfoNet.* Retrieved January 31, 2002 from http://www.acinet.org; National Center for Education Statistics. U.S. Department of Education. *Digest of Education Statistics,* 1997-2000 editions. H1-B data: U.S. Immigration and Naturalization Service. *Leading Employers of Specialty Occupation Workers (H-1B): October 1999 to February 2000,* June 2000. Retrieved February 5, 2002 from http://www.ins.usdoj.gov. U.S. Immigration and Naturalization Service. *Characteristics of Specialty Occupation Workers (H-1B): October 1999 to February 2000,* June 2000. U.S. Immigration and Naturalization Service. *Report on H-1B Petitions: Second Quarter Fiscal Year 2001 January 1, 2001-March 31, 2001.* U.S. Immigration and Naturalization Service. *Report on H-1B Petitions: Annual Report Fiscal Year 2000 October 1, 1999-September 30, 2000.* Foreign Labor Data: Norman Matloff. "High-Tech Cheap Labor." *Washington Post,* September 12, 2000. Retrieved February 5, 2002 from http://www.washingtonpost.com. "H1-B Newsflash." Retrieved February 5, 2002 from http://immigration.about.com/library/blh1b-newsflash.htm. Underemployment data: Kristina J. Shelley "The future of jobs for college graduates." *Monthly Labor Review,* July 1992.

College-Educated Customer Service

Occupations with the Most Openings, 1998-2008

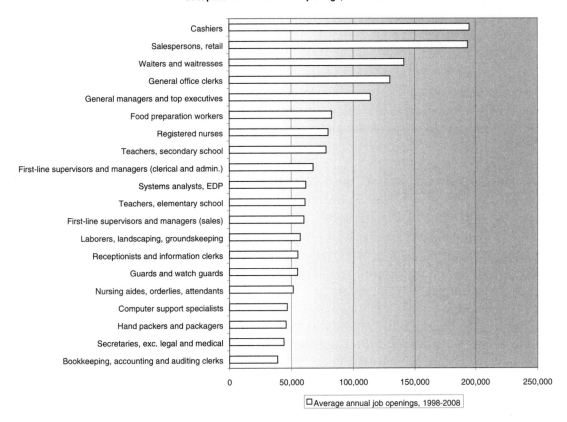

Average annual job openings, 1998-2008

Displayed in this chart are the top 20 occupations that will have the most job openings during the years 1998-2008. Six of the 20 occupations will require at least an associate degree. Only four of 20 will require a bachelor's degree or higher. The other 14 occupations only require work experience or on-the-job training.

What happened to our technological society? More and more people are going to college. Computers have become a part of nearly every aspect of our life. Yet, technology has not created a society based on high-tech jobs. In fact, even when we look at the six occupations in the chart that require a degree, we can see that despite the over-education of society spoken of in a previous panel, five of the six will still face a shortfall of workers[10].

Although more people are receiving degrees, there is a mismatch between degree and job. This is confirmed by a study done by the U.S. Department of Education. The department tracked 1992-1993 bachelor's degree recipients a year after graduation; 43% reported having jobs in which a bachelor's degree was not required; 26% said that their job had no career potential.

---

[10] For a more in depth discussion see the previous panel.

As a society, we still like to see a friendly face in the checkout line at the retail store. We still want salespeople to wait on us and answer our questions. We still prefer to be served in restaurants by waiters and waitresses. Even in fast-food restaurants, we still want our meals our way. There is, thus, a high demand for food preparation workers. Our lawns need cutting. Our flowerbeds need tending. Landscaping and groundskeeping crews are in demand. Our security is important to us; there is a high demand for guards. Some packaging can't be totally automated; therefore, there will be quite a few jobs for packagers. Nursing aides, orderlies, and attendants are needed to tend to the hospital patients' daily needs. In the office, office clerks, receptionists and secretaries have not been totally eliminated by automation. The high demand for bookkeeping, accounting and auditing clerks seems to mean that we prefer knowledgeable people to handle the company finances rather than computer programs.

Despite advances in technology, the jobs with the most job openings in the 1998-2008 period will involve mainly human-to-human rather than human-to-computer interaction. Automation has eliminated some jobs and created new high-tech ones, but despite our fascination with computers, we seem to resist automation in some forms. If automation is one of the driving factors of productivity, and the tendency in the future is to resist automation in some forms, does that mean that productivity[11] will level out? Not as long as educational attainment levels increase.

Automation, technology will continue to push up productivity, as will a more educated workforce. But these patterns of mismatch may be telling us something new: productivity may not be the be-all and the end-all of future development. Educational strategies may have to change to prepare people better for jobs that *are* available — and pay scales may have to improve to attract people to jobs where the "people-to-people" component is predominant and abstract knowledge or machine-skills are less important to deliver a product the customer will value. Anyone who has, lately, "interacted" with a polite but deadly voice-mail system or been served by a surly clerk surely will agree.

Sources: Chart data: "Occupations with the Most Openings." *America's Career Infonet.* Retrieved January 31, 2002 from http://www.acinet.org. McCormick, Alexander C. and Laura J. Horn. *A Descriptive Summary of 1992-93 Bachelor's Degree Recipients: 1 Year Later,* August 1996. National Center for Education Statistics. U.S. Department of Education. *Digest of Education Statistics, 2000.* Paul Decker. "Issues in Focus: Education and worker productivity." *The Condition of Education 1996.* Retrieved February 1, 2002 from http://nces.ed.gov/pubsold/ce96/c96004.html. Underemployment data: Kristina J. Shelley. "The future of jobs for college graduates." *Monthly Labor Review,* July 1992.

---

[11] For a more in depth discussion of productivity see the chapter entitled "People, Technology, and Productivity."

Why Do We Work Multiple Jobs?

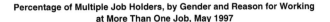

Percentage of Multiple Job Holders, by Gender and Reason for Working
at More Than One Job, May 1997

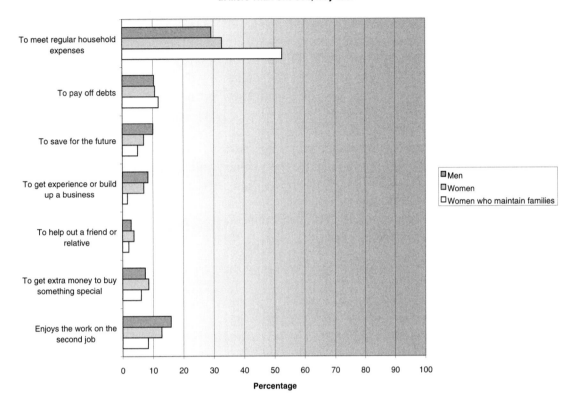

The chart above shows the percentage of multiple jobholders, by gender and the reasons for holding more than one job. More than 8.7 million people held two or more jobs in May 1997. More than 4.7 million were men. Over 4 million were women. Women who worked multiple jobs and maintained families numbered 577,000.

As expected, most people who hold more than one job do so in order to pay daily household expenses. This is especially true of women who maintain families. Fifty-two percent of women who maintain families and have more than one job do so to meet daily living expenses.

The percentage of men and women is nearly equal when it comes to getting a second job to pay off debts. The percentage is a bit higher for those women who maintain families. This could be because women who maintain families incur more debt. Women in general have lower incomes than men and have a tougher time making ends meet.

When the reasons are something other than meeting daily expenses or repaying debts, men and women have different reasons for holding more than one job. More men than women get second jobs to save for the future, to gain work experience, to build a business, or because they like the work on the second job. More women than men, on the

---

other hand, get a second job either to help out a friend (childcare, for example) or to get extra money to buy something special.

Women who maintain families are less likely to get second jobs to gain experience, build a business, or to help out a friend or a relative. These reasons may be seen as too risky (building a business) or unnecessary (gaining work experience when they already work at a job). Women who maintain families may concentrate on the monetary gains of a second job. Therefore, any job seen as not producing instant monetary results, may not appeal to them. Monetary concerns may be part of the reason so few decide to take a second job to help out friends or relatives. Time conflicts with their primary job, or family demands, may be another.

Interestingly, quite a few women who maintain families get second jobs because they enjoy the work. If the expenses are paid by the primary job, a higher priority is given to job satisfaction. Fewer women who maintain families get second jobs to save money.

In the next panel, we discuss the differences between men and women who maintain a full-time work schedule, but work part-time jobs.

Source: Bureau of Labor Statistics. U.S. Department of Labor. "When one job is not enough." *Issues in Labor Statistics,* August 2000.

Part-Time Jobs, Full-time Employment

Percentage of Workers with Part-time Jobs, by Gender and Type of Employment, May 1995

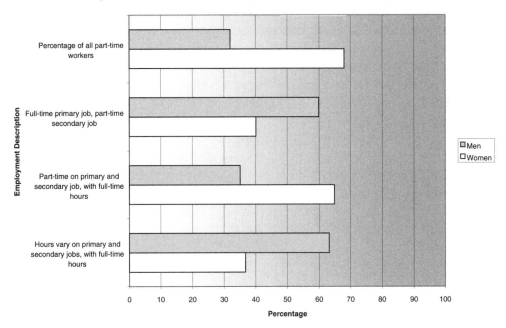

This chart shows the part-time work activity of men and women who also hold full-time jobs (35 hours or more per week). All data are for May 1995. That year, 6.5 million people held a part-time job in addition to a full work schedule. Most (4.4 million) held a full-time primary job and one or more part time jobs. About 975,000 workers combined more than one part-time job into a full-time schedule.

Sixty eight percent of all part-time workers are women. The majority of part-time women workers (72.9%) are 25 years old and older, with 57.2% between the ages of 25 and 54. The men's part-time workforce is more evenly distributed among the age groups, but most workers (53.4%) are 25 years old and older, with 30.3% between the ages of 25 and 54.

More men than women hold a part-time job in addition to their full-time job. Of the men that are in this category, 69.3% are married[12]. Married women in this category make up 44.1%. More married men may choose to supplement their primary incomes with a second job so that their wives can have more free time to take care of the children and household. The second income may also provide enough money so that the wife doesn't have to get a second job herself, or it may provide enough money so that the wife doesn't have to work full time at all. Despite this, nearly half of women who work a part-time job in addition to a full-time job are married. Some reasons for this could be that the combined income of the husband and the wife isn't enough to pay the daily living expenses or

---

[12] In this panel, "married" means "married, with spouse present."

---

debts the couple has accrued. Another reason could be that the extra income provides either extra savings or extra spending money.

More women than men hold two part-time jobs. In this case, 49.5% of women who are in this category are married. Married men make up 41.3% of the men who hold two part-time jobs. The need for a full-time income, but with the flexibility of part-time employment could be the reason for the high percentage of married women holding two part-time jobs. Married men have fewer of the jobs in this category — probably because of the lower income and lack of benefits offered by part-time jobs. The advantage of flexibility is overridden by the need to provide for the family.

More men than women hold two jobs with varying hours. In both cases, the majority of workers are married (71.1% of men and 51.4% of women). Some jobs in this category offer more of an incentive for married men and women because of their higher pay than other part-time jobs, good benefits, and their flexible schedule. Jobs in this category include those in the construction trades, transportation, business services, machine operators, assemblers and laborers.

Sources: Bureau of Labor Statistics. U.S. Department of Labor. "A Different Look at Part-time Employment." *Issues in Labor Statistics,* April 1996. Lonnie Golden. "Flexible work schedules: what are we trading off to get them?" *Monthly Labor Review,* March 2001.

Independent Contractors: Who Are We?

Independent Contractor Characteristics, by Gender, 1995-2001

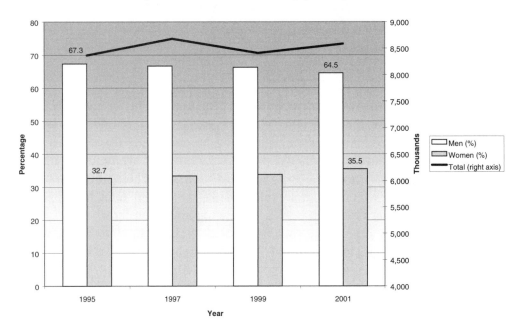

There were some 8.6 million independent contractors in 2001, up from nearly 8.3 million in 1995 (see curve). Men are roughly two-thirds of the total, but with women gaining as participants in this occupational category. Overall, independent contractors represented 6.4% of the workforce in 2001.

As the chart shows, increase in the number of independents has not been steady. When the economy is good, employers are more likely to hire permanent workers. In downturns employers try to save money and look to outsource some of the tasks done by former permanent employees.

Although men make up the majority of independent contractors, their numbers have been shrinking in favor of women. Interestingly, as more women became independent contractors, the number of women-owned individual proprietorships[13] decreased by 482,000 between 1992 and 1997.

Most independent contractors are white married men, over 35 years old. They have a college education but do not necessarily have a degree. The following table shows the makeup of the independent contractor workforce by race for the years 1995 and 2001. Whites had a lower share of this workforce in 2001 than they did in 1995. Both blacks and Hispanics have increased their share. Some of this can be attributed to the overall

---

[13] Individual proprietorships are unincorporated businesses owned by an individual. Self-employed people are included in this category.

growth of black- and Hispanic-owned businesses. By 1997, the number of black individual proprietorships increased by 153,076 since 1992. Hispanic individual proprietorships increased by 338,000 since 1992.

Independent Contractor Workforce, by Race, 1995 and 2001

	1995 (%)	2001 (%)
White	92.3	88.3
Black	5.0	7.0
Hispanic	5.2	7.2

The share of married independent contractors has been decreasing (73.5% in 1995 down to 71.5% in 1999[14]), while the share of never married and divorced singles has been increasing (23.5% in 1995 to 26.5% in 1999). This could be due to the decreased share of men working in this type of arrangement. Independent contractors are twice as likely as traditional workers to work part-time and their jobs are such that there is no guarantee of long-term steady income. It would be more difficult for a married man to support his family being employed in that type of job. When independent contractors do work full-time, they average 3.9 hours more a week than traditional workers. In 1999[3], 15% worked more than 60 hours per week as opposed to 6% of traditional workers. This could be another deterrent to married men: more work hours mean less time spent with family.

Women, however, are three times more likely than men to prefer to work part-time in this type of work arrangement. They have a need to balance work and family responsibilities. Also, there may be a lesser need for a full-time job if the husband's income will pay most or all of the living expenses.

The next panel will show the occupations in which independent contractors work.

Sources: DiNatale, Marisa. "Characteristics and preferences for alternative work arrangements, 1999." *Monthly Labor Review*, March 2001. Bureau of Labor Statistics. U.S. Department of Labor. *Employment and Earnings,* January 2001. Data for 2001: Bureau of Labor Statistics. U.S. Department of Labor. "Table 6. Employed workers with alternative and traditional work arrangements by selected characteristics, February 2001." Retrieved January 18, 2002 from http://www.bls.gov/news.release/conemp.t06.htm; Bureau of Labor Statistics. U.S. Department of Labor. "Table 5. Employed workers with alternative and traditional work arrangements by selected characteristics, February 2001." Retrieved January 18, 2002 from http://www.bls.gov/news.release/conemp.t05.htm. U.S. Census Bureau. *Economic Census, 1992* and *1997.*

---

[14] 2001 data not available at time of printing.

Independent Contractors: Where Do We Work?

Number of Independent Contractors, by Occupation and Gender, February 1999

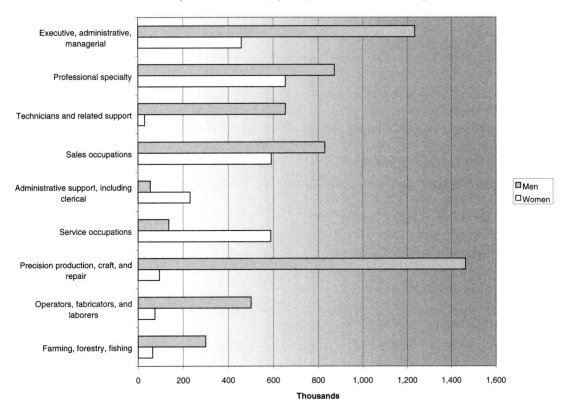

The chart shows the number of independent contractors employed in the various occupations for February 1999. Overall, more men are independent contractors than women, but they do not make up the majority of the workforce in each occupational category. However, they make up the majority in occupations that traditionally employ more men than women. A striking example is in the precision production, craft, and repair field, where there were over 1.4 million men working as independent contractors, while only 95,000 women worked in this same field as independents. But women make up a sizeable proportion of independent contractors in the professional specialty; sales; and executive, administrative, and managerial fields. In the administrative support, clerical, and service occupations, women workers are dominant.

The table on the next page shows the percentage of employees working in the various occupations. The percentage division within the independent contractor work arrangement does not always correspond to the percentage division within the traditional work arrangement. For the most part, employees in traditional work arrangements are evenly distributed among the various occupational categories. Independent contractors, however, are mostly concentrated in the executive, administrative, and managerial; professional specialty; sales; and precision production, craft, and repair fields.

Percentage of Workforce: Independent Contractors vs. Traditional Employees

Occupation	Independent Contractor (%)	Traditional Employees (%)
Executive, administrative, managerial	20.5	14.5
Precision production, craft, and repair	18.9	10.5
Professional specialty	18.5	15.5
Sales occupations	17.3	12.0
Service occupations	8.8	13.7
Operators, fabricators, and laborers	7.0	13.6
Farming, forestry, and fishing	4.4	2.0
Administrative support, incl. clerical	3.4	15.0
Technicians and related support	1.1	3.3

In the next panel we look at the income of independent contractors.

Source: DiNatale, Marisa. "Characteristics of and preference for alternative work arrangements, 1999." *Monthly Labor Review*, March 2001.

Independent Contractors: Can We Make A Living?

Median Annual Earnings: Independent Contractor vs. Traditional Worker, February 1999

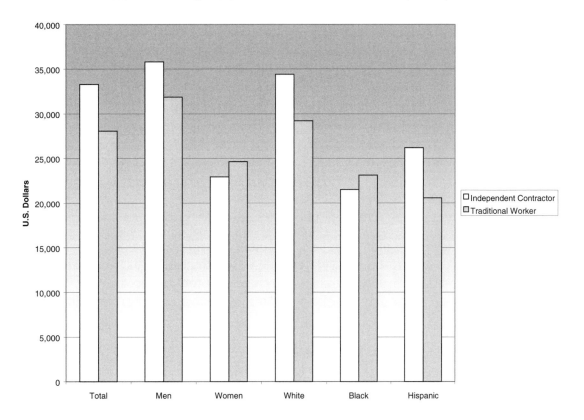

The chart shows the median annual earnings[15] for both full-time independent contractors and full-time traditional workers for February 1999. The chart also shows this comparison by gender and race. Overall, independent contractors earn more than traditional workers. They tend to be highly educated and skilled — else they would not survive. Despite this, women and blacks tend to earn more in the traditional workforce than they do as independent contractors. This could be because women and blacks tend to put in fewer hours in this type of work arrangement. They may also have less experience in their field, or be employed in fields that traditionally pay less.

Most independent contractors may earn more than traditional workers, but they also incur expenses that traditional workers do not. These expenses include work-related expenditures for equipment, transportation, and training; self-employment taxes[16]; federal and state withholding taxes; and health insurance.

---

[15] Figures based on median weekly earnings.

[16] Many business expenses and half of the self-employment tax are deductible.

The next table shows the percentage of independent contractors and traditional employees that have health care coverage. It also shows the percentage of workers that purchased coverage on their own.

Independent Contractor vs. Traditional Employee: Health Care Coverage

	With health insurance coverage (%)				
	Total	Through current employer	Purchased on own[17]	Through spouse or other family member	Other
Independent Contractor	73.3	1.8	33.0	26.7	11.8
Men	71.6	1.8	37.2	20.4	12.2
Women	76.8	1.9	24.8	39.1	11.0
Full-time	72.3	2.1	38.4	23.0	8.8
Part-time	76.4	0.9	18.2	37.4	19.9
Traditional Employee	82.9	61.1	21.1	[3]	0.7
Men	82.2	66.3	14.8	[3]	1.1
Women	83.7	55.4	28.0	[3]	0.3
Full-time	84.8	70.6	13.5	[3]	0.7
Part-time	74.3	16.9	56.7	[3]	0.7

Independent contractors are more likely than traditional employees to purchase their own health insurance. For this reason, clearly, fewer have health insurance coverage. Part-time independents have higher health insurance coverage — probably because they are covered by their spouses; many part-time independents also have coverage through full-time traditional jobs.

Although income tends to be higher for independent contractors, added expenses, such as business expenses, taxes, and health care coverage may offset the higher pay. Their disposable income may not be as high as it may appear on the surface. Independence has a cost.

Source: DiNatale, Marisa. "Characteristics and preferences for alternative work arrangements, 1999." *Monthly Labor Review*, March 2001.

---

[17] The percentages in the column "Purchased on own" for the traditional employees include those that have coverage through their spouses or other family members.

Home-Based Business Popularity

Home-based Business vs. Small Business, 1982-1992

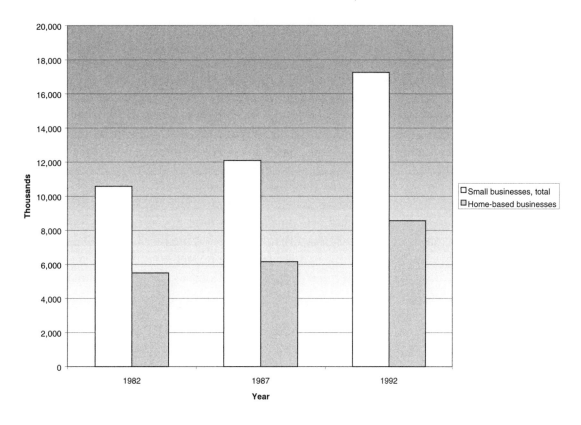

The chart shows the number of small businesses and the number of home-based businesses for the years 1982 to 1992[18]. Although the number of home-based businesses has been rising, their percentage of all small businesses has been decreasing (from 51.9% in 1982 to 49.6% in 1992). In 1992, home-based businesses accounted for 5% of the estimated $6.4 trillion contributed to the economy by all small employer firms, which translates to $320 billion.

Part of the decline in share could be the shift in the types of home-based employment pursued by individuals. Since the 1960s, there has been less employment in family farming. Doctors and lawyers, who once were home-based, are now part of group practices. In many areas, zoning changes are making it more difficult to sell things from the home or to advertise goods or services for sale.

Home-based businesses produce less profit. Many entrepreneurs hope simply to make a living from their small business. As the following table shows, most home-based busi-

---

[18] This was the last year the *Economic Census* reported on home-based businesses.

nesses have receipts totaling less than $25,000. On the other hand, most other small businesses have receipts totaling $25,000 or more; a third have receipts exceeding $100,000.

Percentage of Small and Home-based Businesses[19], by Receipts, 1992

Receipts	Non-home-based business (%)	Home-based business (%)
$0-24,999	45.7	74.0
$25,000-99,999	22.7	19.9
$100,000-999,999	25.5	6.8
$1,000,000+	4.8	0.2

Despite these negatives, there were more home-based businesses in 1992 than in 1982. Many may have been then (and are today) the temporary bases of furloughed people waiting for permanent employment. More than half such businesses (57% in 1992) were started with less than $5,000 in capital, 25% without any capital at all.

Not all persons who have home-based businesses work exclusively from their home. Most only do clerical/office work at home and are out there doing construction, selling, driving vehicles, or doing repair work for others; 61.2% of businesses in 1992 (5.5 million) were of this type. When the work is done from the home, it tends to be manufacturing of some good, delivery of a service (medical, childcare), or sales from the home (home-based retail enterprise).

With advances in technology and the availability of the Internet, the number of home-based businesses may well grow. New technology may create new occupations and new markets for the products and services produced by home-based businesses. The extent of this is not predictable at a time when e-commerce, generally, is undergoing a consolidation.

Sources: Chart data: Kuenzi, Jeffrey J. and Clara A. Reschovsky. "Home-Based Workers in the United States: 1997." *Current Population Report.* December 2001. U.S. Bureau of the Census. "Almost Half of All U.S. Small Businesses Home-Based, Census Bureau Reports." Online. Available: http://www.census.gov/Press.Release/cb97-182.html. January 22, 2002. Office of Advocacy. U.S. Small Business Administration. Pratt, Joanne H. Pratt. "Homebased Business: the Hidden Economy." *Small Business Research Summary.* March 2000. U.S. Bureau of the Census. "Characteristics of Business Owners." *1992 Economic Census,* September 1997. Office of Advocacy. U.S. Small Business Administration. *Small Business Expansions in Electronic Commerce,* June 2000.

---

[19] Percentages may not total 100% due to rounding and some businesses not reporting.

Chapter 4

People and Their Money

In this chapter we attempt to describe the complicated subject of income in 11 panels. The first three look at household income, examining how each fifth of households has fared during the last 30 years. The first panel deals with share of income — and we see that while the richest fifth or quintile has gained in share of the wealth, the other groups have all seen their shares erode. We offer some explanations for this shift. In the second panel we look at this 30-year period in two halves, from 1967 to 1983 and from 1984 to 2000, and also peek at the performance of the top 5% of all households. In the third panel we look at the gap between the richest and the poorest.

In the next two panels we examine how the races and ethnicities have done. All have gained in income. The wealthiest groups are Asians and Pacific Islanders. Men continue to earn more than women, and the gap between their incomes is greater, in constant dollars, in 2000 than it was in 1967 — but in the intervening period, the gap grew much larger during the troubled 1970s.

Next we look at income brackets and the number of households that fit into each. We note that while households with lower incomes have declined in number, those with higher incomes have increased. The largest income bracket is made up of households earning between $50,000 and $74,999 a year. A panel is provided to let you discover how your own household fared in the years 1990 to 2000.

We turn next to the lower income groups in the U.S. and look at poverty. In 2000 about 8.6% of all families were poor — but only 4.7% of families were made up of married couples. Poverty rates increase following economic peaks and persist into the periods of recovery after recessions end. We look next at the minimum wage and note that it has not been keeping up with inflation. We next characterize poor families and note that families headed by women, raising children under 18, are the most likely to be poor. Nearly quarters of such families live in poverty.

The final panel shows how educational attainment affects the incomes of men, women, and families. We note again that men persistently make more money than women irrespective of education — and that it takes two, these days, to bring home the bacon.

Income: The Richest Get Richer

Households' Share of Aggregate Income by Fifths

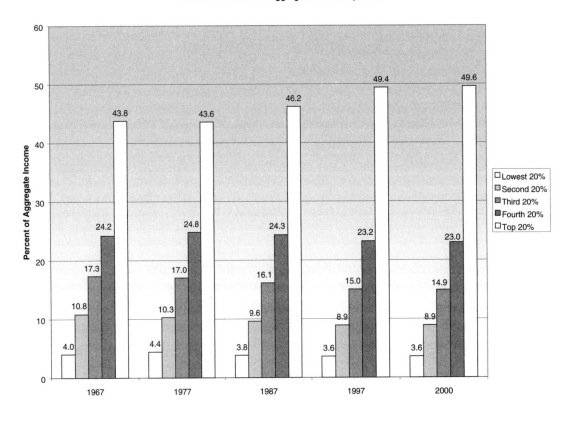

In the period 1967 to 2000, the richest fifth of households in the United States increased its share of aggregate income. All other groups lost ground. The richest got richer, the rest relatively poorer.

To give these households some dimension, the following table shows the average income of each fifth for 1967 and 2000 in constant 2000 dollars:

Average Income of Five U.S. Household Segments (Constant 2000 $)

	Ave. income 1967	Ave. income 2000	Change, 67 to 00 - %
Lowest fifth	7,147	10,190	42.6
Second fifth	19,485	25,334	30.0
Third fifth	31,111	42,361	36.2
Fourth fifth	43,528	65,729	51.0
Highest fifth	78,881	141,620	79.5
Top 5%	125,732	250,146	99.0

All groups saw their incomes rise, but only the top fifth gained share. In 1967, there were 60.8 million households, in 2000 106.4 million. The top 5% (not shown in the graph but included in the top fifth) increased their share of aggregate income from 17.5% to 21.9% — a rate almost twice as high as that shown for the highest fifth of households, the only fifth that showed a growth in share. All other segments lost ground. Thus even within the richest group, the super-rich grew faster than the rich.

This shift in wealth toward the top clearly shows that political efforts to create a more "equal" society were not on the front burner in this era. Many different factors may explain this. Among these might be the following:

- The industrial structure of the U.S. shifted from one centered on heavy industry to one organized around a more diffuse structure of services and, lately, to one based on information. This has eroded the power of unions and, possibly, the popular feeling that everyone was part of a single working-class society. The emphasis on white-collar occupations and higher educational attainment no doubt contributed to a weakening of the collective sense of participation in a middle-class enterprise.

- This period saw the rise of organized minorities, led by the Civil Rights movement, and the proliferation of other groups — women, the disabled, Hispanics (due to relaxation of immigration laws in 1965). As groups separately sought to realize gains and to establish rights by minority-based political efforts, more general initiatives, common during the Depression and World War II, were weakened.

- Many specific programs aimed at fighting poverty through various interventions and tools — housing subsidies, minimum wage, food stamps, legal aid, etc. — had not been unambiguously successful. "Trickle down" theories took hold and were embraced by those who favored less direct government involvement and lower taxes — at a time when the economy was, on the whole, producing jobs.

- International tensions relaxed as the Cold War drew to its end and the Berlin Wall finally fell. These events eroded the sense of a national community laboring against external threats. Entrepreneurial energies were freed up at a time when the Baby Boom was also creating an Economic Boom. Since the 1980s, an almost uninterrupted expansion, one might say an exuberant "free-for-all," has characterized economic times.

- The single largest birth cohorts in American history — the Baby Boomers — matured and began amassing skill and wealth. They greatly stimulated the economy by their sheer size and their demand for goods and services. Also, people in their maturity make the most money, and the elderly have the most assets. Improved health care improved life expectancy in this period and brought about a population more grey than any ever before in history.

In the next panel, we examine this pattern over time and look at income growth. The data show that the shift toward a topside concentration of wealth occurred in the last 20 years of this period.

Source: U.S. Bureau of the Census. *Current Population Survey*. March issues. "Share of Aggregate Income Received by Each Fifth and Top 5 Percent of Households (All Races): 1967 to 2000." 21 March 2000.

Income Trends: Then and Now

Growth in Average Income by Household Segments

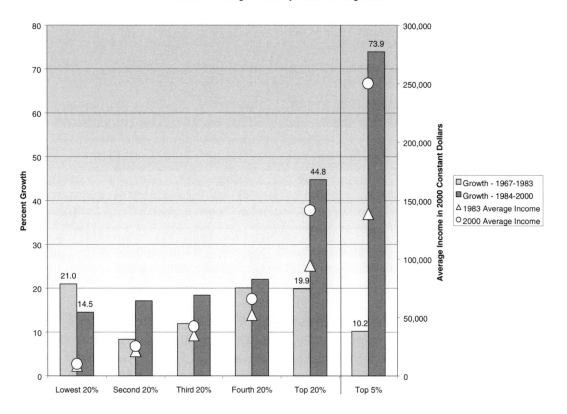

In this graphic, we display growth in household income divided into two periods of roughly equal length: 1967 to 1983 and 1984 to 2000. Results for five population segments of the U.S. are shown as well as the top 5% of households, which are included in the Top 20% category.

In the early part of this 33-year period, the income of the lowest fifth of households grew at a rate just slightly greater than that of the top fifth. In the second half of the period, the lowest fifth saw income growth shy of 15% and the top fifth income growth of nearly 45%.

In the early period, policies of income distribution clearly favored the lowest reaches of society, did not reach the "working poor" which may be represented by the second fifth of households, and held down the growth in income of the very wealthiest 5% of households by high rates of taxation; the top rate in the 1965-1981 period rose to 70% and fell to 50% in 1981.

In the second half of this period, those with more grew more wealthy, and the richer the faster. Income growth of the richest 5% of households went from 10.2% in the 1967-1983 period to an astounding 73.9% in the 1984-2000 period. Average income moved up for all groups in constant, inflation-adjusted dollars, but it leaped for those who were making the most.

Four recessions marked the 1967-1983 period. This period included the darkest days of the Vietnam war, the resignation of a president, an Arab oil embargo, and the Iranian hostage crisis. The 1980s began with the election of Ronald Reagan, brought to power by a resurgence of conservative inclinations. The Berlin Wall fell. The 1980s are now remembered as the years of the "Me Generation" and by phrases like "Greed is good." Children were playing Pac Man as the new computer age dawned; "Apple" no longer simply meant a fruit. This period then rapidly morphed into the age of the Internet. The 1983-2000 period saw a single brief recession (1990-1991); but after that not even a small cloud troubled the bright economic sky.

With the beginning of the 21st century, and the events of September 11, 2001, it is anybody's guess if the "Age of Greed" is with us for the long haul — or if these interestingly uneven patterns of income growth and share are a temporary phenomenon — to be replaced by a more even distribution of income in decades to come.

Source: U.S. Bureau of the Census, *Current Population Survey*, March issues, "Share of Aggregate Income Received by Each Fifth and Top 5 Percent of Households (All Races): 1967 to 2000," March 21, 2000.

The Income Gap Between Rich and Poor

The Rich and the Poor: Income of the Top Fifth and Lowest Fifth

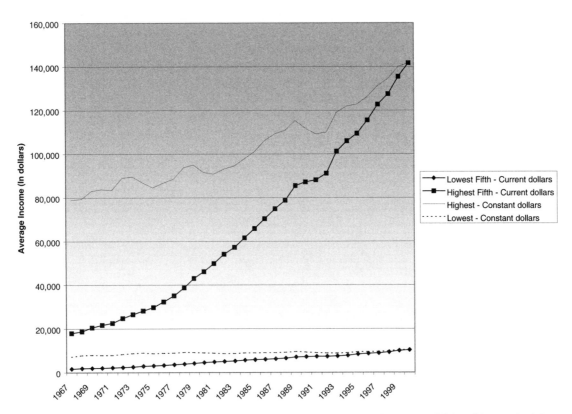

In this graphic we display the average income for the top and lowest fifth of households year by year in current as well as constant dollars to show the widening gap between the two extremes of households during this unusual period.

The income of the top fifth is heading upward like a jet on take-off. The bottom fifth's income is hugging the ground, barely growing. In 1967, the income of the top fifth was 11 times higher than that of the lowest. The gap widened over the next 33 years. In 2000, the top fifth earned nearly 14 times more than the lowest fifth.

Recent Census data indicate that income disparities may have remained flat since 1993. However, researchers have begun to point out that the Census is not an entirely reliable source for trends in income. They do not report capital gains income, for example, which grew from $163 billion in 1993 to $427 billion in 1998. The Census does not record earnings over $999,999; a person making $5 million is classified in the $999,999 and higher bracket.

Data from the IRS seem to offer a more comprehensive look at high-income households. The Center on Budget and Policy Priorities' analysis of IRS data shows that, between 1995 and 1997, the average after-tax income of the 1% of tax filers with the highest income jumped 31% or $121,000. The income of the bottom 90% rose just 3.4%. From

1993-97, the top 1% of tax filers secured after-tax income gains of 41%, while the bottom 90% saw only a 5% percent raise.[1]

Average After-Tax Income

Year	Top 1%	Bottom 90%
1993	366,150	22,757
1994	369,535	22,939
1995	396,545	23,041
1996	448,704	23,168
1997	517,713	23,815
Change 93-97	41.4%	4.6%

The income shown above is adjusted for inflation and expressed in 1997 dollars. Income is "adjusted gross income" minus federal income taxes.

Sources: Shapiro, Isaac, Robert Greenstein and Wendell Primus. "An Analysis of New IRS Income Data." Center on Budget and Policy Priorities. Retrieved November 30, 2001 from the World Wide Web: http://www.cbpp.org; Fones, Arthur F. and Daniel Weinberg, U.S. Census Bureau, Current Population Survey, *The Changing Shape of the Nation's Income Distribution*.

---

[1] The after-tax income of these tax filers is lower than would be expected for two reasons: Families can have more than one tax filer and their income would not be combined into one family; and not all sources of income, most notably government cash assistance, are counted in adjusted gross income. Working in the opposite direction, the data subtract only individual income taxes. Other taxes such as payroll taxes or the corporate income taxes are not considered. Data taken from Center on Budget and Policy Priorities and David Campbell and Michael Parisi "Individual Income Tax Rates and Shares, 1997." *SOI Bulletin, IRS Spring 2000.*

Incomes by Race/Ethnicity

Median Income by Race, 1967-2000

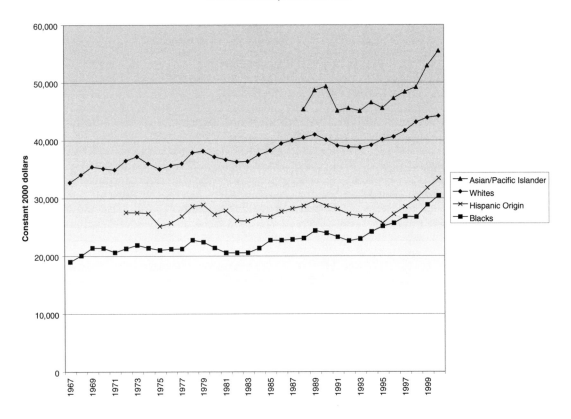

The graphic shows median household income by race in inflation-adjusted constant dollars. Median means that half earn less and half earn more. Overall, for all races, median income was $42,128. Income has increased among all minority categories. The Bureau of the Census began tracking income of Asians separately in 1989, Hispanics in 1972.

All groups saw their income fall slightly during the late 1970s and early1990s — when the economy soured. But income growth seems to have been rather resilient, benefiting no doubt from a healthy economy and increased education and productivity levels. Some groups have made real strides. Among African Americans, median household income reached an all-time high of $30,439, a 5.5% increase from 1999. For Hispanics, household income topped $33,447, up 5.3% in just one year. Asians saw a 5.0% increase to $55,521. The growth for whites was nearly unchanged.

Since 1990, whites have seen the smallest growth in income, with 10.2% ($40,100 to $44,226). Hispanics saw 16.6% ($28,671 to $33,447), Asians 12.4% ($49,369 to $55,521) and blacks saw the biggest increase with 26.9% ($23,979 to $30,439).

In dollars, the gaps among whites and minorities have closed. The difference in income is shown below:

White and Black Differences

	White Income	Black Income	Difference ($ dollars)
1990	40,100	23,979	16,121
2000	44,226	30,439	13,787

White and Hispanic Differences

	White Income	Hispanic Income	Difference ($ dollars)
1990	40,100	28,671	11,429
2000	44,226	33,447	10,779

Sources: U.S. Census Bureau, Current Population Reports, P60-213, *Money Income in the United States, 2000,* U.S. Government Printing Office, Washington D.C. 2001.

Income by Gender

Median Income of Men and Women
(1955 to 2000 in Constant 2000 Dollars)

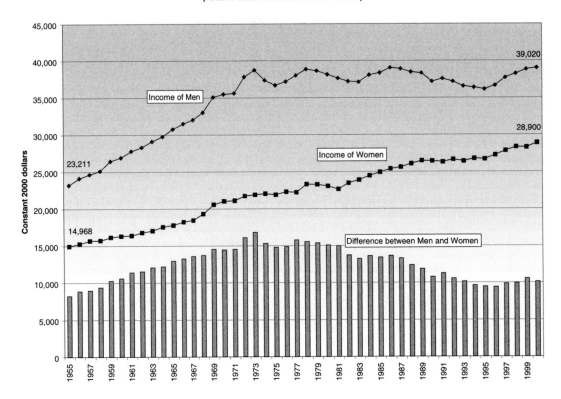

In this series, using deflated, constant dollars, we see that the incomes of men and women have risen steadily in the 1955 to 2000 period — but the gap in income between men and women has not meaningfully closed. In fact, it has grown from $8,243 in 1955 to $10,120 in 2000, with significan widening in 1973 (to $16,820) — just ahead of the 1974-1975 recession. Women's income resists the downward pressures on wages in recessions more than men's; consequently, during the recession, the differential dropped in favor of women but grew again after the recession ended.

The data are median income; half of the population earns more, half earns less. Population here means individuals aged 15 years old and older (14 years and older before 1980).

Whatever other factors might be involved — that women are over-represented in the lower-paying services sector jobs, for instance — the fact remains that there is a persistent gap between the sexes in income. Moreover, not even the high-tech economy had any effect on this gap at the end of this period, when the differential was again rising.

Source: U.S. Bureau of the Census. *Current Population Survey*. March reports. "Full-Time, Year-Round Workers (All Races) by Median Income and Sex: 1955 to 2000." 21 March 2002.

Households by Income Bracket

Change in Number of Households - 1990 to 2000

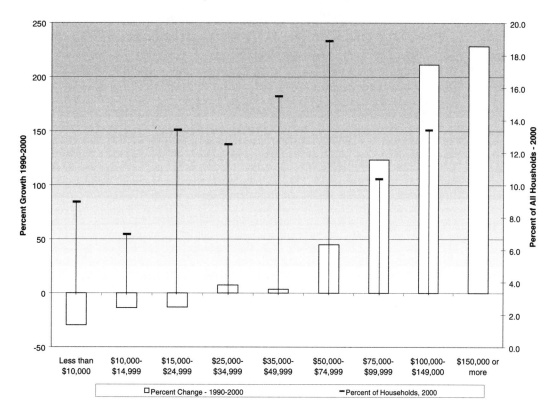

Percent Change - 1990-2000 Percent of Households, 2000

In this graphic we present information on households — not by fifths, as in the previous panels, but by income ranges. The chart shows percentile increases and decreases in the number of households within nine income ranges between the years 1990 and 2000. Data for this period show that households in the lower income ranges were declining, while households in higher income brackets were increasing — as wealth grew in the U.S. over all.

The biggest decrease in households has come in the bracket with less than $10,000 in annual income. Households in the $10,000-$14,999 and $15,000-$24,999 ranges have also declined. The biggest growth has come in the brackets with the highest incomes. Those in the $100,000-$149,000 bracket grew 211.5% and households in the $150,000 or more category a hefty 228.5%.

The line-bars indicate the percentage of all households that each income bracket represented in 2000, to be read on the right axis of the graphic. The line for the $100,000-$149,000 bracket stands for all households with incomes of $100,000 and above. A surprisingly large percentage of households (9%) still earned less than $10,000 a year. The largest income bracket, representing 18.9% of all households, was earning between $50,000 and $74,999. Income distribution is skewed toward the wealthy end — as we have already seen in other panels. One does not see here the well-known "Bell curve" of distribution that one might expect in a naturally evolving system.

The last ten years, in other words, display what is most likely a transitory distribution of income, due to the many factors discussed in the first two panels in this series, most notably the impact of the Baby Boom and shifts in the economic base from heavy industry to technology. To conclude, from these data, that these patterns will persist in the long run is probably risky — although real gains have been scored in the economy through gains in productivity, which are, in turn, resting on higher educational attainment and more efficient arrangements of running enterprises private and public.

Will a new middle class — now a seeming victim of skyrocketing wealth — emerge from this situation as the Baby Boom ages and as the economic gains of the Information Age are absorbed? Most likely. We are now seeing the erosion and disappearance of the very low brackets in favor of those — in terms of this graphic — to the right.

Sources: U.S. Bureau of the Census, "Selected Characteristics of Households, by Total Money Income in 2000," Current Population Survey, December 13, 2001.

Where Does Your Household Income Fall?

Household Income Ranges in Current Dollars

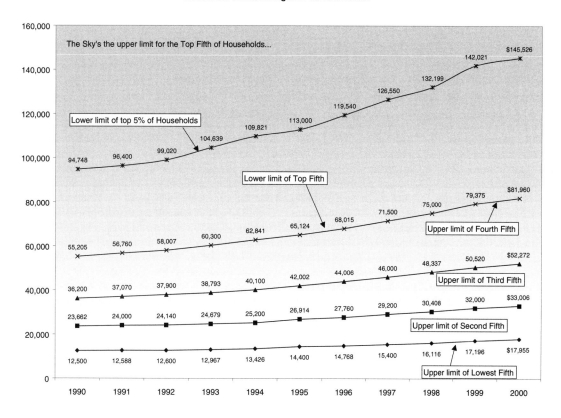

If you would like to find your place in the economic pecking order of the U.S., the graphic above will let you do so. Data show the upper limits of the first four-fifths of all households in current dollars — so that you can check your old Income Tax forms and get a true reading. An example will illustrate the use of this graphic. If, in 1995, your household income was $14,400 or lower, you were in the lowest fifth of households in earning power. If, in that year, your income was higher than $65,124, you were in the top fifth of households. And if your household earned at least $113,000 in 1995, you were in the top 5% of households.

This chart illustrates the expansionary trends of the recent decade. The income curves rise more steeply the higher the income of the quintile of households.

Now that we have contemplated stratospheric income heights, we will turn our attention to the more sobering concerns of making a living wage, the minimum wage, the characteristics of low-wage workers, and to the role of educational attainment in income.

Source: U.S. Bureau of the Census. *Current Population Survey*. March reports. "Income Limits for Each Fifth and Top 5 Percent of Households (All Races): 1967 to 2000." 21 March 2002.

Income and Poverty

Families in Poverty

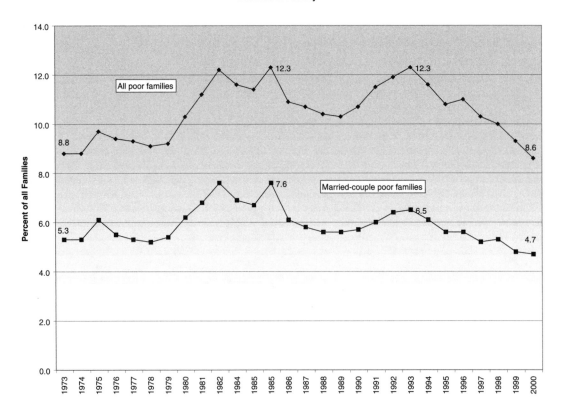

Poverty is — at least superficially — the absence of an adequate income for basic necessities. In the last 30 years or so, about 9% of all families lived in poverty when the economy was in high gear, about 12% when the economy was recovering from recession. As the graphic shows, poor families with a husband and wife both present had a much lower rate of poverty than all families.

Poverty is defined officially by the government. Poverty thresholds are complicated — showing different rates depending on the family unit's composition. The table beginning on the next page shows the rates as defined in 2001 and published by the U.S. Bureau of the Census.

A single individual 65 years old and over was thought to be poor if his or her income was $8,494 a year or lower. A family unit consisting of an adult and seven children under 18 years of age was considered poor if it had income of $35,610 or lower. A family of four, with two children under 18, was poor if it had an income of $17,960 or lower.

Critics sometimes say that poverty is overstated because the dollar figures shown below do not include in-kind assistance like housing subsidies or food stamps. But any reasonable person contemplating the table on the next page will probably conclude that living on incomes such as those shown below, with or without "in-kind" assistance, is likely to be tough at best.

Poverty Thresholds 2001 – in Dollars

| Size of family unit | Related children under 18 years | | | | | | | | |
	None	One	Two	Three	Four	Five	Six	Seven	8 or more
One person									
Under 65 years	9,214								
65 years and over	8,494								
Two persons:									
Householder under 65 years	11,859	12,207							
Householder 65 years and over	10,705	12,161							
Three persons	13,853	14,255	14,269						
Four persons	18,267	18,566	17,960	18,022					
Five persons	22,029	22,349	21,665	21,135	20,812				
Six persons	25,337	25,438	24,914	24,411	23,664	23,221			
Seven persons	29,154	29,336	28,708	28,271	27,456	26,505	25,462		
Eight persons	32,606	32,894	32,302	31,783	31,047	30,112	29,140	28,893	
Nine persons or more	39,223	39,413	38,889	38,449	37,726	36,732	35,833	35,610	34,238

There were 72.4 million families in 2000. Of these 6.2 million were poor. In Census terminology, families and households are not the same thing. Data shown in earlier panels feature households. A family is a grouping of *two or more related individuals living together*, one of whom is the "householder." There were 106.4 million households in 2000. A household is simply a living unit and may be inhabited by one individual or two or more related or unrelated individuals. The 34 million difference between the two figures is made up of people living alone or with friends or a domestic partner.

Poverty rates are shown here by way of giving definition to the income problems of the lowest fifth of households, which had an average income of $10,190 in 2000. Only households made up of a single person under 65 would be ranked above the poverty threshold with the average income of the lowest quintile of households.

Source: U.S. Bureau of the Census, March *Current Population Survey*, "Poverty Status: Status of Families, by Type of Family, Presence of Children, Race, and Hispanic Origin: 1959-2000," February 13, 2002, accessed at http://www.w3.org/TR/REC-html40/loose.dtd.

Income: Living on the Minimum Wage

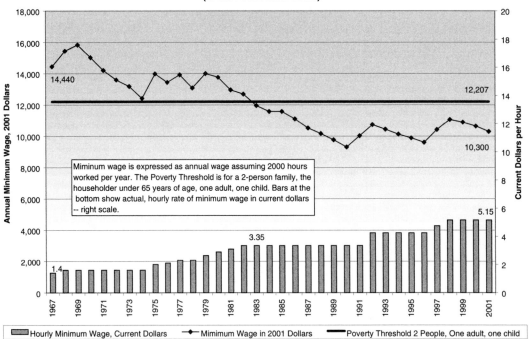

Minimum Wage and Poverty Threshold
(In 2001 Constant Dollars)

Miminum wage is expressed as annual wage assuming 2000 hours worked per year. The Poverty Threshold is for a 2-person family, the householder under 65 years of age, one adult, one child. Bars at the bottom show actual, hourly rate of minimum wage in current dollars -- right scale.

Annual Minimum Wage, 2001 Dollars

Current Dollars per Hour

14,440 12,207 10,300 5.15 3.35 1.4

Hourly Minimum Wage, Current Dollars — Miminum Wage in 2001 Dollars — Poverty Threshold 2 People, One adult, one child

The graphic, above, depicts the minimum wage as income — assuming a work year of 2000 hours. The curve is in inflation-adjusted, constant, 2001 dollars. The line shows the poverty threshold for a family of two people, say a mother and her child, also in 2001 values. This display shows that from 1967 to 1983, the minimum wage was enough to keep this hypothetical family above the poverty line. After 1983, despite three increases in the minimum wage, shown by the bars on the bottom of the chart, the family would have been below the poverty threshold. The minimum wage did not keep up with changes in the cost of living.

The minimum wage now stands at $5.15, with a potential increase by Congress to $6.64. More than 11 million workers fall into the minimum wage category. The vast majority is women over 20 years of age.

From 1950 to 1982, the minimum wage was allowed to fall below 45% of the average hourly wage on only four separate occasions. Since 1982, the minimum wage has never reached 45%, and currently stands at 36% of the average hourly wage.[2]

---

[2] Wartzman, Rick. "As Officials Lost Faith in the Minimum Wage, Pat Williams Lived It." *Wall Street Journal*, July 19, 2001, p. A1.

The minimum wage has advocates and critics. Advocates suggest that only legislative intervention will force up the lowest wage rates and that, without them, wages might even drop. Critics argue that the minimum wage forces small employers to lay off people they would otherwise employ. No unambiguously persuasive data are available or are likely to be offered on this subject. Poverty is, to some extent, a social/cultural phenomenon of an extremely complex nature.

Data in the last panel suggest both that poverty rates *drop* when the economy is in a strong expansion (and labor is pulled into the market — where the minimum wage applies to low-end entrants into the labor force) and that declines in the economy cause poverty to *expand* despite a rising minimum wage. In recent decades expansions have still left 8% of the families in poverty despite the slow up-creep of the minimum wage.

Source: U.S. Department of Labor, "Value of the Federal Minimum Wage, 1938-2000," retrieved December 6, 2001 from http://www. dol.gov.

Profiles: Low-Income Families

Poverty Rates for Working Families

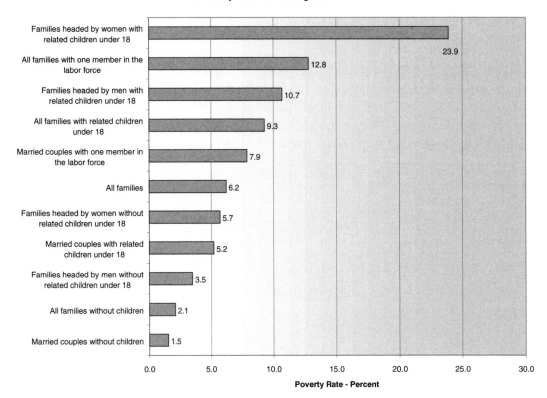

In this panel we continue to look at people with low income — but now using a set of data developed by the U.S. Department of Labor. The Bureau of Labor Statistics reports that, in 1999, 3.8 million families had incomes below the poverty line. The graphic displays the poverty rates of different family arrangements. Rates are all percentages of the respective group shown. Thus, for instance, 6.2% of all families fell below the poverty line; of all families headed by women where children under 18 years were present, 23.9% were poor; finally, of all families made up of married couples without children, 1.5% were poor.

The data reflect some by now, well-known facts:

- Women have a lower average income than men, and when they are the sole support of families, the family is more likely to be living in poverty than a family headed by a single adult male.

- Children cost money to raise and to maintain. Families with children are more likely to be poor than those without children.

- One income does not go as far as two. Households with one individual in the labor force are more likely to be poor than those where two individuals work.

It is clear that the era of the single breadwinner is fading or is altogether past for the great majority of families. This places an extra burden on women, who still carry the disproportionate weight of child-raising chores despite rhetorical flourishes. The evolving economic structure does not favor "family values" in practice — at least as shown by these data. Married couples do better in avoiding poverty — but are most successful when they also avoid having children.

We conclude this series on income by examining the relationship between income and educational attainment in the next panel.

Sources: Beers, Thomas M. U.S. Department of Labor, Bureau of Labor Statistics, *A Profile of The Working Poor*, U.S. Government Printing Office, Washington D.C. ; Winkler, Anne E. "Earnings of Husbands and Wives in Dual-Earner Families, *Monthly Labor Review*, April 1998, p. 42.

Income and Education

Individual and Family Income in 2000 by Educational Attainment

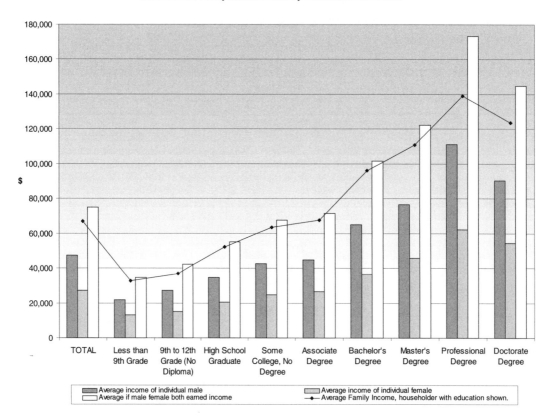

Using the data charted above, taken from the March 2000 *Current Population Survey*, we attempt to sum up several facts about income in the United States in a single graphic. The data show the average income of males and females by educational attainment in 2000. The light bar shows what the average family income *would* be if a male and female, in a single-family unit, both worked and had the same education. The graph shows the *actual* average money income of families headed by a person of a specific educational attainment (the curve).

The first fact that appears is that men consistently earn more than women on average — and this is true even when they are both lawyers or doctors, say, or professors at a university. Women with professional degrees achieved only 55.9% of the income of their male counterparts — quite comparable to women with a 9th to 12th grade education, no diploma, who had 55.4% of men's income with the same qualifications. Women with doctorates came closest to earning the same wages as men — 60.3% of men's income.

Average family income is consistently lower than the combined income of the male and female — strongly suggesting that two adults are working in most families in order to achieve the family's money income, as shown in the following table. The gap between actual family income and the hypothetical male-female combined income grows only as total family income increases — suggesting that those with high incomes have the luxury of choice: one or the other member of the household can stay at home.

Combined Average Male-Female Income and Actual Family Income - 2000

Educational Attainment of Householder	Hypothetical combined male-female income	Actual aver- age annual family income	Family income as % of hypo- thetical com- bined income
Total	$74,886	$67,038	89.5
Less than 9th grade	34,688	32,730	94.4
9-12, no diploma	42,323	36,706	86.7
High school	55,084	52,255	94.9
Associate degree	67,433	63,275	93.4
Some college	71,336	67,515	94.6
Bachelor's degree	101,624	96,024	94.5
Masters degree	122,250	110,924	90.7
Professional degree	173,346	138,933	80.1
Doctorate	144,804	123,561	85.3

The table is drawn from data on individuals who work and are aged 25 and older. Family data do not specify the sex of the householder. These data clearly exclude retired people and those who are not in the labor force — two categories that often contribute dispro-portionately to the ranks of the poor.

But the problem of poverty is also clearly highlighted nonetheless. As shown on an ear-lier panel poverty is most prevalent when the householder is a woman, when there is only one earner in the family unit, and the presence of children add to the cost of the family's maintenance. Families in which the head of household has less than a 9th grade education earned on average $32,730 a year. But a family headed by a single woman would have earned only $12,997.

Source: U.S. Bureau of the Census, *Current Population Survey* "Educational Attainment — Workers 25 Years Old and Over by Mean Earnings and Sex: 1991 to 2000", March 21, 2002, obtained from http://www.w3.org/TR/REC-html40/loose.dtd.

Chapter 5

People, Technology, and Productivity

In the following six panels, we present information on productivity.

The conventional view of productivity is that personal income rises with productivity. And productivity rises because technology enables us to do more in less time. With better tools we can do more. And the more we automate — and let machines do *all* the work — the wealthier we become.

Productivity has had a remarkable growth over the last 50 years or so. The findings developed here clearly show the impact of technology, including a "revival" in productivity growth in the recent Internet Age. But the situation shows considerable complexity. Productivity is a "social phenomenon" in which a number of factors play decisive roles. Technology is one. Public confidence, global events (wars), and the general management of the economy also play roles.

It takes fewer people to produce a measure of output — but the performance is not uniform across the sectors. People are clearly being displaced — but the economy, especially the services sector — absorbs the labor freed up by improvements in productivity.

The presentation begins with a brief tutorial that also serves to show the linkage between productivity and compensation. Next we look at a longer history of productivity and chart its phases; growth declines and then revives. In the third panel, we take a closer look at technology, including computers and software. A 1997 snapshot of the private sector follows; it shows that different industrial sectors have different levels of productivity. Next we compare manufacturing and construction in some detail over a longer period of time. Finally, a sophisticated system of measurement, Multifactor Productivity, is unveiled to show the effect of hidden, "synergistic" factors in the economy.

Productivity in a Nutshell

Indexes of Productivity - Manufacturing
1992 = 100

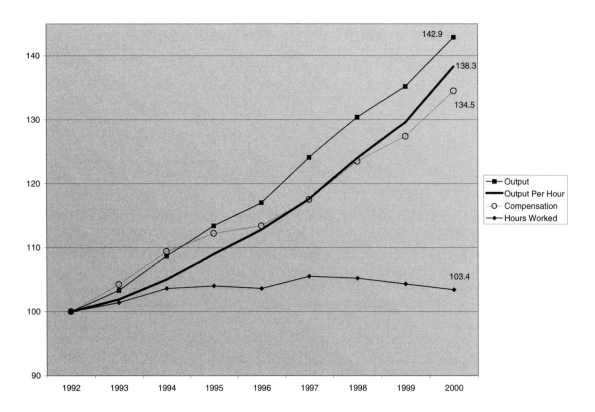

The government's productivity index — much in the news every month — measures output per hour of work. It is shown here for the **Manufacturing** sector as the bold line in the graph above. To simplify this measurement, all output from a sector, usually measured in dollars, is divided by all hours worked by employees, owners, and others (for instance spouses or children in a family-owned enterprise).

Productivity is a ratio. If output rises more than hours, productivity is up. If output drops but hours stay the same, productivity is down. This last condition often prevails in times of economic downturn: sales drop but employment responds more slowly. Therefore the same hours are divided into a smaller total output of goods or services.

The graphic shows some of the measures for Manufacturing in the 1992 to 2000 period. The index used shows 1992 as 100 for all the series; they all start at ground zero, as it were. Hours increased 3.4 percent, output increased 42.9 percent. If you divide the output index (142.9) by the hourly index (103.4), you get the productivity index (138.2); the small difference is due to rounding. In 1994, for instance, an output of 109, divided by hours at 104, produced a productivity index of 105.

Why is productivity so carefully watched? An important reason is that increases in compensation are dependent on productivity. If we produce more in an hour of work, we are likely to share in the increase. Note that, for Manufacturing in this period, compensation closely paralleled productivity; it grew 34.5%; Productivity grew 38.5%. Compensation grew more rapidly early in this period, more slowly later when, perhaps, fears of an economic slowdown, high inventories, and other factors possibly resulted in declines in overtime.

What elements influence productivity? Many factors do. One of these is automation. We shall look at technological factors soon. The next panel explores productivity for all of **Business** over a longer period of time.

Source: Bureau of Labor Statistics, U.S. Department of Labor, http://www.bls.gov/lpc/.

The Steady Rise of Productivity

Business Productivity - All Sectors
1992 = 100

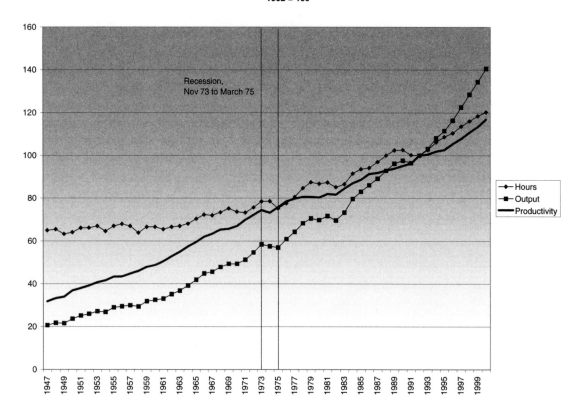

This chart shows productivity — output per hour — steadily rising since 1947. In that 53-year period, productivity increased at a rate of nearly 2.5% a year. A look at various intervals shows that the growth in the early part of this period (1947-1970) was strongest; growth was weaker in the later decades (1970-1990), but shows signs of strengthening again (1990-2000) — especially in the last five years.

Period	% growth per year
1947-1950	5.08
1950-1960	2.83
1960-1970	3.22
1970-1980	1.84
1980-1990	1.70
1990-2000	2.07
1995-2000	2.64

There is growth in all periods when looked at in such increments. Productivity can drop, however. Note above the one period of recession highlighted (others are omitted). It makes a point. Output declined in the first period of the recession by 0.9 index points; hours worked *increased* by 0.1 index points. Consequently productivity fell 1.3 points. Adjustments in employment lagged the decline in output. Therefore slightly more hours produced less in the way of goods and services in the total Business sector, the private economy.

Productivity is the result of more output per person. If fewer people are employed, productivity rises. But employment has increased. The conclusion is that machines, new social arrangements, or some combination of these are making people more productive: they produce more value in the same time. Another factor is that *economic activity* as a whole may lift productivity in good times and depress it in others. A quick look:

- In the immediate post-war years, pent-up demand lifted the economy.

- The 1950s saw tremendous innovation in manufacturing — in all sectors but strongly centered in metals and metalworking, culminating in numerically controlled machine tools.

- The 1960s were a period of explosive developments in materials with plastics, perhaps leading the way supported by important innovations across the board in chemicals.

- The 1970s produced three recessions, the depth and end of the Vietnam war (1973), soaring inflation, and the oil crisis (1979).

- The late 1970s and 1980s saw the rise of the services economy — people-intensive and therefore less capable of leveraging a human hour into dollars. The period was also marked by another recession.

- Beginning in the late 1980s and continuing strongly since, small computers, communications (cell phones), and then the Internet combined to produce an unprecedented period of growth.

In the following panels, we shall take a closer look at this. What is the role of technology? We shall also take a look at the social factor: is labor being transferred to unpaid consumers?

Source: Bureau of Labor Statistics, U.S. Department of Labor, http://www.bls.gov/lpc/.

Domestic Output and the Role of Technology

Gross Domestic Product and Components
(Billions of Chained 1996 Dollars)

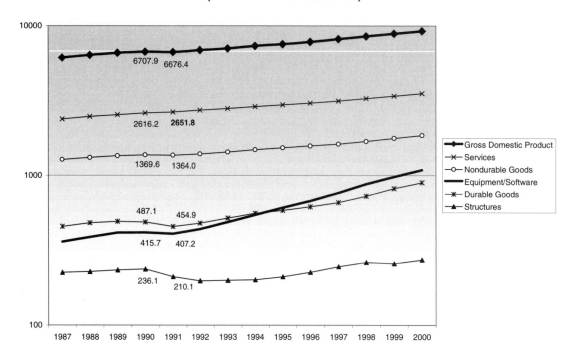

Productivity grows as the quality of tooling grows — machinery, equipment, and software. The nation's Gross Domestic Product (GDP) measures the ultimate output of the economy. The role of "tooling" is shown in the graph above. The top line shows GDP. The other series are selected components. These include three major series — personal expenditures on services, on nondurable goods (food, toiletries, clothing, etc.), and on durable goods (autos, appliances) — and two measures of industrial investment: investment spending on equipment and software (bold line) and investments on nonresidential structures (bottom curve).

In the 1987 to 2000 period, measured here in inflation-adjusted dollars, the largest growth has been experienced by equipment and software (8.8% compounded annual growth, versus GDP's growth of 3.2%). At the beginning of the period, this category was 5.9% of GDP. At the end of the period, it was 11.8%.

The recession of July 1990 to March 1991 caused "Equipment and software" to dip 2.1%; GDP dipped 0.5. Surprisingly, personal consumption expenditures on services did not drop as a consequence of the recession as measured here, year-end to year-end.

While these series do not prove a causal relationship between "machinery" (including software) and "productivity," in the recent periods, strong growth in expenditures on these categories has contributed to steady GDP growth. The use of computers in business, improved communications through cell phones, and the efficiencies introduced in business by the Internet have at least subjectively contributed to productivity.

A look at net stocks of private fixed assets (non-depreciated equipment/software in use by the private sector), shows that much of the growth during the recent period is attributable to growth in computers, software, and communications equipment. Growth rates are cumulative annual rates based on inflation-adjusted 1996 dollars.

Category	1990-2000 annual growth rate (%)
Nonresidential equipment and software	4.82
Information equipment and software	9.41
Computers and peripheral equipment	27.86
Software	13.14
Communication equipment	6.95
Instruments	5.28
Photocopy and related equipment	0.94
Office and accounting equipment	0.37
Industrial equipment	2.33
Transportation equipment	4.77
Other	2.81

Source: U.S. Department of Commerce, Bureau of Economic Analysis, and *Survey of Current Business*, September 2001, published by the same agency.

The Ratio of People to Dollars

Number of Employees Required to Generate $1 Million in Output (1997, Based on Actual Dollars)

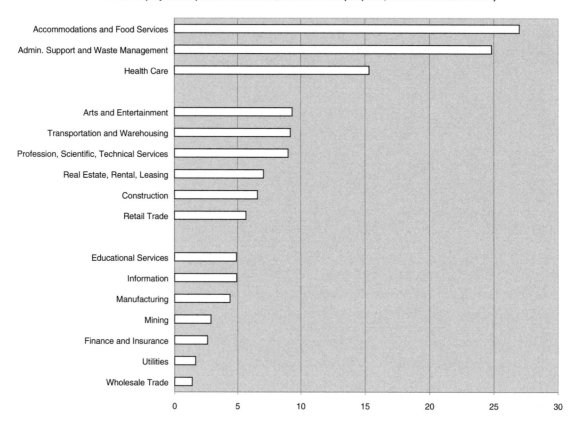

The graphic above provides another look at productivity, this time by economic sector. Shown here are major sectors of the U.S. private economy and the number of people it took in 1997 to produce a million dollars' worth of output.

The largest sector in total output is Wholesale Trade ($4,059 billion) closely followed by Manufacturing ($3,842 billion). The smallest sector is Educational Services ($65 billion) — not to be confused with "Education," a public sector activity, and by far the largest "industry" in the nation.

It is fairly clear from these data that two kinds of industries cluster toward the bottom — the region of highest productivity: (1) capital intensive activities where machinery as replaced people and "embodies" human intelligence (manufacturing, utilities, mining) and (2) activities where symbolic commerce dominates (brokering as in wholesale trade, finance and insurance, educational services, and information services).

In the middle range are industries where people deliver services directly (entertainment, professional and technical services), where automation is particularly difficult (transportation and construction), where the nature of the industry and its geographical dimension require a human agent (real estate), and where people are needed to interact with the customer intensely to make a sale (retail).

Three sectors require intensive human activity. Health care is, undoubtedly, still the most people-to-people of the services. Administrative support includes travel agents, employment agencies, temporary help providers, janitorial services, and waste removal. The hospitality and restaurant sector remains one of the most traditional, still delivering its services very much as it did a hundred years ago; in hotels and restaurants, ample staff often means a better ambiance. In this last grouping of sectors, automation is either inherently impossible (e.g. temporary help agencies), undesirable from the customers' point of view (health care, hotels, restaurants), or very resistant to automation (waste removal).

In the next panel we will show trends in two sectors — one in the first group, manufacturing, and one in the more resistant second group, construction.

Source: U.S. Department of the Census, 1997 Economic Census.

Long-Term Productivity Trends in Two Sectors

**Employees Required to Produce $1 Million in Manufacturing Shipments or in Construction
Put Into Place
(Based on 1996 Dollars)**

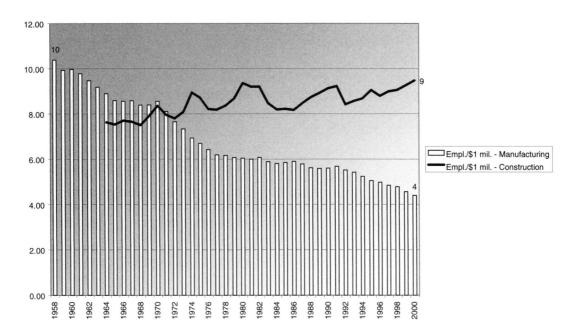

Some of the data from the previous panel — for manufacturing and construction — are shown here to illustrate effects over a longer period of time. In this display the number of employees needed to produce $1 million in output is calculated using deflated 1996 dollars, hence values vary slightly.

Manufacturing is a sector that responds well to innovation and automation. The construction sector does not. Not surprisingly, productivity in manufacturing is growing. In 1958, 10.4 employees produced $1 million in shipments; by 2000, it only took 4.4 people. Notice that in the periods of recession (especially 1960, 1970, 1982, 1991), productivity slowed or reversed. Sales declined more rapidly than employment.

Construction shows quite another pattern. The overall trend shows that it took *more* people to produce $1 million in output (construction put in place) in 2000 (9.48 people) than in 1964 (7.6 people). Notice further that peaks in this jagged curve coincide precisely with years of recession. The peaks may be due to industry dynamics: contractors underbid jobs to keep busy; margins are lower; the same employment produces less in construction put in place. In construction, as elsewhere, employers retain people even as business softens. Declines in total construction put in place, measured in percent, are typically much sharper than declines in employment. The high rate of unionization in construction is also a factor in relatively sluggish employment response to business downturn.

However, productivity trends in construction, as measured here, indicate that this sector is much more dependent on traditional methods of production.

Source: U.S. Bureau of the Census, U.S. Department of Commerce (shipments and construction put in place) and Bureau of Labor Statistics, U.S. Department of Labor (employment data).

Complex Factors of Productivity

Labor and Multifactor Productivity in Manufacturing, 1949 to 2000
Index - 1996 = 100

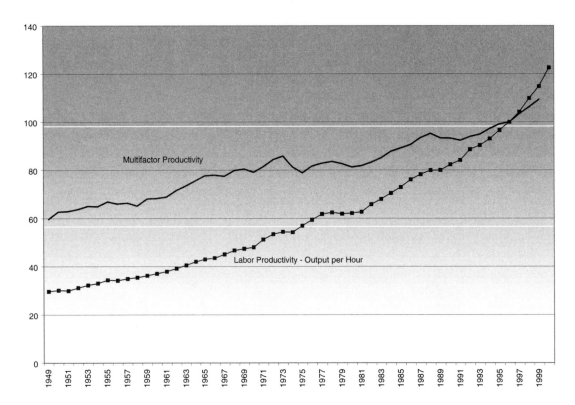

More output per hour of labor indirectly reflects the impact of machines. But why not measure the impact of machines, materials, and other factors directly? The Bureau of Labor Statistics does just that. It produces an index of Multifactor Productivity (MFP). This measure combines the inputs of labor, capital[1], energy, materials, and purchased services into a single index. How the MFP index is produced is described below. First, consider the following:

Multifactor productivity has been growing, albeit at a slower rate then the conventional productivity measure, output per hour. In the 1949 to 1999 period, MFP grew 1.2% (compounded, annual rate); labor productivity grew at 2.7%. But multifactor productivity is a more inclusive measure; it thus provides a more complete picture.[2]

---

[1] Actually the measure includes "services which flow from the stock of capital." By using "services," BLS accounts for variable depreciation rates of capital stock. Thus a dollar of vehicular stock produces more services than a dollar expended on a structure because trucks are depreciated fairly rapidly and buildings over decades of time.

[2] A certain degree of "overcounting" is inherent in MFP because labor productivity, one of the inputs, already reflects some of the impacts of the capital services

---

Multifactor productivity *accounts for* the inputs of labor, capital, energy, materials, and purchased services. It *reflects* factors much more difficult to measure effectively: scale effects (bigger is often better), technological change, reallocation of resources, efficiency improvements, changes in materials and better materials, structural changes, and other factors.

The index is a ratio of outputs to combined inputs. First, data for each *input* are normalized to constant dollars and expressed as an index for each (labor, capital, etc.). Next, the input indexes are combined to reflect the relative importance of each. If labor is 30% and capital 15%, for instance, 30% of the labor index and 15% of the capital index appear in the combined index of inputs. Next, the *output* index is developed in the same manner.

The final multifactor productivity value is the Output divided by the Input. If the Output is 119.57 and the Input is 118.32, the result is 1.0105. This number, multiplied by 100, is the MFP index. Note that only the value greater than 100 reflects the difficult-to-measure, "synergistic" effects of scale, technology, and so on. If the index is 100, it means that all inputs are fully reflected in the output. If the index falls below 100, it means that deterioration has taken place.

Multifactor productivity measures broader aggregates — Business and Non-farm Business (not shown here) — reflect various structural changes in the economy, including "efficiencies" not always appreciated by the consumer. They impose unpaid labor. Examples are the self-service gas stations in many states; labor savings in drive-through car washes; ATM machines that turn us into bank tellers; assemble-your own toys, furniture, and appliances; and that scourge of our age: voice mail.

Source: Bureau of Labor Statistics, U.S. Department of Labor, http://www.bls.gov/mprhome.htm.

People, Education, and Productivity

One of the driving forces of productivity, undoubtedly, has been an ever more educated workforce. In the following several panels, we look a little more closely at people and their education. The traditional measure of educational attainment is "high school and above." Of a hundred adults, picked more or less at random, 84 will qualify for this level. Twenty-five of those people will have four years of college and above. The same look, in 1940, would have found only 24 people with high school and higher and fewer than 5 with college or higher degrees.

In the first panel we try to answer the question: "How educated is the workforce — and what are the trends?" The answer is given above. The trend is toward a flattening of growth in educational achievement as traditionally defined.

Next we examine attainment by looking at major population groups. All groups have been improving their attainment. The most rapid progress has been made by African Americans.

But how does educational attainment relate to compensation — and productivity? Surprising answers are presented in the third panel under "Average Earnings and Productivity." The data show a strong but not "hard" relationship. Productivity rises steadily. Rewards for labor are growing slower and do a lot of rising and falling. In recent years, the college-educated have suffered less from economic swings than those with "high school and above."

The panel on compensation highlighted for us the effects of inflation. This prompted a closer look at the subject. We also looked at four categories of people: those with elementary education, those with high school only, high school and above, and college and higher. Income growth tabulations once more show that those with the most get the most, and those who have least actually lose purchasing power.

The last panel attempts to look ahead to 2010. Substantial changes in ethnic composition of the population and in the different rates of educational attainment these groups have suggest a high and a low boundary for future educational attainment.

Educational Attainment: Key Factor in Productivity

Educational Attainment of Adults, 25 Years and Older
(Percent of Age GroupTotal)

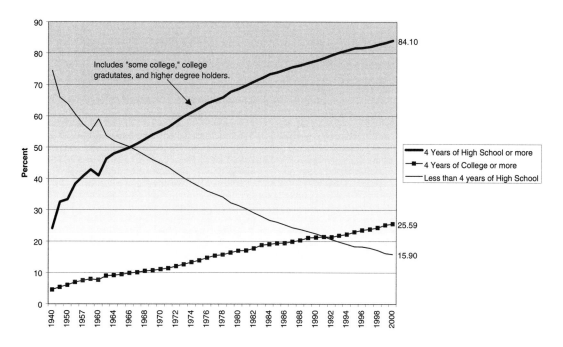

In 2000, more than 84% of some 175 million people aged 25 years or older, had an educational attainment of high school level or higher. Sixty years before, in 1940, when this population was just shy of 75 million, that same attainment was around 24%. Since World War II, we've certainly become a good deal better educated if not necessarily wiser.

The educational level of the population is undoubtedly a major factor in the nation's productivity. Knowledge and the ability to manipulate information have become more important than manual dexterity. One in four people 25 years or older (25.6%) have 4 years of college or a higher degree; they are the fastest-growing group. They are included in the 84% of those with high school and higher attainment but also shown separately on the graphic. Just shy of 16% of the 25-and-over group still has less than a high school diploma — nearly 28 million adults.

Educational attainment now may be at a record high level — and may flatten out or even decline due to demographic factors in the early 21st century. This subject is explored in a later panel. And, at present, there are at least some signs that the economy is taking a skilled workforce for granted. Technological and structural changes — more than increases in educational attainment — may now be driving gains in productivity.

Source: U.S. Census Bureau, U.S. Department of Commerce, *Current Population Survey*, March 2000.

High School and More by Race

Educational Attainment by Race - High School or Higher

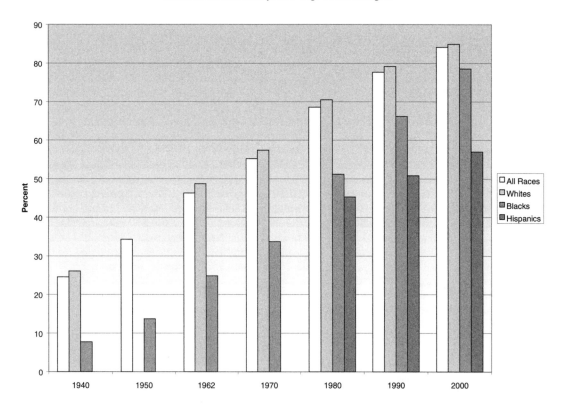

Educational attainment, viewed by major ethnic groupings, shows the same pattern of steady increase. The chart shows the percent of people, 25 years or older, who have four years of high school or higher education. Data for whites are not available for 1950 and data for Hispanics were not reported until 1980; data for 1960 were unavailable; instead, values for 1962 are shown.

The following pattern of increases in qualifications shows the differences between groups shown graphically above:

Racial/Ethnic Group	% gain 1980 to 1990	% gain 1990 to 2000
All Groups	9.0	6.5
Whites	8.6	5.8
Blacks	15.0	12.3
Hispanics	5.5	6.2

Overall results are clearly raised by the strong gains posted by African Americans in these periods. Asian Americans, not shown as a separate category in the Census data used in this analysis, typically have higher educational attainment than whites.

In the 1990 to 2000 decade, the white population 25 years and older grew 5.7%, the black population grew 15.9%, and the Hispanic 49.4%. In 2000, the Hispanic population as a whole (all ages included) was also the youngest: the Hispanic median age was 26.6, the black was 30.5 and the white was 38.5. These factors may affect productivity in the future. We discuss that subject in the last panel in this series.

Source: U.S, Bureau of the Census, U.S. Department of Commerce, Current Population Survey, March 2000. Data on population and median age drawn from *Statistical Abstract of the United States, 2000,* Table 18, p. 19.

Average Earnings and Productivity

**Growth of Productivity and
Average Earnings, 1975 to 1999**

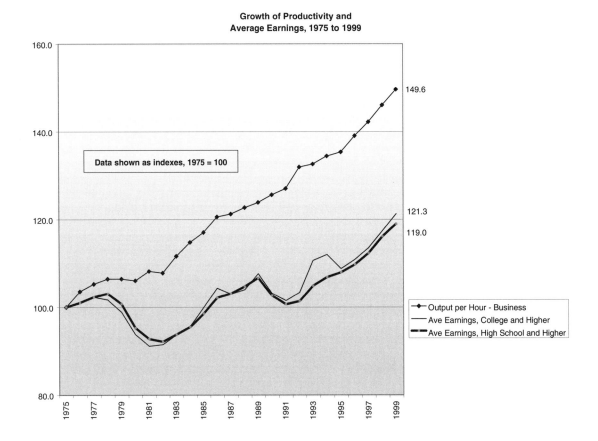

Much as an educated workforce is said to cause productivity to rise, so productivity is said to cause earnings to rise. The complexities hidden behind the last generalization are shown in this chart. It shows indexes for three series: (1) productivity (output per hour for Business), (2) average earnings of those who have college degrees and higher, and (3) average earnings of those who have high school education and higher. The last category includes the second. All series are based on constant dollars (inflation removed) and are expressed in index format where 1975 equals 100.

In the 1975-1999 period, productivity grew 49.6%, earnings of those with college and higher degrees increased 21.3%, and those with high school and higher degrees 19%. (GDP, in that same period, grew 117%).

Aside from the lower overall growth of earnings, note the following points:

Real earnings growth is much more affected by inflation and downturns in the economy than productivity growth. Average earnings headed down as productivity flattened in 1978 and 1979 due to inflationary pressures. Earnings continued to fall as the 1980 and 1981-82 recession hit and also slipped in the 1990-1991 recession, college-plus earnings falling less than those of the larger high school-and-higher group.

Before 1984, in this series, those with college and higher degrees grew at a lower rate than the more inclusive category. After 1984 — with the coming of what might be called the "second computer age," those with higher educational attainments grew earnings at a higher rate than the larger group which includes them.

The growth gap between productivity and earnings has widened. Midway through this period, productivity and earnings were 18 points apart. By the end of this period, productivity and earnings about 30 points apart. As covered in the panels of the last topic, automation and structural alignments are making people more productive; fewer people, especially those of lower educational attainment, are needed. This reflects in earnings growth. Another possible conclusion is that more of the gains of productivity were being converted, in this period, to tool up for the cybernetic age; less of these gains went to people whose primary earnings are salaries and wages.

Earnings data reflect a survey of 144.6 million people of both sexes; of these, those with high school and higher education represent 127.9 million; and of those, people with college and higher were 39 million.

The earnings themselves are presented in the next panel.

Sources: Data on earnings from *Current Population Surveys*, March 2000. Productivity data are from Bureau of Labor Statistics. The Consumer Price Index, published by the BLS, was used to deflate current dollar earnings estimates.

Earnings, Inflation, and Sharing Productivity Gains

Earnings and Inflation in 2000 and Actual Dollars
1975-2000

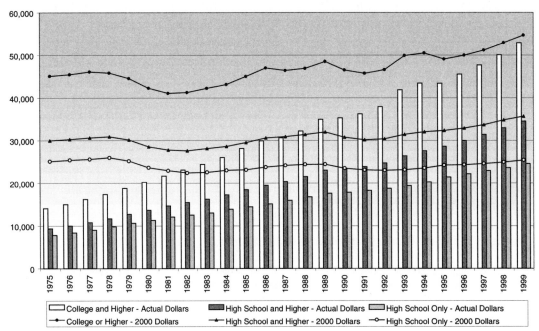

| College and Higher - Actual Dollars | High School and Higher - Actual Dollars | High School Only - Actual Dollars |
| College or Higher - 2000 Dollars | High School and Higher - 2000 Dollars | High School Only - 2000 Dollars |

The data on this busy panel make four important points, one of which is rather obvious: (1) those with more education earn more; (2) earnings in actual, "as earned" dollars grow nicely; (3) when earnings are adjusted for inflation (in this case to 2000 dollars), the earnings curves flatten out; and (4) those with just a high school education benefit almost not at all from sharply rising productivity in the U.S. economy.

The bars represent current dollars, the curves constant dollars. A look at the results for these two groups shows that current dollar gains are impressive but that "real" results, measured in real purchasing power, are less phenomenal.

Educational Attainment	1975 Earnings	1999 Earnings	% Change
College or higher			
Current dollars	14,081	52,883	275.5
2000 dollars	45,069	54,660	21.3
High School or higher			
Current dollars	9,356	34,480	268.5
2000 dollars	29,946	35,693	19.2
High School Only			
Current dollars	7,843	24,572	213.3
Constant dollars	25,103	25,398	1.2
No High School			
Current dollars	6,198	16,121	60.1
Constant dollars	19,838	16,663	**-16.0**

People with college degrees or higher gained most. The second category includes them — averages them in — and also shows the earnings of those with "some college" and with Associate degrees. The High School Only category has increased its earnings in real dollars only by 1.2% in 24 years. In that period, productivity increased 49.6%.

Most tellingly of all, those who have less than a high school education (not included in the graphic) have *lost* earnings power in real terms. They have not only failed to keep up with inflation — much less productivity — they have been marginalized. In the sample from which these data are drawn, they represent 11.6 percent of 144.6 million people aged 18 or older.

The clear conclusion is that the modern economy depends on the better-educated layers of society. It is those from that layer who harvest the fruits of improving productivity. What does this portend for the future? That subject will concern us next.

Sources: Data on earnings from *Current Population Surveys*, March 2000. The Consumer Price Index, published by the Bureau of Labor Statistics, was used to deflate current dollar earnings estimates.

Future Trends in Educational Attainment

Educational Attainment Boundaries
Percent of Adults 25 Years or Older with High School or Higher Education
2000 to 2010

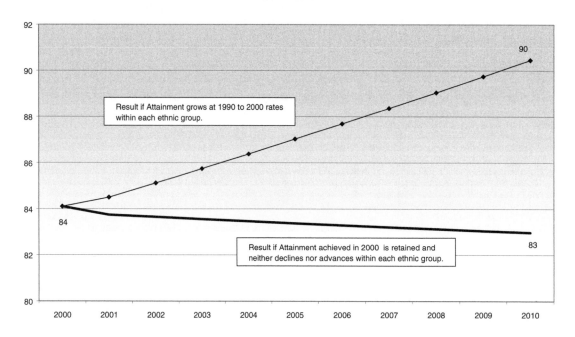

In 2000, around 84% of the adult population, 25 years old and older, had a high school or higher educational attainment. What is the future likely to hold? Continuing growth in educational attainment—which supports growing productivity—is not a certainty. The graphic shows two future vectors. Actual results are likely to fall somewhere between these boundaries.

Growth in educational attainment has been "flattening." Fewer than 4 of 10 born around 1900 had a high school education. There was a lot of room to grow. By 1997, 70% of the oldest group (55 or older) had completed high school. 25 to 34-year-olds and those in the prime working age, 35 to 54, both had 87% high school completion rates. Educational attainment grew in the 20th century because many people who traditionally stopped after elementary school went on — and a quarter of adults went beyond high school. At present high school-and-above educational attainment is growing least among Asians; next in order come whites and Hispanics; African Americans have the highest growth rate:

Attainment and Population Dynamics

Adults 25 and Older

Population Segment	Attainment, High School or Higher in 2000 (%)	% growth in attainment, 1990 to 2000	% of population in 2000	% growth of 25 and older population, 2000 to 2010
Asians	85.6	6.5	3.9	32.0
Whites	84.9	7.3	74.0	4.2
Hispanics	57.0	12.2	10.8	31.4
Blacks	78.5	18.6	11.3	14.9

Note that, with the exception of Hispanics, the higher the attainment, the lower the growth rate. The Hispanic experience is influenced by immigration. The educational attainment of native-born Hispanics in 2000 was 71.8%, just a little lower than that of blacks.

The upper curve in the graphic, leading to an attainment rate just over 90%, assumes that the growth rates shown in the table — both for educational attainment and for population — will actually take place. To some extent this outcome is unrealistic. It assumes that the very high growth rate of the black population will continue; it has been slowing. It also assumes that the white population rate of growth will continue; it has been slowing as well. The projection also assumes that the high rate of Hispanic immigration, which is built into the population forecast, will continue. It may very well slow.

The assumption behind the lower curve, which shows a decline in attainment of about a point, is that each population group will continue to have its 2000 rate of attainment in the future. The declining composite rate will be due to the more rapid growth of groups with lower attainment. Asian Americans, although they have a high attainment rate *and* will be growing at the fastest rate, are a small proportion of the total adult population. The net effect will be a slight decline.

The most realistic projection is that attainment will continue to grow, but at a slower rate, eventually flattening as equilibrium is reached early in the 21st century. Where that equilibrium will be — at 90%, at 85%, lower, or higher, is difficult to predict.

It is not at all unlikely that emphasis will shift from watching "high school and above" to tracking the "college and above" attainment level. In 2000, for the adult population as a whole, this rate was just at 25% (4 years of college and higher). Asian American educational attainment may be the wave of the future. They had just shy of 44% achievement in this category in 2000.

All this, of course, begs an important question, explored in another volume of this series: Is the education actually attained the same education youth got in the 1970s and 1980s? There are indications that in both reading and math, there have been steep declines in actual learning.

Sources: For educational attainment, *Current Population Survey*, March 2000. Population projections from the Middle Series, U.S. Bureau of the Census. Projections made by the authors using these two sources. For a sophisticated analysis of this subject, see Jennifer Cheeseman Day and Kurt J. Bauman, "Have We Reached the Top? Educational Attainment Projections of the U.S. Population," May 2000, Working Paper No. 43, Population Division, U.S. Census Bureau.

Productivity as Reflected in Income - Manufacturing

Wages/Salaries and Productivity in Manufacturing

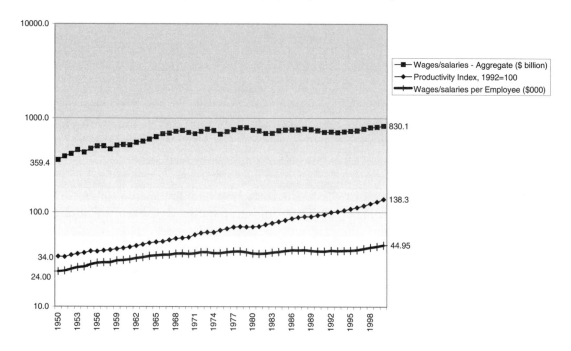

In this panel we want to look more closely at the relationship between productivity and income. Here we look at the Manufacturing Sector — where the effects of technology are clearly reflected. The following panel will show the same data for Business as a whole, with Manufacturing as part of it.

Productivity (output per hour) is shown as an index, with 1992 = 100. The two other series (aggregate wage and salary disbursements and wages and salaries per employee) are in constant 2000 dollars deflated using the Consumer Price Index.

Data are shown on a logarithmic scale; the slopes are therefore comparable. Wages and salaries per employee have shown the least growth. Rates for the last 50 years are these:

Category	Compounded, annual increase - %
Aggregate wages/salaries	1.69
Productivity	2.85
Wages/salaries per employee	1.30
Employment (not shown)	0.39

Productivity has grown much faster than wages/salaries, in the aggregate or on a per employee basis. We have had occasion to note this in the foregoing discussion as well. Productivity is a composite result of human skills, technology, and management. Less of the total yield of increased productivity is going to people, more to other factors — to machines, the "robotic workforce," as investment and to stockholders, as a reward of enterprise. Until about 1970, wages/salaries per employee and productivity moved roughly in parallel. The two curves begin to move in different directions after that time.

In the next panel we look at a broader composite, the Business Sector as a whole. There we also show corporate profits. In the final panel in this series, we shall look at corporate profits in detail.

Sources: Productivity data from Bureau of Labor Statistics, U.S. Department of Labor; wage and salary disbursement data are from the National Income and Product Accounts maintained by the Bureau of Economic Analysis, U.S. Department of Commerce; manufacturing employment data are from the Bureau of Labor Statistics.

Productivity as Reflected in Income - Business

Wages/Salaries and Productivity in the Business Sector

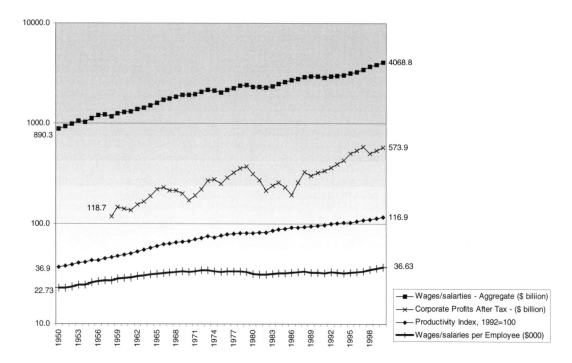

This presentation is like the previous one, but here the entire Business sector is charted. Please note that this sector *includes* Manufacturing. Corporate profits after taxes are added. Two things stand out. The productivity index (output per hour, 1992 = 100) is flatter. It grew at a slower rate, 2.2% a year versus 3.0% in manufacturing. Manufacturing presents more opportunities for automation. The average income per employee is lower, $36,630 in 2000, versus $44,950 in manufacturing. We are dealing here with a much greater part of the economy.

The table of growth rates is shown again, but this time the period used is 1958 to 2000 so that all series can be presented on the same basis; data for corporate profits after taxes in constant dollars are not available prior to 1958. Comparable data for Manufacturing are shown in the last column for all items except corporate profits.

Category	Compounded, annual increase, 58-00 (%)	Data for Manufacturing alone, same period (%)
Aggregate wages/salaries	3.0	1.4
Productivity	2.2	3.0
Wages/salaries per employee	0.7	1.0
Corporate after tax profits	3.8	-
Employment (not shown)	2.3	0.4

Noteworthy here is that aggregate wages and salaries grew at more than double the rate they did in manufacturing; this is explained by the much greater growth in private sector employment as a whole: this period saw the rise of the Services Sector. Productivity has grown at a slower rate because Business as a whole provides fewer opportunities for leveraging technology. Corporate after-tax profits outpaced all of the other indicators shown here. Once again, productivity and wages/salaries per employee diverge.

As manufacturing becomes a smaller percentage of the total economy, it might be logical to assume that productivity growth will flatten. In fact, as shown in an earlier section, productivity has been trending up again in the "second computer revolution" which began in the late 1980s. It may well be that the cyber world will bring productivity increases to the more labor-intensive Services sectors. For that to happen, corporate profits will have to produce the necessary capital. As shown in the graphic, profits are growing healthily. In the next and last panels in this chapter, we take a closer look at corporate profits.

Sources: Productivity data are from the Bureau of Labor Statistics, U.S. Department of Labor; wage and salary disbursement data and data on corporate profits are from the National Income and Product Accounts maintained by the Bureau of Economic Analysis, U.S. Department of Commerce; profits are normalized using the GDP deflator; employment data are from the Bureau of Labor Statistics.

Profits, Investment, and Rewards of Ownership

Corporate Profit After Tax
(Billions of Current Dollars)

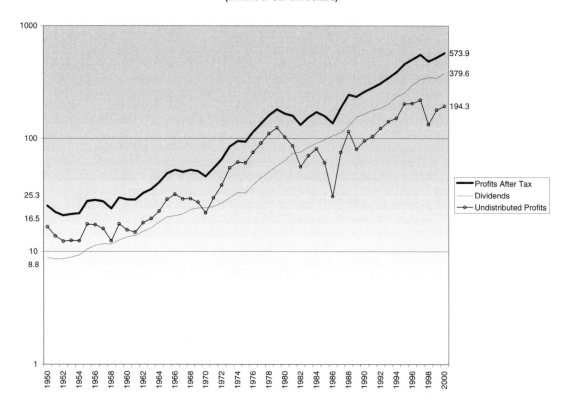

This graphic displays corporate profits after tax (dark line), and its two components — dividends and undistributed profits (circles). Dividends are paid to stockholders, the owners of the enterprise; undistributed profits may be held as cash or invested. Data are shown in current dollars (in the previous panel, the data are in 2000 dollars). A log scale is used so that early years in the series are visible. A fixed scale produces an almost flat line to about 1970 and then a steep surge into the heights — see below:

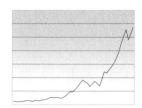

Corporate profits are an important aspect of productivity because they produce the money needed for research and development, technology, machinery, equipment, and structures. These, in combination with methods and management, increase output per hour.

Notice that, until 1981, undistributed profits are generally higher than dividend payments. After that year, they are consistently lower than dividends. The two values, added together, make up profit after tax. Undistributed profits are available to the enterprise for reinvestment. Dividends are stockholders' rewards. The pattern shown here indicates that ownership benefited proportionally more in the latter half of this century than did internal reinvestment. Stockholders, of course, could and did invest their earnings in other enterprises.

It is quite conceivable that this shift in the output of corporations ultimately produced the very substantial investments in the Internet, and related businesses in the last decade of the last century. On this graphic we may be looking at a new phase in productivity — this time in the services sector — or merely at a temporary upsurge in investment that may fade again as other times and other concerns engage the national attention.

Source: U.S. Department of Commerce. Bureau of Economic Analysis. *National Income and Product Accounts*.

Chapter 6

Benefits

Employer provided benefits are an important component of total compensation. This chapter looks at trends in both benefits and retirement.

Over the last 20 years employers' costs for employee benefits have remained reasonably constant as a percentage of total compensation. However, the cost of providing health care insurance has risen. The analysis presented will show that health care coverage is one component of the benefit package that has not fared well over this timeframe. The trend is towards employees absorbing at least a portion of the cost of their health care coverage.

The extent to which this is true varies by size of employer. Small employers tend to offer fewer benefits than do large employers. This is true for all benefits within the employee benefit package, not just health care coverage. Many benefit plans require economies of size in order to be cost effective and it is primarily this that keeps small firms from matching the offerings of larger firms. Laws regulating employee-employer relations recognize this difference and they impose regulations more heavily on employers with more than 25 employees. Panels four and five present data on benefits by size of employer.

Employee benefits are a moving target. They change as the demands of the workforce change. The characteristics of the workforce have changed greatly over the past fifty years. So too have employee benefits. As more women have entered the workforce, the number of employees who are also busy raising children has risen. This increased the need for flexible schedules and provisions for family leave. The sixth panel addresses family leave and points out how trends in family-related benefits are changing.

Computers and the Internet have made remote-working arrangements possible and their adoption is often seen as a benefit. Remote-work arrangements are one of the non-traditional benefits that are discussed in panel five.

Early retirement is a trend that is studied in the final five panels. First, trends in retirement age are charted. In the 1950s the average age of retirement was 67 years. By the year 2000 that number is expected to have dropped to just over 61 years. The opposite trend has been seen in life expectancy. In 1950, life expectancy in the U.S. was 68 years. In 2000 that number is 77 years, and in 2050 it is projected to be 81 years. The question posed in the final panels is, can we afford to continue retiring earlier and earlier and living longer and longer?

Employment Benefits – Are They Headed Up or Down?

**Employer Paid Wages and Benefits for the
Civilian Labor Force -- 1986-99**

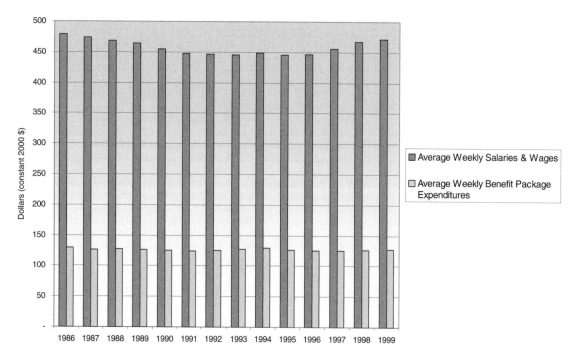

This graph presents what employers pay for people — salaries, wages, and benefits. The costs charted are weekly averages for all employers of the civilian workforce. Constant dollars are used to eliminate the effect of inflation.

Salaries and wages dipped slightly in the early 1990s; benefits remained stable. The cost of benefits rose as a percent of total compensation in the middle of the period while wages declined briefly. The trend has, however, been towards a stable relationship between these costs. Benefits began at 27% of total compensation in 1986 and were again 27% in 1999.

The employee benefit package consists of many items — vacation time, sick leave, health insurance, retirement income accounts, disability insurance, life insurance, to name a few. Before we conclude that all items in the benefit package have remained at consistent levels during the period covered here, we should look more closely at the individual items within these plans. We turn to that matter in the next panel.

Sources: U.S. Department of Labor, Bureau of Labor Statistics, Katherine G. Abraham, Commissioner, *Employer Costs for Employee Compensation, 1986-99*, March 2000, p 3. Data were converted to constant 2000 dollars using the Bureau of Labor Statistics' Consumer Price Index for urban dwellers (CPI-U), All Items series.

Details of the Employment Benefit Package

Different Plans within the Employee Benefit Package - 1986-1999

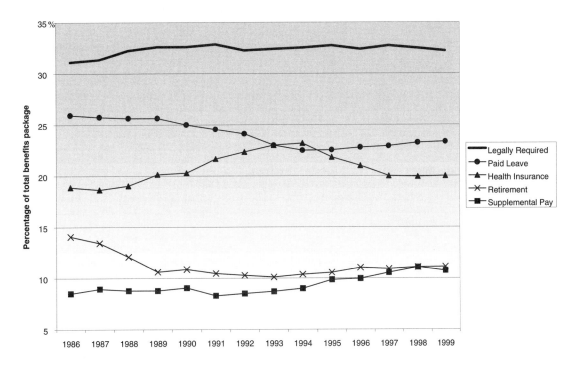

This graphic displays the different components that combine into a standard benefits package for employees. In the display, each component is shown as a percentage of the total package employers funded in the 1986-1999 period. At the top are the legally mandated benefits (e.g. Social Security, Medicare, unemployment taxes). Supplemental pay is at the bottom.

The relationship among the items is reasonably stable. We saw that in the previous panel already. But there has been some shift in the percentage shares of each plan. Three have risen and two have fallen. But changes have been modest.

Expenditures on paid leave fell during the period. In both cases the strong economy was a primary cause. During the tight labor market of the 1990s, employers asked people to work as many hours as possible; time off shrank. New hires were often part time or temporary — categories of employees that are less likely to receive the same benefits as full-time employees. Thus employers spent less on paid leave of all kinds.

The share of retirement plans also shrank. Again, it was the economy. Returns on retirement funds were buoyed up by the strong market, and the amounts employers had to pay to reach predetermined asset balances therefore fell. For plans that required a fixed contribution, higher returns on investment did not alter the employer's cost — but they increased the employees' payout. So, although the expenditure for this benefit category was down, paid-out benefits did not decline.

This brings up an interesting question — Could the opposite also be true? Could one or more of the standard plans have *increased* in cost and yet be yielding a *lower* benefit?

Three components of the "package" cost more at the end of the period than at the beginning: legally mandated benefits, health insurance, and supplemental pay. Mandated contributions affect employers' ability and/or willingness to provide other benefits. They're not discretionary. Supplemental pay was up because a tight labor market required more incentives to hold key staff.

The most interesting of the up-trending benefit plans is health insurance. Health insurance shows the most dynamism on our graphic. Could health insurance be a case in which costs are up but benefits are not?

We look at this issue more closely in the next panel.

Sources: U.S. Department of Labor, Bureau of Labor Statistics, Katherine G. Abraham, Commissioner, *Employer Costs for Employee Compensation, 1986-99*, March 2000, p. 3. Data were converted to constant 2000 dollars using the Bureau of Labor Statistics' Consumer Price Index for urban dwellers (CPI-U), All Items series.

Are Employer-Provided Health Care Benefits Keeping Pace with Health Care Costs?

Health Care Expenditures 1960-1999

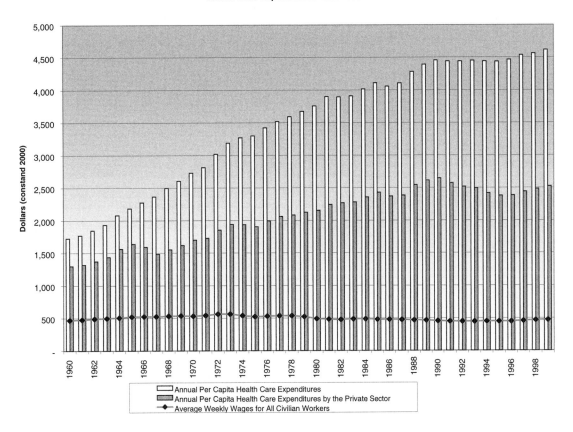

Annual Per Capita Health Care Expenditures
Annual Per Capita Health Care Expenditures by the Private Sector
Average Weekly Wages for All Civilian Workers

Spending on health care has nearly tripled over the last 40 years. "Health care" here includes preventive care, hospital/clinical services, dental care, home health care, mental health services, nursing home care, etc.

The graph shows annual per capita expenditures in constant dollars. Total and private sector expenditures are charted; the "private" portion, of course, is a subset of total. Private sector expenditures include both the employer's contribution and the employee's participation. Public-sector expenditures account for the difference between the two sets of bars in the graph. Public expenditures include payments under Medicare, Medicaid, Department of Defense Medical and Veterans' Administration programs, and all government employee health coverage.

Employer-provided health insurance benefits have remained relatively constant since the mid-1980s (previous panel). But *actual* costs of health care have risen. Weekly average wages and salaries are charted in the graph above; they produce a more or less flat curve at the bottom of graph. This line reflects none of the increased cost of health care experienced during the period shown. Even when looking at the recent 1986 to 1999 period,

---

one sees that spending by the private sector rose 7%. Weekly employer contributions rose only 4%. Who is paying the difference?

The workers! They are getting less health care coverage and/or they pay more of the cost of the coverage they do receive.

Employers are asking workers to carry a larger part of the health care burden. They're also offering this benefit to fewer employees. Health care coverage among full-time employees (of establishments with more than 99 employees) declined from 82% in 1993 to 76 % in 1997.

The overall picture for employee benefits may be mixed, but a clear downward trend emerges in the case of health care. Fewer people are getting medical benefits. More of those who do are paying for part of the package. Rising health insurance costs largely explain this. Employer-provided health care benefits are not keeping pace with the cost of the coverage.

Percent of employees with health care coverage asked to contribute towards the cost of coverage.

Year	Single Coverage	Family Coverage
1980	26	NA
1982	27	NA
1984	36	NA
1986	43	NA
1988	44	64
1989	47	66
1991	51	69
1993	61	76
1995	67	78
1997	69	80

NA – Not Available

The next panel takes a look at the traditional set of benefit plans and how participation in them differs by size of employer.

Sources: Wage data are from the Council of Economic Advisers' *Economic Report for the President*, January 2001, Table B37 – Civilian employment by demographic characteristic, 1955-2000, Table B47 – Hours and earnings in private nonagricultural industries, 1959-2000. Health expenditure data are from the U.S. Department of Commerce, Bureau of the Census, Health Cost Financing Administration's web site http://www.hcfa.gov/stats/nhe-oact/tables/nhe99.csv, October 2001. Population data are from the U.S. Department of Commerce, Bureau of the Census, Table B34 – Population by age group, 1929-2000, available online at http://w3.access.gpo.gov/usbudget/fy2002/erp.html#erp2. Table of employee contributions to employer health plans is from the U.S. Department of Labor, Bureau of Labor Statistics' *Employment Benefits Survey* 1998, available online at http://146.142.24/cgi-bin/surveymost?eb. Figures for the percentage of employees receiving health care coverage by size of firm are from the U. S. Department of Labor's *Employee Benefits in Medium and Large Private Establishments, 1997*, September 1999, Chapter 1. Expenditure data were converted to constant 2000 dollars using the Bureau of Labor Statistics' Consumer Price Index for urban dwellers (CPI), Health Costs Series (for the health cost expenditures) and All Items Series (for all other expenditures).

Small Firms, Smaller Benefits Packages
Large Firms, Larger Benefits Packages

Participation in Different Benefit Plans by Size of Private Sector Employer

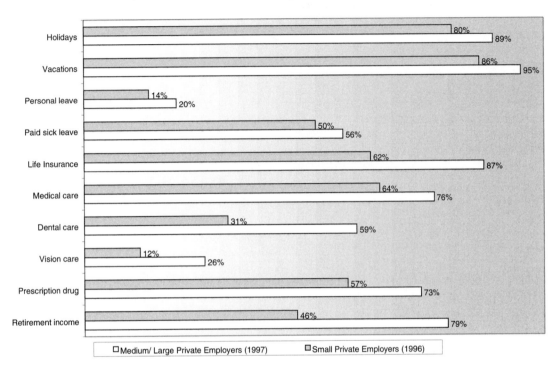

Medium/ Large Private Employers (1997)   Small Private Employers (1996)

A standard employee benefit package includes most of the plans listed above. This graph shows the percentage of full-time employees that participate in each plan. We show data separately for small and large employers. Where participation rates are high, many employers offer the plans.

Medium-to-large employers have 100 or more employees. Small employers have 99 or fewer people. The category "Small Employer" covers the corner florist shop with one part-time assistant as well as the computer-networking firm with ten vans and a city-wide client list. Each of these categories covers a wide range of diverse establishments.

Not surprisingly, medium-to-large employers offer benefits to more of their employees than do small employers. On average, 1.3 times as many full-time employees of medium-to-large establishments receive the benefits than do full-time employees of small companies/organizations.

There are many reasons for this. Small firms don't enjoy the benefit of scale. For example, medium-to-large firms can purchase insurance policies at lower cost. By spreading liability over a large number of participants, premiums are lower. Larger firms need more people and, especially in labor-short boom times, need incentives to recruit. They also tend to have more employees who are covered by collective bargaining contracts.

In addition to the benefit plans listed here, there is a set of newer benefit plans still in the process of becoming popularized. In the next panel we look at participation rates in these non-core benefit plans.

Source: For data on small private sector employers: U.S. Department of Labor, Bureau of Labor Statistics, *Employee Benefits in Small Private Establishments, 1996*, Tables 1 & 3. For data on medium and large private sector employers: U.S. Department of Labor, Bureau of Labor Statistics, *Employee Benefits in Medium & Large Private Establishments, 1997*, Tables 1 & 3.

New Trends in Employee Benefits

Participation in Different Non-Core Benefit Plans by Size of Private Sector Employer

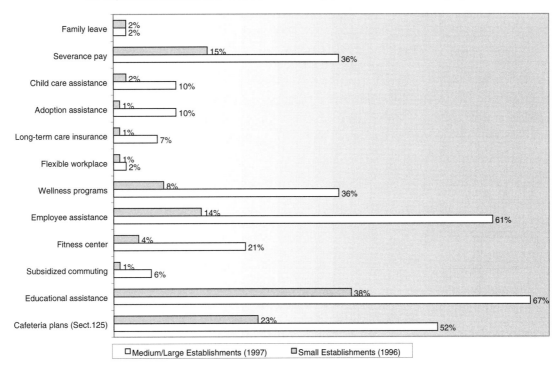

| □ Medium/Large Establishments (1997) | □ Small Establishments (1996) |

One clear trend in benefits is their tendency to expand over time in periods of economic growth. This graph shows participation rates by full-time employees in 12 so-called non-core benefit plans. Non-core plans are those offered in addition to a standard "package." Historical patterns indicate that, as these non-core benefits become more and more popular, they "graduate" into the standard benefit package.

On average, employees of medium-to-large enterprises (100+ employees) are 3 times more likely to be offered a set of these non-core benefits than are employees of small enterprises (1 to 99 employees).

As more companies offer these plans, institutions tend to arise that make the administration of such programs less burdensome to the employer. Then they come into the range of the smaller firms as well.

In addition to the plans shown above, other plans are offered, but comprehensive data on these are not being collected yet, and statistical tracking is therefore difficult.

Indicators about newly emerging benefits are available. For example, health care insurance is frequently offered to the employee and his/her family members. That's pretty standard. But the definition of "family" for this purpose is changing. Same-sex partners as well as the opposite sex but unmarried partners of employees are now sometimes included in plans that cover family members. According to the Human Rights Campaign, the extension of domestic partner benefits by Fortune 500 companies more than doubled in recent years — from 61 companies in 1998 to 145 companies in 2001.

The extension of health care benefits to same-sex partners is, according to an annual survey conducted by Mercer/Foster Higgins, even more widely exercised in small firms (10-499 workers) than in large firms (500+ workers). In 1999 they report that 16% of small firms offered same-sex partner benefits while only 11% of large firms offered the same.

This finding shows that small firms are sometimes quicker to implement new benefits than are large firms. Because small firms, as defined in the Mercer/Foster Higgins study, include enterprises that employ 10 to 499 workers, findings exclude the very small firms that have between 1 and 9 workers. These firms have significantly lower benefit offerings.

Over the five-year period, 1997 to 2001, all of the following benefit types experienced increased usage, according to the Society of Human Resource Managers.

Paid time-off plans

Domestic partner benefits

Flexible scheduling

Flexible spending accounts

Retirement and financial planning assistance

1997 to 2001 was a period of healthy economic growth. In such times benefit plans proliferate. Economic downturns cause such benefits to wither. In a depressed economy, the job itself is the benefit.

Over time, the demographic makeup of a workforce changes. As it does, so too do employment benefit packages. Although the pace of change is hard to forecast, benefit plans will change to reflect the needs of the workforce. Family-related benefits present a dramatic area of change. We look at "family leave" in the next panel.

Sources: U.S. Department of Labor. Bureau of Labor Statistics. *Employee Benefits in Small Private Establishments, 1996*. Tables 1 and 3; *Employee Benefits in Medium & Large Private Establishments, 1997*, Tables 1 and 3. Human Rights Campaign. *Report on Number of Employers Offering Domestic Partner Benefits*. Online. Available: http://www.hrc.org/newsreleases/2001/index.asp. Carrey, Anne and Frank Pompa. *USA TODAY*, 10 August, 2000, page B1. Society for Human Resource Management. Summary of *SHRM 2001 Benefits Survey*. Online. Available: http://www.shrm.org/hrnews/articles/default.asp?page=041801b.htm

Family Leave — A Benefit on the Move

Family Leave Coverage in the 1990s

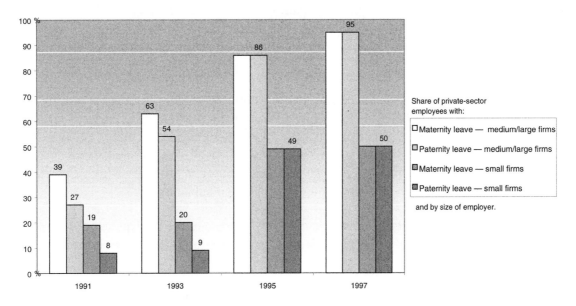

Share of private-sector employees with:

☐ Maternity leave — medium/large firms

☐ Paternity leave — medium/large firms

☐ Maternity leave — small firms

☐ Paternity leave — small firms

and by size of employer.

No discussion of employment benefits would be complete without a look at trends in family-related benefits. These "benefits" are often difficult to track by following what employers pay — because the costs associated with them are indirect. But their impact on the workplace and workforce is very direct.

Changes in the labor force — increasing numbers of women, single parents, and families in which both parents work outside the home — have created enormous pressure on employers and on the political system to legislate for family-related benefits. One of these benefits, family leave, is an example of the trend.

The graph presents data on the percentage of full-time, private-sector employees with family leave coverage during the 1990s. Data are presented for both employees of medium and large establishments (100+ employees) and for employees of small enterprises (1 to 99 employees). Before 1994, family leave data were segregated into maternity leave and paternity leave. After 1993 this distinction is no longer made; data, therefore, are charted as equivalent in 1996 and 1997.

The period covered is particularly interesting. It provides a look at the status of family leave before and after the passage and enactment in 1993 of the Family and Medical Leave Act (FMLA). This act requires that public-sector employers and private employers of 50 or more employees, offer 12 weeks of unpaid family or medical leave every year to qualified employees[1]. Although the law does not require that the leave be paid, it does mandate that the employer maintain any health-care insurance already in place for the duration of the employee's absence.

Results of the legislation are apparent. Family-leave coverage increased dramatically during the 1990s. Passage of the FMLA has increased family leave coverage for private-sector employees more than twofold, and in the case of paternity leave, the increase has been greater yet.

Part-time employees have benefited too. Although not covered by the legislation, 54% of part-time employees of medium and large firms were offered family leave benefits in 1997, up 34% for women and 40% for men over their respective rates in 1991. Also worth noting, the increase in family leave coverage for employees of small firms includes the change for firms with fewer than 50 employees, another group to which the FMLA legislation does not apply. Yet, their numbers are also up substantially.

Passage of the FMLA reflects intense societal desire to make the workplace more amenable to the demands of family life. More legislation of a similar kind may be expected in the future.

"As federal and state lawmakers revisit family leave for medical reasons, more states look at mandating time-off for workers to attend their children's school functions."[2]

Also brewing on the horizon are efforts to make family leave "paid time-off." Just how to pay for such a benefit is what is now being discussed. In early 2001 eight state legislatures had introduced paid family leave legislation.[3]

The way in which employers handle the needs of their employees for time off to care for children and elderly and sick family members is changing. All signs point towards continued changes in this area of employment policy, as well as in other family-related benefit policies.

Source: Waldfogel, Jane. "Family leave coverage in the 1990s." U.S. Department of Labor. *Monthly Labor Review*, October 1999, p. 13.

---

[1] Qualified employees are those who worked for at least 1,250 hours for the employer in the previous year. Family leave may be taken for use in the care of a newborn, a newly adopted child, or a newly placed foster child, to care for a child, spouse, or parent who has a serious health condition, or to treat one's own serious health condition.

[2] "School Break: States take a new look at classroom leave," *Wall Street Journal*, January 15, 2002, page 1

[3] Richards, Cindy. "Eight States Introduce Paid Family Leave Bills," *Women's News*, downloaded on January 14, 2002, available online at http://www.womensenews.org

Retiring Earlier, Living Longer

Median Age at Retirement 1950-2005

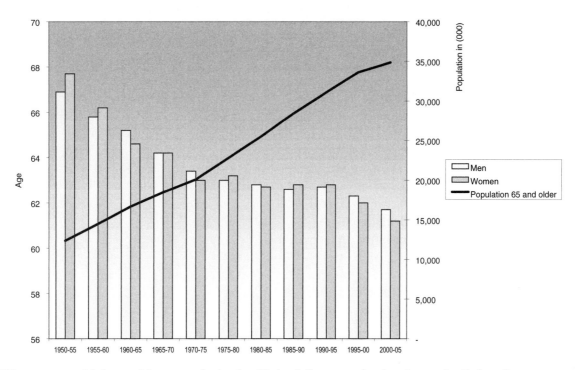

The age at which working people in the United States retire has been declining for many decades. The graph charts the median age at retirement for men and women for the 5-year periods 1950-55 to 2000-2005. All data for years after 1995 are projections made by the Bureau of Labor Statistics (BLS). Total population aged 65 years or older is also charted as a solid line.

Counting the number of retired people is more difficult than at first it may appear. The two ways the federal government employed in reaching the numbers provided here are by (1) counting the number of persons receiving a pension, private or public, and (2) counting the number of people leaving the labor force at an advanced age for reasons other than death.

The inherent problem with counting the retired population in this manner stems from the fact that many people are returning to work after "retiring" from one job by taking on another while receiving pension payments from the first. Nonetheless, it is the best method found by the BLS to date.

In 1950, men and women both retired in their late 60s. Interestingly, women worked almost a year longer than men did on average in the early 50s. By the first years of the new century, this difference is expected to have reversed. Women will be retiring 6.5 years younger than they did in 1950-55 at the age of 61.2. Men too will be retiring earlier than they did in the 1950s but they will be doing so a half year older than their female counterparts, at the age of 61.7.

The trend is clear. We are retiring earlier and living longer. The population age 65 and older has grown steadily over the last century, not only in real numbers but also as a percent of the total population.

Can we afford to continue this trend of retiring ever earlier and living longer? This is a question we will address in the next few panels.

Source: Age of retirement data: Gendell, Murray and Jacob S. Siegel. "Trends in retirement age by sex, 1950-2005." U.S. Department of Labor. *Monthly Labor Review*, July 1992, p. 27. Population data: *Historical Statistics of the United States*, Colonial Times to 1970, U.S. Bureau of the Census. Vol. 1, p.10. More recent data: Online. Available: http://www.census.gov/. Working after retirement data: Herz, Diane E. "Working after early retirement: an increasing trend among men." U.S. Department of Labor. *Monthly Labor Review*, April 1995, p. 13.

Retiring Early, Living Longer, a Burden on the Middle?

Dependency Ratio 1900--2000 and Projections to 2030

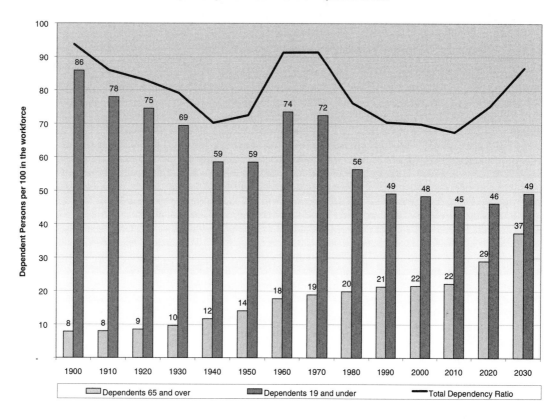

The ratio between the size of the workforce-aged population and the combined young and old population is called the dependency ratio. The higher the dependency ratio the greater the burden on society to support its more dependent sectors. Though it is true that not all youth or elderly people need support and not everyone of working age works, this ratio is a measure of the population's ability to support those not in the labor force.

The graph presents the U.S. dependency ratio for more than a century. Figures are presented for the youth dependency ratio (those aged 0 to 20 per 100 aged 20 to 64), the elderly dependency ratio (those aged 65 or older per 100 aged 20 to 64), and the combined dependency ratio. In 1980, for example, there were 20 people aged 65 or older for every hundred people aged 20 to 64.

What the graph clearly shows is the trend towards a steadily growing elderly dependency ratio and an increasing total dependency ratio into the 21st century. These ratios tend to be cyclical. Their peaks have traditionally occurred during periods of population growth. The mid-century Baby Boom is seen clearly in the data for 1960 and 1970, each showing growth rates for the preceding decade. The new trend in the dependency ratio arises from the increasing percentage of this "dependent" population that is in the 65 and over age cohort. The elderly portion of the dependency ratio is growing steadily and will continue to do so through the early 21st century.

In the previous panel we saw that the average age of retirement is declining. As of the year 2000, the average age of retirement was 61.5. If, to the dependency ratio data presented here, we make the necessary alterations to more accurately reflect all retired people, instead of only those over the age of 64, the dependency ratio will increase even more rapidly.

The Social Security system was established as an insurance policy that would provide us with a small income in retirement. In order to assess our ability as a society to support our expanding period of retirement, we should look next at projections for this system.

Source: Population data for 1900–70: U.S. Bureau of the Census. *Historical Statistics of the United States*, Colonial Times – 1970. Series A29-49 p. 10. Population data for 1980 and projections to 2030: U.S. Bureau of the Census. *Annual Projections of the Resident Population by Age, Sex, Race, and Hispanic Origin: 1999 to 2100*. Online. Available: http://www.census.gov/population/www/projections/natdet-D1A.html

Social Security – Is It Designed to Support Us For 20 Plus Years?

Social Security Funds as Percent of GDP 2000--2050

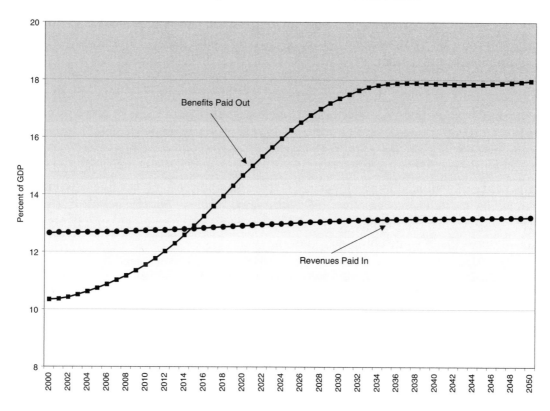

Social Security Funds as Percent of GDP 2000--2050

The Social Security system in the U.S. is a major source of retirement income for many. Thus Social Security is a logical place to start answering the question: Can we afford to continue this trend of retiring ever earlier and living longer?

The graph presents projected income and expense for the Social Security fund from 2000 to 2050. These projections are made by the Social Security Administration. The figures for both income-tax revenues and benefits paid out are presented as a percentage of Gross Domestic Product. The picture is sobering. It highlights the coming deficits in a system on which so many Americans depend for at least a part of their livelihood during retirement.

The gap between revenue and expense arises because of demographic shifts. The aging of the Baby Boom and life-extending medical advances combine to create an imbalance in the Social Security system as designed.

The system was established in 1935 and was intended as an insurance policy against a poverty-ridden old age, a not uncommon fate for the elderly during the first decades of the 20th century. Those in the workforce pay into a fund; upon retirement, they receive a small income from the fund.

In the 1930s, life expectancy in the U.S. was 59.7 years; many people never reached the age of retirement. In 2001, life expectancy was 77.6 years; most people today live for quite a while on Golden Pond. We're living longer and drawing from the Social Security fund for more years with each passing generation. The declining age of retirement only exacerbates this trend.

In simple terms, if the number of those paying into the fund drops as the number of those drawing from it rises, an imbalance is sure to develop in the future.[4] As we saw in the last panel, just such a shift is coming.

Barring any restructuring of the system beforehand, Social Security expenses will exceed revenues in the year 2015. At that point the system will begin to use reserves to meet its obligations. According to Social Security Administration estimates, these reserves will carry the system through the mid-2030s. At that point, if not sooner, one of two things will need to be done: (1) the Social Security tax rate will need to be increased, or (2) benefits paid out will need to be reduced. The second solution may involve extending the retirement age to 70 or an even older age. Since none of these options is politically palatable (the elderly have the highest voting rate), it remains to be seen which will be implemented — most likely some combination of the two.

Since three out of every 10 Americans aged 65 or older depend on Social Security payments for 90% or more of their income (and 3 out of 5 depend on Social Security for 50% or more of their income) we must ask an important question: Are those of us now in our 30s and 40s planning on an alternative or supplemental retirement income? The next panels will address this question.

Source: Social Security Administration. *The 2000 Annual Report of the Board of Trustees of the Federal Old-Age and Survivors Insurance and Disability Insurance Trust Funds*. March 30, 2000. Online. Available: http://www.ssa.gov/OACT/TR/ TR00/Ir3C1-2.html. For data on the dependence of persons 65 years and older on Social Security payments: U.S. Bureau of the Census. *Current Population Survey*. . March 2000 Income Supplement. Reproduced in Social *Security Bulletin*, Annual Statistics Supplement 2000.

---

[4] The system is, of course, far more complex than this statement suggests. The Social Security System has been expanded many times since its inception. It now covers workers, disabled persons, and the dependents of each. The system also adjusts benefits for inflation annually, something that was not done in its first four decades. All of this complicates the statement that if fewer pay in than withdraw from the system the well will run dry. However, the essence of any insurance fund relies on the fact that it will take in at least as much as it pays out.

Household Income After Retirement: Is It Enough to Live On?

Household Income and Expense -- 1985--1999

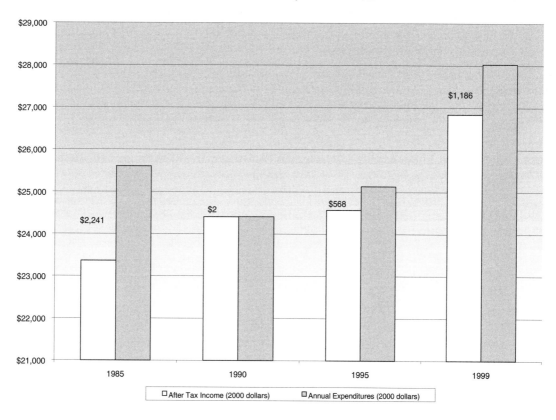

This graph presents the average annual income and expenses of those U.S. households in which the householder is at least 65 years of age. In every year, expenses exceed income. The amount by which expenses exceed income appears above the income column for each year. That amount is, for example, $2 in 1990 and $1,186 in 1999.

The average household headed by someone 65 years or older spends more than it takes in per year. Households in this category spend money earned and accumulated earlier in life. They depend for at least a portion of their livelihood on savings.

Detail Listing of the Sources of Income for Households Headed by Someone 65 years or older

Source of Income	1985	1990	1995	1999
Self-employment Income	923	885	845	1,448
SS & Private Pensions	13,992	16,050	16,912	16,991
Interest, Dividends, etc...	3,889	3,496	2,113	2,996
Unemployment & Workers Comp.	163	201	202	75
Public Assistance	204	224	334	251
Other Income	202	212	196	290
Total Money Income Before Tax	**25,481**	**25,970**	**25,824**	**28,170**
All taxes Paid	-2,119	-1,568	-1,258	-1,330
Total Expenditures	-25,603	-24,404	-25,133	-28,026
Deficit Spending	**2,241**	**2**	**568**	**1,186**

These households derive income from four primary sources: (1) wages and salaries (often of someone other than the head-of-household), (2) self-employment income, (3) Social Security and private-pension payments, and (4) interest and dividend income. There is one additional source of income, not listed in the table above — household savings, those that are used to cover deficit spending.

This brings up a very simple question: Are we now saving at a rate that will provide us with the supplemental income necessary to live comfortably for many years after retiring? As the previous panel showed, the Social Security system would be unable, at current rates, to provide more than an ever-smaller portion of a person's expected retirement income. The resources with which we enter retirement will become an ever more important factor in determining whether or not we are able to retire "early."

Personal savings rates are, therefore, our next area of investigation. Are we saving enough now to provide for our retirement?

Source: U.S. Department of Labor. *Consumer Expenditure Survey 1985–1999.* Online. Available: ftp://ftp.bls.gov/pub/special.requests/ce/standard/1990/age.txt. All dollar amounts have been normalized to the year 2000 using the Bureau of Labor Statistic Consumer Price Index.

A Comfortable Retirement Will Require Proper Savings

Personal Savings Rate 1960 - 2000

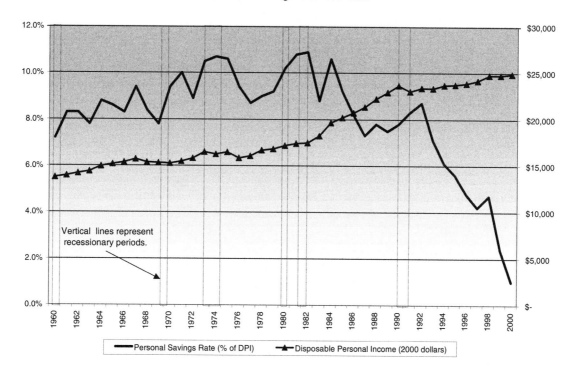

The U. S. personal savings rate is the measure of all personal savings as a percentage of disposable personal income. How much of what we earn and receive in the way of support payments — less taxes — do we save? The graph presents data on both disposable income and savings rates for the last 40 years. The trends in these two series could not be clearer. We are saving less and less while our disposable income steadily rises. The disposable income is in constant dollars, the savings rate in percent of disposable income.

Many factors influence the rate at which we save. Confidence is one important factor. Periods of recession, marked on the graph by vertical lines, tend to be periods in which confidence is low. When we are uncertain, we tend to hunker down, reduce our spending and save money. The personal savings rate rises during these periods.

The decade of the 1990s was a period of growth and optimism. Savings rates plummeted as we began to spend freely. The personal savings rates seen in the late 1990s are the lowest recorded since these data have been collected (1946). Economists attribute this, in part, to the "wealth effect." This term refers to the tendency of households to increase spending levels as the value of their assets (homes, mutual funds, investments of all kinds) increase. During the 1990s the stock market, in which more Americans than ever are now invested, rose sharply as did home values. Together, these changes account for the dramatic reduction in the savings rate.[5]

What impact will this low savings rate have on the trend towards early retirement? It will likely end the trend. It may even reverse that trend.

In essence, the "wealth effect" described above can operate in reverse. Households will tend to decrease spending as the value of their asset-base decreases. During the end of 2000 and in 2001, the stock market showed sharp declines. The value of pensions and savings invested in the market also declined. The economy slowed. Households began to spend less. In this environment people are far less likely to choose early voluntary retirement. But will the trend towards early retirement reassert itself once the economy recovers?

A quick look at two scenarios suggests that the answer to that question is No.

1. The economy recovers strongly – In this case, the demand for well-educated workers will also increase. Since the Baby Boom generation is followed by two smaller generations, there will be pressure to keep as many of the Baby Boom generation working as long as possible. Pressure to remain in the workforce will be high.

2. The economy is slow for an extended time — We did not save money at high rates during the economically strong 1990s. This period was followed by an economic slowdown and by a sharp decline in the stock market. The value of our asset-base declined. Under these circumstances, it is unlikely that people will voluntarily retire early. They will, more likely, remain in the workforce until the age of 65 at which point full Social Security benefits become available. Furthermore, if the age at which full Social Security benefits come into effect is increased, then the pressure to stay in the workforce even longer will increase as well.

Our failure to save money, our lengthening life spans, and the demographic pressures of the Baby Boom will almost certainly combine to stop, and possibly reverse, the trend towards early retirement during the beginning of the 21st century.

Source: U.S. Department of Commerce. Bureau of Economic Analysis. *Personal Income and Its Disposition*. Online. Available: http://www.bea.doc.gov/.

---

[5] If this explanation of a drop in the savings rates is correct, one can expect to see rates begin to climb again starting in 2001 as the economy slows and stock prices fall.

Chapter 7

Workplace Issues

The workplace has changed greatly over the last quarter century. As we have seen in earlier chapters, the demographic makeup of the workforce has changed. Computers are ubiquitous in the workplace and were not so common just 25 years ago. The very nature of the work that is done has shifted from being slightly weighted towards production to being slightly weighted towards services. How have these changes played out in terms of safety and equal treatment on-the-job? This is the question we will contemplate in this chapter.

First, a look at occupational safety issues. In general, the trends in this area are very positive. The number of occupational fatalities has declined despite increasing numbers of people in the workplace. There has also been a steady decline in the number of occupational injuries and illnesses suffered between 1973 and 2000. This decline in occupational injuries and illnesses has been much greater (59%) for the less serious injuries than for injuries that resulted in lost work days (12%). The third panel in this chapter looks at the injuries we suffered in 1999 by type — cuts, bruises, chemical burns, amputations, etc...

The topic of occupational safety concludes with two panels. One addresses the fact that far more men than women are killed and injured on the job. In 1999 a total of 6,023 people were fatally injured while working. Of these, 97% were men. The last panel on this subject addresses the dramatic declines in the number of people assaulted at work. With the exception of those working in law enforcement and those working with the mentally ill, we are all safer from assault at work than we are in the world at large. In 1999 for every 1,000 people in the workforce, 9 were the victims of a violent act. In the society at large, 33 out of every 1,000 people over the age of 12 was victimized.

Safety from discrimination and harassment is another subject covered in this chapter. Six panels are used to cover the subject of trends in workplace discrimination and sexual harassment. Data on this subject have been gathered on a consistent and nationwide basis by the U.S. Equal Employment Opportunity Commission (EEOC). This commission, established in 1964, enforces all of the nation's civil rights laws, regulations and policies. The data they collect and publish on the subject are the basis for the analysis presented here. In short, charges of discrimination and sexual harassment filed with the EEOC are up. The number of charges resolved by the EEOC is up. Charges resolved in favor of the plaintiff are up. But most significant, monetary benefits awarded are up by 111% between 1992 and 2001. The panels discuss what all of this might mean.

The last panel in the chapter is about workplace safety concerns since September 11, 2001. It highlights areas in which attention is being directed. These may or may not become lasting trends. They are certainly of high interest as we enter the new century.

Dying at Work

Fatal Occupational Injuries - 1993-2000

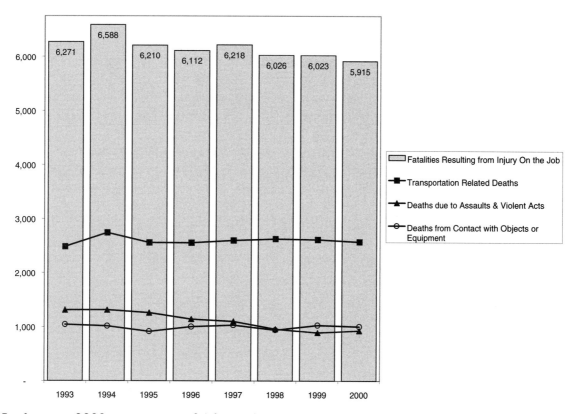

In the year 2000 an average of 16 people a day were killed while working in the United States. As startling as this figure may seem, it represents an improvement over prior years. The graph presents total occupational fatalities as well as the totals for the three categories that account together for three-fourths of these deaths.

Fatalities resulting from on-the-job injuries are classified into seven categories. In 2000, a total of 5,915 people died as a result of injuries suffered on the job. The pie chart to the left shows a percentage breakdown of these fatalities by category.

The category with the most fatalities is Transportation. This has been the case for many years. The category includes all deaths resulting from vehicular accidents both on and off the highway, involving also water vehicles, railroad cars, and aircraft. The occupations most at risk for these sorts of deaths are transportation workers (truck drivers in particular), agricultural workers, those working in the services sector, and construction workers.

Overall, industrial workers most at risk are laboring in construction; they suffer 19.5% of all occupational fatalities. Not surprisingly, far more men than women are killed on the job — far more men than women are employed in the most dangerous occupations.

The distribution of fatal injuries by occupational category and by type of accident has not changed much over the last decade. But the total number of fatalities has dropped from 1.7 per million workers in 1993 to 1.4 per million workers in 2000. One category that has seen slightly more decline than the others is that of Assaults and Violent Acts. These acts include homicides (most of which are associated with robberies), suicides, and assaults by animals[1]. In 1993, assaults and acts of violence accounted for 21% of occupational fatalities (1,311). In 2000, they accounted for 16% of on-the-job fatalities (929).

On-the-job fatalities are declining both in real terms and on a per-worker basis.[2] Is the same true for non-fatal injuries suffered on the job? We will try to answer the question in the next panel.

Source: National Census of Fatal Occupational Injuries in 2000, U.S. Department of Labor, Bureau of Labor Statistics, available on-line at http://stats.bls.gov/oshhome.htm.

---

[1] Victims of assaults by animals are almost always those in the agricultural work force. They are rarely lion trainers or rodeo clowns, as those of us with a vivid imagination might presume.

[2] The year 2001 will prove an exception to this trend as the enormous death toll suffered on or as a result of the events of September 11 is calculated and becomes part of the national total of fatal occupational injuries for the year.

The Workplace is Safer and Safer

Occupational Injury and Illness Rate, 1973-2000

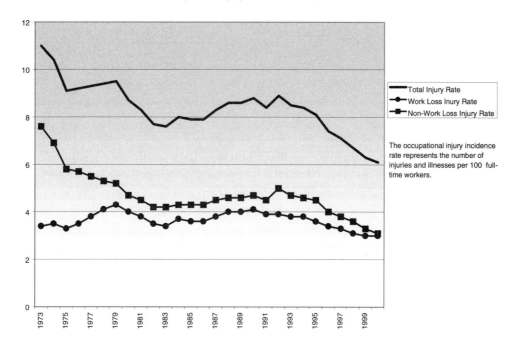

The occupational injury incidence rate represents the number of injuries and illnesses per 100 full-time workers.

This graph presents data on all nonfatal workplace injuries and illnesses. As in the case of fatal on-the-job injuries, here too we see a declining rate of injury. The number of on-the-job injuries is down. This is true both for injuries causing no more than a partial day of lost work time (the day on which the injury occurred) and for injuries or illnesses that result in lost work time.

The trend is clear, but the decline is greater for less serious injuries. Non-work-loss injuries — those that involve no more time loss than a partial day's work on the day the injury is suffered — are down over the period by 59%. Lost work time injuries are down by 12%.

Several factors together are believed to explain this decline. In 1992, expenditures on workers' compensation claims reached $45.7 billion, more than twice the $22.3 billion spent in 1985. This notable rise in expenditures spurred cost control efforts and made it more cost effective to spend larger sums on safety and health programs.[3]

Another factor believed to have influenced the injury and illness rate is a series of changes made in Occupational Safety & Health Administration (OSHA) policies and en-

---

[3] This subject is covered in detail in a study by Hugh Conway and Jens Svenson, published in the November 1998 *Monthly Labor Review*. See the source notes for a full citation.

forcement procedures. In the mid-1990s, OSHA refocused its resources. The agency spent less time inspecting establishments and more time providing compliance assistance.

Some suspect that inaccurate reporting of minor injuries is on the rise and that this accounts for some of the reduced rate of non-work-loss injuries. But such claims are difficult to verify.

Another possible factor sometimes cited as an explanation for declining injury rates is the transition from an industrial to a services economy; the former has a much higher injury rate than the latter. But studies of this factor have shown that the shift did not contribute particularly to the decline.[4]

What is clear is that both fatal workplace injuries and all other occupational injuries and illnesses are down — good news and particularly encouraging because the change occurred during a time of growth. Periods of expansion are particularly susceptible to rises in workplace injury rates: the pace of work tends to speed up as orders pile up and demand is great; the hiring of new employees to meet greater demand means there are more inexperienced workers on the job. Thus the period presented in the graph provides a very positive view of the efforts being made to improve safety in the workplace.

Although the injuries and illnesses presented here did not result in death, they do represent a wide range of severity. They cover everything from minor cuts and bruises to dismemberment and seriously disabling sorts of injuries. The next panel will take a look at the distribution of occupational injuries by type.

Source: Data presented in the graph are from: U.S. Department of Labor, Bureau of Labor Statistics, "Incidence rate of occupational injuries and illness for private industry by selected case types, 1973-2000," available online at: http://www/bls.gov/news.release/ osha.t06.htm. Information about the likely reasons for a declining rate of injury are from: Hugh Conway and Jens Svenson, *Occupational Injury and Illness Rates, 1992-96: Why They Fell*, Bureau of Labor Statistics, *Monthly Labor Review*, November 1998.

---

[4] Ibid.

Ouch! — The Injuries We Get At Work

Lost-Worktime Injuries and Illnesses by Category and Gender -- 1999

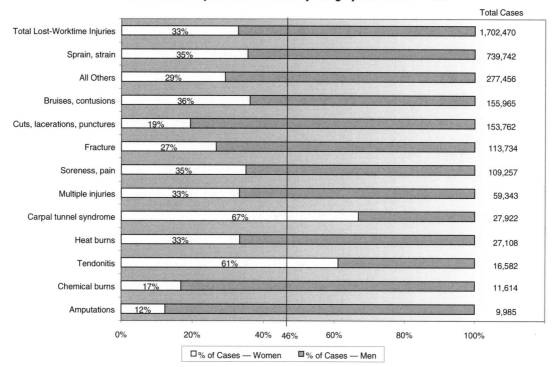

Total Cases

Category	%	Total Cases
Total Lost-Worktime Injuries	33%	1,702,470
Sprain, strain	35%	739,742
All Others	29%	277,456
Bruises, contusions	36%	155,965
Cuts, lacerations, punctures	19%	153,762
Fracture	27%	113,734
Soreness, pain	35%	109,257
Multiple injuries	33%	59,343
Carpal tunnel syndrome	67%	27,922
Heat burns	33%	27,108
Tendonitis	61%	16,582
Chemical burns	17%	11,614
Amputations	12%	9,985

0%   20%   40%   46%   60%   80%   100%

☐ % of Cases — Women   ▦ % of Cases — Men

This chart provides data on the number of non-fatal injuries and illnesses that were reported in the United States in 1999 and resulted in lost work time. The injuries are categorized by type, in descending order, and by gender of the injured party.

A line has been placed at the 46% mark because this is the percentage of the workforce that was, in 1999, made up of women. Although men make up 54% of the workforce, they suffer 67% of all non-fatal occupational injuries and represent more than 54% of injuries suffered in all but two categories. Those categories are Carpal Tunnel Syndrome and Tendinitis, which together represented only 2.6% of occupational injuries in 1999.

Carpal Tunnel Syndrome and Tendinitis are suffered disproportionately by women. They are caused by tasks that require repetitive motions — typing, keying, fitting parts, gripping and twisting actions, etc… As the use of PCs expanded in the 1980s and 90s, so too did cases of Carpal Tunnel Syndrome and Tendinitis. Nonetheless, these types of injuries have declined in the late 1990s, as has the incidence of injuries in all categories.

It appears that the workplace is becoming a safer and safer place to be, at least when it comes to physical wellbeing. We will look more closely at the gender difference in those suffering injuries at work in the next panel.

Source: U.S. Department of Labor, Bureau of Labor Statistics, *Case and Demographic Characteristics for Work-related Injuries and Illnesses Involving Days Away From Work — 1999*, available online at: http://www.bls.gov/iif/oshcdnew.htm — Resource Table Categories.

The Workplace is More Dangerous for Men

Occupational Injuries by Industry -- 1999

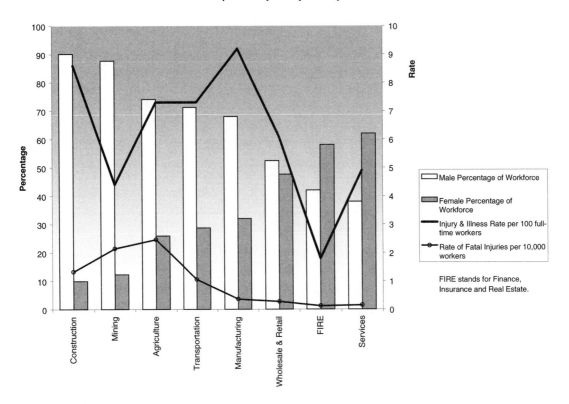

Men are injured and killed on the job at far higher rates than women. This graph shows why. We saw in preceding panels that both fatal and non-fatal occupational injuries and illnesses have declined over the last decades. In this panel we look at the rates of on-the-job injuries by industry and gender. One can see clearly why the workplace, although becoming safer, is still more dangerous for men than it is for women.

The graph shows the percentage of males and females employed in each of the eight major industries of the private sector in 1999. Rates for both fatal and non-fatal on-the-job injuries are plotted against the right scale. The non-fatal injury rate is a rate of injury per 100 full-time employees. Rates for fatal injuries are calculated as cases per 10,000 workers. The result is clear. Men represent a higher percentage of the workforce in the industries that suffer the highest rates of occupational injuries.

The trend is towards a safer workplace, and although men are at greater risk of injury on the job than women, the risk level for both has declined in the 1990s. Is the same thing true if we confine our investigation to violent acts in the workplace? The next panel answers this question.

Source: U.S. Bureau of the Census. *Statistical Abstract of the United States 2001*, Tables 596 and 633; *Statistical Abstract of the United States 2000*, Table 672.

Assaulted On the Job

In Which Occupations Are You at Most Risk?

Decline in the Rate of Violent Victimizations per 1,000 Workers between 1993 and 1999

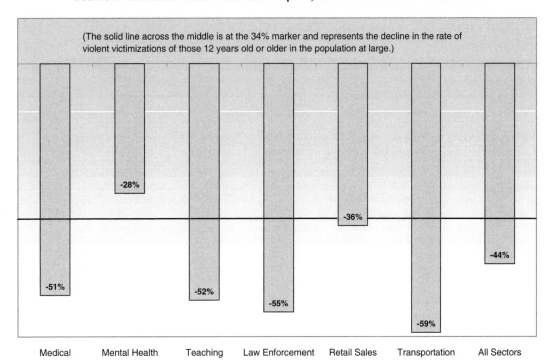

(The solid line across the middle is at the 34% marker and represents the decline in the rate of violent victimizations of those 12 years old or older in the population at large.)

| Medical | Mental Health | Teaching | Law Enforcement | Retail Sales | Transportation | All Sectors |

-28% -51% -52% -55% -36% -59% -44%

Assaults in the workplace are down. This graph presents data on the decline in the number of violent incidents in the workplace between 1993 and 1999. The six individual employment categories presented have the dubious distinction of being the categories with the highest rates of violent criminal victimization. Police officers, nurses, psychiatrists, cab drivers, and cashiers all are at high risk of being assaulted on-the-job. A total workplace figure is provided under the heading "All Sectors."

The trend is clear. Violent acts in the workplace have declined sharply. For the workplace as a whole, the decline between 1993 and 1999 was 44%, a full 10% greater than the decline experienced by the society as a whole. Violent crime in the general population fell 34% during this period. A line has been drawn across the graph at the 34% mark to highlight the decline in violent crime in society overall. Bars passing that line all show "better" results than society as a whole.

In all but one of the most vulnerable employment categories, the rates of violent crime dropped by more than the rate for all violent crimes. This exception was for those who work with the mentally ill. But even in this category, improvement has been significant.

The graphic shows change over time. The table below shows the extent to which different groups of workers are vulnerable to violent assault. Here one can see how frequently those employed in the six categories are victimized. With the exception of those who work in law enforcement or those who work with the mentally ill, workers are safer on the job than in the public square. For every 1,000 people aged 12 years or older, 33 were the victims of a violent act in 1999, down by 34% from the rate of 50 per 1,000 people in 1993. Violent acts are down, both in the workplace and in the society at large and it is still more likely that one will be assaulted off the job than on the job. A somewhat less than reassuring fact.

Rates of Violent Victimization per 1,000 Workers

Category	1993	1999
Industry		
Law Enforcement	163.1	74.1
Mental Health	64.4	46.1
Teaching	25.8	12.4
Retail Sales	21.9	14.1
Transportation	20.6	8.4
Medical Fields	20.3	10.0
All Private Employment	16.0	9.0
Society at Large *	50.0	33.0

* In the case of the "society at large," rates are per 1,000 people aged 12 years or older.

The preceding panels have shown that the people are safer in the workplace, both from accidental injury and from assault. Have employees also become safer from discrimination and harassment during the 1990s? We shall look at this question in the next panel.

Source: U.S. Department of Justice, Bureau of Justice Statistics, *Violent Crime Victimization Survey 2000*, table entitled "Violence in the Workplace, 1993-99," available online at http://www.ojp.usdoj.gov/bjs/abstract/cvusst.htm. For data on the rates of violent crime generally: U.S. Department of Justice, Bureau of Justice Statistics, National Crime Victimization Survey, *Criminal Victimization 1999, Changes 1998-99 with Trends 1993-99*, page 1.

Workplace Discrimination

Discrimination Cases Filed with The Equal Employment Opportunity Commission (EEOC), 1993-2001

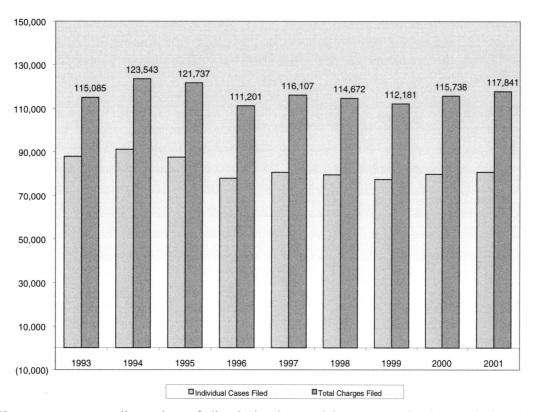

We turn now to a discussion of discrimination and harassment in the workplace. The chart presents data on the number of charges that were filed with the United States Equal Employment Opportunity Commission (EEOC) between 1993 and 2001. The EEOC is the federal agency responsible for the administrative and judicial enforcement of our federal civil rights laws. This chart shows the number of individual cases filed each year and the total number of charges filed. A case may include more than one charge. Cases filed in 2001 averaged 1.46 charges per case, up from 1.31 charges per case in 1993.

The number of cases filed in 2001 is lower than the number filed in 1993. But charges per case are up. Fewer individuals filed cases containing more charges.

Discrimination and harassment in the workplace are inherently difficult social phenomena to track. The range of potentially discriminatory acts is great. Generalizing about them is difficult. The legal definitions for discrimination and harassment have changed over time. This, again, makes it difficult to compare cases over time. Finally, a large percentage of claims arise as the result of layoffs. During times of low unemployment and strong economic growth, the number of people laid off drops.

Some people argue that workplace discrimination and harassment are much more common than are reported. There are no reliable data to quantify this assertion. We therefore rely on the statistical data collected by the EEOC in an effort to chart trends in the workplace.

By charting the number of cases and charges brought before the EEOC over a period of years, we get an overview of the subject. But it is important to realize that fewer than half of all cases (48%) are determined, by the EEOC, to be based on "reasonable cause." More than half are abandoned, withdrawn, or dismissed on a finding of "no reasonable cause." During the period shown, fewer than one out of five plaintiffs won the case that he or she filed.

As a result, in our next panels we will concentrate on those cases found to *have* reasonable cause. In an attempt to understand the trends in discrimination, we will look next at cases by eight categories — those based on discrimination because of age, disability, national origin, pregnancy, race, religion, and sex — and at sexual harassment cases.

Source: U.S. Equal Employment Opportunity Commission, *Charge Statistics FY 1992 through FY 2001*, available online at http://www.eeoc.gov/stats/charges.html.

Discrimination and Harassment Cases by Category

Cases of Discrimination Found to Have Reasonable Cause by Category Brought Before the EEOC, 1993-2001

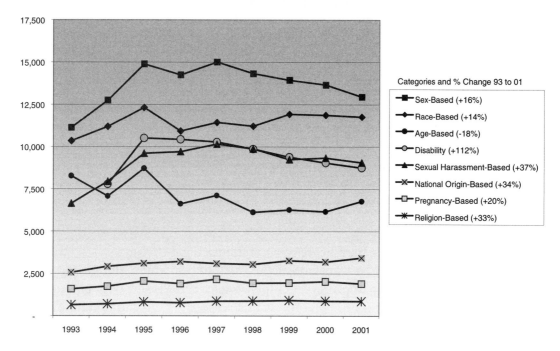

This chart presents data on discrimination charges filed with the U.S. Equal Employment Opportunity Commission (EEOC). We focus on cases determined to have reasonable cause. We will call these resolved cases[5]. Discrimination and harassment charges fall into eight categories; these, in turn, are covered by four legislative statutes[6] that EEOC enforces.

The graph shows data on resolved cases for each of the eight categories of discrimination. Sex-based cases lead the parade, closely followed by race-based discrimination claims. Both of these categories saw increased "resolutions" over the period. But case filings did not increase dramatically. They did in the other categories.

With one exception, all categories of discrimination saw significant increases in the number of cases resolved. The exception was age-based discrimination. One possible reason for this is the strong economy of the 1990s. Most age-based charges arise from claims of

---

[5] The EEOC uses the term "resolved cases" to mean any case upon which it has ruled, regardless of whether or not a finding of reasonable cause was made. Here, we will use the term "resolved case" to mean a case or charge the EEOC has found to be based on a reasonable cause to believe that discrimination occurred.

[6] The four statutes are, (1) Title VII of the Civil Rights Act of 1964, frequently referred to as Title VII; (2) Equal Pay Act of 1963 (EPA); (3) Age Discrimination in Employment Act of 1967 (ADEA); (4) Americans with Disabilities Act of 1990 (ADA).

---

wrongful termination. As demand for labor grew, pressure on older workers to leave the labor force diminished. Those asked to leave were generally offered early retirement packages. In 2000 and 2001 the economy began to slow and jobs were cut. In 2001 the number of age-based case resolutions rose — the consequence of an increased number of cases filed in 2000. Cause and effect were at work. There is an average one-year delay between filing a charge of discrimination with the EEOC and resolution of that charge[7].

The strong economy of the 1990s may have been expected to have a similarly dampening effect on all categories of workplace discrimination as employers focused on providing as accommodating an environment as possible for workers in short supply. Not so. Case resolutions in all categories — except age-based — rose during the period 1993 to 2001. This suggests that age-based charges are based primarily on claims of wrongful termination — rather than other forms of discrimination. What other factors influence discrimination charges and resolutions?

Various factors influence these rates. First and most obviously, where discrimination is present, cases will be filed.

Second, changes in the law — new legislation and new legal precedents — have a profound impact on filing rates. Laws establish the rules under which charges are judged. They also establish limits on monetary compensation. Lawyers and clients are more likely to file charges if a successful outcome seems reasonably easy to obtain. The availability of punitive damages is also a motivating factor in entering what can be a lengthy and difficult journey.

Finally, filing rates are influenced by the level of public attention given to a particular type of discriminatory action. Heavy media coverage of high-profile cases serves as a trigger — Tailhook, Anita Hill and Clarence Thomas come to mind. A more thorough look at this subject will be offered in the panel on sexual harassment.

In the next panel we will look further at the changing levels of discrimination case resolutions by category.

Source: U.S. Equal Employment Opportunity Commission, Charge Statistics FY 1992 through FY 2001, available online at http://www.eeoc.gov/stats/charges.html.

---

[7] This delay between filing charges and charge resolutions also explains why we chose to list disability-based cases starting in 1994. This category of discrimination was only established in 1992, and 1993 was the first full year in which charges based on disability were filed.

Trends in Discrimination and Harassment Charge Resolutions

Percentage Change in EEOC Cases Resolved, by Category, 1993 to 2001

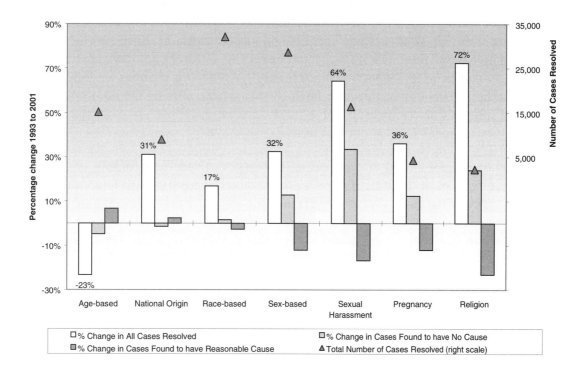

This chart presents data on the percentage change in discrimination charges resolved by the U.S. Equal Employment Opportunity Commission (EEOC) between 1993 and 2001. The chart shows trends. The first and lightest bar shows the change in the number of cases resolved, regardless of outcome[8]. The second bar shows the percentage change in the number of cases resolved by a finding of "no reasonable cause" (charges were dismissed). The third bar shows the change in the percentage of cases that EEOC found reasonable enough to investigate.

The one clear trend is towards resolving more cases. In all but one category, age-based discrimination, the number of cases resolved rose sharply during the period. See the previous panel for an explanation about trends in age-based discrimination.

In all other categories, the number of cases resolved at the end of the period is much higher than at the beginning. Religion-based discrimination is up the most, having increased by 72%. The total number of religion-based discrimination cases is small, only 2,127 filed in 2001 or 1.8% of all filings. Nonetheless, the large percentage increase in

---

[8] In this panel we will use the EEOC definition of the term resolved. Therefore, "cases resolved" include cases that were dismissed based on a lack of reasonable cause to believe that discrimination occurred.

---

resolved cases makes it an interesting category. What is going on in this area of discrimination to cause such an increase?

One important factor fueling these charges may be the growing religious diversity of the labor force. A recent survey[9] found that 36% of the human resource professionals surveyed reported having a greater number of faiths represented in their workforces than had been the case only five years earlier. This change has created a need for new accommodations for employees' religious practices and beliefs — different holidays, altered break schedules that can be used for such things as daily prayers, and changes to policies covering work attire. Many companies have been slow to adjust, leaving the door open to accusations of religious discrimination. Have these accusations borne up under the scrutiny of EEOC investigations? Only about two in five cases have.

The number of religion-based discrimination charges resolved by a finding of "no reasonable cause" has risen. In 2001 61% of cases resolved were found to have no reasonable cause. Many of the cases filed never get past the initial EEOC investigation.

A similar pattern is found for pregnancy-based charges as well as those brought under either of the gender-based categories. In these categories too, the numbers of cases resolved are growing but so are the numbers of cases found to be without merit.

We have seen that the number of discrimination cases filed is up slightly. We have also seen that the number of resolved cases is up sharply. Does this mean that the EEOC is receiving many more cases that it believes are based on true instances of discriminatory behaviors, policies, or actions? We will look at trends in the cases that are won by plaintiffs to try and answer this question.

But first we will take a closer look at the trends in sexual harassment charges. The sexual harassment category saw the second largest increase in cases resolved but the highest increase in cases dismissed for lack of reasonable cause. It is an interesting category and deserves a closer look.

Source: U.S. Equal Employment Opportunity Commission, Charge Statistics FY 1992 through FY 2001, available online at http://www.eeoc.gov/stats/charges.html. The percentages reported on human resource managers surveyed: *Thou Shalt Accommodate Employees' Religious Beliefs*, Hot Topics in Employment Law, November 26, 2001, an e-mail newsletter published by Alexander Hamilton Institute, Inc. and available at http://www.ahipubs.com/newsletter/.

---

[9] This survey was conducted by the Society for Human Resource Managers and the Tanenbaum Center for Interreligous Understanding. For a full citation see the source note.

Sexual Harassment in the Workplace

EEOC Sexual Harassment Charges in 1993 and 2001

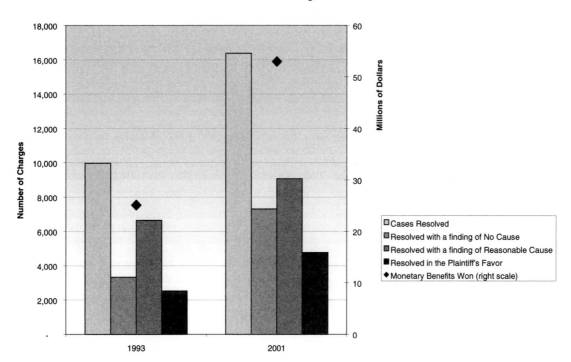

This chart presents data on the number of charges filed with the U.S. Equal Employment Opportunity Commission (EEOC) based on allegations of sexual harassment. Data for two years are provided to demonstrate changes over the period 1993 to 2001.

The clear trend is towards greater activity in all aspects of sexual harassment filings. The EEOC resolved many more cases in 2001 than it did in 1993 and reduced the backlog of cases it has tended to carry. Case resolutions are up 64%. Cases dismissed on a finding of no reasonable cause are up 119%. Cases found to have reasonable cause are up too, by 37% and those resolved in favor of the plaintiff, up by 89%. Can we say conclusively from these data that more people are being sexually harassed at work in 2001 than were in 1993? Probably not.

One high-profile discrimination case can have an important impact on trends in filing legal charges of a similar kind. In the case of sexual harassment discrimination, the 1990s had three very prominent, high profile cases that brought sexual harassment to the forefront of public discourse in a way never seen before.

First, in 1991, came sexual harassment allegations during confirmation hearings of Clarence Thomas for a seat on the United State Supreme Court. Professor Anita Hill asserted that Thomas had harassed her while they were both employed, coincidentally, by the EEOC. Her graphic comments were made public, and subsequent hearings were broadcast widely.

The second case was the Tailhook scandal in which women attending a naval aviator's convention were sexually harassed, groped, and assaulted. After one of these women, Lt. Paula Coughlin, complained to her superior officer — only to be told, "that's what you get when you go on the third deck full of drunk aviators"[10] — she filed an official complaint that lead to a lengthy and much publicized investigation.

Finally, in 1994, came allegations by Paula Jones that then President Clinton had sexually harassed her in 1991 while he was governor of Arkansas. These charges were investigated and litigated and covered prominently in the press until they were thrown out in 1998. Some may argue that the coverage continues.

Together, these cases served to keep sexual harassment front-and-center in the media for almost the entirety of the 1990s. All of this public attention was accompanied by legislative changes. In late 1991 the Senate amended the Civil Rights Act and made it possible for victims of sexual harassment to sue for punitive damages, not just back pay.

The cumulative result has been increasing numbers of case filings, charge resolutions, and money awarded to successful plaintiffs. On the chart are shown monetary benefits earned by successful plaintiffs. Charges resolved in favor of the plaintiff were up 89% between 1993 and 2001. Monetary benefits won increased by 111% to $53 million.

Can conclude that instances of sexual harassment are on the rise? No, not with any great degree of certainty. The underlying problem is that we have little reliable data from which to start. What we can say is that the likelihood of an incident of sexual harassment going unreported has probably dropped. It may even be true that attention to the subject, and quickly growing liability to employers, has helped to encourage the establishment of aggressive policies to protect employees from being sexually discriminated against and harassed.

This area of the law is very much in flux. As the legal system deals with defining *hostile environment,* human resource managers try to craft policies that will allow co-workers their freedom and privacy while preventing harmful behavior. The problem for employers is that "no one has figured out exactly what that policy should be — least of all the lawyers and judges who keep adding new loops and threads to the complex web of sexual harassment law." [11]

Source: U.S. Equal Employment Opportunity Commission. *Charge Statistics FY 1992 through FY 2001.* Online. Available: http://www.eeoc.gov/stats/charges.html. Quote by Admiral Snyder is from: *Women's Rights on Trial.* 1st Edition. Gale, 1997, p. 312. Quote by John Cloud is from: Cloud, John. *Sex And The Law.* March 23, 1998, Vol. 151, No.11. Online. Available: http://www.time.com/time/%85magazine/1998/ March 11, 2002.

[10] A statement allegedly made by Admiral John W. Snyder. See the source note for a full citation.

[11] This statement was made by John Cloud in an article entitled *Sex and The Law.* See the source note for a full citation.

Winning Discrimination Cases

Cases Resolved in the Plaintiff's Favor -- Merit Resolutions -- 1993-2001

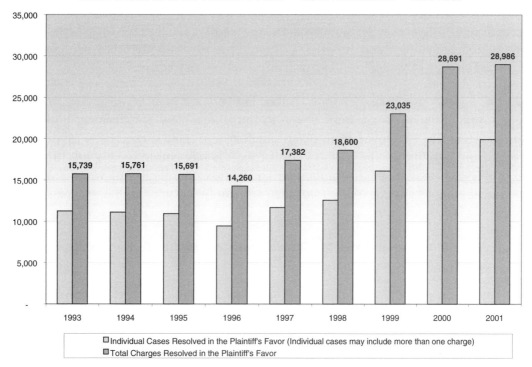

☐ Individual Cases Resolved in the Plaintiff's Favor (Individual cases may include more than one charge)
☐ Total Charges Resolved in the Plaintiff's Favor

Discrimination is either on the rise or being successfully fought more often since 1993. The number of charges of discrimination and harassment brought before the U.S. Equal Employment Opportunity Commission (EEOC) and won by the plaintiff rose 84% between 1993 and 2001. The trend is clear. Nearly twice as many employees are winning employment discrimination cases in 2001 than did in 1993.

% Change, 1993-2001 Resolutions in Favor of Plaintiff	
Category	%
Age-based	3
Disability-based	355
National Origin	137
Pregnancy-based	37
Race-based	65
Religion-based	100
Sex-based	76
Sexual Harassment	89
Total	84

The upward trend holds for all categories of discrimination, although some categories have experienced greater percentage increase than others. The table to the left lists the percentage increase in charges brought and resolved in favor of the plaintiff, by category.

It should be noted that 1993 was the first full year in which charges based on disability were filed. Since resolutions lag filings by an average of one year, much of the increase in this category may be explained as the result of newness in this area of employment discrimination law. However, this alone does not explain everything. The category has seen steady growth throughout the period. The change from 1996 to 2001 was a respectable 103%.

Most of the preceding panels on the subject have addressed discrimination case filings, or cases found to be based on a "reasonable cause" to believe that discrimination has occurred. This panel looks at the most decisive cases, those for which the EEOC made a ruling that discrimination had taken place and that some remedy was due the employee making the charge.

The rate of meritorious case resolutions is rising steadily. This is true for all categories of discrimination including those for which the number of cases filed has dropped during the period. The area of workplace discrimination law is very active.

The EEOC is busy processing charges. Labor lawyers are busy representing employees and employers. Employers are busy trying to implement new employment policies that will protect both the employee from discriminatory and harassing actions as well as the employer from liability for the harmful acts of individuals within its employ. If attention to the problem of workplace discrimination and harassment is part of what is needed to reduce the number of cases experienced, then we can be optimistic that progress is being made.

Our final panel on this subject will look at the monetary awards that are being won by the plaintiffs of successfully made charges.

Source: U.S. Equal Employment Opportunity Commission, Charge Statistics FY 1992 through FY 2001, available online at http://www.eeoc.gov/stats/charges.html.

Following the Money

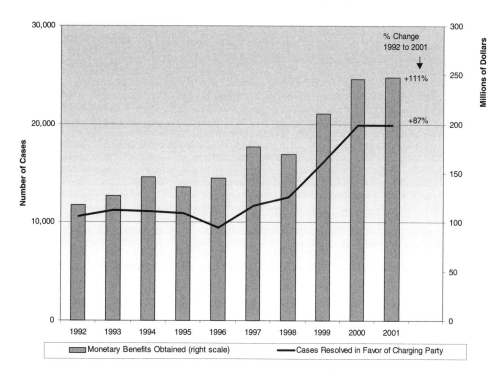

Following the money awarded to those bringing successful claims of discrimination and/or harassment before the U.S. Equal Employment Opportunity Commission (EEOC) is a steep, uphill climb. Monetary awards rose by 111% between 1992 and 2001.

This chart presents data on the number of discrimination charges brought before the EEOC and resolved in favor of the plaintiff. The bars represent the monetary awards obtained by these plaintiffs for the years 1992 through 2001.

The number of charges filed has increased greatly during in this ten-year period, as we have seen in previous panels. The number of resolutions has also risen sharply, as have cases resolved in favor of plaintiffs. But it is the number of dollars awarded to successful plaintiffs that has risen most of all.

The overall pattern in this chart shows that monetary benefits are rising very much in conjunction with the number of charges of discrimination found to be true, legally definable cases of discrimination. The rate at which monetary awards increased (111%) is higher than the rate at which successful case resolutions increased (89%), but the lines run in a parallel pattern.

A similar pattern of steady increase can be seen in the median values of jury awards given to plaintiffs who win discrimination cases that are litigated in the court system. The monetary awards in the chart above are those determined by the EEOC and do not include awards issued by the judicial system in cases brought in the courts. The table below provides a look at the value of court awards. Shown are the annual median values of jury awards for all cases of employment discrimination and harassment decided in the years 1994 through 1999. The median award value rose 115% over this six-year period.

As employers pay more and more for claims of discrimination, their motivation to reduce this sort of liability grows. It should be noted that employer expenses related to these matters are not limited to awards paid to plaintiffs. Even in cases that are dismissed or dropped by the plaintiff before a ruling is made, employers may have extensive legal and administrative costs resulting from compliance with EEOC procedures.

Median Compensatory Jury Awards for Employment-Practice Liability Cases

1994	$93,000
1995	$111,000
1996	$127,500
1997	$133,700
1998	$178,000
1999	$200,000

Many firms — in an attempt to control the growing liability associated with discrimination charges — are regularly sending their employees to seminars designed to educate them on the right ways to interact with supervisors, colleagues and subordinates. Recent court rulings have reinforced the value to employers of such training programs.

A U.S. Supreme Court ruling in 1999[12] established restrictions in the punitive damages for which employers who implement effective anti-discrimination programs are liable. Programs deemed to be effective are those that strictly define acceptable and unacceptable behavior, establish procedures for reporting violations in confidence and for investigating such claims, and set aside time for the training of personnel in these matters.

The trend towards larger awards in employment discrimination actions throughout the 1990s is clear. Whether or not this trend towards greater awards will continue is very hard to say. Clearly, some people believe that it will. A new form of commercial liability insurance has emerged during the 1990s in answer to the rising costs associated with employment discrimination actions. The Employment Practices Liability Insurance (EPLI) policy may, one day, be a standard part of the commercial insurance package.

One can hope that the net effect of all this activity — beyond the work that it provides to labor lawyers and insurance companies — is to reduce the number of cases in which a person is discriminated against, harassed, or harmed on the job.

Source: U.S. Equal Employment Opportunity Commission, Charge Statistics FY 1992 through FY 2001, available online at http://www.eeoc.gov/stats/charges.html. The figures on median jury award values are from: Jury Verdict Research press release dated January 23, 2001, available online at http://www.juryverdictresearch.com...s/Verdict_study/verdict_study.html. Original data from Jury Verdict Research's report *Employment Practice Liability: Jury Award Trends and Statistics — 2001*.

---

[12] The case in question was *Kolstad v. American Dental Association*, 119 S. Ct. 2118 (1999).

Survey of Safety Issues Post September 11, 2001

Summary of Corporate Responses to a Safety Survey Conducted After September 11, 2001

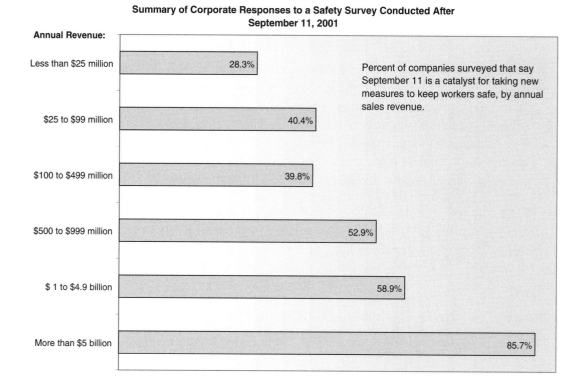

Annual Revenue:

Less than $25 million — 28.3%

$25 to $99 million — 40.4%

$100 to $499 million — 39.8%

$500 to $999 million — 52.9%

$ 1 to $4.9 billion — 58.9%

More than $5 billion — 85.7%

Percent of companies surveyed that say September 11 is a catalyst for taking new measures to keep workers safe, by annual sales revenue.

As a result of the terrorist attacks that took place on September 11, 2001 issues of safety in the workplace have taken on a new urgency. The term "home security" has been coined to designate a large range of security measures being put into place in the wake of September 11 as well as the bio-terror actions involving anthrax that followed in the Fall of 2001. Here we will look at home security issues in the workplace.

The chart presents data collected by Financial Executives International and Duke University's Fuqua School of Business in a survey conducted in late 2001. It shows the number of corporate chief financial offices surveyed that believe the new environment of risk makes it necessary to implement additional security measures to keep workers safe. The size of the business appears to be an important factor in augmenting the desire to implement such new security measures. The larger the firm the more likely it is to be in the process of implementing changes in response to the increased threat of terrorist attack.

What sorts of measures are being considered and implemented? Security measures are being beefed up across the board. Disaster plans and emergency response policies are being established or brought out of file cabinets and re-examined. Access to facilities is being limited or, in the case where passkeys were already in place, more strictly monitored. New and elaborate mail sorting processes are being implemented in mailrooms across the country. Business travel limitations and restrictions remain in place for many companies although the level of business travel has increased since coming to an almost screeching halt immediately after September 11.

The hiring process has been greatly affected in the period since September 2001. Pre-employment background checks are on the rise. Automated Data Processing Inc. (ADP) saw a 30% increase in the number of background checks that its Screening and Selection Services Division carried out in the 12-month period ending January 2002. It estimates that half of this increase is the result of post September 11, employer concern.

As employee screening and background checks increase, so too do concerns about infringement of privacy and profiling based on race or national origin. Federal and state laws prohibit discrimination in employment on the basis of race and national origin, among others. Therefore, employers find themselves confronted with a growing tension between protecting employees while complying with civil rights and anti-discrimination laws. This tension, which is also being played out in the society at large, will likely continue as new security standards are established and implemented.

What is clear is that attention to the area of workplace security has been greatly heightened since the fall of 2001. New measures are being put in place to try and reduce the risk of future losses. The impact that all of these measures will have on the workplace in general is not yet clear. These are trends that we will all watch and attempt to gauge as the situation evolves.

Source: *Safety Since 9/11: Are You Protecting Your Company Against the Real Threats?*, an online newsletter published by the Institute of Management and Administration, February 1, 2002, page 1. The data on background checks are from: Joann S. Lublin, *Check, Please, Who are those people working alongside you? Too often, nobody has bothered to ask*. Wall Street Journal, March 11, 2002, page R11.

Chapter 8

The Family and Free Time

This chapter serves as an introduction to the second half of this book: leisure in America.

The opening panels in this section will address fundamental questions: how long are we at work and how often do we relax? The common belief is that we are working longer hours. Is this true? Another belief is that we have less free time to enjoy. Recent data suggest that time for recreation has been consistent over recent decades.

Other panels will look at leisure hours through the lens of family life. Quite simply, do we have enough time to get things done? Can we hold a job and a run a home? Are we on our way to being overstressed? We'll look at the dollars we spend on entertainment and recreation. As more of our free time is spent at home, some questions must be posed: do we socialize enough? How do we meet new people?

Again, this chapter is an introduction. The rest of this book will look at aspects of leisure more closely: the arts, vacations, sports, and volunteering.

Is Our Work Week Getting Longer?

Average Weekly Hours Worked, 1969-1998

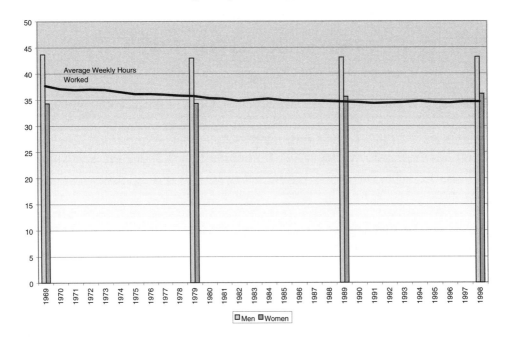

A number of analysts have reported that we are working longer hours and that leisure time is declining — in spite of increased productivity rates and growing incomes. The media so frequently repeat that we are overworked that the notion has become a commonplace. But are we?

The panel charts the average hours worked by men and women for private sector employers from 1967 to 1998. There was a steady decline during this period. The average workweek fell from 38 hours in 1967 to 34.6 hours in 1998.[1] The workweek has been fairly stable along gender lines as well, with men seeing a small decrease in their hours. Women have seen a small spike — as more women entered the workforce and worked year round.

What about our actual work arrangements? Are some of us working longer weeks? The answer is, Yes. Those working more than 49 hours a week grew from 13% to 19.9% of workers. But the share of those working 40 hours a week or less has dropped. Those working between 41 and 48 hours a week remained almost the same.

---

[1] Data shown come from the Current Employment Statistics (CES) Survey, which provides data on the average paid hours for production workers in goods-producing industries and nonsupervisory workers in service-producing industries. This information comes from employers and is based on payroll records. Another method is the Current Population Survey (CPS), which uses different methodology. It featured a drop in hours too, although a slightly less dramatic one: 40 hours to 39.2 hours.

Distribution of Workers by Time Worked, 1976 and 2000

Hours	1976 (%)	2000 (%)	Change, 76 to 00
1-34	24.5	22.9	-1.6
35-39	7.3	6.6	-0.7
40	44.6	39.3	-5.3
41-48	10.6	11.3	0.7
49 and over	13.0	19.9	6.9

These data indicate that the percentage of those who work 40 hours or less decreased from 76.4% to 68.8% of the workforce between 1976 and 2000. Those who work more than 40 hours a week routinely went up from 23.6% to 32.2%. It seems that long hours have it, by a nose — although the Department of Labor, in another study, suggests that the hours of managers and professionals, those most likely to work long weeks, have more or less held steady without much variation since 1982 at around 42 hours a week.

Men and women are thus on the job slightly longer over the course of a year than they used to be. Many families now have two people in the workforce as women's participation rates rise. This suggests that work may be encroaching on our leisure time — as the media claim.

Source: "Are Managers and Professionals Really Working More?" *Issues in Labor Statistics*, May 12, 2000; "Overwork Overstated." Retrieved online March 8, 2002 from http://www.ncpa.org; Elaine L. Chao, U.S. Department of Labor, *Report on the American Workforce.*

How Much Leisure Time Do We Get?

Median Hours Spent at Work and Play Per Week

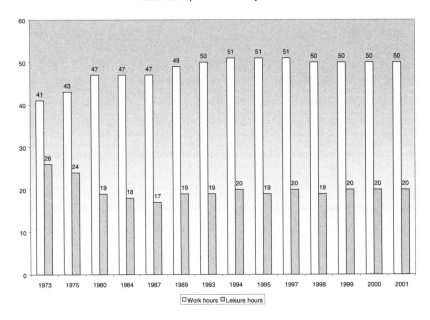

Do we have less free time? We long for an extra hour in the day to clear off our desks at work, run errands, cook a real dinner, or sit and read the morning paper. How much time do we have for work and play? The panel above shows the results of a survey by Harris. It suggests that the amount of our work and leisure time has been rather consistent for two decades. [2]

The median time available to people to relax, watch television, play sports, indulge their hobbies, or socialize with friends was 20 hours in 2001. This figure has remained nearly unchanged since 1980, but nine hours were lost between 1973 and 1987. Some of this must come from the changing role of women. More females left the home to enter the workforce; women also moved into executive positions that made more demands on their time.

The survey also asked about people's work hours, which include time on the job, keeping house, and going to school (including travel time). People reported spending more hours in their work. People spent 41 hours working in 1973; they reported working 50 hours in 2001. This is an increase of 9 hours – more than the typical 8-hour workday. Do we have busier lives now than in 1973?

_____

[2] The Harris Poll was conducted by telephone within the United States between June 13-18, 2001 among a nationwide cross section off 1,010 adults. Figures for age, sex, race, education, number of adults and number of voice/telephone lines in the household were weighted where necessary to align them with their actual proportions in the population.

Let's look at these numbers a little more closely. There are 168 hours in a week; we spend roughly 56 of them asleep (if we're lucky). This leaves 112 hours open. In 1973, people spent 67 hours at work and relaxation; in 2001, they spent 70. This leaves 45 hours a week (6.4 hours a day) up for grabs in 1973; 42 hours (6 hours a day) remained in 2001. Is this time devoted to personal care? Or was it perhaps devoted to childcare? Childcare was not included in the survey — perhaps because, as any parent doing such work can attest, it is heavy labor.

	1973 Hours	2001 Hours
Hours in Week	168	168
Hours Asleep	56	56
Hours Work/Leisure	67	70
Remaining Hours Per Week	45	42

It's possible that the survey respondents overestimated their time spent on various activities. They did not keep time logs. Logs tend to offer more accurate representations of how people actually spend their time. The survey is useful in the questions it raises: Are we losing our free time? Over the last decade, have some of us found some balance between our work and recreational lives?

The next panel will examine how we feel about our work and free time.

Source: "Reading, TV, Spending Time With Family, Gardening and Fishing Top List of Favorite Leisure-Time Activities." *PR Newswire*. 8 August 2001.

Where Are We Happiest?

I'd Rather Be Golfing? Our Time At and Off Work

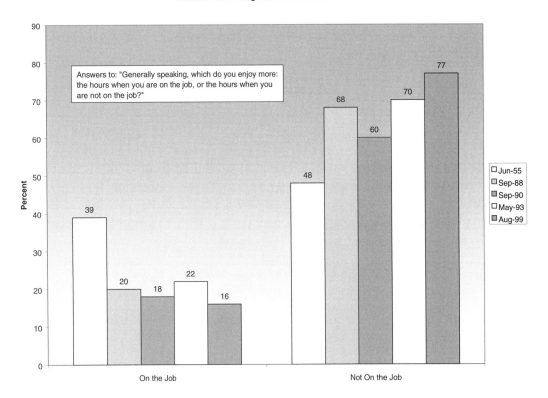

Answers to: "Generally speaking, which do you enjoy more: the hours when you are on the job, or the hours when you are not on the job?"

How do we feel about our work and free time? The panel above shows the results of a Gallup Survey included in the publication *Attitudes About Work and Leisure In America.*

Not too surprisingly, people seem to enjoy their time away from work. This is time spent with family and friends or playing sports and pursuing hobbies. Respondents in June 1955 had the most favorable attitudes about their employment: 39% claimed to enjoy their hours on the job more than their hours at home. By May 1999, a noticeable gap had formed: only 16% of people claimed to prefer their time at work; 77% preferred their free hours.

More of us clearly cherish our time away from the office. We read, surf the Internet, play a sport, take classes, and socialize with friends. Has there been a shift in our view of the office and home? How do we see each place? According to another survey, 48% of interviewees in 1975 felt that "work is the important thing — and the purpose of leisure time is to recharge people's batteries so they can do a better job." In 2000, only 34% of respondents gave that answer. In 1975, 36% agreed with the statement: "Leisure time is the important thing — and the purpose of work is to make it possible to have the leisure time to enjoy life and pursue one's interests." In 2000, 43% of people agreed with that statement.

We seem more inclined, these days; to draw a sharp line between our work and our leisure, but it is a slow transition — if indeed it is real. Technology such as cellular phones and e-mail, which should simplify our work lives, often keep us connected to the office. We feel the need to "check in" to see how things are doing in the midst of a vacation. Why? For many people, work is their life and identity, and it is hard to make a clean break. We are a long way from our counterparts in Europe who see vacation time as mandatory. There it is not uncommon for some companies simply to shut down for weeks or a month.

In the next few panels, we take a look at home life.

Source: Bowman, Karlyn. *Attitudes About Work and Leisure in America*. Online. Available: http://www. aei.org. September 28, 2001. Source includes several surveys. The question: "Generally speaking: which do you enjoy more – the hours when you are on the job, or when you are not on the job?" comes from a Gallup poll. The questions "Work is the important thing — and the purpose of leisure time is to recharge people's batteries so they can do a better job" and "Leisure time is the important thing — and the purpose of work is to make it possible to have the leisure time to enjoy life and pursue one's interests" come from a Roper Starch Worldwide poll.

The Family Dinner Remains Intact

Dining In and Dining Out

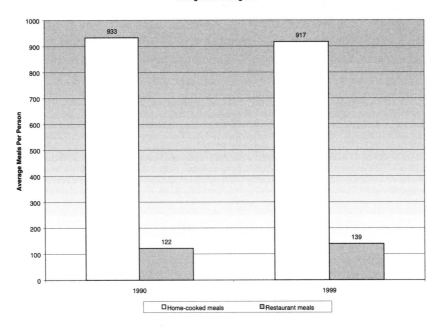

In our busy lives, do families still sit down to share a meal together? What kind of meals do they have?

NPD, a market research firm, annually charts the diets of Americans in their survey *Annual Report on Eating Patterns in America*. According to their research, in the 1990s, the family dinner seemed to be holding strong. Per capita home-cooked meals fell just 1.7% from 933 meals to 917 meals. Dinners at restaurants increased 14% during the same period.

We dined out more in the 1990s. But where? At fast-food franchises. NPD reports that 80% of the growth in restaurant meals over the last five years came from the fast food industry. Of our meals out, 18% are ordered from a drive-in window. Not good news for the waistlines of some families out there.

The point is, however, that we do still seem to make time for a traditional sit-down dinner. This in spite of our busy lives — both parents working and children with their own jobs and activities.

Source: "NPD Sees Focus On Cost, Convenience Reshaping Eating Patterns in America." Online. Available: http://www.npd.com. 19 March, 2002.

Running the Household

Time Spent On Household Activities

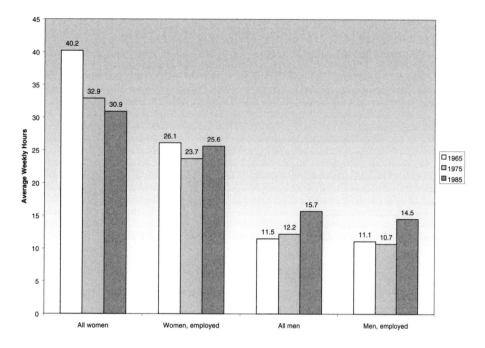

Time Spent On Household Activities

Our leisure time is not just dictated by our time away from the office. We spend significant time each week simply maintaining our homes: cooking dinners, raking leaves, and paying bills. Women have traditionally run the household, with men bringing home the paycheck. Is this still the case?

The panel shows the average weekly hours spent by married and employed women and men in total family care. (As might be expected the hours were higher for the unemployed — they have more time to do chores.) The figures, taken from U.S. Department of Labor and Time *for Life: Surprising Ways Americans Use Their Time*, show how the work gets divided. Women still handle more of the responsibilities than men and are generally spending less time at them. Women spent 40.2 hours a week doing housework, shopping and caring for children in 1965 and 30.9 in 1985, a decline of 23% in two decades. Females who work spent nearly the same amount of time at their chores, with 26.1 hours a week in 1965 and 25.6 in 1985, a decrease of only 2%.

Men are helping more around the house: their time spent on chores increased 36.5% from 11.5 hours to 15.7 hours. What accounts for the increase? With men remaining single longer, perhaps some men are more willing to perform household chores themselves. In spite of all the discussion of gender roles, however, the traditional roles in marriage still seem intact: the task of maintaining a household still falls to women.

What's going on here? Women worked roughly 40 hours a week running the household and raising children in 1965 — the time spent at a typical job. Together, men and women spent 51.7 hours running the home. By 1985, women were spending 30.9 hours per-

---

forming the same tasks. Together, men and women spent 45.4 hours running the home. Are we simply more efficient? Or are we spending less time because we have so little to spare?

A point worth making: we are spending less time on housework as our houses have been getting bigger. According to government statistics, the average square footage of a new privately owned home grew 48.3% from 1,500 square feet in 1970 to 2,255 in 1999. Those homes with 2.5 bathrooms or more increased 244% for the same period; homes with 4 or more bedrooms increased 41.6%.

Source: Chao, Elaine L. U.S. Department of Labor. *Report on the American Workforce, 2001*, p. 123.

Do Kids Get Enough Time With Their Parents?

Children's Time With Mom and Dad

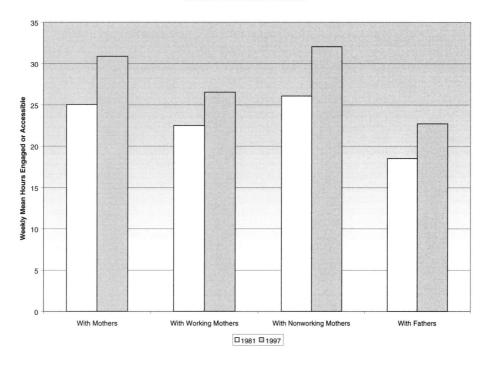

One recent study claims that children are spending more time with their parents than they did two decades ago.

The study, by the University of Michigan, found that children between the ages of 3 and 12 in two-parent families spent 25 hours with their mothers in 1981 and about 31 hours a week with their mothers in 1997. They spent more time with their fathers as well: mean weekly hours increased from about 19 to 23 hours a week.[3]

Unsurprisingly, children spent the most time with stay-at-home moms. But even when mother is working, the time difference is smaller than some might expect: 3.5 hours in 1981 and 5.5 hours in 1997.

What's going on here? One reason is that couples are having smaller families; the typical woman will have about two children during her childbearing years (down from the three she would have had in the 1930s, according to the source). A smaller family means that children have a better opportunity to spend time with their parents.

---

[3] The study is based on a comparison of time diary data from two nationally representative samples of U.S. families, both conducted by the Institute for Social Research. The 1980 sample included information on 243 children, and the 1997 sample included information on 2,125 children. The children (helped by a parent if necessary) filled out two time diaries, one each for a weekday and a weekend day, describing what they did, with whom they did it, and who was present. The time diaries include activities parents engaged in with children as well as time spent just being in the same room with them.

Of course, there are many children out there in need of more attention from their parents. But is it possible that some trends are reversing? Are kids getting "quantity" *and* "quality" time? Pro-family messages have been all over talk shows and Washington D.C. Men have seen their roles as fathers dramatically redefined: they are encouraged to be more nurturing and to take active roles in their children's lives. The percentage of working mothers has declined for the first time, from 59% in 1998 to 55% in 2000.

Source: "Children Spend More Time With Parents Than They Used To." Online. Available: http://www. umich.edu. November 16, 2001.

How We Spend Our Recreational Time (and Dollars)

Selected Recreational Spending

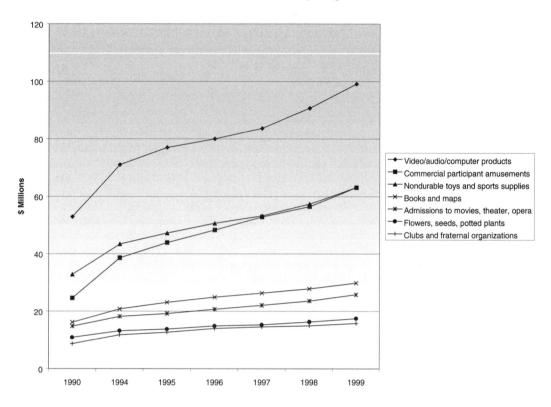

The panel tracks spending on selected leisure pursuits over recent years and offers some insight into our recreational time.[4] It raises the question: is the majority of leisure time spent by ourselves?

The leading categories are all for products or services that provide a largely solitary (and sedentary) pleasure. The top category was audio, video, and computer products. Our leisure time is increasingly centered in the home, and we are seeking to make it as comfortable as possible: from big-screen televisions to the newest computer to help us access the Internet. Spending on books and toys has been stable through the 1990s, but again: these dollars support solitary pursuits.

We're buying plenty of stuff. Are we devoting enough of our leisure time to socializing? The "commercial participant amusements" category covers a wide range of activities: we bowl, shoot pool, golf, swim, skate, and gamble. The figures show a steady incline (much

---

[4] Chart definitions: Commercial participant amusements consists of billiard parlors, bowling alleys, dancing, riding, shooting, skating and swimming places; amusement devices and parks, golf courses, sightseeing buses and guides, private flying operations, casino gambling and other commercial participant amusements.

of which probably comes from the gambling component of the category) from $24.6 billion in 1990 to $63.1 billion in 1999. There are questions the data do not address: Are we doing these things by ourselves? With a friend or spouse?

We do these things because we enjoy them. But is that enough? Are we becoming increasingly isolated? Do we need to reach out more? We are more likely to be tending our own garden than someone else's: more money was spent on flowers and plants than in clubs and fraternal organizations.

Source: U.S. Bureau of the Census. *Statistical Abstract of the United States 2001*. 121st ed. Washington DC: U.S. Government Printing Office, 2001.

How Do We Compare With Other Countries?

Work and Play Around the World

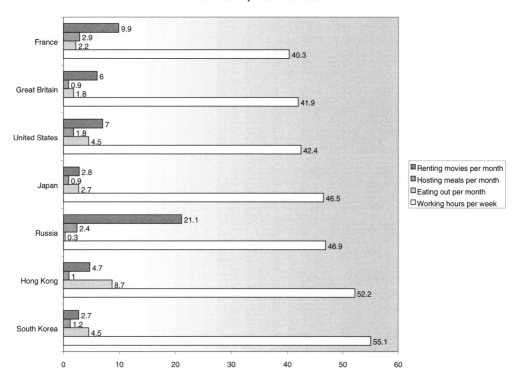

The United States ranks lowest in the world for vacation time allotted by employers: 13 days, compared to 42 days for Italy, 37 for France and 35 for Germany. What about our free time in general?

Roper Starch Worldwide conducted a study of 30,000 people in 32 nations to determine how people spend their leisure time. Some of the results, shown in the graphic above, offer some insight as to how we compare with other countries.

Russia was tops in movie rentals, with a rate of 21.1 times a month, which is triple the global rate of 7.7 times. Other nations that ranked high on the list were Malaysia, Czech Republic, and Poland (not shown). One possible explanation for their high rates: video piracy often puts Hollywood blockbusters at discount prices on the streets of these countries mere days after a film's release.

Hong Kong was tops in eating out, surprising, considering the cost of living in the nation. Russians were also the least likely to eat out — possibly because it is too expensive.

Indonesia (not shown) was actually the leader in hosting meals (6.1), followed by Turkey (5.4), and India (3.9). Americans, with a rate of 1.8 times per month, are far less likely to invite friends and family over to share a meal. Are we too busy? Are we too antisocial?

How does America fare overall? We are a reasonably hospitable nation, ranking 20th on the list of nations having people over dinner. In spite of Hollywood, we ranked 14th on the list of movie renting countries.

Source: "No Work, All Play?" *U.S. News & World Report.* 18 June 2001, p. 10; "Hong Kong Eats Out Most, New Roper 32-Country Study Shows." Online. Available: http://www.roperasw.com. March 8, 2002.

Chapter 9

Vacations and Travel

We all look forward to "getting away from it all." But *how* do we do it? *Where* do we do it? Many changes have taken place in the travel industry in recent years, and the following panels will address some of the more intriguing trends.

The first panel presents an overview of the two major types of travel: business and pleasure. The image of the executive who is "just in town for business" may be a thing of the past; technology such as e-mail, videoconferencing and cellular phones guarantee that we now can be reached anytime, anyplace.

But is that a good thing? Do we need more vacation time? We'll see that we get (and take) less vacation time than most other industrialized nations. We still like to travel and do so; the travel industry has begun to respond to the unique needs of travelers. They market to everyone from seniors and singles; and offer everything from adventure holidays — rock climbing, anyone? — to trips to antique shops and museums.

We'll also see the role the Internet has played in how we travel — from tracking down cheap fares, to finding that out-of-the-way inn, to checking the temperature a continent away. We'll examine another crucial part of taking vacations — having the money to do so. The explosion of wealth over the last decade has allowed people to invest in their own vacation properties. Second homes, timeshares and condominiums offer a refreshing change from standard (and expensive) hotels.

Do We Travel For Business or Pleasure?

The Types of Trips We Take

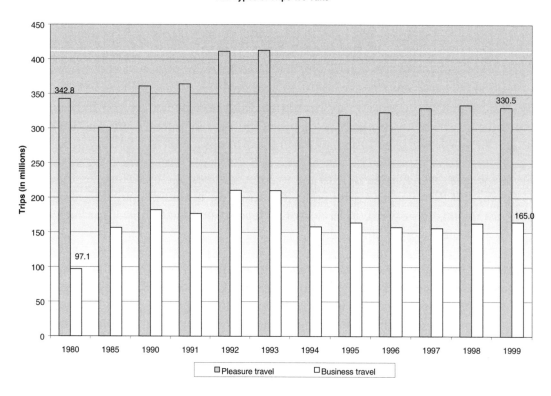

We're often seen as a country constantly on the move, hitting the open road or taking to the skies. Travel Industry Association of America (TIA) has analyzed the types of trips we have been taking, and its data for the last two decades are shown above.

As expected, the majority of our trips are for pleasure, and the number has been increasing (1999 figures were the most recent available; the final effect of September 11 remains to be seen). The bulk of our spending in the $584 billion industry takes place in five states: California, Florida, New York, Texas and Illinois. Most of our travel is done on the highways we love so much: 76% of our trips were taken by car, truck, or RV. Only 18% were taken by plane.

Spending on vacations jumped in the early 1990s, perhaps because of the growing affluence of the time; people could, quite simply, afford to take a trip. Spending fell from 1993 to 1994, fallout perhaps from the brief recession. The number of business excursions continues to grow too, at the same rate as those for pleasure: both grew 4% over the last five years. Some sources expect the number of business trips to fall as companies rethink their spending during this slowing economy. Some companies have used videoconferencing and similar technologies to address their needs. Some travel just has been postponed.

We are taking a moderate number of more trips — but we're taking different *kinds* of trips. The family vacation appears to be making a comeback: the number of adults traveling with kids grew 10%; interestingly, there was a 10% increase in the number of adults taking children on business trips as well! Perhaps this speaks to some companies being family friendly and including children in travel arrangements. It could also be the effort of parents to juggle work and home responsibilities.

Another point to make: it isn't just mom and dad organizing these trips. Roughly 15% of singles have been on a vacation with their nephews and nieces. Twenty-one percent of adults traveled with a grandchild in 2000, up from just 13% in 1999, according to the TIA data for Meredith Corp. Indeed, the travel industry has adopted the term "grandtravel" to address this blossoming market.

Seniors aren't the only segment of the population the travel industry has had its eye on. More attention is being paid to the single traveler. There are now accommodations being made for dogs and cats: more than 29 million people traveled with a pet during the last three years. Tours and travel packages are aimed at gay and lesbian vacationers.

We like our getaways — and we are taking more of them. But they are for shorter periods of time: the big two-week vacation seems to be history. Do we take enough time? What price are we paying for not doing so?

Sources: "More Family Vacations Include Kids"; "Mature Travelers Comprise Nearly One-Third Of All U.S. Traveler"; "Traveling Singles Represent 15.9 Million U.S. Household"; "Fluffy and Fido Prove to be Popular Travel Companions"; "TIA Releases Travel Forecast Through 2003." Retrieved January 9, 2002 from the World Wide Web: http://www.tia.org; "The New Family Vacation," *American Demographics*, August 1, 2001, p. 42.

Are Weekend Trips the New Vacation Trend?

The Growth of Weekend Travel

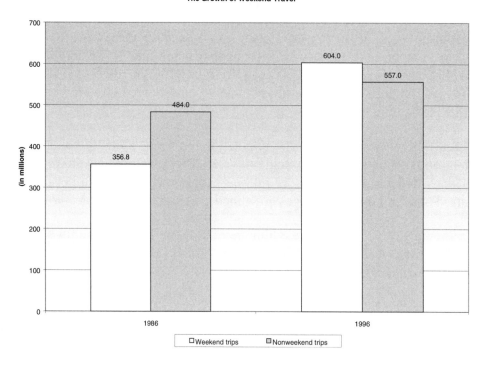

The Travel Industry Association of America is forecasting 2.5% to 4% growth annually in travel over the next decade. In 1999 we took 1.3 billion leisure trips and spent $540 billion on travel.

But Americans have the least amount of vacation time compared to other countries: roughly 13 days, compared to 42 days in Italy, 37 days in France, and 28 in Great Britain, according to the World Trade Organization. Nearly a day of time has been shaved off this total over the last decade. So how do we spend these precious days? Instead of the traditional two-week vacation, we're taking more vacations for shorter periods.

The number of weekend trips grew 70% between 1986 and 1996, rising from 356.8 million trips to 604 million (weekend travel includes a Friday and/or a Saturday night stay, at least 50 miles from home). The number of non-weekend trips saw growth of only 15% during this period, with trips rising from 484 million to 557 million. What's responsible for the increase? The time crunch many people suffer, our unwillingness to be away from work for an extended period, "getaway packages" marketed by the travel industry.

In a 2001 survey, half of all adults said they take at least one weekend trip a year; 29% reported taking five or more a year. As well, over half of weekend travelers with household annual incomes between $50,000 and $74,999 make last-minute plans for these weekend trips, compared to 32% for those with income of $75,000 or more and 40% for those under $50,000. Could this be because these middle-class families are feeling stressed and feel the need to suddenly "get out of town" for a couple of days?

But are these abbreviated vacations enough? Are we still just too stressed and too pressed for time?

Source: "Popularity of Weekend Travel Grows." Retrieved January 9, 2002 from the World Wide Web: http://www.tia.org.

Trends in Second Homes

Median Price of Homes

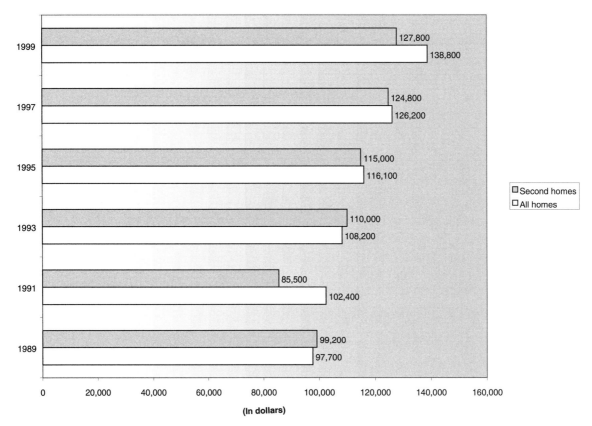

	Second homes	All homes
1999	127,800	138,800
1997	124,800	126,200
1995	115,000	116,100
1993	110,000	108,200
1991	85,500	102,400
1989	99,200	97,700

(In dollars)

According to the Census Bureau, there were about 6 million second homes in 1999, including condominiums and time shares, up from 5.4 million in 1994 and up 288,000 from 1989. Industry analysts estimate the number to reach 9.8 million by 2010, an increase of 53% from the current year. Sales have been increasing steadily since 1991, with sales of 264,000 homes in that year, to 345,000 in 1997, to 377,000 in 1999, according to the National Association of Realtors. Unit sales have increased 30% between 1989 and 1999.

About 6% of homes purchased each year are second homes, although other sources have placed it higher (for example, analysis by Acxiom/DataQuick saw 13.1% of sales going to second homes, or 800,000 units in 1999).

People are not only buying more second homes, they're buying more expensive homes. The panel above compares median prices for all homes and second homes. Median prices mean that half are more expensive, half less expensive. Some of the increase, of course, comes from the increase in the cost of homes. Interestingly, the prices were nearly equal between 1993 and 1997. No doubt many second homes were purchased in expensive housing markets. But there is probably another reason: the willingness of people to spend more money on these residences. They seek "all the comforts of home." At the same time, this past decade saw an increase in the number of affluent people. Quite simply, many people could afford to make this type of purchase: as investment, vacation property, or both.

Who is making these purchases? The Census puts the median age of vacation homeowners at 52. In short, the Baby Boomer generation. As we've seen elsewhere in this book, they are retiring earlier and have increasingly active lifestyles. Many buy a place at the lake and entertain the grandkids on the weekend. An increasing number of homes involve no mortgage — they are paid for with cash, which speaks to the affluence of the purchasers.

What about other types of vacation properties? There are now more than 2 million time-share owners in the United States. The U.S. leads the world in the number of owners. Sales have risen from $1.33 billion in 1992 to an estimated $4 billion in 2000, a 200% increase!

Will we ever stay in a hotel again?

Sources: Fogerty, Thomas A. "New Wealth Brings Surge in Two-Home Families." USA Today, February 11, 2000; "Second Homes/Recreational Property." Online. Available: http://www.realtor.org. January 16, 2002; "State of the U.S. Vacation Ownership Industry." Online. Available: http://www.arda.org. January 16, 2002; "Historical Census of Housing Tables Vacation Homes." Online. Available: http://www.census.gov. January 16, 2002.

Changes in the Travel Industry

Who Gets the Travel Dollar

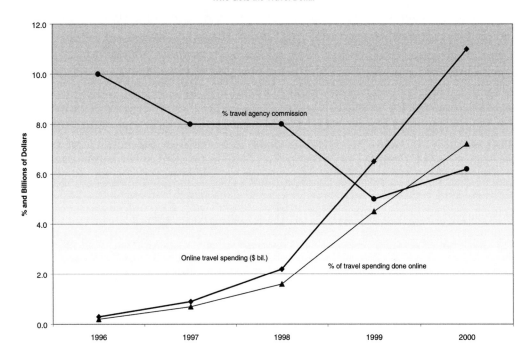

The Internet has brought enormous changes to the business and leisure communities. With its rise in the 1990s, electronic commerce offered a new option in how to shop and gather information. One area in which it has had enormous influence is the travel industry.

Travel regularly ranks at the top of electronic commerce spending studies. The panel shows the growth in online travel spending, from $300 million in 1996 to $11 billion in 2000, a growth of 3,566%. The data above are based on figures from Jupiter Communications. (It's worth noting that, as with many market research groups, other organizations have similar but slightly different numbers.) Keep in mind the travel industry covers more than airline tickets. Cruises, hotels, and car-rental firms have all reaped benefits from online sales efforts.

The traveler can use the Internet for several purposes. According to the Travel Industry Association of America, 52.2 million travelers used the Internet to plan their travel in 1999, a 54% increase from 1998. A smaller but still significant number actually make reservations: according to travel intelligence firm PhoCusWright, 21 million people bought travel online in 2000, nearly doubling the Internet travel market for the second year.

So, what has this meant for travel agencies? Travel agencies once held the role of neutral comparison shopper for the consumer. But, as Pam Dixon points out in her article "Fare Game" the rise of the Internet in the early 1990s gave airlines and consumers a means to communicate directly with each other. The user can search for the cheapest, most convenient ticket or package on his own.

Several sources have pointed out that surely it is no coincidence that airlines made their first cuts in commissions paid to travel agents for booking airfare during this period. The first cuts came in 1995. Most major airlines put a cap of $50 on round-trip domestic flights; a cap on international flights would come three years later. The panel above charts how the base commission rate fell from 10% to 8% in 1997; it fell to 5% near the end of 1999. The figure rose in 2000, according to the American Society of Travel Agents. However, the maximum earned on a ticket fell from $50 to just $20. As a result, more travel agencies started charging service fees to make up for lost revenues. Many agencies could not compete and closed; the number of agencies has decreased 20% since 1991 to 18,489 in 2000.

While locations may close (and some agents simply become independents), agencies still see the lion's share of the travel market. The panel above shows that only 0.2% of travel spending came from the Web in 1996; by 2000, that share reached 7.2% of the total. But a shift is taking place. Some travel agencies have been looking beyond air travel to cruises and packaged tours, which are expected to see a rise in popularity (particularly after September 11). Another sign of the Web's growing control of ticketing and travel: the top companies in the airline ticket market have all been recent arrivals and are not airline companies: Travelocity, Expedia and Priceline. Southwest is the leader among airlines.

The Internet has been a "place" where many people can make informed decisions about how they use their leisure time. The traditional travel agency probably will not become extinct. Rather, it will reinvent itself in this age of increasing technology and information.

*Sources:*Dixon, Pam. "Fare Game: Airlines, Travel Agents Duke It Out Over the Web," *San-Diego Union-Tribune,* January 9, 2000, p. F1.; "Jupiter: Triple Digit Growth Rates to Fade in Internet Travel Market." Online. Available: http://www.businesswire.com. April 17, 2000; Tricia A. Holly. "Welcome to the Outside." *Travel Agent*, April 23, 2001, p. 18; "PhoCusWright Survey Reveals 21 Million Americans Bought Travel Online in 2000." Online. Available: http://www.phocuswright.com. January 29, 2002; "Internet Usage by Travelers Continues to Soar." Online. Available: http://www.tia.org. January 29, 2002.

Chapter 10

People and Sports

Sports is certainly one of the leading leisure activities. In this chapter, we look at amateur and professional sports and examine some of the trends that shape the world of sports.

The first panel presents a look at the fastest growing fitness activities over recent years. Some sports, of course, will always be popular. But have new ones captured our imagination? What does this say about us?

In the next few panels we look at teenagers and sports. What fitness activities are they pursuing? We'll examine the curious trends surrounding their activities: they have basically invented the entire "extreme sports" phenomenon, but they have turned away from some traditional sports, such as baseball. They have also turned away from "physical" sports. Are children getting enough exercise?

After high school sports, the next panel is about college sports. We examine the differences in male and female athletic programs and briefly analyze the sports women have pursued in recent years.

The final panels in the chapter are devoted to professional sports, and examine attendance figures, television viewing, and ticket costs. Are we watching as much sports as we used to? Is the rising cost of tickets keeping some fans out of the stadium?

What Are The Fastest Growing Sports?

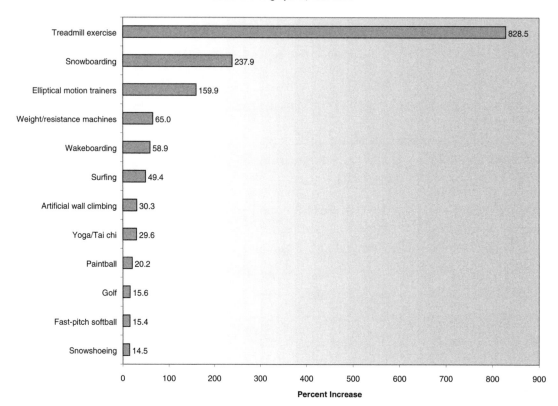

Fastest Growing Sports, 1987-2000

Sport	Percent Increase
Treadmill exercise	828.5
Snowboarding	237.9
Elliptical motion trainers	159.9
Weight/resistance machines	65.0
Wakeboarding	58.9
Surfing	49.4
Artificial wall climbing	30.3
Yoga/Tai chi	29.6
Paintball	20.2
Golf	15.6
Fast-pitch softball	15.4
Snowshoeing	14.5

There are probably no real surprises in a list of the most popular sports of the year 2000: swimming, walking, bowling, bicycling, and fishing. These are sports that appeal to young and old, can be done anywhere, and can be enjoyed regardless of level of skill. They also have appeal because they have a social aspect: people enjoy walking together; fishing boats and bowling leagues offer camaraderie. But what are the new fitness activities? What explains their growth?

The panel shows the sports that enjoyed the highest growth rate from 1987 to 2000 according to American Sports Data. Treadmills were at the top of the list, with an astounding growth of almost 829%. Snowboarding was next with almost 238%, followed by elliptical motion trainers with almost 160% and weight resistance machines with 65%. What's responsible for these numbers? The boom of the health club industry. We've become increasingly health-conscious over the last 15 years, and we have hit the gym: memberships jumped 89.5% during the period, hitting 32.8 million as of December 2000, according to the International Health, Racquet and Sportsclub Association.

Weight machines, treadmills and elliptical motion trainers have seen high growth because they offer solid workout opportunities for young and old. They are good low-impact, aerobic activities. We enjoy them at home or at the gym. It isn't just young people at health clubs anymore either: while 18-34 year olds still see the highest portion of gym memberships, those 55 and older now make up a quarter of gym members (their numbers grew 379% between 1987 and 2000).

Some activities saw growth because they're simply "hot," some new sport to invigorate our fitness and leisure time. Wakeboarding, paintball, wall climbing, and snowboarding are all part of the "extreme sports" category, activities for Generation-Y'ers that offer some adrenaline rush to their workout. For those interested in getting in touch with their inner (and thinner?) Zen, there are yoga and tai chi. While they saw high growth rates, the number of participants in these new sports is fairly low: 7.1 million people played paintball and 2.1 million surfed during 2000, compared to 40.8 million people who exercised on a treadmill. Will these new fitness activities stick around?

In the next panels we examine the sports activities of teenagers.

Sources: "Extreme Sports Participation Surges Ahead While Old Favorites Falter." *Research Alert*, June 1, 2001, p. 1; "The Scope of the Health Club Industry." Retrieved February 5, 2002 from the World Wide Web: http://www.ihrsa.org.

Popular Sports for Teenagers

Popular Sports For 12-17 Year Olds (per 100 people)

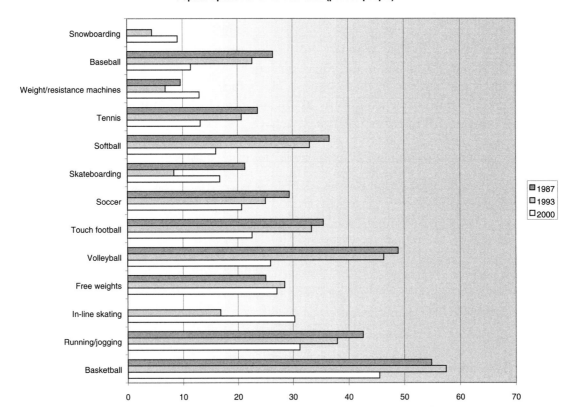

The graphic shows the most popular physical activities for youths between the ages of 12 and 17 according to figures from American Sports Data. Figures are rates per 100 people; teens had to do an activity once over the past year.

The survey shows steady declines in almost every category. The biggest decline was in volleyball; nearly 49 teens of 100 played volleyball in 1987; only 26 of 100 did so in 2000. Other categories that saw steep declines were in sports seen as American institutions: softball, baseball, and touch football. Even basketball, at the top of the list, saw its numbers fall from 57.4 to 45.5 in seven years. There are some troubling ramifications here. Youths are rejecting team sports and the character-building experiences they can offer: working with others, good conduct, and making friends. Baseball's audience has been shrinking and is not gaining new participants who play and follow the sport. What will happen to our national pastime?

Some sports have seen an increase in activity. More teens are using weight machines, no doubt trying to attain the "perfect body" as a boost to their self esteem and sexual desirability. In-line skating and snowboarding are new arrivals, not having shown up on the 1987 survey. These are new and trendy sports and, as "extreme sports," have attracted a certain type of daredevil young man and woman; they give the sports flash and visibility.

A point needs to be made here: sports allow teenagers to get the regular, strenuous physical workout that they need. A good part of kids' exercise has traditionally come from organized sports and physical education classes. But there has been a marked drop-off in kids attending gym classes. According to the Centers for Disease Control, the percent of teens that attend gym class fell from 32% in 1991 to 27% in 1997. According to the report, *Shape of the Nation*, by the National Association for Sport and Physical Education, the majority of high school students take physical education for only one year between the ninth and twelfth grades. Half of all states allow substitutions for gym class; some students, such as band members, may get exemptions.

The lack of physical exercise is troubling particularly in light of statistics on children's obesity rates. Roughly 5% of teenagers were overweight at the end of 1980; that figure has almost tripled in recent years according to the Centers for Disease Control. One's weight is related to exercise and eating patterns, of course. But many experts argue that the patterns we establish in our youth affect how we behave as adults: an overweight teenager is likely to be overweight in middle age. If we exercise regularly when we are young, we're also likely to be active as adults.

Organized sports offer an excellent opportunity for teenagers to stay fit. What is the status of high school sports? How many teenagers are pursuing these activities? The answers, covered in the next panel, are somewhat more reassuring.

Sources: "Older Americans Exercise More While Teenagers Take It Easy." *Research Alert.* 3 August 2001, p. 3; "Exercise Edged Out of High Schools." *USA TODAY.* 11 October 2001, p. 9D; Centers for Disease Control and Prevention. National Center for Health Statistics. *Health 2001*; National Association for Sport and Physical Education, *Shape of the Nation, 2001*.

Part of the Team: Organized Sports and Young People

High School Athletes: By the Numbers

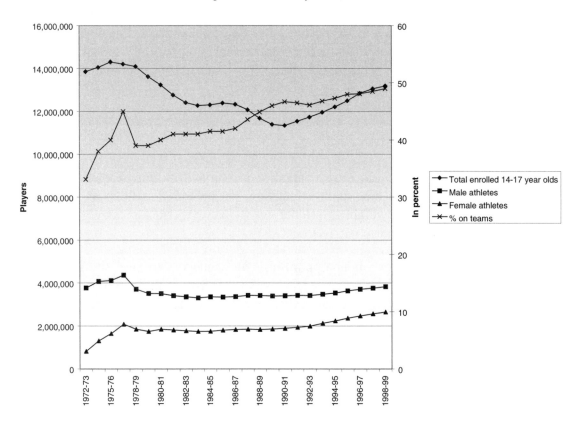

Between 20 million and 30 million young people participate in some sort of organized sport. According to statistics quoted by the Orthopedics Society of America, roughly half of boys and a quarter of girls between 8 and 16 compete in an organized sport at least once during the year. Three-quarters of junior high schools and middle schools have competitive sports programs. Roughly 7 million athletes compete at the high school level.

The panel tracks participation from 1972 to the present. The number of women players grew steadily over the next five years. The reasons for this include the passing of Title IX to ensure female players enjoyed the same opportunities as men. Some of it is due to societal changes: women's roles were being reinvented across every aspect of our culture; that it took place on the playing field as well is hardly surprising. The number of young male athletes increased as well; perhaps the ruling stimulated interest in sports in general, and more boys went out for teams.

The numbers of young men and women who joined high school teams stayed fairly consistent from roughly 1980 to 1994. However, the number of enrolled 14-17 year olds (grades 9-12) fell during the early 1980s, leveled out and then dipped again in the late 1980s before starting to climb again. Therefore, because of declining enrollment, the *percentage* of students on sports teams actually grew. As enrollment fell from 12.38 million in Fall 1995 to 11.6 million in Fall 1998, for example, the percentage of student athletes grew from 41% to 45%.

Why do these teenagers pursue athletics? Boys will always try out for the football team. High school sports are a religion in some communities; to be on the football team is a badge of honor for young men. Some youths are looking for ways to get physically fit. Perhaps others are looking to become more "well rounded" and have a sport to put on college applications. Perhaps others are influenced by their parents or friends. Intriguingly, both men's and women's teams have seen steady growth since 1994 (top sports for boys: football and basketball; for women: basketball and track & field).

The trend for more young people to pursue organized sports can be seen elsewhere. Membership in Boy Scouts and Girl Scouts — groups that value team playing and physical fitness — has been growing steadily (since 1994 actually, the same year as high school sports!). Little League membership has increased from about 2.6 million players in 1992 to 2.9 million players in 1999, a jump of 8% (the league had 70,000 players in 1954).

But there are issues here. Parents often have to make a sizeable investment in equipment purchases, pay for expensive lessons, and take time driving kids to and from practice. There are increasing incidents of violent or threatening behavior at kids' games by parents. What is the effect on children? Roughly 70% of children drop out of league games by the age of 13, according to one survey. The number one reason? It had ceased to be fun for them. Kids also get hurt at these games. According to the National Electronic Injury Surveillance System, more than 3.5 million sports-related injuries in kids under age 15 needed medical attention.

Other questions come to mind: Whatever happened to unstructured play, groups of kids who just get together in the neighborhood? Is this a thing of the past? Are affluent kids over-managed? According to a survey by Urban Youth Sports, 15% of urban children participate in organized sports, while 85-90% play in the suburbs. Affluence plays a role in all this, of course: it takes money for uniforms, equipment, and for the maintenance of proper practice space.

Sources: "The Dark Side of Kids' Sports." *The Physician and Sportsmedicine*, September 2001; "Urban Youth Sports." Retrieved February 9, 2002 from the World Wide Web: http://www.sportinsociety.com; "Young Athletes." Retrieved February 9, 2002 from the World Wide Web: http://www.orthopedicsosa.com; athlete figures from U.S. Bureau of the Census, *Statistical Handbook of the United States*, Washington D.C.; enrollment figures from U.S. Department of Education, National Center for Education Statistics, *Statistics of State School Systems: Statistics of Public Elementary and Secondary School Systems; Statistics of Nonpublic Elementary and Secondary Schools: Projections of Education Statistics to 2010*.

Spending on College Teams

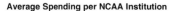

Average Spending per NCAA Institution

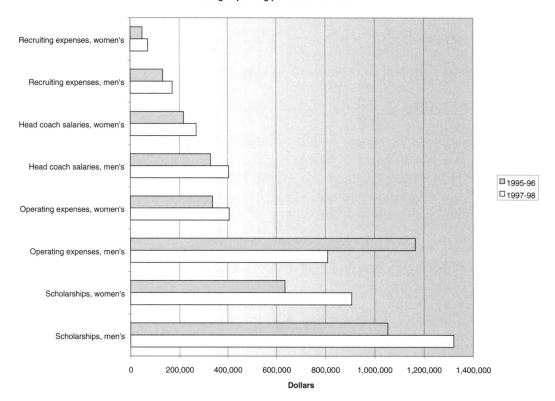

The panel compares the average spending per institution on selected aspects of male and female athletic programs. Data come from a survey of Division I programs conducted by the National Collegiate Athletic Association.

Athletics programs for women have been receiving attention since the passing of Title IX in 1972. This federal law prohibited gender discrimination in public classrooms and athletic fields. Just as women entered college and the workforce in large numbers, so too did they pursue athletics: the number of women in college sports quintupled from 32,000 to 163,000. The trend hasn't just affected college sports either. In 1972, only one in 27 girls participated in high-school sports; today, one in three girls do, according to the source.

More money is spent on recruitment and scholarships for men's programs than women's'. Men receive roughly two-thirds of recruitment budgets across all athletic divisions.

But spending on scholarships for women grew 43%, compared to only 25% for men. Indeed, according to the *Chronicle of Higher Education*, women have been getting slightly more scholarship money than is required by federal guidelines. Female athletes, who make up 41.5% of varsity athletes, received 43% of scholarship dollars in 1999-2000 (the Department of Education told colleges that the proportion of scholarship aid must be within one percentage point of the proportion of women on varsity teams). Many schools actually spend more money on scholarships than they are required to.

More dollars were spent on head coach salaries for men's programs than women's' programs. No surprise here: men have always made more money than women have. But the growth in spending was higher for women: spending jumped 25.2% from 1995-96 to 1997-98, while the increase for men was only 22.3%. Is there more of an effort to attract both coaching and athletic talent for women's teams?

Women's sports are coming into their own. The Women's Sports Foundation claims that the number of 18-34 year olds who watch sports has increased by 40% over the last 25 years. Sports sponsorship has crossed the $1 billion threshold, according to *American Demographics*.

But men's sports teams are still the big moneymakers (football and basketball make up roughly 70% of the average NCAA Division I athletic budget, according to *USA Today*). Because of this, the dollars will follow suit. According to *USA Today*, between 1972 and 1997, for every new dollar spent on women's sports, $2 was added to men's sports. Between 1992 and 1997, for every new dollar spent on women's sports, $3 was spent on men's sports.

What kind of sports are college women pursuing? The next panel examines this question.

Sources: "Suit Unfairly Attacks Effort to Boost Women's Sports." *USA TODAY*, January 21, 2002; Welch Suggs. "Scholarships for Women Exceed Federal Guidelines.*" Chronicle of Higher Education*, May 18, 2001, p. 1; "No Longer Just Fun and Games." *American Demographics*, May 1, 2001, p. 36.

Women Embrace College Sports

Women's Participation in NCAA Sports

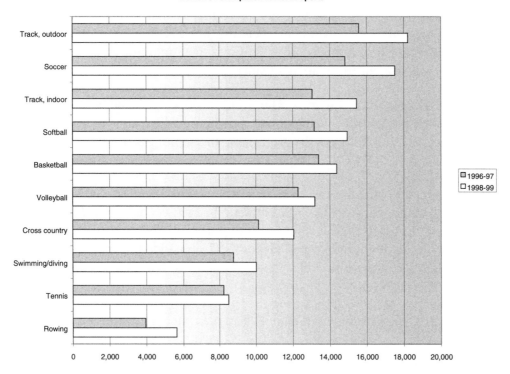

The number of female athletes at the college level grew 16% from 1996-97 to 1998-99 according to statistics from the National Collegiate Athletic Association. The total number of athletes jumped from 128,209 to 148,803. Roughly 8 million women attended public and private universities during this period. The panel above shows the number of women by sport.

There have been impressive growth rates within these sports as well. The table below shows the percent growth in female athletes during these periods.

Increase in Women Athletes by Sport, 1996-97 and 1998-99

Sport	Growth (%)
Rowing	42.1
Cross country	18.7
Track, indoor	18.3
Soccer	18.1
Track, outdoor	16.9
Swimming/diving	14.4
Softball	13.4
Volleyball	7.4
Basketball	7.2
Tennis	3.2

There are probably several reasons these sports have seen such interest. Women have increasingly embraced healthy lifestyles; they are simply playing sports they have participated in their entire lives. Indeed, many of these sports were the most popular sports for high school girls, suggesting women are drawn to these sports simply because they enjoy them. The top sports for high school girls in 1999 are shown below:

Sport	Participants
Basketball	456,873
Track & field (outdoor)	405,163
Volleyball	380,994
Softball (fast pitch)	340,480
Soccer	257,586
Tennis	156,505
Cross country	155,529
Swimming & diving	133,235

Another possible influence on women's sports has been the increasing prominence and role model potential of female athletes such as Mia Hamm and Picabo Street. More colleges are perhaps putting a stronger emphasis on their programs for women, through funding and scholarships.

What of the men? Their numbers saw a modest 5% increase in this period, from 200,627 in 1996-97 to 211,273 in 1997-98. The big sport for men, football, saw about the same growth. Participation in men's sports programs seem quite stable, and it is the women's programs that show the most dynamic activity.

Source: U.S. Census Bureau, *Statistical Abstract of the United States*, Washington D.C. 2000.

The Loyal Fans: The State of Professional Sports

Who We Root For: 10 Years of Professional Sports Attendance

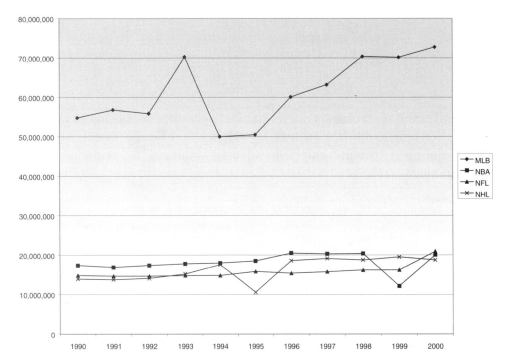

Ah, the big game! We watch it from way up in the bleachers, from luxury box seats, or simply from the comfort of our recliner on Sunday afternoon. We can quote statistics on our favorite athlete. We spend millions on apparel with the logo of our favorite team. But how many of us are still going to the stadiums or arenas?

The panel charts attendance at the big four sports over the last decade. Over 1 billion attended a game during this period, with the top attendance belonging to our national pastime: Major League Baseball. Baseball has more games in a year than the other sports (over 2,400), and people have more opportunities to attend games. National Football League attendance has grown for the third year in a row. Perhaps surprisingly, considering its popularity in our culture, football saw the lowest attendance of the big four. Cost may have something to do with it. It was the second most expensive sport for a family to attend in 2000 according to statistics from Team Marketing Report (the next panel will look at ticket costs more closely).

A word of explanation on the attendance dips in 1994, 1995, and 1999. These were the years of lockouts/strikes (experienced by every sport but the National Football League). Fewer games were played — which meant fewer people in the seats. The number of games for Major League Baseball fell from 2,269 in 1993 to 1,600 in 1994, for example. Attendance fell from 70.2 to 50 million.

Multiple factors influence attendance. New facilities have been built recently, and luxury seating will attract visitors, according to industry consultant Rick Horrow in *Amusement*

Business magazine. Corporations will pay the money for club seats and boxes to entertain important clients. Fans and teams, of course, play a major role; a team with a winning season will bring in more viewers.

What about sports viewed on TV? With the rise of satellite television, a number of sports networks have been brought into households, providing more coverage of professional and college games. But with even more viewing options, we don't seem to be watching more. According to Nielsen ratings, the number of viewers for Monday Night Football has been dropping for the last few years; its most recent season ratings dropped from a 13.7 share to a 12.7 share (although it is always one of the most watched shows on television). The most recent Olympics saw low ratings. The chart below shows the change in viewing audience from 1996-2000 according to Sports Business News statistics quoted in *Sports Business Journal*.

Sport	Change in Viewers
National Basketball Association (NBA)	+34.0
All golf	+11.5
Major League Baseball (MLB)	-3.8
National Football League (NFL)	-13.0
National Association for Stock Car Auto Racing (NASCAR)	-21.3
National Hockey League (NHL)	-38.1

What explains some of these growth rates? The popularity of Tiger Woods must have played a major role in the growth of the golf audience. Similarly, the fans of Michael Jordan will always show up to watch him play. Perhaps the death of racer Dale Earnhardt played some role in NASCAR's smaller audience. The other sports probably have more games broadcast than NASCAR and hockey.

In the next panel we take a look at a major issue for fans: ticket prices.

Sources: Doyle, Tom. "The Baseball & Softball Participation Paradox." *Sporting Goods Dealer*, November-December 2001, p. 42; Tom Powell. "Big Four Sports Draw A Billion In A Decade." *Amusement Business*, December 27, 1999, p. 26; John Morrell, "New Stadiums Pay Off For Professional Teams." *Amusement Business*, December 25, 2000, p. 44.

Going...Going...Gone! The Cost of Salaries and Tickets

Average Growth in Ticket Prices and Player Salaries
1991-2000

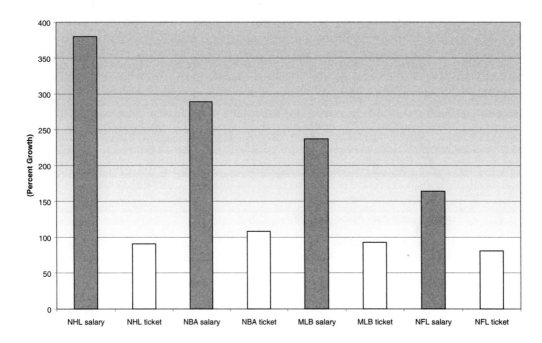

From 1991 to 2000, the average ticket price for the top four sports increased 80% according to statistics quoted in *Sports Illustrated*. They point out the rate was four times higher than the Consumer Price Index and exceeded growth rates for tickets for similar events such as concerts and movies. Player salaries have increased at stunning rates as well, from a low of 81% to a high of 380% during the period.

Most analysts agree that the salaries of athletes play some role in the high cost of tickets. Ticket costs vary by sport. For the most recent year, basketball had the most expensive ticket price at $51.02, followed by football at $48.97, hockey at $47.69 and baseball at $18.99. The table shows the ticket price and percent increase from 1990.

Sport	Average Ticket Price 2000 ($)	% Increase 1990- 2000
National Basketball Association (NBA)	51.02	108
Major League Baseball (MLB)	18.99	93
National Hockey League (NHL)	47.69	93
National Football League (NFL)	48.97	81

But any trip to the big game usually involves more than just the ticket. Team Marketing Report measures the average cost for a family of four, including tickets, two beers, four small soft drinks, four hot dogs, parking, programs, and two adult-sized souvenir caps (and, clearly, two free-spending parents). The numbers suddenly become substantial: a family trip to see a basketball game in 2000 cost, on average, $266.6; a football game cost $256.72; hockey cost $255.80; baseball $144.98. Again, these figures are averages;

in some cases the numbers are even higher. A trip to a New York Knicks game during the 1999-2000 season cost a family of four $455.26 for mid-range seats, tickets, food, parking, and souvenirs, according to Team Marketing Report and *Sports Illustrated*.

So, what's happening here? Some analysts have been pointing towards leagues making a push for more affluent fans to help pay for salaries and new stadiums. Statistics point to growing wealth among the young people the sports industry is targeting. In short, more people have the money to pay for pricey tickets. There is also some thinking that there will always be people who will pay to see their favorite team, no matter what the cost.

Dennis Howard, a professor of sports marketing, quoted in the *Christian Science Monitor*, points out that the majority of ticket holders have annual household incomes of at least $80,000 (except for baseball, where ticket costs are the lowest). His research places most sports goers at roughly 15% of American households.

Sports for the wealthy? Exclusively? How many families can afford the expense of tickets? The fans are becoming more vocal about their displeasure. They complain about the performance of overpaid players, bad coaches, and blind officials. That seems to be more satisfying than cheering the team on.

Sources: Swift, E.M. "Hey, Fans, Sit On It!" *Sports Illustrated*. 15 May 2000, p. 70. "High Cost of Pro-Sports Fandom May Ease." *Christian Science Monitor*. 19 November p. 16.

Chapter 11

Arts and Culture

The panels in this chapter will take a look at some of the major changes in the field of arts and culture.

The first charts will offer a general look at the cultural events that we enjoy. How do we spend our free time? Some of us write poetry on the side, have discovered ballroom dancing, or enjoy taking a stroll through a park on a Saturday afternoon. We'll see that some activities still exist — opera has a small but devoted following — while others have experienced surprising rebirths.

Other panels will take a closer look at some of the mainstays of the world of art and culture. We'll see that museums have managed to reinvent themselves by blending popular exhibits with programs that entertain families and address important social turns in our history. Later, we'll examine how technology has begun to shape our entertainment. Computers, the Internet, and pay television are all competing for our attention. But will all our electronic gadgets change us? Are they making us less social?

Indeed, with all this technology, we must not forget about the beloved book. We can wander through stadium-sized megastores, drinking lattes, and browse to our hearts' content. But are we still buying books? Are we still reading? And what of young people, weaned on electronics and MTV. Can the book still compete?

We'll also take a look at another great American pursuit: going to the movies. Statistics offer a surprising review of the film industry. The last panel will look at the topic of ratings: is entertainment getting too adult? What will this mean?

What Are Our Favorite Cultural Activities?

The ArtsThat We Support

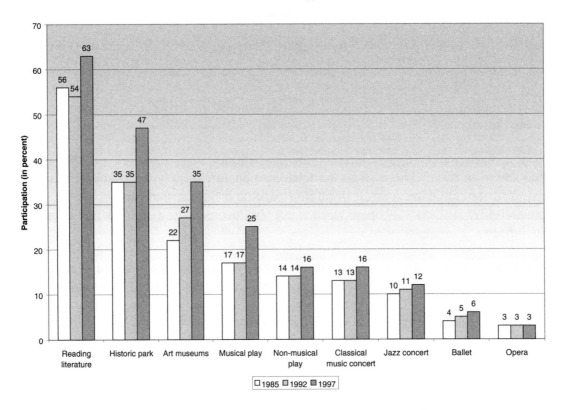

The graphic shows participation rates for leading arts activities. We're looking here at people who are 18 years old and older who read a book or attended a performance at least once during the previous year. The National Endowment for the Arts conducted the survey that yielded these data.

The chart offers some interesting insights into the cultural programs we support. Reading was king of the category, with 63% having read a novel, book of poetry, or a play over the previous year. Historic parks had the second highest participation rate in 1997; reasons for this include the growth of the outdoor sports category (camping, snowboarding, etc.) and that parks are "G"-rated entertainment — something the whole family can enjoy. Indeed, participation rates are very similar when broken down by age: 46% of 18-24 year olds had visited a park; 52% of 35-44 year olds had; 45% of 55-64 year olds did as well.

Museums saw a steady increase in traffic: from 22% in 1985 to 27% in 1992 to 35% in 1997. They also enjoyed the highest growth rate in participation: the rate increased almost 60% between 1985 and 1997. Why the increase? Museums are cheap, quality entertainment (many charge no admission); we shall also see later in this chapter that these institutions have altered their image and have been rewarded with more visitors.

But some activities don't draw us. While we did see more musicals, our interest in traditional plays was static in 1985 and 1992, with a modest increase in 1997; keep in mind, however, that this simply might have been that there were fewer shows to see. Because of budget constraints, many regional theatres were fighting to stay open in the early 1990s. We seem gradually to be warming up to jazz concerts and willing to broaden our horizons, put on a tux or our best dress, and attend the ballet. Clearly, opera still feels elitist or boring to people; its attendance rates have not changed since 1985. Perhaps ballet and opera performances are being kept alive by revenue from regular season ticket holders; they simply just aren't drawing new people in.

Part of the reason the performing arts rank at the bottom may be an accessibility issue. Ballet and operas tend to be found in big cities; the only way some people may get to see such performances is in touring productions. We'll take a closer look at these pursuits later in this section.

So, what types of art do we actually *do*?

Sources: U.S. Bureau of the Census, *Statistical Abstract of the United States*, Washington D.C. and the U.S. National Endowment for the Arts, *Survey of Public Participation in the Arts* Research Division.

How We Express Our Creative Side

The Art We Do

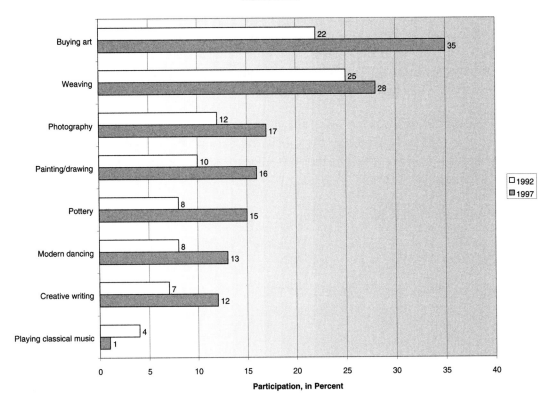

Participation, in Percent

The graph shows the types of cultural activities in which we participate. It refers to people over the age of 18 who have enjoyed each activity at least once during the year. Data comes from a survey by the National Endowment for the Arts.

Buying artwork was the leading way in which we indulged our creative passions. Our appreciation transcends age, race, and education. It was the top pursuit for 18-24 year olds (42%) just as it was for their 45-54 year old parents (40%). It was the top pursuit for blacks, whites, and Hispanics. It was the top activity for those with a high school education (35%), and those with a graduate degree (41%).

Surprisingly, the weaving category, which includes sewing, crocheting, and quilting, saw the second highest participation rates in 1992 and 1997. These are big businesses: needlecraft had 34% of the $23 billion hobby industry, or almost $8 billion; quilting is a $1.8 billion industry. Arts and crafts products are also big business, generating billions in sales each year. This also applies to pottery, which includes ceramics, jewelry making and metalworking. Perhaps part of the appeal of sewing is that it's a hobby one can do by oneself — anytime and anywhere. Painting and photography have also seen big boosts in participation rates.

Another point to make here: Men are indulging their creative impulses just as much as women are. The "let's get our hands dirty and build something" quality of pottery perhaps speaks to men in some way (slightly more men participated than women did, as opposed to the weaving field, which was dominated by women). But let's not be sexist: men also edged out women in modern dancing, with 13% to 12% participation rates in 1997, according to the report. More of them bought art (36% to 34%) and they are only slightly less likely than women to do some creative writing (14% for women, 10% for men).

Those of us who play classical music are a dying breed. Are lessons too expensive? Are we unwilling/unable to investment the time to practice? We still *like* classical music; the previous panel showed how attendance at classical music concerts has actually increased. What's the message from this? Those who can't play, listen?

Source: U.S. Bureau of the Census, *Statistical Abstract of the United States*, Washington D.C; National Endowment for the Arts, *Survey of Public Participation in the Arts;* Jerry Siebenmark. "New Ken Quilt Owners Expecting to Double Company Sales." *Wichita Business Journal*, August 24, 2001, p. 6; "Keeping On Track: Spending on Hobbies." *Christian Science Monitor*, August 12, 2001, p. 27.

Are We Still Reading?

Who Buys Books?

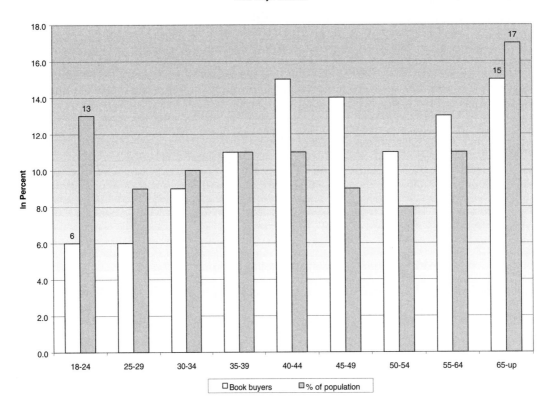

The panel above shows the percent of book buyers compared with percent of population, according to *USA Today*. Thus, 18 to 24 year olds represent 6% of book buyers but 13% of the population 18 and older.

The most interesting piece of information shown here is that more than two thirds of book buyers are over 40 according to the original source, *Consumer Research Study on Book Purchasing*. Almost 70% fell under the book buyers' category, while they made up less than 60% of the population. Senior citizens in particular make a strong showing; not only are they a significant share of the population (17%), but they are the highest book-buying segment (15%). What of the twenty- and thirty-somethings? They are probably too busy in the workforce or consumed by family life; they are probably reading — computer screens, not books.

So, who exactly is buying books? According to 1997 figures from the American Booksellers Association, buyers tend to be college educated, married, and about 42 years old; they have a median annual income of $39,900. A survey by the research firm NPD makes similar observations: the majority of book purchases were made by people with less than $50,000 in income. Fiction, of course, remains the top category. We buy books mostly at large chains. This has spelled trouble for independent book retailers; they find it hard to compete with chains' prices and number of titles. Independents have lost market share to chain bookstores (their share fell from 32.5% in 1991 to 17.2% in 1997). Some have been forced to close, but many independents survive because of their faithful clientele.

A recent Gallup poll revealed that 84% of Americans had read all or part of at least one book during the past year, a figure that has been constant for two decades. Thirty percent reported reading 1-5 books; 7% reported reading more than 50. Women read more than men did: 64% of women had read six or more books, while only 42% of men had.

So is the old cliché about "no one reading anymore" true? And what about juveniles? The table below shows millions of adult and juvenile books over recent years.

Year	Juvenile books	Adult books
1980	144	315
1994	526	1,018
1995	511	1,028
1996	535	1,060
1997	519	1,067
1998	487	1,037
1999	481	1,071

These data came out before children began to fully embrace Harry Potter (the first book, *Harry Potter and the Sorcerer's Stone,* appeared in late 1998). The children's book industry is expected to see strong sales in the coming years. The adult segment also has seen some turnaround.

Data from the National Education Association provide further hope for the future of reading. Eighty-seven percent of teens ranked it as exciting or informative. Minority youth gave reading higher ratings than did whites. Indeed, minority teens were much more likely to read aloud to someone — parent, younger child, senior citizen — a few times a week than white youths were. Much of this, the report suggests, comes from parental involvement.

In spite of all the options we have for leisure time, we are still reading.

Sources: "The Age of Book Buyers." *USA TODAY*, March 24, 1999, p. D1; "Most Americans Still Read." *Research Alert*, February 4, 2001; "Teen Book Club." *American Demographics*, July 1, 2001, p. 12; Marcia Mogelonsky. "Book Biz Boon." *American Demographics*, March 1999; Jim Milliott, "Leaders of the Pack." *Publishers Weekly*, October 30, 1995, p. 31.sales figures from American Booksellers Association and Book Industry Study Group.

Are We Still Going to the Movies?

Wanna See A Movie? Yeah, But Where?

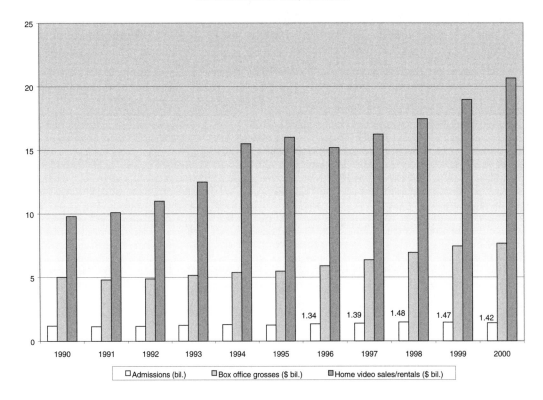

Going to the movies is one of the great American leisure pursuits. Over the last decade, we have seen the rise of the "blockbuster" — films with big stars that make big money on their opening weekends. We've seen stars make huge paychecks. We've gone to our local multiplex and taken out second mortgages to pay for tickets and popcorn. So the industry must be doing pretty well, right?

Well, not exactly. The graph above charts admissions and box-office revenues over the last decade. Some things to notice here: The industry has seen box office revenues rise steadily, with grosses jumping 2.7% to hit $7.7 billion in 2000. However, fewer people are actually going to the movies. Admissions have dropped for two consecutive years, from 1.48 billion in 1998 to 1.47 billion in 1999 to 1.42 billion in 2000. Several sources have pointed out what accounts for the increased revenues: the increase in ticket prices. The average price of a ticket is now $5.39, up 28% from 1990. In large cities, the cost of a ticket is far higher.

The industry is suffering in another way: oversupply. The number of screens has increased 52% over the last decade, with a total of 36,264 screens in 2000. The multiplexes that seemed to spring up on every corner simply could not generate enough revenues to keep going.

This ties in to the other point to be made from the panel. People aren't going to the movies as much because they watch them at home. The home video market has seen some troubles too as preferences shifted between rental and direct sales and DVD began capturing share from VHS. This market has consistently generated billions (the rental segment generated over $8 billion in 2000, beating theaters for the second year). This is another example of one of the major themes of this book's leisure section: Americans are cocooning. People are spending more time at home; families are trying to spend more time together.

Sources: "Media Forecast: Strong Spending." *USA TODAY*, July 25, 1997, p. 2B; Jim McCullaugh. "Special Interest Looks for Retail Respect." *Billboard*, October 31, 1992, data from the Motion Picture Industry of America; some home video figures are estimated.

The Status of the Performing Arts

Performing Arts Attendance

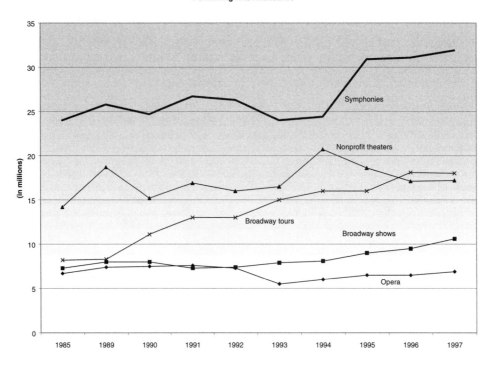

The previous panels have shown our favorite cultural events and activities. The performing arts continue to occupy the bottom of the scale. Why? Who attends the opera, symphonies and theatre? Does "Middle America" have access to this type of entertainment?

A look at the panel above shows the rocky histories of some segments of the performing arts. Symphonies have seen some decline in attendance, but still are the most popular form of performance entertainment. Opera attendance appears to be returning to peak level achieved in 1992; nonprofit theatres saw full houses until 1994, saw a drop-off, and now see audiences returning. The "Great White Way" of Broadway has seen record attendance levels. These industries have seen budgets get cut and expenses soar. Who has been attending?

Performing arts do seem to speak to a narrow segment of the population. Take Broadway shows, for example: according to a study by the League of American Theatres and Producers, the majority of theatregoers were women (61%, a figure consistent for two decades), and their average age was 40. Roughly three-quarters of theatregoers over the age of 25 had completed college, and 36% held a graduate degree (about 21% of the U.S. population have completed college). The average annual household income was $94,000 and, most significantly, roughly 80% of them were white.

Similar trends can be found in other areas. According to statistics from the National Endowment for the Arts, those who attended a concert or an opera were most likely to be women, of the Baby Boomer generation, affluent and white (although more Asians reported attending the opera, which perhaps isn't surprising considering the medium's rich history in some cultures).

Some effort has been made to bring more diverse product to the stage. In some cases it has paid off as well. There has been a 140% increase in the number of Broadway theatre-goers under the age of 18 for example, from 500,000 attendees in 1991 to 1.2 million in 2000.

The number of new productions on Broadway has been fairly consistent over the period. However, new productions by opera companies are up 12% from 1985 and 1997. Symphonies did even better; there was a 38% increase in shows over the period. These groups all saw boosts in income as well. A closer look at attendance figures shows how strong the support can be. Figures show the increase in millions of visitors.

Change in Attendance 1985 and 1997

Event	1985	1997	% Change
Broadway shows	7.3	10.6	+45.2
Broadway tours	8.2	18.0	+119.5
Operas	6.7	6.9	+2.9
Symphonies	24.9	31.9	+32.9

The most startling point shown above is that Broadway tours have seen an increase of 120% in attendance. This type of entertainment is finding its way to us and we are supporting it. But how many regions have suitable venues for such performances? How many people still have to drive some distance to see a concert or attend the theatre? Are some people kept away from downtown because they perceive it as unsafe at night?

Sources: U.S. Census Bureau, *Statistical Abstract of the United States*, Washington D.C., 1999; "Who Goes to Broadway?" Retrieved November 16, 2001 from the World Wide Web: http://www.livebroadway.com.

What Will Bring Entertainment Into Our Homes?

What's in the Typical Home?

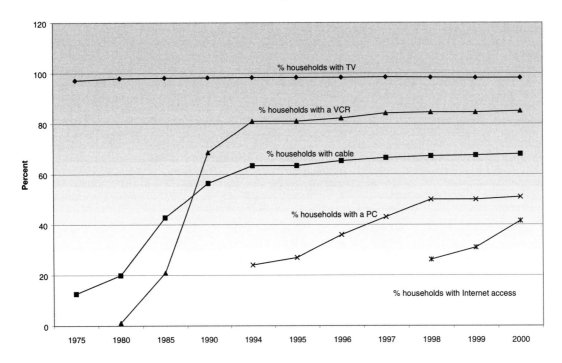

For many years, the television was the champ of home entertainment, network broadcasters sitting comfortably on top of the hill. Over the last decade, however, technology has offered an array of new options to consumers — in short, the personal computer entered the American home. Is TV on its way out? Will our entertainment come from the desktop?

The graph charts the ownership rates for the most popular forms of technology. The percent of households with a television has been consistent since 1965 (just to back up even further: 9% of households had a television in 1950, while 64.5% of them did just 5 years later). In 1975, HBO beamed down signals from a satellite, and cable broadcasting entered a whole new phase: 12.6% of homes had cable in that year, hitting 56.4% penetration 15 years later. It continues to grow towards the 70% mark.

Then along came the personal computer. It brought us the phenomenon of "home computing" and, of course, the Internet. Half of the homes in America now own a computer (many have more than one). The technology and entertainment industries seemed to order themselves around these innovations; suddenly we saw personal digital assistants, cellular phones that can access the Internet, MP3 recorders, the ability to access music and video straight from the Web, screenphones, and personal recording devices. Some of these new products have done well. Others have struggled to see the bright sales originally forecast for them.

Where do we stand now? Americans seem to want their home-lives to be comfortable. We want to cocoon on the couch and to be entertained. When exactly did the phrase "couch potato" originate? Not very long ago. The table below lists the estimated growth in sales of selected items for 2000-2001 according to the Consumer Electronics Association.

Most Purchased Electronics

Item	Percent Change 2000-2001 (%)
Digital TV sets	+119.9
Home theater in a box	+94.5
Video game console systems	+63.8
Home component DVD players	+53.0
DVD players	+52.9
Satellite TV receivers	+50.2
MP3 players	+32.0
Personal computers	-12.2

It is televisions and related equipment that are seeing the high growth rates. After years of strong sales, the PC is expected to see its first drop in sales. Is the bulk of our leisure time going to be spent in the home? Probably not. Change is everything.

Sources: Snider, Mike. "Safe at Home and All Plugged In." *USA TODAY*, January 8, 2002, p. D1. Broadcasting data from Television Bureau of Advertising; Computer and Internet data from Dataquest and U.S. Department of Commerce, using U.S. Bureau of the Census *Current Population Survey* supplements.

How Museums Are Changing With Us

Museums Established by Decade

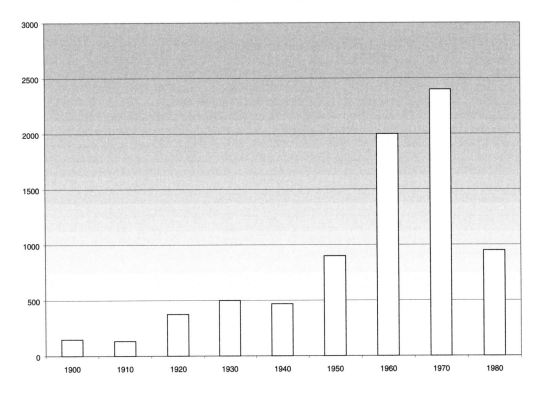

The graphic above shows the number of museums established by decade. A significant increase occurred during the late 1940s when arts programs were funded by the federal government. The numbers increased dramatically during the 1960s and 1970s. The number fell sharply in the 1980s. This corresponds to a time when arts funding and the National Endowment for the Arts fell under scrutiny for controversial shows.

There are currently 15,000 museums in the United States. They average 865 million visits a year, or over 2 million visits a day, an increase of 50% over a decade ago. Indeed, we have seen in previous panels that museums have become quite popular. Many museums have been booking very popular exhibits and have seen boosts in foot traffic and ticket revenues (particularly vital when so many are battling for funding and contributions). But while the great artists still brings in the crowds — Van Gogh, John Philip Sargent, and Jackson Pollock exhibits were among the top museum shows in 1999 — museums have begun to become more than buildings that house a variety of art. They have begun to take on identities.

While final statistics for the 1990s are not yet available, the number of new museums established between 1998-2000 makes this interesting point:

New Museums, 1998-2000

Type of Museum	% of Total
Specialized	25.4
History	18.1
Science	16.3
Art	12.7
Children's	10.9
Natural history	7.2
Aquarium	5.4
General	3.6

Over a quarter of new museums were "specialized," dealing with social or ethnic issues. Recent museums include those devoted to women, African Americans, and the Oklahoma City tragedy. Science museums are popular because they often entertain as well as inform; many contain exhibits in which visitors can witness or perform experiments. The trend toward combining entertainment and education explains the popularity of children's museums. Such institutions have been around longer than one might think — the first children's museum opened in 1899 — but they have become an attractive tool for schools and parents. Attendance figures support this: the number of visitors jumped 144% between 1996 and 1998.

There are many niche museums in this country addressing a variety of aspects of our culture.

Source: Mihm, Stephen. "Museums: Firsts, Facts and Figures." *New York Times*, April 19, 2000, p. 20.

What Happened to Family Entertainment?

Types of Films Released between 1980 and 1998

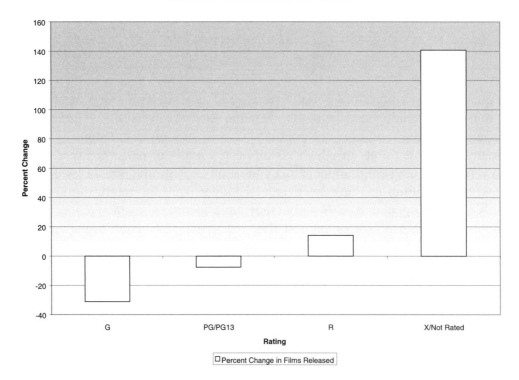

A great deal of recent attention has been paid to the content of programs served up by the entertainment industry. Some argue that it is becoming increasingly explicit and that it caters too much to the appetites of children and teenagers. Others balk at the idea of any censorship; people are free to change the radio station or turn off the television. Have we made improvements? Are we too reactionary? Or are all of these protests falling on deaf ears?

The graphic shows the change in the types of films released between 1980 and 1998. The G-rated movie isn't quite dead, although it is barely breathing; the number of actual films made fell from 16 to 11 in this period, or 31%. The number of PG/PG-13 films fell too, although by only 7.6%. The number of R-rated films did not see the increase some might expect; 155 films were made in 1980, while 177 were made in 1998, for a 14% jump. It was the number of films that received no rating that saw a dramatic increase, 140%, up from 27 in 1980 to 65 in 1998.

A little cinema history here: new ratings were developed over this period. The PG-13 rating was started in 1984; it was intended as a rating for films suitable for teens but not for children. It also, of course, allowed studios to market films more closely to teenagers, a large segment of moviegoers and a population with millions (now billions) in disposable income.

The NC-17 rating (No children under 17 admitted) started in 1990, is a replacement for the X, which theatres would not show and for which newspapers would not accept advertising. These were films deemed to have artistic merit and adult content. *Last Tango in Paris* and *A Clockwork Orange* received X-ratings on their release. Another point that explains the 140% increase: as more films are made independently, they are bypassing the Motion Picture Association of America and remain unrated. An unrated film does not necessarily mean an explicit film. But the viewing public is offered no guidance about the film's content.

However, perhaps the family does win out. In 1998, according to data from Exhibitor Relations and published in *The Christian Science Monitor*, PG-13 films not only grossed more money but had a higher average gross per screen. They generated $2.2 billion in box office grosses (R-rated films made $2 billion) and had average per-screen grosses of $35 million (R-rated films made $11 million).

The box office champs of the 1990s were also often PG-13 films: *Titanic, Stars Wars: Episode I-The Phantom Menace, Jurassic Park, Forrest Gump, Toy Story 2*. Disney films continue to do extremely well financially. Clearly, families hunger for family entertainment.

What of other entertainment? The video game industry is still under scrutiny for producing games with violent or sexual content. According to 1999 data released by the Entertainment Software Ratings Board, 71% of all titles were rated "everyone;" 19% were rated "teen;" 7% were rated "mature." More than 7,000 games have been rated since 1994. Surprisingly, the average age of the user is 28. Television? Watchdog groups have long complained about the content of prime-time television: for example, The Kaiser Family Foundation's report, *Sex on TV*, claimed sexual content had increased from 56% of shows in the 1997-1998 season to 68% in the 1999-2000 season. It all comes down to taste, of course: some of what these groups protest range from fairly innocuous to truly objectionable.

There's a bigger point to make here. Are these ratings accurate and relevant? Is the envelope continually being pushed? Is too much adult material slipped into PG-13 films? Should one profanity bring a film an R-rating? Do we need a more refined system? If we support quality entertainment, will it continue to be produced?

Sources: Sterritt, David. "Movie Ratings — from G to X: Are They Out of Focus?" *Christian Science Monitor*. 16 September 1982; video game ratings: Online. Available: http://www.esrb.org January 16, 2002; Kaiser Foundation report *Sex On TV*. Online. Available: http://www.kaiser.org; "How Many and How Much." *Christian Science Monitor*. 24 December 1998, p. B10.

Chapter 12

Leisure Time in Our Community

Our community. It can be our neighborhood, our city, or the world-at-large. How do we spend our leisure time in our communities? Do we take advantage of the resources offered to us? Do we offer our time and talents to our community? This chapter discusses some of the ways in which people spend their time (and in some cases money) within their communities.

The first panel presents data on charitable giving vs. volunteerism. More of us are donating to charitable organizations and we are donating more than ever before. Has the spirit of volunteerism followed? The next four panels present the characteristics of volunteers over time. Who volunteers the most, men or women? Do college graduates volunteer more than high school dropouts? Those between the ages of 35 and 54 volunteer the most, but has this always been the case? What about other age groups? Are their percentages increasing or decreasing? Whites have always volunteered in higher percentages than blacks or Hispanics, but have blacks always volunteered more than Hispanics?

The next two panels discuss where we contribute our money and our time. The overall percentage of households that contribute to charity rose in the late 1990s. Does this mean that all types of charitable organizations also saw an increase in the percentage of households contributing to them? Are the types of charities we give money to the ones we volunteer for?

The population of the United States has been growing, as has religious membership. Yet, our society is more secular than ever before. The next panel discusses this phenomenon. The following two panels present information about adult and youth religious attendance. The United States has become a more racially diverse nation. It has become a more religiously diverse one also. We look at the fastest-growing religions in the past decade.

Public libraries. Are they still needed with the Internet in most of our homes? The number of libraries has grown in the past decade. Funding has increased tremendously. Visits to public libraries have also increased since 1993. We cover this subject in three panels.

Participation in adult education soared in the 1990s. Why are we taking classes in our spare time? Do these reasons change based on gender and educational attainment? Have the reasons changed over time? Have colleges and universities adapted to meet the needs of this type of nontraditional student? The final three panels cover these issues.

Helping The Less Fortunate

Volunteering and Contributing to Charity, 1987-2000

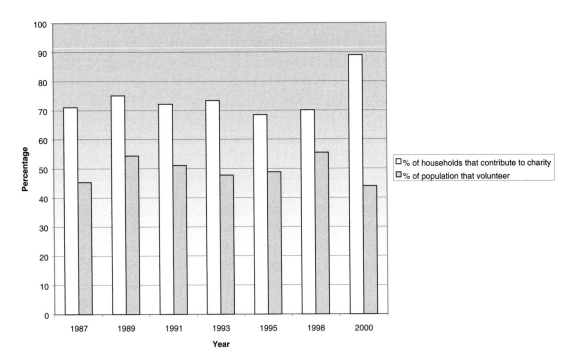

The chart shows the percentage of households that gave to charity — and the percentage of adults who volunteered during the 1987 to 2000 period. In 2000, 89% of households gave to charity. Of these the average household gave $1,620 — up from a figure of $1,075 contributed in 1998. Forty-four percent of the adult population volunteered in 2000, lower than the participation rate in 1998, which was 55.5%. Some 25.5 million volunteers disappeared in just two years: 109.4 million volunteered in 1998, 83.9 million in 2000. Why the sudden jump in contributions, the decline in volunteering?

During the 1987 to1998 period, the survey producing these data included those aged 18 to 20. Beginning in 2000, only those 21 and older were included. Thus the earlier data and 2000 data are not directly comparable. But the shift indicates, indirectly, the role that younger people play. They seem to give less but to volunteer more. Of course, the increase in contributions and the drop in volunteers may not entirely be due to this shift in survey methodology.

Overall, more of us are donating, and we're giving more. Are we contributing equally based on our income? The table on the next page provides some answers. Although those in the higher income bracket give the most money, it's those in the lowest brackets who contribute the highest percentage of their income to the needy. The exception to this was in 1993. In that year those earning $100,000 and over contributed 0.5% more of their income than those earning under $10,000. But from 1995 to 1998, those in the top two income brackets gave less of their income to charity, those in the two lowest brackets more.

In 1998, those earning under $10,000 gave an average of 3% more of their income than those earning $100,000 or more.

Amount Given by All Contributing Households, 1991-1998

Household income	Average dollar amount given				Percent of household income			
	1991	1993	1995	1998	1991	1993	1995	1998
Under $10,000	239	207	295	329	3.6	2.7	4.3	5.2
$10,000-$19,999	507	332	425	495	3.4	2.3	2.8	3.3
$20,000-$29,000	617	668	578	552	2.5	2.7	2.3	2.2
$30,000-$39,999	640	715	722	734	1.8	2.0	2.1	2.1
$40,000-$49,000	1,038	572	576	951	2.3	1.3	1.3	2.1
$50,000-$59,999	1,293	632	1,001	1,041	2.4	1.1	1.8	1.9
$60,000-$74,999	1,180	1,572	1,301	1,696	1.7	2.3	1.9	2.6
$75,000-$99,999	1,666	1,720	1,582	1,394	1.9	2.0	1.8	1.6
$100,000 and over	2,450	3,213	3,379	2,550	2.5	3.2	3.4	2.2

How did we make our contributions? In 1998, 84% of households reported giving contributions of food or clothing. Around 80% purchased goods or services from charitable organizations and gave cash or checks. And, despite the growing popularity of the Internet, only 1.2% of 1998 contributions was made online. This rose to 2% in 2000. But, of those with Internet access, 13% used the Internet to research charitable organizations in 2000. And, of those, 12% made a donation online.

Who's volunteering? In 1998, the typical volunteer was a white woman, between the ages of 35 and 54, with at least some college education and an income level between $60,000 and $74,999. Has this picture changed over time? In the next panel we look at gender differences in volunteering.

Sources: Chart data (1987-1998), household contribution data and Internet giving data, 1998: *Giving and Volunteering in the United States, 1999: Key Findings,* Washington D.C.: INDEPENDENT SECTOR, 2000. Retrieved October 3, 2001 from http://www.indep sec.org/GandV. Chart data, household contribution, and Internet giving data, 2000: *Giving and Volunteering in the United States, 2001: Key Findings,* Washington D.C.: INDEPENDENT SECTOR, 2002. Retrieved February 6, 2002 from http://www.independent sector. org/PDFs/GV01keyfind.pdf. U.S. Census Bureau. *Statistical Abstract of the United States: 1994, 1996, 1999* and *2000.*

Characteristics of Volunteers: Gender

Percentage of Volunteers, 1974-2000

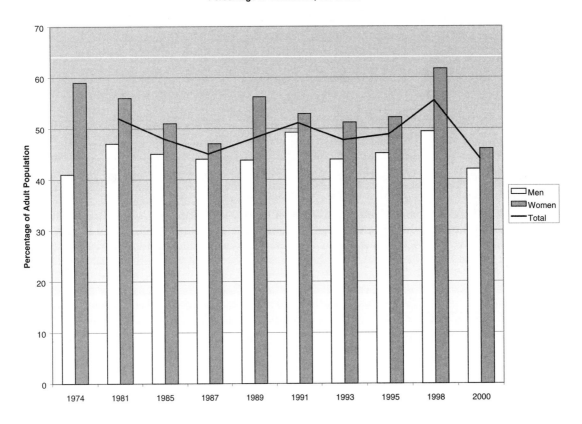

The graphic divides volunteers engaged in charitable causes by gender for the years 1974-2000[1]. It also shows the total percentage of adult volunteers for the years 1981-2000. The curve shows that volunteering has its seasons too, now rising and now falling. The pattern does not match the economic cycle precisely. There was a recession in 1991, but not one in 1998, another peak of voluntary activity.

But while volunteering has cycled over time, the participation of men and women is something of a constant. A consistently higher percentage of women volunteer. Women, of course, outnumber men, but that's not the sole explanation. 1974, 1989, and 1998 saw the biggest spread between the participation of the sexes. Men's participation is more steady and, over this period, has fluctuated around the 45% mark. Women's participation averages at a higher rate (in the middle 50s), but has been trending down. Women may respond more to causes, issues, and perceptions of need. When volunteering declines overall, women leave the ranks in greater numbers than men. But when volunteering surges, more women respond.

---

[1] 1974-1985 data includes those 14 years old and over. 1989 data includes those 16 years and over. 1987 and 1991-1998 data includes those 18 years old and over. 2000 data includes those 21 years old and over.

For most years the percentages of men and women volunteers increased or declined in tandem. This was not the case in three periods: 1974-1981, 1987-1989, and 1989-1991. From 1974 to 1981 and from 1989 to 1991, the percentage of women volunteering went down, the proportion of men volunteering went up. During the 1987 to 1989 time period, the percentage of men volunteering dropped slightly, women's participation went up. No one has analyzed the overall phenomenon in sufficient detail to explain these fluctuations.

The next panel discusses the educational attainment characteristics of volunteers.

Sources: Chart data, 1974-1998: U.S. Census Bureau. *Statistical Abstract of the United States: 1980, 1991, 1994, 1996, 1999,* and *2001.* 2000 data: *Giving and Volunteering in the United States 2001: Key Findings*, Washington D.C.: INDEPENDENT SECTOR, 2002.

Characteristics of Volunteers: Educational Attainment

Educational Attainment of Adult Volunteers, 1981-1998

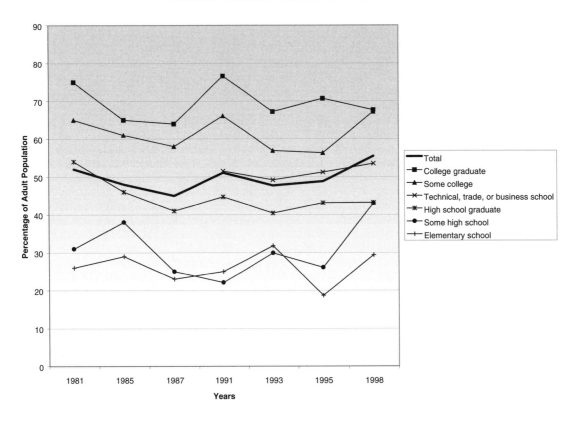

The chart shows the percentage of the adult population who volunteer based on educational attainment. Volunteerism among groups has fluctuated greatly over the 1981-1998 period. Overall, the percentage of people volunteering dropped between 1981 and 1987. Volunteering then saw an upswing from 1987 to 1991. 1991 to 1993 saw another downturn, but the popularity of volunteering rose again after 1993.

For the most part, the popularity of volunteering among those with at least a high school diploma follows this overall pattern — with a couple of exceptions. While overall volunteerism was on the rise from 1995 to 1998, volunteerism among high school and college graduates declined. Those with less than a high school diploma tended to follow an opposite pattern. When overall volunteerism was down, these groups saw an increase in volunteerism, and vice versa. The only exceptions were 1985 to 1987 and 1995 to 1998. From 1985 to 1987, both overall volunteerism and volunteerism among those with less than a high school diploma were down. From 1995 to 1998, volunteerism was increasing overall, as was volunteerism among those with less than a high school diploma.

The next panel discusses the age characteristics of volunteers.

Sources: U.S. Census Bureau. *Statistical Abstract of the United States: 1991, 1994, 1996, 1999,* and *2001.*

Characteristics of Volunteers: Age

Adult Volunteers, by Age, 1987-1998

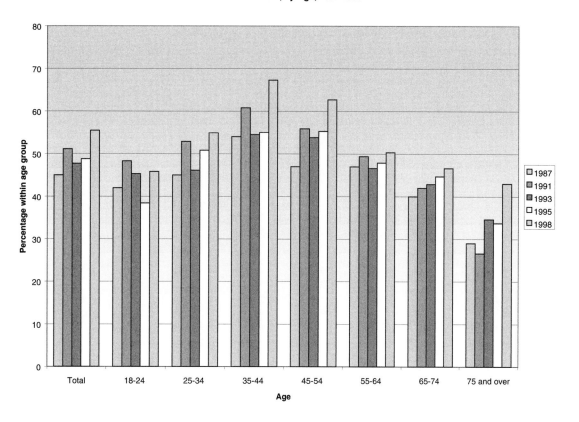

The chart above shows the percentage of adult volunteers by age group for the years 1987-1998. The pattern of volunteerism among many of the age groups follows the over-all pattern of volunteerism. There are some exceptions. One exception is in the 18-24 year old range. While overall volunteerism increased between 1993 and 1995, the per-centage of 18-24 year olds volunteering decreased. Another exception was in the 65-74 year old range. From 1991 to 1993, overall volunteerism decreased, but this group's per-centage of volunteers increased. This group also has seen a steady increase of volunteers, unlike the volatile fluctuations in volunteerism among the rest of the age groups.

Those in the 75 year old and older group have a different pattern than other groups. From year to year, when total volunteerism was up, those in the 75-year-old and over group saw their percentage of volunteers go down, and vice versa. The only exception was from 1995 to 1998. In this case, both overall volunteerism and the percentage of volunteers 75 years old and over went up. An interesting pattern to note: from 1991 to 1998, the volun-teerism pattern of those with only an elementary school education (as seen in the previous panel) and those who were 75 years old and over were identical. The pattern was the op-posite from 1985-1991 for these two groups.

Throughout all the years shown, those within the 35-44 and 45-54 year old range had the highest percentage of volunteers. They were also the only age groups that had a higher percentage of volunteers than average In 1998, 67.3% of 35-44 year olds and 62.7% of 45-54 year olds volunteered compared to 55.5% of the entire adult population. Children in their high school and college age groups, at one end of the spectrum, and aging parents at the other may be part of the explanation for these high rates of participation.

The next panel discusses the racial characteristics of volunteers.

Sources: U.S. Census Bureau. Statistical Abstract of the United States: 1991, 1994, 1996, 1999, and 2001.

Characteristics of Volunteers: Race

Adult Volunteers, by Race, 1991-1998

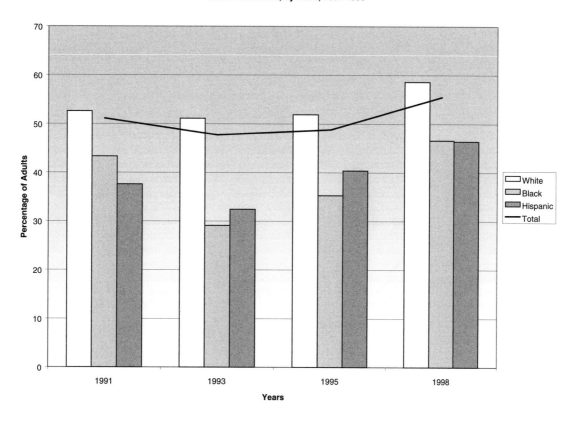

The chart above shows the percentage of the adult population that volunteer based on race. The chart also shows the total percentage of volunteers for the years 1991 to 1998 as a curve. All the races tend to follow the overall pattern of volunteerism, but the fluctuations in the percentage of white volunteers are not as great as that for blacks and Hispanics. Also, the percentage of whites who volunteer is consistently higher than average.

A higher percentage of whites volunteer than blacks or Hispanics. In 1991 and 1998, a higher percentage of blacks volunteered than Hispanics. In 1991 the percentage difference was 5.7%; in 1998 the difference was only 0.2%. The opposite was true in 1993 and 1995, when Hispanics volunteered at a higher rate than blacks (the percentage difference was 3.3% and 5.1%, respectively).

The next two panels discuss where we contribute our money and where we volunteer our time.

Sources: U.S. Census Bureau. *Statistical Abstract of the United States: 1994, 1996, 1999,* and *2001.*

Where is Our Money Going?

Where We Contribute, 1987-1998

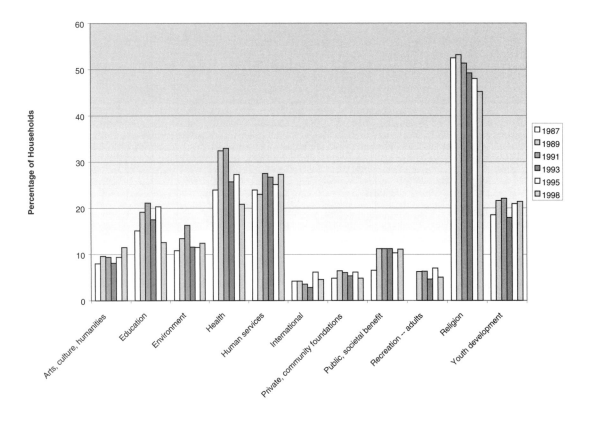

In 1999[2], there were 217,910 public charities in the United States, which took in a total of $143.6 billion in charitable contributions from the public. This represents a 47.6% increase in the number of public charities and a 56.3% increase (constant 2000 dollars) in charitable contributions since 1992. Over this time period, most types of charities saw the percentage of household contributors remain fairly steady or rise. The graphic shows the percentage of households that gave to various types of charities for the years 1987-1998.

Religious charities did not share in the increases. These types of charities had the highest percentage of household contributors — but they have seen a steady decrease in that percentage over most of this time period. One simple reason might be a decline in attendance at religious services: 59% of the population attended religious services[3] in 1990-1991 compared to 55% in 1995-1998.

---

[2] No monetary total data are available for the years in the graph. Data are only available for 1992 and 1999.

[3] Percentage attending religious services at least once a month. Data from "Table 7 – Changes in Attendance at Religious Services." Retrieved February 8, 2002 from http//www.umich.edu.

Educational, environmental, and health charities all saw large increases in the percentage of household contributors between 1987 and 1991; but they have also seen large decreases in the percentage of household contributors between 1991 and 1998. Only environmental charities have seen a bit of an increase (0.9%) from 1995 to 1998. The others saw dramatic decreases (-7.7% for educational charities and –6.5% for health charities) between these two years.

There are no data handy to explain the unusual giving pattern for educational charities. But the increase in the percentages of households that gave to environmental charities could have been due to media coverage of the Exxon Valdez oil spill and cleanup effort in 1989. In 1990, the Spotted owl was put on the threatened species list, which led to standoffs between the timber industry, the government, and environmental groups. The Clean Air Act also was passed in 1990, and changes in such legislation generate a strong drumbeat of interest. In 1991, Biosphere II[4] was in the news.

The spike in the percentage of households giving to health charities from 1987 to 1991 (a 9% increase) could partially be explained by the publicity given to the AIDS epidemic during these years. In 1989, the NAMES Project AIDS Memorial Quilt[5] was nominated for a Nobel Prize. The quilt was also touring the country to bring attention to the victims of HIV and AIDS. In 1990, the quilt was profiled in a feature-length documentary called "Common Threads." The movie won an Academy Award that year. The red ribbons that have become common on the lapels of stage, screen and music stars in recent years were introduced in 1991. In the medical world, new drugs to fight HIV and AIDS were in the news. In the sports world, Magic Johnson announced that he was HIV positive. Later that year he created the Magic Johnson Foundation, which raises funds for community organizations that provide education about treatment and prevention of HIV and AIDS.

In later years, as media attention to these events waned, so, seemingly, did the interest in giving to environmental and health-related charities.

Although giving to international charities has been steady over the years, there was an increase (3.3%) in the percentage of household contributors between 1993 and 1995. This rise coincided with the 10th anniversary of Live Aid, a concert to raise money for the victims of famine in Africa. Publicity and news reports on conditions in Africa may have spurred more people to give. This enthusiasm waned, but a higher percentage of households were giving to international charities in 1998 than in each of the years[6] before 1995.

---

[4] Four men and four women were sealed in a dome in the Arizona desert to determine if a self-sustained ecosystem could be maintained. The experiment ultimately failed.

[5] The quilt is an international memorial to those who have died of AIDS. It was begun in June 1987 in San Francisco as one man's protest against the AIDS epidemic. Cleve Jones spray-painted his friend's name on a piece of cloth the size of a grave. Soon, thousands of people were adding panels as a tribute to their loved ones who died. In 1995, there were more than 27,000 panels.

[6] Years shown in the graph.

Regardless of whether or not a higher percentage of the population contributes to a certain type of charity, the amount contributed in each category has increased dramatically since 1992.

Public Support of Charitable Organizations[7], 1992 and 1999

Type of Charity	% change (1992-1999)	1992 ($ mil)	1999 ($ mil)
Total	*56.3*	*94,995.3*	*148,433.7*
Environment	126.3	1,191.0	2,694.7
Public, societal benefit	85.2	6,584.7	12,194.2
Religion, spiritual development	84.1	2,122.9	3,909.0
Recreation	78.1	973.4	1,733.5
International	70.0	3,372.8	5,732.5
Arts, culture, humanities	62.2	6,766.0	10,973.1
Youth development	58.4	1,475.3	2,336.2
Human services	57.4	27,676.3	43,563.5
Education	51.6	24,490.6	37,132.6
Health	45.3	20,118.4	29,240.2

The next panel discusses where we volunteered our time.

Sources: U.S. Census Bureau. *Statistical Abstract of the United States: 1990, 1991, 1994, 1996, 1999,* and *2001.* National Center for Charitable Statistics. "Reporting Public Charities in the United States by Type, Circa 1999." Retrieved February 8, 2002 from http://nccs.urban.org. National Center for Charitable Statistics. "Reporting Charitable Organizations and Their Finances by Type and Selected NTEE Classification in the United States, circa 1992." Retrieved February 8, 2002 from http://nccs.urban.org. "Campus to Show AIDS Quilt Apr. 22." *Columbia University Record,* April 14, 1995. Retrieved February 13, 2002 from http://www.columbia. edu. The Magic Johnson Foundation. "About the Foundation." Retrieved February 13, 2002 from http://www.magicjohnson.org. The Park Community: Shelter. "Welcome to the Dealing with HIV/AIDS pages." Retrieved February 13, 2002 from http://www.the-park.com/volunteer/safehaven/hiv/hiv.htm. Neville Hodgkinson. "The Cure That Failed." *The Sunday Times,* April 4, 1993. Retrieved February 13, 2002 from http://www.duesberg.com/nhcure.html. Environmental history data: "Timeline of the 80's, 1989." Retrieved February 15, 2002 from http://www.inthe80s.com/time1989.shtml. "Timeline of the 90's, 1990." Retrieved February 15, 2002 from http://www.inthe90s.com/time1990.shtml. "Timeline of the 90's, 1991." Retrieved February 15, 2002 from http://www.inthe90s.com/time1991.shtml.

---

[7]In constant 2000 dollars. Includes gifts, grants, and contributions from government and private sources.

Where is Our Time Spent?

Where We Volunteer, 1991-1998

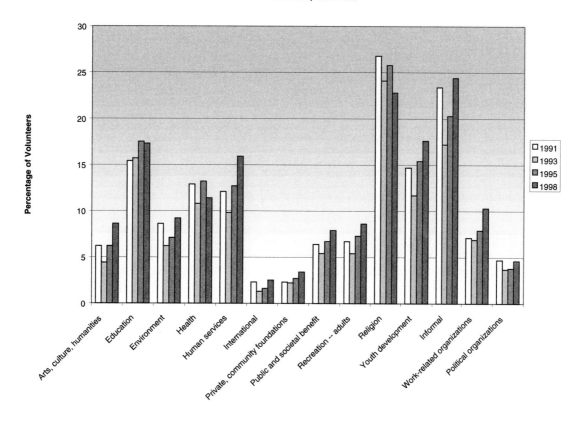

In 1998, 55.5% of the population volunteered (109.4 million people), putting in a total of 15.8 billion hours of volunteer time, an increase of 15.2 million people and 600 million hours over 1991. Where did we do it? The graphic shows the percentage of volunteers who participated in various charitable activities in selected years between 1991 and 1998.

Over this period of time, most volunteer organizations had an overall increase in the percentage of volunteers. Three exceptions to this were religious, health, and political organizations. All organizations except educational charities experienced a decline in the percentage of volunteers from 1991 to 1993. From 1993 to 1995, all charities saw an increase in volunteerism. Most charities had another increase in volunteerism from 1995 to 1998, except for educational, health, and religious organizations.

The year 1998 saw the highest participation rate in the last 17 years. The following table shows the percentage change in volunteerism from 1991 to 1998. The table also shows the percentage change from 1995 to 1998, a period of dramatic shifts.

Percentage Change in Volunteerism, 1991-1998 and 1995-1998

	% change	
	1991-1998	1995-1998
Total	*4.4*	*6.7*
Human services	3.8	3.2
Work-related organizations	3.2	2.4
Youth development	2.9	2.2
Arts, culture, humanities	2.4	2.4
Recreation – adults	1.9	1.3
Education	1.9	-0.2
Public, societal benefit	1.5	1.2
Private, community foundations	1.1	0.7
Informal	1.0	4.1
Environment	0.6	2.1
International	0.2	0.9
Political organizations	-0.1	0.8
Health	-1.5	-1.8
Religion	-4.0	-3.0

Although no data are available to explain the pattern of volunteerism over the years, some of the increased popularity of this activity, from 1995 to 1998, may be traced to the Internet and what has come to be called "virtual volunteering"[8]. Ten percent of those with Internet access used the Internet to research volunteer opportunities and organizations. According to *VolunteerMatch*[9] *2001 Annual Report,* 600,000 volunteer referrals were made through their website, resulting in 78% volunteering at least once. In the United States, 3% of those with Internet access performed some virtual volunteering such as mentoring, tutoring, or website development in 2000.

Volunteerism declined from 1998 to 2000, but in response to the terrorist attacks on September 11, 2001, millions of people volunteered their time to help the victims of the attacks and the victims of the war in Afghanistan. Building on this spirit of volunteerism, in the State of the Union Address of January 29, 2002, President George W. Bush proposed that every American volunteer at least 4,000 hours over the rest of his or her lifetime. Will America answer this call?

Sources: U.S. Census Bureau. *Statistical Abstract of the United States*: *1994, 1996, 1998, 1999,* and *2001. Giving and Volunteering in the United States, 2001: Key Findings*, Washington D.C.: INDEPENDENT SECTOR, 2002. Retrieved February 6, 2002 from http://www.independentsector.org/PDFs/GV01keyfind.pdf. *VolunteerMatch 2001 Annual Report.* Retrieved February 14, 2002 from http://www.impactonline.org/about/VM2001AR.pdf. Points of Light Foundation."President Bush's State of the Union Address – Excerpts." Retrieved February 14, 2002 from http://www.pointsoflight.org/pressroom/StateofUnion .htm.

---

[8] Volunteers work out of the home using a computer. In February 2002, The VolunteerMatch website posted over 4,600 virtual volunteering opportunities. Data from http://www.impactonline.org/virtual/.

[9] VolunteerMatch is an online resource for matching volunteers and organizations nationwide. Organizations looking for volunteers post ads on the VolunteerMatch website. Potential volunteers search the database of volunteer opportunities and are directed to the organization needing the volunteer.

Religious Membership

Membership of Religious Bodies, 1890-2001

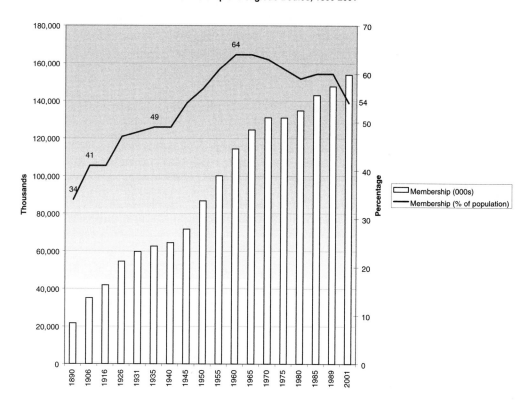

Membership in religious bodies has been rising steadily — with the population — since 1890, the first year of reliable figures, but membership as a percent of the total population has been in decline since its peak in 1960, when 64% of the population belonged to churches of some kind.

The curve is the most interesting feature of this graphic. It seems to suggest that the late 19th century was, in some way, much less "religious" than mid-20th century America or, for that matter, America in the first year of the 21st century. In 1890, only 34% of the U.S. population was enrolled in religious organizations. In 2001, the number was 54%. Are we looking at "religiousness" or at something else? Most people, if asked, might say that people in the past were much more religious than they are now.

The first issue to explore is the nature of the data. Membership in religious bodies is not a question asked in the 10-year censuses of the United States. It is information collected by each religious body, and different denominations or faiths have different definitions of membership; these also have changed over time. Some churches report all baptisms; others report only "communicants," usually persons 13 years and older. Large denominations collect data in a systematic manner and record results on forms. Others use baptismal records. Yet others poll local churches for estimates. Data published by the Census often have been "the latest available data," not data for a given year. People collecting and transmitting data may be highly trained in statistical methods or trained not at all.

All this, perhaps, underlines the meaning of "separation of church and state." In fact, these data may be considered just rough approximations. In general, reporting included *fewer* actual members in the early portion of this series than in later — in one case heads of households only were reported by a major group, later all members of the religion. Therefore the low figures in the early years and the much higher ones in later years probably come from changing definitions, the mix of religious denominations, and other similar factors — not least urbanization and growing statistical sophistication as time advanced.

The increase in membership that peaked in 1960 — and the decline thereafter — might be understood (all things being equal) as yet another phenomenon of the Baby Boom — which was itself the consequence of war, another condition that causes people to look inward. The sharp rise in membership, as a percent of population, begins in 1940 and peaks as the Baby Boom approaches its maturity. Many families become active in religious bodies as their children reach a certain age. The falling off in membership that comes thereafter very well may be largely a demographic phenomenon, although cultural forces probably play a role as well.

In the next panel, we look at attendance at religious services as it relates to membership in religious bodies.

Sources: U.S. Census Bureau. *Statistical Abstract of the United States*: 1980, 1992 and *2001.* U.S. Census Bureau. *Historical Statistics of the United States: Colonial Times to 1970.* 2001 data: U.S. Census Bureau. "National Population Estimates." Retrieved February 15, 2002 from http://eire.census.gov/popest/data/national.php. Barry A. Kosmin, et. al. *American Religious Identification Survey 2001,* December 19, 2001. Retrieved February 15, 2002 from http://www.gc.cuny.edu/studies/aris.pdf.

Religious Attendance

Adult Religious Membership vs. Attendance, 1957-2000

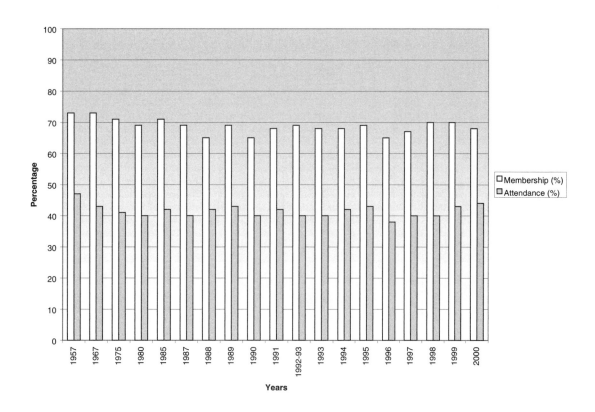

The chart shows the percentage of the adult population who are members of a religion and the percentage of the population that attend religious services. Adult religious membership and attendance has remained fairly steady over the years. A little more than half of those claiming membership in a religion actually attend religious services.

During most years, as religious membership increased, so did attendance, and vice versa. In 1992-1993, however, membership went up, but attendance went down. The opposite was true for 1988 and 2000. In both of these years, membership was down, but attendance went up from the previous year. Therefore, there isn't always a direct relationship between membership in a religion and attendance at religious services.

The next panel discusses youth religious attendance.

Sources: U.S. Census Bureau. *Statistical Abstract of the United States*: *1990, 1991, 1995, 1996*, and *2001*.

Our Youth: Religious Attitudes and Attendance

Religious Attitudes and Attendance: 12th Graders

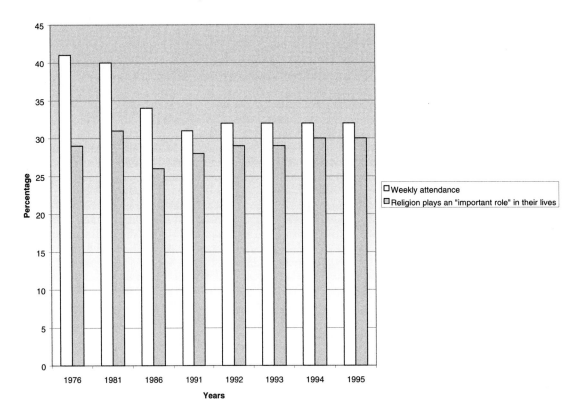

Religious attendance by 12th graders has fallen off sharply since the mid-1970s, but the percentage of 12th graders that feel religion has an important role in their lives has increased. Since 1986, the percentage has been rising and by 1995, the percentage that attend religious services and who feel religion plays an important role in their lives was nearly identical. In recent years, many religious bodies have tried new ways of worship to appeal to youth. Has it been working?

What about attitudes and attendance of younger children? The following table shows the percentage of 8th and 10th graders who attend weekly religious services and the percentage of those who feel that religion plays an important role in their lives. As the table on the next page and the graph above show, consistently just shy of a third of all 8th, 10th, and 12th graders feel that religion plays an important part in their lives, but as children get older, the percentage attending weekly religious services drops. In 1995, 42% of 8th graders attended weekly religious services. That same year, only 32% of 12th graders attended weekly religious services.

Religious Attitudes and Attendance: Percentage of 8th and 10th Graders

	1991	1992	1993	1994	1995
8th graders:					
Weekly attendance	46	43	42	42	42
Religion plays an "important role" in their lives	29	27	30	30	30
10th graders:					
Weekly attendance	38	39	40	37	37
Religion plays an "important role" in their lives	29	28	29	28	29

The next panel shows the 15 religions that have seen the largest growth from 1990-2000.

Source: Office of the Assistant Secretary for Planning and Evaluation. U.S. Department of Health and Human Services. *Trends in the Well-Being of America's Children and Youth, 1997 Edition*, 1997. Retrieved February 11, 2002 from http://aspe.hhs.gov/hsp/97trends/sd1-3.htm.

Top Growing Religions, 1990-2000

Top 15 Growing Religions, 1990-2000

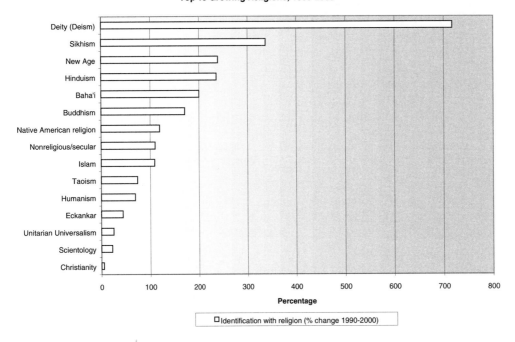

The chart shows the top 15 religions that showed the biggest percentage increase in membership from 1990 to 2000 in the United States. This list reflects the growing diversity of the American population. In some ways it also reflects a growing openness to new ideas, as reflected by the growth in New Age religions. It also reflects a growing secularism in our society: those identifying themselves as having no religion grew by 110% (14.4 million people) in this time period[10]. Although not seen on the graph, two religions that saw declines in their population were Judaism (a decrease of 306,000 people) and Agnosticism (a decrease of 195,000).

Keep in mind that the graphic shows percent growth — not actual numbers of people. Groups with the highest rates of growth, in the graph, have relatively low numbers. The table on the next page provides actual counts for the belief systems shown on the graph. The first column shows changes in the number of people identifying with the belief. The second column provides the actual count of people who hold these beliefs. The system with the greatest *numerical* growth has been Secularism, followed by Christianity. Deity, leading on the chart, is a small group of only 49,000 people — most of whom have embraced Deity since 1990.

---

[10] The growth of Deism also relates to the growing secularism in our society. A Deist believes in God, but denies religion. His beliefs are based on nature and reason, rather than faith.

Population Change, 1990-2000 and Adult Population Per Religion, 2001

	Population change (1990-2000)	Adult population (2001 est.)
Nonreligious/secular	14,423,000	27,539,000
Christianity	7,805,000	159,030,000
Buddhism	681,000	1,082,000
Islam	577,000	1,104,000[11]
Hinduism	539,000	766,000
Unitarian Universalism	127,000	629,000
Baha'i	56,000	84,000
Native American religion	56,000	103,000
New Age	48,000	68,000
Sikhism	44,000	57,000
Deity (Deism)	43,000	49,000
Humanist	20,000	49,000
Taoism	17,000	40,000
Scientology	10,000	55,000
Eckankar	8,000	26,000

Source: "Largest Religious Groups in the United States of America." Retrieved February 7, 2002 from http://adherents.com/rel_USA.html. "Deism Defined." Retrieved February 22, 2002 from http://www.deism.com/deism_defined.htm.

---

[11] This number reflects data in the source used by the editor. Other sources estimate the number of American Muslims between 2.8 million (a study released by the American Jewish Committee in October 2001) and 8 million (newspaper accounts in 2001). The 2000 edition of *Yearbook of American and Canadian Churches* estimates there are 3,950,000 Muslims in America.

Public Libraries and Bookmobiles

Public Libraries and Bookmobiles, 1993-1999

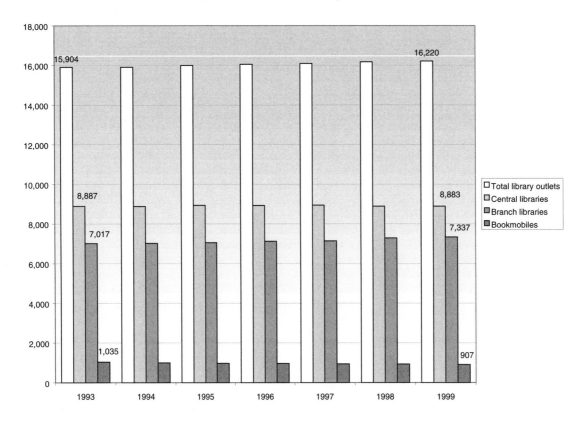

The number of public libraries[12] in the United States has increased since 1993 and the number of people served by them also has increased (from 255.5 million in 1994 to 270.9 million in 1999). In 1993 there were 8,929 public libraries. By 1999, this number had grown to 9,046. This growth has not been steady. In 1996 there were 35 fewer public libraries than in 1995. 1997 saw an increase of 21 public libraries but 1998 saw three fewer. 1999, however, saw an increase of 82 public libraries.

The chart above shows the total number of library outlets[1], the number of central libraries and branch libraries, and the number of bookmobiles for the years 1993-1999. The total number of library outlets has gone up over the years, much of this due to the expansion of branch libraries. The number of central libraries has decreased, as has the number of bookmobiles. This suggests that libraries are consolidating their administrative services, but building more branches to reach out to more neighborhoods. With more branches in the neighborhoods, the need for bookmobiles has decreased. Will this trend continue?

---

[12] A public library is an administrative entity. It may or may not have branch libraries. If it has branch libraries, the public library becomes a central library and contains the administrative services that oversee the branch libraries' operations. A public library outlet is either a central public library or a branch library.

On February 4, 2002, President George W. Bush proposed a $13 million increase in funding for public libraries ($181.7 million total spending for libraries) in his administration's fiscal year 2003 budget. On the same day, the state of Hawaii announced that it would have to close some library branches and cut hours and service at others. According to the same news report, a new public library branch in Kapolei (set to open in July 2003) may have to stand empty due to budget constraints. How can this happen?

The next panel looks at the funding of public libraries.

Sources: Chart data: National Center for Education Statistics. U.S. Department of Education. *Public Libraries in the United States: 1993, 1994, 1995, 1996, 1997, 1998,* and *1999,* various publication dates. Retrieved February 18, 2002 from http://nces.ed.gov. "Bush Budget Boosts Recruitment, Funds School Libraries." *American Libraries*, February 11, 2002. "Hawaii's Libraries Face Cuts in Hours, Service." *American Libraries*, February 11, 2002.

Public Library Funding

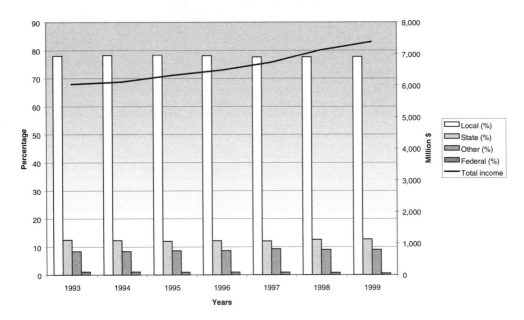

Public Library Funding, 1993-1999
Total income in constant 2000 dollars (right axis)

The chart shows the total income (in constant 2000 dollars) of public libraries and the percentage of that income paid by the various levels of government and other sources from 1993-1998. The amount of funding libraries receive has risen sharply since 1993. Funding has increased by more than $1.3 billion from 1993, reaching $7.3 billion in 1999. Local governments average 78% of the funding burden, with state government coming in a distant second, picking up an average 12.3%. Funds from other sources, such as fees, private philanthropy, and fundraising averaged 8.8% of the total. The Federal government only contributed an average of 0.9% to the total funding of public libraries.

This type of funding structure relies heavily on local tax millages and, in some cases, penal fines to fund public libraries. Therefore, the amount public libraries receive varies from city to city and county to county. Some advocates for funding reform have done studies pointing out the inequities in funding legislation at the state level as well. In Michigan, for example, a study by the Public Library Funding Initiative Group (PLFIG) showed that state legislation shortchanged public libraries in that state by more than $22 million in 1998 alone – it did not take inflation into consideration.

Despite the inequities and relatively heavy tax burden, in 2001 taxpayers passed more library funding referenda than they rejected. In Ohio and Virginia, for example, many municipalities approved funding measures for libraries while rejecting other tax issues.

Where is the funding going? Most of it is not going towards books, magazines, or other media. During this time period (1993-1999), 64.6% of the funding went for staff salaries, 20.2% went for such things as repair or replacement of furnishings and equipment and maintenance and operational costs of the buildings. Only 15.1% of the funding was spent on library collections[13]. More libraries are providing access to electronic services and the Internet (Internet access increased from 20.9% of libraries having the service in 1994 to 92.4% having it in 1999). Expenditures on these services averaged 3.6% of the total operating expenditures[14].

With the Internet bringing virtual libraries such as The Internet Public Library (http://www.ipl.org) into 50.5% of homes in the United States in 2001 (an increase of 24.3% since 1998), do most people still use their local public library?

Sources: Chart data and funding averages: National Center for Education Statistics. U.S. Department of Education. *Public Libraries in the United States: 1993, 1994, 1995, 1996, 1997, 1998,* and *1999,* various publication dates. Retrieved February 18, 2002 from http://nces.ed.gov. 2000 constant dollar data was extrapolated using CPI data from the U.S. Bureau of Labor Statistics and the U.S. Bureau of Economic Analysis. Michigan data: Charles R. McClure, et. al. *Creating Stability and Equity in Michigan Public Libraries: Ending the Crisis,* January 2001. Retrieved February 20, 2002 from http://www.kpl.gov/plfig/final_report.htm. Referendum data: "Referenda Roundup 2001: Libraries Get the Voters' Approval." *American Libraries,* 2001. Retrieved February 19, 2002 from http://www.ala.org/alonline/news/ referenda2001.html. Internet data: Economic and Statistics Administration. U.S. Department of Commerce. "Percent of U.S. Households with Internet Access, By U.S., Rural, Urban, and Central Cities, 1998, 2000, 2001." Retrieved February 19, 2002 from http://www.esa.doc.gov; Sarah Ormes and Charles R. McClure. "A Comparison of Public Library Internet Connectivity in the USA and UK." Retrieved February 20, 2002 from http://www.ukoln.ac.uk/publib/USAUK1.htm

---

[13] All percentages are averages for the years 1993-1999. The sum of percentages will not equal 100 due to rounding.

[14] Averages are for the years 1997-1999. No data were collected on expenditures for access to electronic services and the Internet before 1997.

Public Library Usage

Library Usage, in Millions, 1993-1999

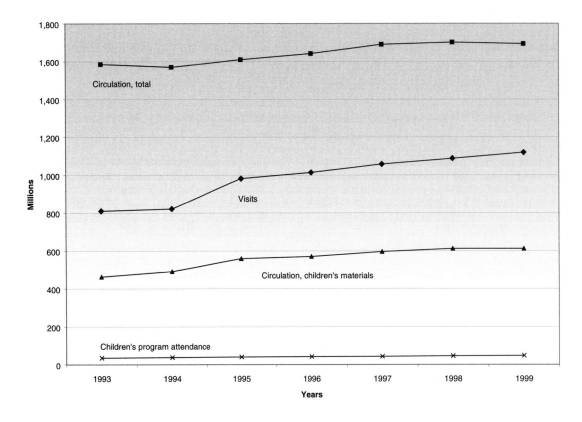

Overall, the number of visits, circulation, and attendance at children's program at libraries has increased throughout the 1993 to 1999 period. But the number of visits to a public library (4.3 per capita in 1999) has increased at a greater rate than circulation. In fact, total circulation went down by about 7.8 million materials between the years 1998 and 1999 while the number of visits went up by over 31.7 million. This may indicate that more people went to the library solely to take advantage of Internet access offered. In 1998, only 26.2% of households had Internet access at home, but 87.8% of libraries offered this service. Although the percentage of households with Internet access at home increased 58% from 1998 to 2000, a majority of households still did not have Internet access at home in 2000. However, 95.7% of libraries offered the service in 2000. In 2001, 5.4% of the population (15.4 million) accessed the Internet from public libraries.

More of us continue to take advantage of all the services offered by public libraries. The following table shows the number of households using the various public library services in 1996[15]. A little over a third of households didn't use any public library services.

Households Using Public Library Services in the Past Month, 1996

	Number of households (estimate)[16]
Borrow or drop off books or tapes	35,671,680
Other purpose, such as a lecture, story hour, or use of equipment	17,835,840
Calling library to renew books or for information other than hours or directions	13,872,320
Using a home computer to link to a public library	3,963,520
Having library materials mailed or delivered to the home	1,981,760
Visiting a bookmobile	1,981,760
Not using a public library in the past month	55,489,280

Why did we use public library services? The following table shows the percentage of households that use the library for selected reasons. The percentages do not add to 100 because a single household could have multiple reasons for using a public library. Also, some households did not use a public library in the previous month.

Reasons for Using a Public Library, 1996

	% of all households (estimate)
Enjoyment of hobbies, including borrowing books or tapes or attending activities	32
To get information for personal use, such as consumer or health issues, investments, etc.	20
For a school or class assignment	19
For a work assignment or to keep up to date at work	8
To get information to help find a job	5
For a program or activity designed for children ages 6 to 12	4
For an activity for children under age 6	4
To work with a tutor or take a class to learn to read	1

Sources: National Center for Education Statistics. U.S. Department of Education. *Public Libraries in the United States: 1993, 1994, 1995, 1996, 1997, 1998,* and *1999,* various publication dates. Retrieved February 18, 2002 from http://nces.ed.gov. Internet data: U.S. Census Bureau. *National Population Estimates.* Retrieved February 20, 2002 from http://eire.census.gov/popest/ data/national.php. U.S. Department of Commerce. *A Nation Online: How Americans Are Expanding Their Use of the Internet.* February 2002. Retrieved February 19, 2002 from http://www.esa.doc.gov. Data for 1996 tables: National Center for Education Statistics. U.S. Department of Education. "Use of Public Library Services by Households in the United States: 1996." *Statistics in Brief,* February 1997. Retrieved February 18, 2002 from http://nces.ed.gov/pubs/97446.pdf. U.S. Census Bureau. *Statistical Abstract of the United States: 2001.*

---

[15] The last year for which data is available. Data based on survey questions relating to public library use for the past month. Interviews were conducted from January 1996 to April 1996, therefore data are based on library use from December 1995-March 1996.

[16] A single household could be included in multiple activities.

Adult Education: Job Training or Leisure Activity?

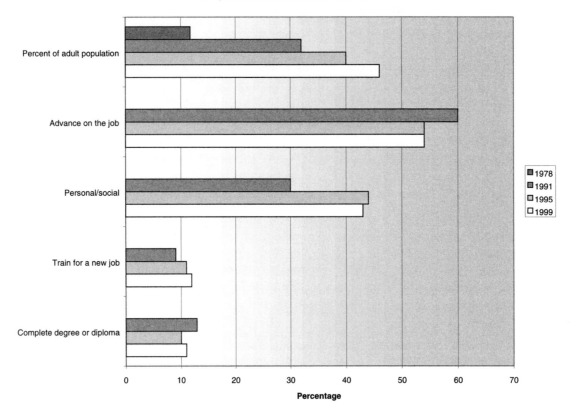

The chart above shows the percentage of the adult population that participated in adult education during the years 1978-1999. The chart also shows the percentage of those participating for various reasons from 1991 to 1999[17].

The percentage of the adult population participating in adult education has soared since 1978 (from 11.8% of the adult population in 1978 to 46% in 1999). In 1978, 18.2 million people were enrolled in adult education classes. By 1999, the number had reached 90 million. By contrast, the number of adults enrolled in degree programs at colleges and universities was 11.3 million and 15 million, respectively.

Advancement on the job continues to be the top reason people participate in adult education, but in the mid- to late-1990s, participation in adult education was becoming more and more of a social activity. From 1991 to 1999, 6% fewer adults took adult education classes to advance on their job, but 13% more adults took classes for personal development and socializing.

---

[17] Because participants in adult education may have more than one reason for taking adult education classes, percentages may not add to 100.

A higher percentage of adults are also taking adult education classes to train for a new job, but a lower percentage of adults participated in order to complete a degree or obtain a diploma.

Do men and women participate in adult education equally? Do they both have the same reasons for taking adult education courses? Have these reasons changed over time? The next panel will look at gender differences in adult education.

Sources: U.S. Census Bureau. *Statistical Abstract of the United States: 1980, 1994, 1996,* and *2001.* Kwang Kim and Sean Creighton. "Participation in Adult Education in the United States: 1998-99." *Statistics in Brief,* November 1999. Retrieved February 21, 2002 from http://nces.ed.gov.

Adult Education: Are Men and Women Equal?

Gender Differences in Adult Education, 1991 and 1999

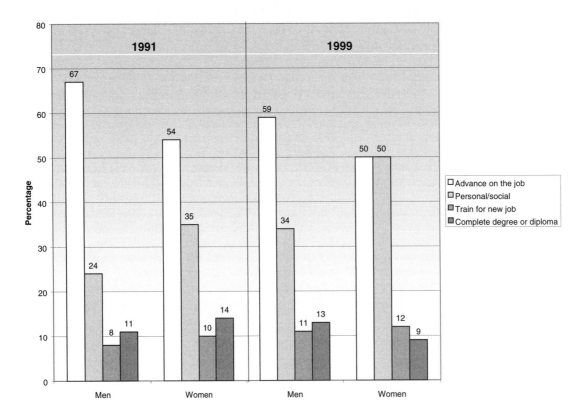

Do men and women attend adult education classes just to meet each other, to socialize, to achieve personal goals? No. The predominant object, both in 1991 and in 1999, for both sexes, was advancement on the job, if more so for men than for women. But the trend toward education to achieve personal goals is certainly there. This motivation increased among men and reached to a level nearly equal to that for women eight years earlier in 1999, and, among the ladies, advancement on the job and personal goals had the same rank for seeking adult education in 1999.

Large numbers of adults are engaged in this form of education. In 1991, 32% of both adult males and females — 25.9 million men and 31.5 million women — were going to classes. By 1999, a smaller proportion of men (43%) and a larger of women (48%) were pressing school benches — 40.2 and 48.6 million respectively.

If "training for a job" is lumped in with "advancement on the job," then the overwhelming motivation for adult education is job related, in both periods, for men as well as women, and with increases in absolute numbers as well in percentages taken into account, the trends is that we are — ambitious. Again, the men slightly more so than the women. But, in the red-hot economy of the late 1990s, slightly less so than earlier.

Completing a degree or obtaining a diploma ranked third among both sexes in 1991, third among men only in 1999. But this category, in any case, hovers just at or above the 10% mark throughout this period.

In the next panel we try to factor in the educational attainment of those taking adult education? How many are engaged in education as a quest that should never end?

Sources: U.S. Census Bureau. *Statistical Abstract of the United States: 1994* and *2001*.

Adult Education: Supplement to a College Degree?

Reasons for Participating in Adult Education, by Educational Attainment, 1999

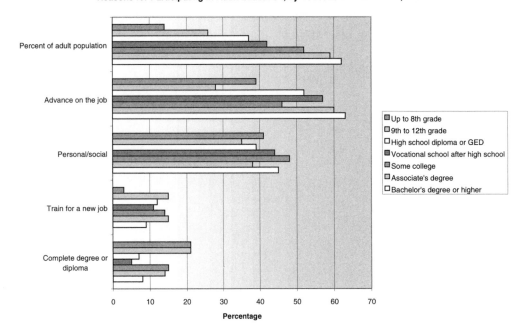

The chart above shows the percentage of the adult population who participates in adult education by educational attainment level. The chart also shows the reasons participants take adult education classes (percentage of participants by educational attainment level[18]).

The more educated people are, the greater likelihood of them taking adult education classes. Sixty-two percent of adults with a Bachelor's degree or higher took adult education classes in 1999, but only 14% of adults with up to an 8th grade education took adult education classes that same year — the educated get more educated.

The table below ranks the reasons adults participate in adult education by educational attainment level. Advancement on the job remains the top reason for taking classes for those with a high school diploma, GED, vocational school education, or Associate's degree or higher. In fact, those with a Bachelor's degree or higher have the highest percentage of participants (63%) in this category. Those with a 9th to 12th grade education are the least likely (28%) to take classes for this reason. Personal development and social interaction is the second most popular reason for taking adult education classes for those with a diploma, GED, degree, or vocational education after high school.

---

[18] Percentages may not add to 100 because participants may have more than one reason for taking adult education classes.

For those with less than a high school diploma and for those with some college, but no degree, the top reason for taking adult education classes was personal development and social interaction, followed by advancement on the job. Those with some college had the highest percentage in this category (48%), and those with a 9th to 12th grade education had the lowest percentage at 35%.

Those with less than a high school diploma and those with some college or an Associate's degree are more likely than any other group to be taking adult education classes to complete a degree or a diploma. Those with vocational school education after high school are the least likely to take classes to complete a degree.

Training for a new job is the third most popular reason for taking adult education classes among those with an Associate's degree. Those with a 9th to 12th grade education are just as likely to train for a new job by using adult education as those with an Associate's degree (15% for both). Those with up to an 8th grade education are the least likely to be taking adult education classes for this reason (3%).

Reasons for Participating in Adult Education, Ranked Within Educational Attainment Categories, 1999

Educational attainment	Advance on the job	Personal/ social	Train for a new job	Complete degree or diploma
Up to 8th grade	2	1	4	3
9th to 12th grade	2	1	4	3
High school diploma or GED	1	2	3	4
Vocational school after high school	1	2	3	4
Some college	2	1	4	3
Associate's degree	1	2	3	4
Bachelor's degree or higher	1	2	3	4

Does all this signal a trend in continuing education? What does this say about the value of a high school diploma or college degree? Advancing technology and increased globalization has led to the need for many employees to update their knowledge and skills in their current field every few years. Many colleges and universities have adapted to this type of student. Many offer evening and weekend classes. Some schools have branches out in the community, or, in the case of The University of Phoenix, branches in multiple states. Some set up branches within company buildings. Santa Clara University, for example, set up a branch within National Semiconductor in Sunnyvale, California. Distance learning has also become more popular. According to the United States Distance Learning Association, 2.3 million students will be taking distance learning courses over the next few years.

All work and no play? Not necessarily. Taking adult education classes for personal development or social interaction ranks either first or second among all educational attainment levels. With the Baby Boomers retiring and having more leisure time to pursue personal interests, will personal development and social interaction become the top reason overall for adults participating in adult education? Maybe — if the markets don't dip.

Sources: U.S. Bureau of the Census. *Statistical Abstract of the United States 2001*. 121st ed. Washington, DC: U.S. Government Printing Office, 2002. Speer, Tibbet L. "A Nation of Students." *American Demographics* (August 1996). United States Distance Learning Association. "Resources: Distance Learning Link Program (DLLP)." Online. Available: http://www.usdla.org/html/resources/dllp.htm. February 22, 2002.

Chapter 13

People and the Internet

In December 1969, ARPA (Advanced Research Projects Agency) went online, connecting four major universities. It was for research, education, and government purposes, and provided a communications network in the event of a national emergency. This research and communications network would soon be known as the Internet.

As the technology became more advanced, the system rapidly developed. According to the Internet Society, the earliest e-mail was introduced in 1972; domain names such as .com and .edu appeared in 1984; the term "World Wide Web" appeared about 1989; commerce sites were established around 1994. With the good comes the bad, however: for all those pesky marketing e-mails, we coined the term "spamming" in the same year.

The Internet is now reference tool and entertainment device. We play games, send photos to Grandma, order the latest bestsellers, try on new identities in chatrooms and do research for the big report due on Monday. This chapter offers some insight into this technology that has so changed our lives.

The first panels in this chapter offer an overview of the Internet. Searching the Internet clearly has become one of our favorite leisure activities, while others (reading) have paid a price. Other panels will address the basic question: who is using the Internet? Recent data dispel the myth that the World Wide Web is just for the young and affluent.

Final panels in this chapter address some of the highlights of the Web: auctions, online term searching and online dating (a different kind of searching altogether). These panels are slightly lighter in tone. We'll look at the most popular search terms to see what they reveal about our interests and habits. We'll look at the phenomenon of eBay auctions. We'll also look at online personals and dating to see if this technology helps us find true love.

The Shift to High-Tech Entertainment

Our Time Spent On Selected Entertainment

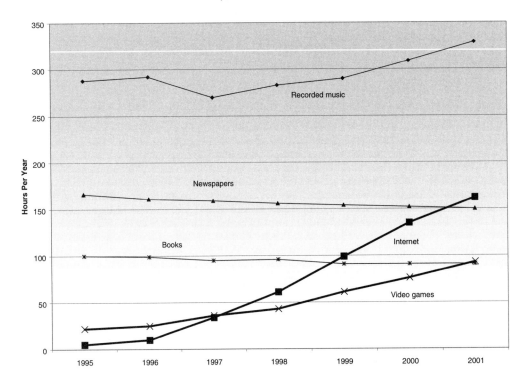

The graph shows the hours spent per person per year on selected entertainment. Figures come from the *Communications Industry Forecast* by Veronis, Suhler & Associates. Data for 2000 and 2001 are projected.

The figures show how quickly the Internet and home video games have found a place in our lives. The average estimated time spent online jumped from 5 hours per person in 2000 to 162 hours per person in 2001. Playing video games saw a steady increase as well; average per-person time jumped from an estimated 22 hours to 93 hours a year.

It's interesting to see how this compares to other leisure activities. The champion of home entertainment is still television (not shown) which has seen only a minor increase in time spent watching since the 1,580 hours estimated to have been spent on it in 1995. We are spending more time listening to music, true; however, generally we are "multi-tasking" (doing something else at the same time). Also, with the growth of online music services and music trading, there could be a link between the music and Internet categories.

So, what's going on here? Clearly, more items are competing for leisure time. The Internet and video games have stolen away time spent reading; we're spending less time, per person, on books and newspapers. Newspapers in particular saw a drop in time used. Why? We get our news and social commentary from television, radio, and online sources. Indeed, the newspaper industry has seen a rash of consolidations and a drop in circulation and advertising. But research offers one interesting anomaly: Internet users — and particularly those who read their news online — are more likely than other Americans to be print newspaper readers, too, according to the Newspaper Association of America and *Research Alert.*

Our leisure time increasingly is becoming ordered around the television and computer: either in pay television and high-definition TV sets or in MP3 players and digital picture processing. So, who is online? What do they do there?

The following panels will present data on the demographics of the online world.

Sources: "Entertainment & Leisure." *Research Alert*, January 5, 2001, p. 6. U.S. Census Bureau, *Statistical Abstract of the United States: 2001*, Washington D.C. 2001.

Who Uses the Internet: By Race

Internet Population by Race

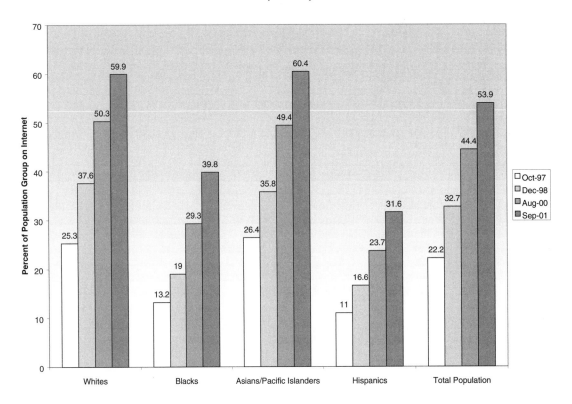

According to the Department of Commerce, as of September 2001, roughly 149 million Americans were using the Internet (about 54% of the population). Two million new Internet users join the Internet every month.

The graphic shows the online population by race from 1997 to 2001. Access has increased across the board, with African Americans and Hispanics seeing the strongest rates of growth. Between 1997 and 2001, black participation on the Internet increased by 201.5%, Hispanic participation by 187.3%, Asian/Pacific Islander presence by 128.8%, and white participation by 136.8%.

Populations with the highest household incomes were first on the Internet. Those with less disposable income typically adopt new technologies more slowly and cautiously. In this period, the importance of the Internet became widely known, and everybody has been joining in. At the same time, the costs of PCs and Internet access also have been trending down.

Among the races and ethnic groups, whites and Asians/Pacific Islanders have Internet participation shares higher than their shares in the population, as shown in the table on the following page, blacks and people of Hispanic origin have lower participation shares. But the gaps are closing.

Population Shares and Internet Participation Shares

Race/Ethnic Group	2000		2001	
	Population %	Internet participation %	Population %	Internet participation %
White – non-Hispanic	71.5	81.0	71.0	78.9
Black – non-Hispanic	12.2	8.0	12.2	9.0
Asian/Pacific Islander	3.8	4.2	4.0	4.4
Hispanic Origin	11.8	6.3	12.1	7.1

This shows that while 59.9% of whites had Internet access in 2001, whites had 78.9% of all Internet collections. Another fact is shown: While non-Hispanic whites had a 71% share of the population, they had a 78.9% share of Internet Access. Blacks and Hispanics have some distance to go before they are as "wired" as the other two population groups.

Source: U.S. Department of Commerce, Economics and Statistics Administration, National Telecommunications and Information Administration, *A Nation Online: How Americans Are Expanding Their Use of the Internet*, February 2002.

Who Uses the Internet? By Age

Internet Population by Age Group

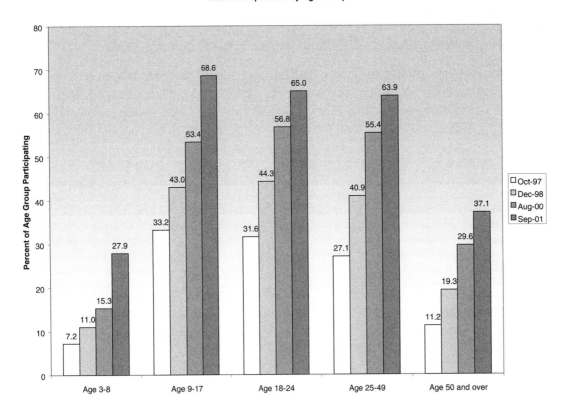

We've seen that more than half of the American population goes online. Computers and technology are traditionally seen as the domain of the young. But is this true? This panel examines the Internet population by age.

The data above offer some keen insights into the online phenomenon. The fact that the data begin with preschoolers and toddlers speaks to how the Internet has come to dominate our lives: children go online both for educational and entertainment purposes and, accordingly, many online organizations have taken notice and focused their marketing efforts on children (for better or worse).

Those 24 years old and younger had high percentages of their age groups online. This age group does tend to be techno-savvy and its members use the Internet for research, entertainment, and communicating with friends. But those 25 years and older saw the most dynamic growth rates: people 50 and older are the fastest growing segment of the group.

The online population also roughly follows the demographics of the general population, as seen in the table below (statistics come from Mediamark Research). The median age of online users is slightly lower than is the median age of the population, although not by much: 39 years old vs. 43 years old.

General Population vs. Internet Population

Age	All U.S. Adults (%)	Online Users (%)
18-24	13	17
25-34	20	23
35-44	23	26
45-54	17	21
55-64	11	9
65 and over	16	4

Another way to carve up these numbers: from 1996 to 2000, the share of the online population 35 and older has increased from 52% to 62%; the share for 18-34 year-olds has fallen from 48% to 38%. According to *A Nation Online,* while 18-35 year-olds tend to use the Web more for entertainment, those 35 and above have a different agenda. On-line banking, shopping, and gathering health information all ranked high on the list of their frequent activities (and keeping in contact with loved ones through e-mail, of course — this is every group's favorite activity).

Source: U.S. Department of Commerce, Economics and Statistics Administration, National Telecommunications and Information Administration, *A Nation Online: How Americans Are Expanding Their Use of the Internet*, February 2002.

Who Uses the Internet? By Income

Internet Households by Income

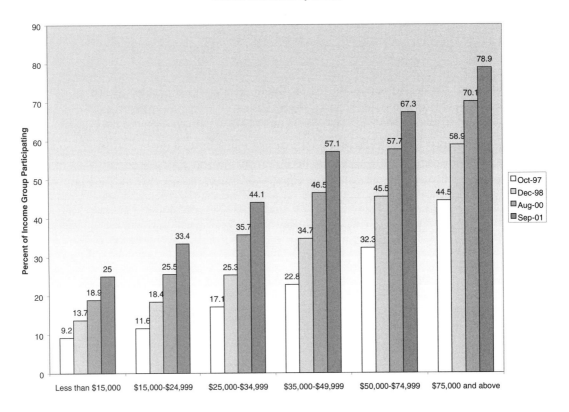

The panel examines the online population by income. Those with higher income do have a stronger presence online; however, it is important to see that the Internet has been embraced by every segment of the population.

Those with an income of $75,000 or more make up roughly 30% of online households. This figure is expected to fall to about 25% by 2005 (according to Jupiter Research) as individuals with lower incomes move onto the Internet. Between December 1998 and September 2001, Internet use by individuals in the lowest income range (those earning less than $15,000 a year) saw a 25% annual growth rate. Those in the highest range ($75,000 or more a year) saw an annual growth of 11%.

Is the average Internet user wealthier than the average American? Yes. But the field is becoming more level, depending on whose numbers you use. According to Jupiter Research, the average income of the online user has fallen from about $63,000 in 1996 to $59,000 in 2000. This is just above the mean income of $57,045 for all households. A study by Insight Express found the typical online household's income fell from $62,700 in 1996 to $49,800 in 2001, which is slightly more than the $42,148 median income for all households (according to the Census). Mediamark Research placed the median income of Internet users at $65,466 in Spring 2000. While the numbers may vary, they all make the same point: that income is becoming less of an impediment to participating on the

World Wide Web. Similarly, the online population and general population are beginning to look identical. One is inclined to nod in agreement. It's everywhere, it's everywhere!

Sources: "Access Up, Divide Shrinks." *Industry Standard*, June 26, 2000, p. 186; Michael Pastore. "Online Customers Now the Average Consumer." Retrieved February 1, 2002 from the World Wide Web: http://cyberatlas.internet.com; "Online Households." *Investor's Business Daily*, November 27, 2000, p. A10; U.S. Department of Commerce, Economics and Statistics Administration, National Telecommunications and Information Administration, *A Nation Online: How Americans Are Expanding Their Use of the Internet*, February 2002.

Who Uses the Internet? By Gender

Online Population by Gender

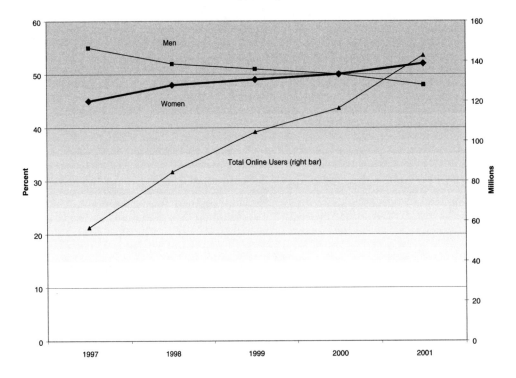

Recent statistics show that more women use the Internet than men do.

Roughly 73 million women were Internet users as of September 2001, compared to 69.5 million men for this period. According to the source, women between the ages of 20 and 50 are more likely than men are to be Internet users; however, of those 60 and above, men have higher rates of Internet use than women do.

There may be more women on the Internet, but men spend more time there. According to Nielsen/NetRatings, men spent more time online, logged on more often, and viewed more pages:

Time Spent On Line

Measure	Male Surfers Dec. 2000	Female Surfers Dec. 2000	Male Surfers Dec. 2001	Female Surfers December 2001
Average time spent (hh:mm:ss)	9:42:14	7:44:57	11:20:27	9:06:51
Number of sessions	18	15	21	17
Average pages viewed	667	503	801	573

The source points out that during this period, men viewed 40% more pages than women did and logged onto the Internet 24% more times than women did.

What have women been doing online? According to *A Nation Online*, women used e-mail and searched for jobs at roughly the same rates as men. Women are more inclined to search for health information online than men are (39.8% compared to 29.6%). More men still shop online than women do, but the numbers for females have been spiking: 29% of online shoppers in September 1997 were female, while 38% of them were in April 1999, according to a study by CommerceNet Consortium and Nielsen Media Research. The same study found that the number of online purchases by women had increased 80%, with growth rates over 100% in categories such as CDs, videos, clothing, and computer hardware.

Sources: "Number of Female Web Surfers Grow Faster Than Overall Internet Population, According to Nielsen/NetRatings." Retrieved from the World Wide Web: http://www.nielsen-netratings.com; Chart data: "Access Up, Divide Shrinks." *Industry Standard*, June 26, 2000, p. 186; "Flexing Their Online Muscles." *New York Times*, July 12, 1999, p. C4. U.S. Census Bureau, *Statistical Abstract of the United States: 2001*, Washington D.C. 2001.

Who Uses the Internet? Young People

Kids and Teens Take to the Web

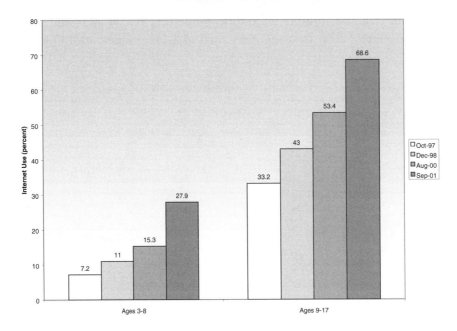

According to *A Nation Online*, more than 31 million individuals under the age of eighteen were using the Internet as of September 2001 (there are more than 65 million people under 18 in the United States). Slightly more than 13 million were using the Web in September 1997. The presence of young people on the Web is quite impressive: those between the ages of 12 and 17 now make up 12% of the Internet population in the United States, according to Media Metrix (an interesting side note: the figure is the same in Europe).

The graphic shows the percent of the age group that is Internet users. The numbers are vivid and fairly easy to explain: computers are simply a common and integral part of young people's lives. More than 50% of households with children own a computer, according to Computer Intelligence. The number of kids with classroom Web access is expected to jump from 1.5 million in 1996 to 20.2 million in 2002, according to Jupiter Research.

The favorite online activities for these age groups are probably no surprise. Kids 5-12 ranked e-mail, homework research, and game playing as their top online pursuits; top activities for teenagers were e-mail, using search engines, and instant messaging. There is a surprise to be found here, however: Jupiter Media Metrix shows that adults spent more time online than teenagers did and accessed the Web more often.

Average Monthly Net Use in Minutes

Date	Teens	Adults
June 2000	321	728
November 2000	272	858
April 2001	264	837

Average Monthly Net Access In Days

Date	Teens	Adults
June 2000	8.6	14.7
November 2000	8.9	15.7
April 2001	8.5	15.3

Why the discrepancy? Jupiter analysts have attributed it to teenagers' active schedules, having to share a computer with other family members, and perceiving the PC as an entertainment rather than as a productivity tool.

Teenagers aren't big online shoppers, either. Jupiter reports that in a recent survey, only 15% of teens purchased items online. Those who did purchased lower-priced items like CDs and books. Considering teenagers' limited income, this makes sense. Children, the next generation of credit card holders, are getting the message, too: a survey by NFO Interactive found that more than 50% of children have asked their parents to buy products they have seen while surfing the Internet. Kids and teens are expected to spend $4.9 billion in 2005, but the spending they promote offline is expected to exceed $21 billion for the same year. In short, advertising to teenagers and children pays off.

Some final observations about the data in the chart. Almost 30% of 3-8 year olds are online. Is this too young? Are they supervised? In a telling comment about children's technical proficiency with computers, *Wired* magazine quotes the general manager of Disclaiming: "it's rather common for a 3-year-old to understand the basics of using a mouse and clicking on pictures on a computer screen." Only a few years ago, "kids weren't usually comfortable using a mouse until the age of 6 or so."

What happened to stuffed animals, a good book, and an even better imagination?

Sources: Lake, David. "Teens Turn On, Tune In, Log Off." *Industry Standard*, July 23, 2001; Annette Hamilton. "Online Kids…Tomorrow's Opportunity." Retrieved online at http://zdnet.com.com/2001-11-0. Joanna Glaser. "Kid Surfers: Time to Buck Up!" *Wired,* September 2000; Michael Pastore. "Marketing to the Net's Future Means Marketing to Youths." Retrieved March 6, 2002 from http://cyberatlas.internet.com.

The Rise in Computer Hacking

As the Internet Grows, So Do Computer Attacks

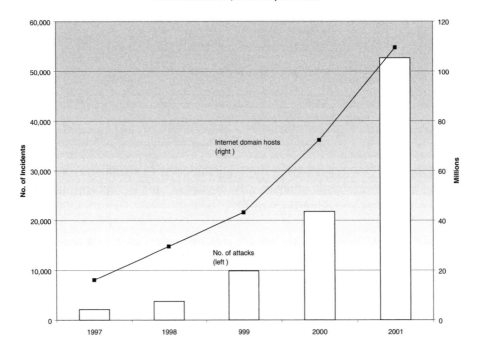

There has been a disturbing rise in the number of computer attacks, and experts expect that the numbers will increase. One study by the Omni Consulting Group showed that out of 3,000 surveyed businesses, security gaps cost between 5.7-7.7% of their annual revenue. Most losses come from viruses and worms and e-mail, although the cost in equipment and wasted hours can be enormous. Collins Consulting Group estimated the damages done by viruses and computer "cracking" in the U.S. at $266 billion in 1999. They estimate worldwide losses due to downtime from security breaches and virus attacks at $1.6 trillion.

From 1997 to 2001, the number of reported incidents skyrocketed from 2,134 in 1997 to 52,658 in 2001. Some of the monikers of these bugs and viruses will surely ring some bells: The Love Bug (2000) is estimated to have had $8.8 billion in economic impact worldwide; Code Red (2001) had about $2.6 billion; Melissa (1999) had roughly $1.1 billion.

During this same period the Internet took off. More homes steadily gained Internet access. Electronic commerce blossomed. We became a "global marketplace" and sensitive information was increasingly distributed electronically. The graphic shows the number of hosts as a way of showing how quickly the Internet grew to accommodate a population that was increasingly coming online: the number of Internet hosts increased from about 16.1 million in January 1997 to 109.5 million in January 2001.

How are we handling this growing threat? The research firm International Data Corp. reported in *USA TODAY* that companies and organizations are expected to spend $14 billion by 2005 to fend off threats to their computer networks, a 180% increase over spending in 2000. The nation drafted its first infrastructure-protection plan in 1999, a program to protect vital systems in case of a cyber attack. E-mails are regularly distributed about some new potential virus making its way through networks.

But we don't always take the message so seriously. Software giant Microsoft reports that downloads to fix a bug in their new XP operating system have been slow; the glitch leaves users with high-speed access vulnerable to a hackers.

One final observation: hackers have their own culture and vocabulary to explain (justify?) their actions. A PBS report points out that there is a code of ethics for hacking. A hacker will explore a computer system, but will not steal or vandalize; many actually feel it is their duty to identify security holes and report them to systems administrators. One who enters a computer system with the intent to vandalize it is considered a *cracker*.

Sources: Acohido, Byron. "Agency Raise the Bar On Tech Security." *USA TODAY*, February 27, 2002, p. 7B; "Internet Domain Survey." Retrieved February 28, 2002 from the World Wide Web: http://www.isc.org; "Enterprise Security Solutions to Combat Cyber-Terrorism." Retrieved online: http://www.collinscg.com; "Hacker Profile." Retrieved online: http://www.pbs.org.

The Most Popular Online Search Terms

Top Search Terms, March 1999 - January 2001

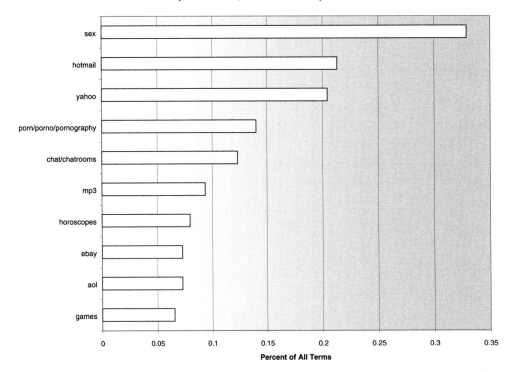

Alexa Research conducted a two-year study on the most popular search terms used in searching the Internet. Data are based on an examination of 42 million search pages viewed in aggregate by users of the Alexa toolbar at 10 of the Internet's leading portals and search engines: altavista.com, aol.com, excite.com, go.com, google.com, goto.com, lycos.com, msn.com, netscape.com and yahoo.com.

The most striking discovery in their research was that an alarming number of users are not particularly skilled in reaching their online destinations. Many portals were reached by typing the web address into the search engine as opposed to directly into the address field. In short, people searched for AOL by aol, aol.com and www.aol.com; yahoo was searched for as yahoo, yahoo.com and www.yahoo.com; hotmail and ebay were searched for using similar methods. This amazing discovery seems to suggest that even though more people own PCs and have Internet access, they don't seem to understand how these technologies work.

The popularity of sex terms probably isn't surprising. Sex was the top search term, comprising 0.3289% of all searches (or roughly 1 in every 300 terms). But we may not be as driven by our carnal impulses as it may look: according to the firm, the top 50 search terms account for less than 3% of all search terms views. We have some varied interests, to be sure. But they also point out that the 50 most popular Web sites receive 25 percent of the traffic. In spite of how varied out searching tastes may be, the Web is a lot more concentrated. We keep coming back to the same sites.

What, out of curiosity, were the most searched terms for the rest of 2001? The table below shows the top terms on two popular search engines (terms are ranked).

Lycos	Yahoo
Dragonball	Playstation 2
Britney Spears	Britney Spears
Napster	WWF
Tattoos	Dragon Ball Z
Osama Bin Laden	Napster
IRS	World Trade Center
Pokemon	Harry Potter & the Sorcerer's Stone
World Trade Center	Dale Earnhardt
Nostradamus	NASCAR
WWF	Internal Revenue Service

Some terms were more popular on one site than the other, but the table offers some insight into our preoccupations: online game playing (Dragonball, Playstation 2), celebrities (Britney Spears, Dale Earnhardt), researching information (IRS), or current events (Osama Bin Laden, World Trade Center).

Another point to make here: many of these terms speak to the interests of children. We've seen elsewhere in this chapter how children have taken to the Internet. Terms such as Dragonball and Harry Potter & the Sorcerer's Stone show how willing and adept children are at researching their interests.

Sources: "Search Engines, Browsers Still Confusing Many Web Users." Retrieved February 6, 2002 from the World Wide Web: http://www.cyberatlas.internet.com; "Lycos Web Most Wanted." Retrieved online at: http://50.lycos.com; "SearchDay." Retrieved online: http://www.searchenginewatch.com.

Looking for Love in All the Wired Places

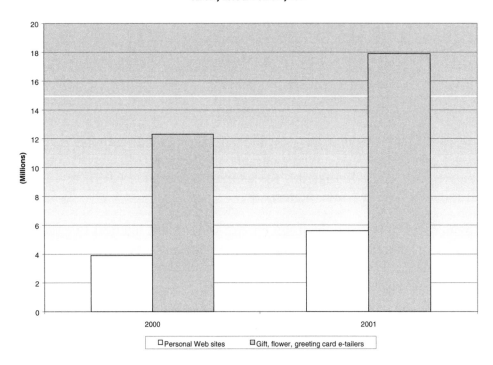

Visitors to "Relationship" Web Sites
January 2000 and January 2001

According the Census, in the year 2000 there were 48.2 million people over the age of 18 who have never married, 13.7 million who have been widowed and 19.8 million who are divorced. Some of these, of course, are people who are in some sort of serious relationship. But a number of these are unattached and looking for Mr. or Ms. Right (or *both*, for you swingers out there). They are fed up with sitting home with a good book on a Saturday night or enduring being fixed up with someone's cousin from out of town. They are turning to the Internet.

It makes perfect sense: the Internet has become a meeting place for all sorts of people of varying ages, intellects and interests. Just as we search for information on health care or shop for books and CDs, so have we begun shopping for mates. Part of the appeal must certainly come from the safety and anonymity that the online experience affords.

The panel above is an attempt to show that we use the Internet in our personal relationships. The number of visitors to matchmaking/dating web sites jumped from 3.9 million visitors in January 2000 to 5.8 million in January 2001, an increase of 48.7%. Data suggest that there are more than a few romantics out there too: visitors to sites that specialize in flowers and greeting cards increased by 45.6%, from 12.3 million to 17.3 million.

Online dating sites include Matchmaker.com, Oneandonly.com and Match.com. One of the leading sites is Match.com, which signed 4.1 million members in 2000, bringing its database to 10 million (roughly 2 million people maintain active profiles on the site). It costs less than $20 for members to post photos and descriptions of themselves, and communicate with members.

Most would consider this money well spent. And money *is* being spent: Jupiter Media Metrix estimates revenue from online dating to grow from $41 million in 2001 to $85 million in 2006, an increase of 107%.

Who is visiting these sites? Jupiter reports that 58.3% of men who visit the site are 18 and older; 34.6% of women are 18 and older. The numbers are definitely in the ladies' favor: there are roughly 4 million more men than women who have never taken a walk down the aisle (26.1 million men and 22.1 million women in 2000). Some sites have offered single women free memberships to balance out their rosters.

Personal sites have caught on that we're all looking for *somebody*. There are sites that cater especially to Jews, Christians, Gays, and the Disabled. Keep in mind that these are personal sites too; no doubt many more people meet in informal ways — in chat rooms or in newsgroups.

Sources: Mullins, Robert. "Love Silicon Valley Style." *Silicon Valley/San Jose Business Journal*, June 22, 2001: "Valentine's Day Lights E-Commerce Fire." Retrieved February 27, 2002 from the World Wide Web: http://www.ecommercetimes.com; "Online Love in the Time of Calamity." Knight-Ridder/Tribune News Service, December 31, 2001, U.S. Census Bureau, *Statistical Abstract of the United States: 2001*, Washington D.C. 2001.

Money is No Object: A Quick Look at Online Auctions

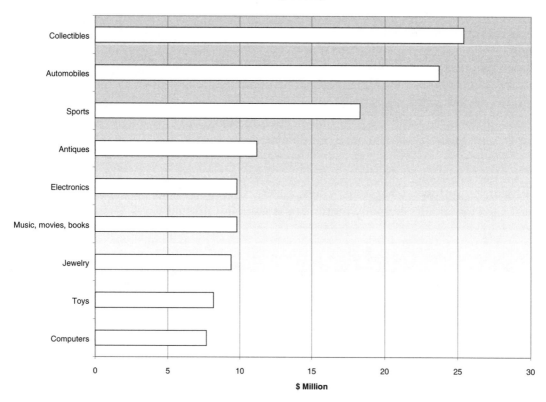

What Do We Buy On eBay?

About 35 million Americans participate in online auctions, according to a survey by Harris Interactive for the National Consumers League. The online site eBay handles roughly 70% of these transactions (the first eBay auction took place in 1995).

The panel shows the top sales categories on eBay according to research by Morgan Stanley. What category generated the most activity? Collectibles. You think no one on earth wants the set of ceramic orange pigs that Aunt Edna got you as a wedding present? Guess again. Think you'll never find a Captain Galaxy doll like you had when you were a kid? Guess again. Or *bid* again, as the case may be. These mementos and knickknacks are big business, and you may be surprised at what people will pay to round out their collections. And let's not forget the sellers: many generate handsome profits by selling items at multiple auctions.

But it isn't just the antiques or the one-of-a-kinds that get sold at the site. It offers electronics, jewelry, apparel, and books. eBay has, in short, turned into big business. It's also become sophisticated: the site is arranged according to categories and subcategories, and feedback on transactions is left by buyers and sellers. A high feedback rating often means that a seller gets more bids and better prices for his or her wares. But this comes with some peril: 41% of online auction buyers reported some problem with their transactions to the National Consumers League.

So, you may get a deal. You may find yourself in a bidding war with several people and have to reach deep in your pockets to get what you want.

But hey, isn't Captain Galaxy worth it?

Sources: Brown, Eryn. "How Can a Dot-Com Be This Hot?" *Fortune*, January 21, 2002, p. 78; ". 6 Million Americans Participated in Online Auctions; 41 percent of Buyers Encountered Problems, Survey Reports." *US Newswire*, January 31, 2001.

Part II

Data Presentation

Data used to create graphics in the first part of this book are present in Part II in tabular format. The tables are arranged by chapter and follow the same sequence as the panels in the chapters. Locating the appropriate table should, therefore, be easy.

In most instances, the data shown are the same as those used to generate the graphics. From time to time, however, additional time series are presented or data are presented for more years. For an explanation of the data, please consult the panel in which they are used. The tables carry some explanatory notes, but the relevance of the data — and the reasons they were selected — are not spelled out.

Tables carry source notes. However, for more information on the subject, including other sources of information, please consult the source notes and (if present), the footnotes shown in the relevant panel in Part I of this volume.

Chapter 1
EMPLOYMENT TRENDS

100 Years of Sectoral Change

Thousands of employees and percent of total.

	Employment 1900	Employment 2000	Percent 1900	Percent 2000
Agriculture	11,680	3,281	43.5	2.4
Goods	7,252	25,710	27.0	18.8
Services	6,832	85,370	25.4	62.5
Government	1,094	22,131	4.1	16.2
Total	26,858	136,492	100.0	100.0

Source: Bureau of the Census, *Historical Statistics of the United States*, Washington, DC, 1975 (for 1900 data); Bureau of Labor Statistics and Bureau of the Census for data on the 2000 structure of employment.

Major Sectors over 20 Years

Values in thousands of employees.

	1980	1990	2000
Agriculture	3,364	3,223	3,281
Goods Producing	25,658	24,905	25,710
Services Producing	48,506	66,194	85,370
Government	18,292	20,348	22,131

Source: Bureau of Labor Statistics, *Employees on nonfarm payrolls by major industry*, 1950 to date, downloaded January 2002 from http://www.bls.gov/ces/home.htm. Data for agricultural employment, from BLS, was published in *Statistical Abstract of the United States, 2000*, Table 672, p. 420. Included in totals for the government are data not reported by BLS but obtained from U.S. Department of Defense, published in *Statistical Abstract, 2000*, Table 579, p. 168. The military on active duty for the year 2000, included but not shown, was estimated from 1998 data by the editors.

The Services Producing Sector's Component Elements

In thousands and employees.

	1980	1990	2000
Transportation and Public Utilities	5,146	5,777	7,019
Wholesale Trade	5,292	6,173	7,024
Retail Trade	15,018	19,601	23,307
Finance and Real Estate	5,160	6,709	7,560
Services	17,890	27,934	40,460

Source: Bureau of Labor Statistics, *Employees on nonfarm payrolls by major industry,* 1950 to date, downloaded January 2002 from http://www.bls.gov/ces/home.htm.

Government Employment, by Level of Government

In thousands of employees.

	Local Government	State Government	Federal Government
1992	9,606	3,836	2,737
1993	9,552	3,891	2,704
1994	9,996	3,917	2,644
1995	10,119	3,971	2,580
1997	10,227	3,987	2,492
1998	10,505	3,985	2,447
1999	10,715	4,034	2,449
2000	10,995	4,083	2,426

Source: U.S. Bureau of the Census, *Public Employment and Payroll,* http://www.census.gov/govs/www/apes.html, downloaded December 21, 2001. Federal employment excludes military.

Elementary and High School Education - Staff and Enrollment (in thousands) and Student-to-Staff Ratio

	Teachers & Support Staff (000)	Elem./Secondary Enroll-ment (000)
1992	4,754	42,823
1993	5,016	43,465
1994	5,279	44,111
1995	5,341	44,841
1996	5,415	45,484
1997	5,489	46,127

[Continued]

Elementary and High School Education - Staff and Enrollment (in thousands) and Student-to-Staff Ratio

[Continued]

	Teachers & Support Staff (000)	Elem./Secondary Enroll-ment (000)
1998	5,684	46,535
1999	5,782	47,244
2000	5,959	47,533

Source: U.S. Bureau of the Census, *Public Employment and Payroll*, http://www.census.gov/govs/www/apes.html, downloaded December 21, 2001. Values for 1996 are extrapolated. School enrollment data are from U.S. Center for Education Statistics, published in *Statistical Abstract of the United States, 2000*, Table 239, p. 151.

Defense and Postal Service as Elements of Federal Employment

In thousands of employees.

	Total Federal Employment	Defense Dep. Civilian Employment	Postal Service Employment	Defense as % of Total	Post Office - % of Total
1992	2,737	959	595	35.0	21.8
1993	2,704	901	629	33.3	23.3
1994	2,644	858	640	32.4	24.2
1995	2,580	808	651	31.3	25.2
1996	2,536	782	653	30.8	25.7
1997	2,492	755	654	30.3	26.2
1998	2,447	718	653	29.3	26.7
1999	2,449	693	670	28.3	27.4
2000	2,426	675	672	27.8	27.7

Source: U.S. Bureau of the Census, *Public Employment and Payroll*, http://www.census.gov/govs/www/apes.html, downloaded December 21, 2001. Values for 1996 are extrapolated.

Percentage of Workforce Which is Union Member
or is Covered by a Union

Values are in percent of the workforce

	% Union Member	% Covered by a Union
1964	29.3	-
1965	28.9	-
1966	28.4	-
1967	28.3	-
1968	28.2	-
1969	28.0	-
1970	27.8	-
1971	27.2	-
1972	26.6	-
1973	26.6	-
1974	26.2	-
1975	24.6	-
1976	24.5	-
1977	24.1	26.9
1978	23.4	26.2
1979	24.4	27.4
1980	23.3	26.1
1981	21.7	24.3
1982	21.0	24.0
1983	20.3	23.6
1984	19.1	21.9
1985	18.2	20.8
1986	17.7	20.2
1987	17.3	19.4
1988	17.0	19.2
1989	16.6	18.8
1990	16.3	18.6
1991	16.3	18.5
1992	16.0	18.1
1993	16.0	18.0
1994	15.7	17.7
1995	15.1	16.9
1996	14.7	16.4
1997	14.2	15.8
1998	14.1	15.6
1999	14.0	15.5
2000	13.6	15.0

Source: Barry T. Hirsch, David A. Macpherson, and Wayne G. Vroman, "Estimates of union density by state," *Monthly Labor Review*, July 2001.

Median Weekly Pay, Selected Years, Unionized, Covered by Union Contract, and All Workers

All data are in 2000 constant dollars.

	Pay of Union Member	Pay of Person Covered by Union	Pay of Non-Union Person	Average of All Employees	Dollar Difference Union and All
1983	670.8	662.2	497.9	541.2	129.7
1988	698.7	692.9	518.2	560.4	138.3
1989	690.2	686.0	516.6	554.1	136.1
1991	645.6	640.7	495.9	527.8	117.8
1993	685.2	678.1	507.7	551.8	133.5
1994	687.9	682.1	502.0	542.6	145.2
1995	680.2	675.7	505.1	541.2	139.0
1996	675.0	669.5	507.1	537.8	137.2
1997	686.7	678.1	512.8	539.7	147.0
1998	696.2	689.9	527.2	552.5	143.7
1999	694.6	689.4	533.3	567.5	127.1
2000	696.0	691.0	542.0	576.0	120.0

Source: Statistical Abstract of the United States, 1980-2001, United States Department of Commerce. Data have been normalized to 2000 dollars using the Bureau of Labor Statistics' Consumer Price Index, All Items series.

Chapter 2
THE WORKFORCE

Percentage of Workers per Occupational Category by Age, March 2000

Total employee numbers in thousands.

	Total Employees	% Distribution by Age	
		18-34 Years Old	35-64 Years Old
Exec., admin., managerial	19,050	27.4	72.6
Professional specialty	20,060	32.2	67.8
Technical & related support	4,342	40.6	59.4
Sales	14,757	42.1	57.2
Admin. support, including clerical	18,137	39.6	60.4
Private household service	779	31.5	68.5
Other service	16,258	46.4	53.6
Prec. prod., crafts, and repair	14,066	34.3	65.7
Mach. oper., assemb., and inspectors	7,181	38.6	61.4
Transport. & material moving	5,071	35.1	64.9
Handlers, equip. cleaners, & laborers	4,907	55.0	45.0
Farming, forestry and fishing	2,839	36.5	63.5

Source: U.S. Census Bureau. "Table 6. Educational Attainment of Employed Civilians 18 to 64 Years, by Occupation, Age, Sex, Race, and Hispanic Origin: March 2000," December 19, 2000. Retrieved December 12, 2001 from http://www.census.gov/population/socdemo/education/p20-536/tab06.txt.

Retirement and Job Openings — 2000-10

Numbers in thousands, except where indicated.

	Jobs Created by Retirement	Job Openings Needed To Be Filled	% Change in Retirement, 1993-98 to 2003
Airline pilots, navigators	27	38	172.7
Management analysts	44	189	152.0
Teachers, special education	57	197	135.4
Photographers	26	48	94.8
Teachers aides	264	565	91.8
Industrial engineers	26	33	87.6
Social welfare clerks	45	34	85.0
Human resources	38	66	83.6
Postal clerks, ex mail carriers	2	18	81.0

[Continued]

Retirement and Job Openings — 2000-10

[Continued]

	Jobs Created by Retirement	Job Openings Needed To Be Filled	% Change in Retirement, 1993-98 to 2003
Police, detective supervisors	32	48	80.2
Plumbers, pipe- and steamfitters	83	134	73.6
Financial managers	101	223	73.1
Psychologists	42	75	73.0
Social workers	52	193	72.0
Lawyers	45	168	71.6
Administrators, education	117	178	70.6
Teachers, elementary	349	551	68.8
Registered nurses	443	1,004	62.6
Chemists	27	43	57.6

Source: Dohm, Arlene. "Gauging the labor force effects of retiring baby- boomers." *Monthly Labor Review*, July 2000. Retrieved November 26, 2001 from http://www.bls.gov/opub/mlr/2000/07/art2full.pdf; Daniel E. Hecker "Occupational employment projections to 2010." *Monthly Labor Review*, November 2001.

Job Openings and Number of Degrees Conferred, by Occupation

Numbers in thousands. Projections are based on data from 1993-1998. Over this 5-year period, the number of degrees conferred has remained steady. Degrees conferred under the occupation Registered nurses include all nursing degrees. Degrees conferred under Social workers include only Master's degree or higher. The standard requirement for a job in social work is a Master's degree. Degrees conferred under the occupation Management analysts include all business administration and management degrees.

	Total Job Openings, 2000-2010	Degrees Conferred, 1998-2008
Registered nurses	1,004	538
Teachers, elementary school	551	602
Financial managers	223	262
Teachers, special education	197	214
Social workers	193	152
Management analysts	189	1,422
Administrators, education and related	178	140
Lawyers	168	398
Psychologists	75	38
Personnel and labor relations managers	66	16
Photographers	48	10
Chemists	43	146
Industrial engineers	33	56

Source: Dohm, Arlene. "Gauging the labor force effects of retiring baby- boomers." *Monthly Labor Review*, July 2000. Retrieved November 26, 2001 from http://www.bls.gov/opub/mlr/2000/07/art2full.pdf; Daniel E. Hecker. "Occupational employment projections to 2010." *Monthly Labor Review*, November 2001. National Center for Education Statistics. U.S. Department of Education. *Digest of Education Statistics*, 1997-2000 editions. Washington D.C.: U.S. Government Printing Office, various publication dates.

Projected Job Openings (2000-2010) as Percentage of Total 2010 Employment in Occupation

Numbers in thousands, except where indicated.

	Job Openings (2000-10) as % of Total 2010 Employment	Job Openings 2000-2010	Employment 2010
Supervisors, police and detective	35.3	48	136
Eligibility clerks, government programs	32.1	34	106
Aircraft pilots and flight engineers	29.5	38	129
Plumbers, pipefitters, and steamfitters	24.2	134	554
Postal service clerks	23.7	18	76

Source: Hecker, Daniel E. "Occupational employment projections to 2010." *Monthly Labor Review*, November 2001.

Percentage of the Labor Force by Gender and Participation Rates, 1950-2025

Numbers in percent.

	% of Workforce		Participation Rate	
	Men	Women	Men	Women
1950	70.4	29.6	86.4	33.9
1960	66.6	33.4	83.3	37.7
1970	61.9	38.1	79.7	43.3
1980	57.5	42.5	77.4	51.5
1990	54.8	45.2	76.1	57.5
1998	53.7	46.3	74.9	59.8
2015	52.0	48.0	72.2	61.9
2025	52.3	47.7	68.8	58.1

Source: Fullerton Jr., Howard N., "Labor force participation: 75 years of change, 1950-98 and 1998-2025." *Monthly Labor Review*, December 1999.

Women as Percentage of Total Workforce by Occupation, 1975, 1995, 2000

Numbers in percent.

	1975	1995	2000
Managerial and professional specialty	34.8	48.0	49.9
Technical, sales, administrative support	61.3	64.4	64.2
Service occupations	61.0	60.0	60.1
Precision production, craft, repair	5.5	8.9	9.8

[Continued]

Women as Percentage of Total Workforce by Occupation, 1975, 1995, 2000

[Continued]

	1975	1995	2000
Operators, fabricators, laborers	24.4	24.3	23.3
Farming, forestry, fishing	14.0	19.9	22.5

Source: Wooten, Barbara H., "Gender differences in occupational employment", *Monthly Labor Review*, April 1997. Retrieved December 6, 2001 from http://www.bls.gov/opub/mlr/1997/04/art2full.pdf; U.S. Census Bureau. Special Populations Branch, Population Division. "Table 11. Major Occupation Group of thePopulation 16 Years and Over by Sex: March 2000." *Current Population Survey*, March 2000. Retrieved December 6, 2001 from http://www.census.gov.

Job Losses and Gains by Gender During Periods of Decline and Recovery in Employment, 1970-1993

Numbers in thousands, except where indicated.

	% of Jobs Gained or Lost		Total Number of Jobs Gained or Lost
	Men	Women	
March 1970-Nov. 1970	-92.1	-7.9	-1,051
Nov. 1970-Sept. 1971	59.5	40.5	1,231
Oct. 1974-April 1975	-72.3	-27.7	-2,271
April 1975-Feb. 1976	49.3	50.7	2,308
March 1980-July 1980	-87.3	-12.7	-1,319
July 1980-Jan. 1981	40.9	59.1	1,327
July 1981-Nov. 1982	-95.1	-4.9	-2,761
Nov. 1982-Nov. 1983	48.0	52.0	3,078
June 1990-Feb. 1992	-94.1	-5.9	-2,092
Feb. 1992-April 1993	46.5	53.5	2,029

Source: Goodman, William, "Women and jobs in recoveries: 1970-93." *Monthly Labor Review*, July 1994. Retrieved December 6, 2001 from http://www.bls.gov/opub/mlr/1994/07/art4full.pdf.

Distribution of the Labor Force, 16 Years Old and Older, 1988-2008

Numbers in thousands, except where indicated.

	Total Employment			% of Workforce Population		
	1988	1998	2008	1988	1998	2008
White	104,756	115,415	126,665	86.1	83.8	81.9
Black	13,205	15,982	19,101	10.9	11.6	12.4
Hispanic	8,982	14,317	19,585	7.4	10.4	12.7
Asian	3,708	6,278	8,809	3.0	4.6	5.7

Source: Fullerton, Jr. Howard N.. "Labor force projections to 2008: steady growth and changing composition." *Monthly Labor Review*, November 1999.

Percentage of Labor Force by Race, Entrants and Leavers, 1988-1998

Numbers in thousands, except where indicated.

	Total Labor Force, 1998	Percentage of		
		Entrants	Leavers	Difference
White non-Hispanic	101,767	21.0	15.5	5.5
Black non-Hispanic	15,589	29.6	12.8	16.8
Hispanic	14,317	43.7	6.4	37.3
Asian, and other non-Hispanic	6,000	46.4	5.8	40.6

Source: Fullerton, Jr., Howard N., "Labor force projections to 2008: steady growth and changing composition." *Monthly Labor Review*, November 1999.

High School and College Completion Rates, by Rates, 1974-2000

Numbers in percent.

	High School			College		
	White	Black	Hispanic	White	Black	Hispanic
1974	NA	NA	NA	14.0	5.5	5.5
1975	NA	NA	NA	14.5	6.4	6.3
1976	NA	NA	NA	15.4	6.6	6.1
1977	NA	NA	NA	16.1	7.2	6.2
1978	NA	NA	NA	16.4	7.2	7.0
1979	NA	NA	NA	17.2	7.9	6.7
1980	70.5	51.2	45.3	17.8	7.9	7.9
1981	71.6	52.9	44.5	17.8	8.2	7.7
1982	72.8	54.9	45.9	18.5	8.8	7.8
1983	73.8	56.8	46.2	19.5	9.5	7.9
1984	75.0	58.5	47.1	19.8	10.4	8.2
1985	75.5	59.8	47.9	20.0	11.1	8.5
1986	76.2	62.3	48.5	20.1	10.9	8.4
1987	77.0	63.4	50.9	20.5	10.7	8.6
1988	77.7	63.5	51.0	20.9	11.2	10.1
1989	78.4	64.6	50.9	21.8	11.8	9.9
1990	79.1	66.2	50.8	22.0	11.3	9.2
1991	79.9	66.7	51.3	22.2	11.5	9.7
1992	80.9	67.7	52.6	22.1	11.9	9.3
1993	81.5	70.4	53.1	22.6	12.2	9.0
1994	82.0	72.9	53.3	22.9	12.9	9.1
1995	83.0	73.8	53.4	24.0	13.2	9.3
1996	82.8	74.3	53.1	24.3	13.6	9.3
1997	83.0	74.9	54.7	24.6	13.3	10.3
1998	83.7	76.0	55.5	25.0	14.7	11.0

[Continued]

High School and College Completion Rates, by Rates, 1974-2000

[Continued]

	High School			College		
	White	Black	Hispanic	White	Black	Hispanic
1999	84.3	77.0	56.1	25.9	15.4	10.9
2000	84.9	78.5	57.0	26.1	16.5	10.6

Source: U.S. Census Bureau. "Table A-2. Percent of People 25 Years Old and Over Who Have Completed High School or College, by Race, Hispanic Origin and Sex: Selected Years 1940-2000." December 19, 2000. *Note:* NA stands for data not available.

Foreign Born Population, 1960 and 2000

Numbers in thousands, except where indicated. Data include only those for which region of birth was reported.

	Number of Foreign Born		% Distribution	
	1960	2000	1960	2000
Total	9,678	28,379	100	100
Europe	7,256	4,355	75	15
Asia	491	7,246	5	25
Latin America	908	14,477	9	51
Other	1,023	2,301	11	9

Source: U.S. Census Bureau. "Table 2. Region of Birth of the Foreign-Born Population: 1850 to 1930 and 1960 to 1990," March 9, 1999. Retrieved March 26, 2002 from http://www.census.gov; U.S. Census Bureau. "Table 3.1 Foreign-Born Population by Sex, Age, and World Region of Birth: March 2000," January 3, 2001. Retrieved March 26, 2002 from http://www.census.gov.

15- to 17-Year Olds Working Illegally as a Percentage of Total Youth Labor Force: 1971-1997

	% of 15- to 17-Year Old Workers Working			% of 15- to 17-Year Olds Who Work
	In Hazardous Occupations	Excessive Hours	Illegally	
1971-75	2.6	2.4	4.9	25.8
1976-80	2.4	2.6	4.8	27.7
1981-85	2.1	2.0	4.0	24.5
1986-90	1.9	2.1	3.9	26.0
1991-94	1.6	1.5	3.0	21.4
1995-97	1.9	1.4	3.1	24.3

Source: Kruse, Douglas and Douglas Mahony. National Bureau of Economic Research. "Illegal Child Labor in the United States: Prevalence and Characteristics." *Working Paper 6479*, March 1998.

Detected Illegal Employment of Minors, 1990-2000

For 1990, data for number of violations found rather than the number of workplaces with violations.

	1990	1992	1994	1996	1998	2000
Workplaces with violations	42,000	16,410	9,148	7,322	9,776	10,806
Illegally employed minors	38,000	8,537	12,959	7,577	16,535	6,098
Total inspections	NA	NA	48,918	48,414	49,288	52,401
Child labor enforcement officers (average)	NA	36.5	40.0	8.5	22.0	40.0

Source: Child Labor Coalition. "Overview on enforcement." *Child Labor in the US.* Retrieved November 30, 2001 from http:// www.stopchildlabor.org/USchildlabor/enforcementoverview.htm. Child Labor Coalition. "State Survey Chart on Child Labor." *Child Labor in the US.* Retrieved November 30, 2001 from http://www.stopchildlabor.org/USchildlabor/kidchart.htm. *Notes:* NA stands for data not available.

Estimated Illegal Workforce Population for Top 10 Country of Origin, 1996

	1996
Total	3,340,000
Mexico	1,795,500
El Salvador	222,775
Guatemala	109,725
Canada	80,160
Haiti	70,140
Philippines	63,460
Honduras	59,850
Dominican Republic	49,875
Poland	46,760
Nicaragua	46,760

Source: U.S. Immigration and Naturalization Service. *Statistical Yearbook of the Immigration and Naturalization Service, 1996.* Retrieved November 26, 2001 from http:// www.ins.usdoj.gov/graphics/aboutins/repsstudies/report.pdf. Bureau of Labor Statistics. U.S. Department of Labor. "Table 5. Civilian labor force participation rates for selected demographic groups, annual averages, 1948-2000." Retrieved December 3, 2001 from http:// www.bls.gov/opub/rtaw/pdf/table05.pdf.

Total Illegal Workers Arrested by the U.S. Immigration and Naturalization Service, 1994-1999

The estimates for 1998 and 1999 were derived by the editor using a figure of 450,000 illegal immigrants. The U.S. Census Bureau estimates that between 400,000 and 500,000 illegal immigrants entered the U.S. annually in the 1990's.

	Illegal Immigrants	Illegal Workers, est.	Arrests	Arrest (%)
1994	4,755,000	3,166,830	7,554	0.00238
1997	5,120,000	3,435,520	17,552	0.00511
1998	5,570,000	3,737,470	13,914	0.00372
1999	6,020,000	4,039,420	2,849	0.00071

Source: U.S. Immigration and Naturalization Service. *Statistical Yearbook of the Immigration and Naturalization Service*, 1997-1999 editions. Retrieved November 28, 2001 from http:// www.ins.usdoj.gov/. *Note:* est. stands for estimated.

Chapter 3
TRENDS IN OCCUPATIONS

Top 20 Fastest Growing Occupations, 2000-2010

Occupation	Growth (%)
Computer software engineers, applications	100
Computer support specialists	97
Computer software engineers, systems software	90
Network and computer systems administrators	82
Network systems and data communications analysts	77
Desktop publishers	67
Database administrators	66
Personal home care aides	62
Computer systems analysts	60
Medical assistants	57
Social and human services assistants	54
Physician assistants	53
Medical records and health information technicians	49
Computer and information systems managers	48
Home health aides	47
Audiologists	45
Physical therapist assistants	45
Computer and information scientist, research	40
Fitness trainers and aerobics instructors	40
Veterinary assistants and laboratory animal caretakers	40

Source: Hecker, Daniel E. "Occupational employment projections to 2010." *Monthly Labor Review*

Top 20 Occupations With The Largest Job Decline, 2000-2010

Occupations	Decline (%)
Railroad brake, signal, and switch operators	61
Telephone operators	35
Loan interviewers and clerks	28
Meter readers, utilities	26
Farmers and ranchers	25
Order clerks	20
Insurance claims and policy processing clerks	20
Word processors and typists	19

[Continued]

Top 20 Occupations With The Largest Job Decline, 2000-2010

[Continued]

Occupations	Decline (%)
Office machine operators, except computer	19
Railroad conductors and yardmasters	19
Computer operators	17
Switchboard operators, including answering service	16
Prepress technicians and workers	16
Sewing machine operators	13
Tellers	12
Machine feeders and offbearers	12
Procurement clerks	12
Barbers	12
Wholesale and retail buyers, except farm products	9
Butchers and meat cutters	9

Source: Bureau of Labor Statistics. U.S. Department of Labor. "Table 5. Occupations with the largest job decline, 2000-10." Retrieved December 14, 2001 from http://stats.bls.gov/emp/mlrtab5.pdf.

Educational Attainment of Civilian Labor Force, 16 years and over, 1993-2000

Data in percent.

	Some College or Less, no Degree	Bachelor's Degree or Higher	Associate Degree
1993	68.8	24.1	7.2
1994	68.1	24.1	7.8
1995	67.2	24.9	7.9
1996	66.8	25.3	7.9
1997	66.9	25.3	7.9
1998	66.1	25.7	8.1
1999	65.6	26.4	8.0
2000	65.1	26.7	8.2

Source: U.S. Census Bureau. *Current Population Survey,* annual.

Job Openings and Degrees Conferred, 1998-2008

Numbers in thousands.

Occupations	Degrees Conferred	Job Openings
General managers and top executives	1,422.6	1,139.7
Registered & licensed practical nurses	538.1	1,078.5
Teachers, secondary school	549.1	777.7
Systems analysts, EDP	60.6	615.6
Teachers, elementary school	601.0	609.9
Computer support specialists	361.7	466.0
Computer engineers	37.7	341.4
Physicians and surgeons	173.8	212.1
Financial managers	261.8	207.1
Lawyers	397.2	191.8
Marketing, advertising, & public relations managers	240.7	179.1
Teachers, special education	213.4	171.7
Education administrators	140.6	170.6
Electrical and electronic engineers	228.5	168.7
Teachers, preschool	85.7	165.2

Source: "Occupations with the Most Openings Requiring a Bachelor's Degree or Higher." *America's Career Infonet.* Retrieved January 31, 2002 from http://www.acinet.org; "Occupations with the Most Openings Requiring Post- Secondary Training or an Associate's Degree." *America's Career Infonet.* Retrieved January 31, 2002 from http://www.acinet.org; National Center for Education Statistics. U.S. Department of Education. *Digest of Education Statistics,* 1997-2000 editions.

Occupations with the Most Openings, 1998-2008

Occupations	Average Annual Job Openings, 1998-2008
Cashiers	194,970
Salespersons, retail	193,800
Waiters and waitresses	141,520
General office clerks	129,960
General managers and top executives	113,970
Food preparation workers	82,270
Registered nurses	79,400
Teachers, secondary school	77,770
First-line supervisors and managers (clerical and admin.)	67,540
Systems analysts, EDP	61,560
Teachers, elementary school	60,990
First-line supervisors and managers (sales)	60,070
Laborers, landscaping, groundskeeping	57,150
Receptionists and information clerks	55,300
Guards and watch guards	55,020
Nursing aides, orderlies, attendants	51,510
Computer support specialists	46,600

[Continued]

Occupations with the Most Openings, 1998-2008

[Continued]

Occupations	Average Annual Job Openings, 1998-2008
Hand packers and packagers	45,630
Secretaries, exc. legal and medical	43,910
Bookkeeping, accounting and auditing clerks	38,780

Source: "Occupations with the Most Openings." *America's Career Infonet.* Retrieved January 31, 2002 from http://www.acinet.org.

Percentage of Multiple Job Holders, by Gender and Reason for Working at More Than One Job, May 1997

Data in percent.

	Men	Women	Women Who Maintain Families
To meet regular household expenses	29.3	32.7	52.6
To pay off debts	10.4	10.7	11.9
To save for the future	10.1	7.0	5.0
To get experience or build up a business	8.4	7.0	1.6
To help out a friend or relative	2.8	3.7	2.0
To get extra money to buy something special	7.4	8.5	6.1
Enjoys the work on the second job	15.9	12.8	8.3

Source: Bureau of Labor Statistics. U.S. Department of Labor. "When one job is not enough." *Issues in Labor Statistics*, August 2000.

Percentage of Workers with Part-time Jobs, by Gender and Type of Employment, May 1995

Data in percent.

	Men	Women
Percentage of all part-time workers	32.0	68.0
Full-time primary job, part-time secondary job	59.9	40.1
Part-time on primary and secondary job, with full-time hours	35.1	64.9
Hours vary on primary and secondary jobs, with full-time hours	63.2	36.8

Source: Bureau of Labor Statistics. U.S. Department of Labor. "A Different Look at Part-Time Employment." *Issues in Labor Statistics*, April 1996.

Independent Contractor Characteristics, by Gender, 1995-2001

	Total	Men (%)	Women (%)
1995	8,368	67.3	32.7
1997	8,680	66.6	33.4
1999	8,409	66.2	33.8
2001	8,585	64.5	35.5

Source: DiNatalie, Marisa. "Characteristics and preferences for alternative work arrangements, 1999." *Monthly Labor Review*, March 2001; Bureau of Labor Statistics. U.S. Department of Labor. "Table 6. Employed workers with alternative and traditional work arrangements by selected characteristics, February 2001." Retrieved January 18, 2002 from http://www.bls.gov/news.release/conemp.t06.htm.

Number of Independent Contractors, by Occupation and Gender, February 1999

Numbers in thousands.

	Total	Men	Women
Farming, forestry, fishing	364	300	64
Operators, fabricators, and laborers	577	502	75
Precision production, craft, and repair	1,558	1,463	95
Service occupations	724	136	588
Administrative support, including clerical	286	55	231
Sales occupations	1,421	830	591
Technicians and related support	685	655	30
Professional specialty	1,528	873	655
Executive, administrative, managerial	1,694	1,234	460

Source: DiNatalie, Marisa. "Characteristics and preferences for alternative work arrangements, 1999." *Monthly Labor Review*, March 2001.

Median Annual Earnings: Independent Contractor vs. Traditional Worker, February 1999

Data in U.S. dollars.

	Independent Contractor	Traditional Worker
Total	33,280	28,080
Men	35,828	31,876
Women	22,932	24,648
White	34,424	29,224
Black	21,528	23,140
Hispanic	26,208	20,592

Source: DiNatale, Marisa. "Characteristics of and preference for alternative work arrangements, 1999." *Monthly Labor Review*, March 2001.

Home-based Business vs. Small Business, 1982-1992

	Small Businesses, Total	Home-based Businesses	Home Businesses as % of Small Businesses
1982	10,584	5,493	51.9
1987	12,093	6,156	50.9
1992	17,253	8,557	49.6

Source: Kuenzi, Jeffrey J. and Clara A. Reschovsky. "Home-Based Workers in the United States: 1997." *Current Population Reports*, December 2001.

Chapter 4
PEOPLE AND THEIR MONEY

Average Income Received by Each Fifth and Top 5 Percent of Households (All Races): 1967 to 2000

Inflation-adjusted constant dollars based on the Consumer Price Index.

Year	Current Dollars						2000 Constant Dollars					
	Lowest Fifth	Second Fifth	Third Fifth	Fourth Fifth	Highest Fifth	Top 5 Percent	Lowest Fifth	Second Fifth	Third Fifth	Fourth Fifth	Highest Fifth	Top 5 Percent
1967	1,626	4,433	7,078	9,903	17,946	28,605	7,147	19,485	31,111	43,528	78,881	125,732
1968	1,832	4,842	7,679	10,713	18,762	29,048	7,742	20,463	32,452	45,275	79,291	122,761
1969	1,957	5,216	8,335	11,674	20,520	31,586	7,925	21,124	33,755	47,277	83,101	127,916
1970	2,029	5,395	8,688	12,247	21,684	33,283	7,839	20,845	33,568	47,319	83,781	128,596
1971	2,126	5,529	8,965	12,745	22,583	34,637	7,865	20,454	33,165	47,149	83,544	128,137
1972	2,316	5,898	9,625	13,817	24,806	38,447	8,312	21,167	34,543	49,588	89,026	137,983
1973	2,568	6,366	10,402	14,954	26,521	40,417	8,673	21,501	35,133	50,507	89,575	136,509
1974	2,911	6,973	11,206	16,181	28,259	41,669	8,946	21,429	34,437	49,726	86,842	128,052
1975	3,034	7,204	11,787	17,117	29,809	43,940	8,611	20,445	33,452	48,578	84,599	124,703
1976	3,278	7,780	12,762	18,521	32,320	47,805	8,798	20,882	34,254	49,711	86,748	128,311
1977	3,513	8,291	13,671	20,018	35,091	51,792	8,863	20,918	34,492	50,505	88,535	130,671
1978	3,807	9,112	15,010	21,980	38,791	57,625	9,209	22,042	36,309	53,169	93,835	139,394
1979	4,114	10,021	16,495	24,193	42,990	64,197	9,097	22,159	36,474	53,496	95,060	141,954
1980	4,483	10,819	17,807	26,219	46,053	66,617	8,920	21,527	35,431	52,169	91,634	132,551
1981	4,836	11,589	19,141	28,512	49,942	71,095	8,797	21,081	34,818	51,864	90,846	129,324
1982	5,003	12,238	20,195	30,026	54,164	78,945	8,598	21,033	34,708	51,605	93,090	135,680
1983	5,239	12,796	21,105	31,667	57,303	83,943	8,645	21,115	34,825	52,254	94,556	138,514
1984	5,606	13,634	22,547	33,944	61,648	90,629	8,896	21,634	35,777	53,862	97,823	143,809
1985	5,797	14,330	23,735	35,694	65,841	98,946	8,896	21,992	36,425	54,779	101,044	151,850
1986	5,944	14,961	24,979	37,622	70,340	107,444	8,964	22,562	37,670	56,737	106,078	162,033
1987	6,167	15,584	26,055	39,383	74,897	118,000	8,994	22,727	37,998	57,435	109,228	172,089
1988	6,504	16,317	27,291	41,254	78,759	124,215	9,152	22,960	38,402	58,050	110,825	174,788
1989	7,021	17,401	28,925	43,753	85,529	138,185	9,468	23,465	39,005	59,000	115,334	186,339
1990	7,195	18,030	29,781	44,901	87,137	138,756	9,238	23,150	38,238	57,652	111,881	178,158
1991	7,263	18,149	30,147	45,957	88,130	137,532	8,996	22,479	37,340	56,922	109,157	170,345
1992	7,288	18,181	30,631	47,021	91,110	144,608	8,794	21,937	36,959	56,736	109,933	174,484
1993	7,412	18,656	31,272	48,599	101,253	173,784	8,718	21,944	36,783	57,163	119,096	204,409
1994	7,762	19,224	32,385	50,395	105,945	183,044	8,934	22,127	37,275	58,005	121,943	210,684
1995	8,350	20,397	34,106	52,429	109,411	188,828	9,376	22,902	38,295	58,869	122,850	212,022
1996	8,596	21,097	35,486	54,922	115,514	201,220	9,397	23,062	38,792	60,038	126,275	219,964
1997	8,872	22,098	37,177	57,582	122,764	215,436	9,493	23,644	39,778	61,611	131,354	230,511
1998	9,223	23,288	38,967	60,266	127,529	222,283	9,732	24,574	41,118	63,593	134,569	234,555
1999	9,940	24,436	40,879	63,555	135,401	235,392	10,274	25,257	42,252	65,690	139,949	243,299
2000	10,190	25,334	42,361	65,729	141,620	250,146	10,190	25,334	42,361	65,729	141,620	250,146

Source: U.S. Bureau of the Census, *Current Population Survey*, March issues, "Share of Aggregate Income Received by Each Fifth and Top 5 Percent of Households (All Races): 1967 to 2000", March 21, 2000.

Growth in Average Income by Household Segments

Dollar data in constant 2000 dollars; growth rates based on constant dollars.

	Households					
	Lowest Quintile	Second Quintile	Third Quintile	Fourth Quintile	Top Quintile	Top 5%
Income Growth - 1967-1983 - %	21.0	8.4	11.9	20.0	19.9	10.2
Income Growth - 1984-2000 - %	14.5	17.1	18.4	22.0	44.8	73.9
Average Income in 1983 - $	8,645.0	21,115.0	34,825.0	52,254.0	94,556.0	138,514.0
Average Income in 2000 - $	10,190.0	25,334.0	42,361.0	65,729.0	141,620.0	250,146.0

Source: U.S. Bureau of the Census, *Current Population Survey*, March issues, "Share of Aggregate Income Received by Each Fifth and Top 5 Percent of Households (All Races): 1967 to 2000", March 21, 2000.

Income of the Lowest and Highest Fifth of U.S. Households, in Current and Constant Dollars, 1967 to 2000

	Current $		Constant 2000 $		Income Gap in 2000 $	Lowest as % of Highest (2000 $)	Top to Bottom Ratio (2000 $)
	Lowest Quintile	Highest Quintile	Lowest Quintile	Highest Quintile			
1967	1,625	17,946	7,147	78,881	71,734	9.0	11.0
1968	1,832	18,762	7,742	79,291	71,549	9.3	10.2
1969	1,957	20,520	7,925	83,101	75,176	9.5	10.5
1970	2,029	21,684	7,839	83,781	75,942	9.4	10.7
1971	2,126	22,583	7,865	83,544	75,679	8.8	10.6
1972	2,316	24,806	8,312	89,026	80,714	9.3	10.7
1973	2,568	26,521	8,673	89,575	80,902	10.0	10.3
1974	2,911	28,259	8,946	86,842	77,896	10.6	9.7
1975	3,034	29,809	8,611	84,599	75,988	9.9	9.8
1976	3,278	32,320	8,798	86,748	77,950	9.9	9.9
1977	3,513	35,091	8,863	88,535	79,672	9.4	10.0
1978	3,807	38,791	9,209	93,835	84,626	9.7	10.2
1979	4,114	42,990	9,097	95,060	85,963	9.9	10.4
1980	4,483	46,053	8,920	91,634	82,714	9.8	10.3
1981	4,836	49,942	8,797	90,846	82,049	9.4	10.3
1982	5,003	54,164	8,598	93,090	84,492	9.1	10.8
1983	5,239	57,303	8,645	94,556	85,911	8.8	10.9
1984	5,606	61,648	8,896	97,823	88,927	8.8	11.0
1985	5,797	65,841	8,896	101,044	92,148	8.4	11.4
1986	5,944	70,340	8,964	106,078	97,114	8.2	11.8
1987	6,167	74,897	8,994	109,228	100,234	8.1	12.1
1988	6,504	78,759	9,152	110,825	101,673	7.9	12.1
1989	7,021	85,529	9,468	115,334	105,866	8.5	12.2
1990	7,195	87,137	9,238	111,881	102,643	8.5	12.1
1991	7,263	88,130	8,996	109,157	100,161	8.2	12.1
1992	7,288	91,110	8,794	109,933	101,139	7.4	12.5
1993	7,412	101,253	8,718	119,096	110,378	7.1	13.7

[Continued]

Income of the Lowest and Highest Fifth of U.S. Households, in Current and Constant Dollars, 1967 to 2000

[Continued]

	Current $		Constant 2000 $		Income Gap in 2000 $	Lowest as % of Highest (2000 $)	Top to Bottom Ratio (2000 $)
	Lowest Quintile	Highest Quintile	Lowest Quintile	Highest Quintile			
1994	7,762	105,945	8,934	121,943	113,009	7.3	13.6
1995	8,350	109,411	9,376	122,850	113,474	7.4	13.1
1996	8,596	115,514	9,397	126,275	116,878	7.2	13.4
1997	8,872	122,764	9,493	131,354	121,861	7.1	13.8
1998	9,223	127,529	9,732	134,569	124,837	7.0	13.8
1999	9,940	135,401	10,274	139,949	129,675	7.3	13.6
2000	10,190	141,620	10,190	141,620	131,430	7.2	13.9

Source: U.S. Bureau of the Census, *Current Population Survey*, March issues, "Share of Aggregate Income Received by Each Fifth and Top 5 Percent of Households (All Races): 1967 to 2000," March 21, 2000.

Median Annual Income by Race/Ethnicity, 1967-2000

Data in 2000 constant dollars. Median means that half earned more and half earned less.

	Whites	Blacks	Pacific Islanders	Hispanic Origin
1967	32,742	19,010	-	-
1968	34,071	20,091	-	-
1969	35,456	21,431	-	-
1970	35,148	21,393	-	-
1971	34,934	20,635	-	-
1972	36,510	21,311	-	27,552
1973	37,210	21,903	-	27,506
1974	35,986	21,401	-	27,369
1975	35,021	21,024	-	25,159
1976	35,668	21,209	-	25,684
1977	36,008	21,249	-	26,862
1978	37,881	22,765	-	28,551
1979	38,163	22,406	-	28,839
1980	37,176	21,418	-	27,162
1981	36,659	20,571	-	27,831
1982	36,293	20,569	-	26,086
1983	36,360	20,582	-	26,062
1984	37,523	21,376	-	26,963
1985	38,226	22,742	-	26,803
1986	39,474	22,742	-	27,676
1987	40,004	22,856	-	28,199
1988	40,499	23,087	45,404	28,648
1989	41,002	24,385	48,683	29,560
1990	40,100	23,979	49,369	28,671

[Continued]

Median Annual Income by Race/Ethnicity, 1967-2000

[Continued]

	Whites	Blacks	Pacific Islanders	Hispanic Origin
1991	39,101	23,294	45,145	28,105
1992	38,863	22,630	45,610	27,226
1993	38,768	22,975	45,105	26,919
1994	39,166	24,202	46,595	26,958
1995	40,159	25,144	45,603	25,668
1996	40,623	25,669	47,307	27,226
1997	41,699	26,803	48,415	28,491
1998	43,171	26,751	49,212	29,894
1999	43,932	28,848	52,925	31,767
2000	44,226	30,439	55,521	33,447

Source: U.S. Census Bureau, *Current Population Reports*, P60-213, Money Income in the United States, 2000, U.S. Government Printing Office, Washington D.C. 2001

Median Annual Income of Men and Women

Data in constant 2000 dollars. Median means that half earned more and half earned less.

	Constant 2000 $			Women as % of Men	Male to Female Ratio
	Men	Women	Difference Men and Women		
1955	23,211	14,968	8,243	64.5	1.551
1956	24,133	15,284	8,849	63.3	1.579
1957	24,666	15,707	8,959	63.7	1.570
1958	25,123	15,742	9,381	62.7	1.596
1959	26,446	16,177	10,269	61.2	1.635
1960	26,935	16,338	10,597	60.7	1.649
1961	27,797	16,400	11,397	59.0	1.695
1962	28,322	16,805	11,517	59.3	1.685
1963	29,115	17,057	12,058	58.6	1.707
1964	29,746	17,562	12,184	59.0	1.694
1965	30,770	17,796	12,974	57.8	1.729
1966	31,504	18,236	13,268	57.9	1.728
1967	32,039	18,452	13,587	57.6	1.736
1968	33,023	19,305	13,718	58.5	1.711
1969	35,103	20,561	14,542	58.6	1.707
1970	35,484	21,019	14,465	59.2	1.688
1971	35,629	21,090	14,539	59.2	1.689
1972	37,820	21,724	16,096	57.4	1.741
1973	38,733	21,913	16,820	56.6	1.768
1974	37,375	22,046	15,329	59.0	1.695
1975	36,707	21,907	14,800	59.7	1.676
1976	37,198	22,310	14,888	60.0	1.667
1977	38,022	22,238	15,784	58.5	1.710

[Continued]

Median Annual Income of Men and Women

[Continued]

	Constant 2000 $			Women as % of Men	Male to Female Ratio
	Men	Women	Difference Men and Women		
1978	38,854	23,321	15,533	60.0	1.666
1979	38,650	23,286	15,364	60.2	1.660
1980	38,149	23,063	15,086	60.5	1.654
1981	37,639	22,660	14,979	60.2	1.661
1982	37,218	23,482	13,736	63.1	1.585
1983	37,140	23,892	13,248	64.3	1.554
1984	38,089	24,472	13,617	64.2	1.556
1985	38,365	24,941	13,424	65.0	1.538
1986	39,050	25,400	13,650	65.0	1.537
1987	38,911	25,615	13,296	65.8	1.519
1988	38,474	26,095	12,379	67.8	1.474
1989	38,322	26,481	11,841	69.1	1.447
1990	37,208	26,438	10,770	71.1	1.407
1991	37,568	26,314	11,254	70.0	1.428
1992	37,202	26,657	10,545	71.7	1.396
1993	36,554	26,429	10,125	72.3	1.383
1994	36,386	26,778	9,608	73.6	1.359
1995	36,154	26,698	9,456	73.8	1.354
1996	36,662	27,258	9,404	74.3	1.345
1997	37,714	27,850	9,864	73.8	1.354
1998	38,253	28,338	9,915	74.1	1.350
1999	38,836	28,289	10,547	72.8	1.373
2000	39,020	28,900	10,120	74.1	1.350

Source: U.S. Bureau of the Census, March *Current Population Survey*, "Full- Time, Year-Round Workers (All Races) by Median Income and Sex: 1955 to 2000," March 21, 2002.

Change in Number of Households by Income Range, 1990 to 2000

Income Range	Percent Change	Percent of all Households
Less than $10,000	-29.5	9.0
$10,000-$14,999	-13.5	7.0
$15,000-$24,999	-13.0	13.4
$25,000-$34,999	7.5	12.5
$35,000-$49,999	3.6	15.5
$50,000-$74,999	44.9	18.9
$75,000-$99,999	123.4	10.4

[Continued]

Change in Number of Households by Income Range, 1990 to 2000

[Continued]

Income Range	Percent Change	Percent of all Households
$100,000-$149,000	211.5	13.4[1]
$150,000 or more	228.5	-

Source: "Challenging Changes." *Investor's Business Daily*, August 8, 2001, p. A20; U.S. Bureau of the Census. *Notes:* 1. The value of 13.4% is for all households earning $100,000 or higher.

Household Annual Income Ranges in Current Dollars

Current dollars are dollars as valued in the year - not adjusted for inflation.

	Upper Limit of Each Fifth				Lower Limit of Top 5 Percent
	Lowest	Second	Third	Fourth	
1967	3,000	5,850	8,306	11,841	19,000
1968	3,323	6,300	9,030	12,688	19,850
1969	3,574	6,860	9,920	13,900	21,800
1970	3,687	7,064	10,276	14,661	23,178
1971	3,800	7,244	10,660	15,200	24,138
1972	4,050	7,800	11,530	16,500	26,560
1973	4,418	8,393	12,450	17,985	28,509
1974	4,923	9,094	13,400	19,453	31,085
1975	5,025	9,450	14,246	20,496	32,681
1976	5,479	10,133	15,423	22,192	35,382
1977	5,813	10,900	16,531	24,100	38,961
1978	6,384	12,000	18,146	26,425	42,572
1979	7,009	13,035	20,025	29,097	47,465
1980	7,556	14,100	21,610	31,700	51,500
1981	8,160	15,034	23,396	34,600	56,300
1982	8,520	16,010	24,560	36,670	61,107
1983	9,000	16,773	25,718	38,898	64,600
1984	9,600	17,904	27,506	41,600	69,590
1985	10,000	18,852	29,022	43,809	73,263
1986	10,358	19,783	30,555	46,120	78,226
1987	10,800	20,500	32,000	48,363	80,928
1988	11,382	21,500	33,506	50,593	85,640
1989	12,096	23,000	35,350	53,710	91,750
1990	12,500	23,662	36,200	55,205	94,748
1991	12,588	24,000	37,070	56,760	96,400
1992	12,600	24,140	37,900	58,007	99,020
1993	12,967	24,679	38,793	60,300	104,639
1994	13,426	25,200	40,100	62,841	109,821
1995	14,400	26,914	42,002	65,124	113,000

[Continued]

Household Annual Income Ranges in Current Dollars
[Continued]

	Upper Limit of Each Fifth				Lower Limit of Top 5 Percent
	Lowest	Second	Third	Fourth	
1996	14,768	27,760	44,006	68,015	119,540
1997	15,400	29,200	46,000	71,500	126,550
1998	16,116	30,408	48,337	75,000	132,199
1999	17,196	32,000	50,520	79,375	142,021
2000	17,955	33,006	52,272	81,960	145,526

Source: U.S. Bureau of the Census, March Current Population Survey, "Income Limits for Each Fifth and Top 5 Percent of Households (All Races): 1967 to 2000," March 21, 2002.

Poverty Rate of All Families and Married-Couple Families, 1973-2000

	All Families			Married-Couple Families			Couples as % of Total
	Total	Below Poverty Level		Total	Below Poverty Level		
		Number	Percent		Number	Percent	
1973	55,053	4,828	8.8	46,812	2,482	5.3	85.0
1974	55,698	4,922	8.8	47,069	2,474	5.3	84.5
1975	56,245	5,450	9.7	47,318	2,904	6.1	84.1
1976	56,710	5,311	9.4	47,497	2,606	5.5	83.8
1977	57,215	5,311	9.3	47,385	2,524	5.3	82.8
1978	57,804	5,280	9.1	47,692	2,474	5.2	82.5
1979	59,550	5,461	9.2	49,112	2,640	5.4	82.5
1980	60,309	6,217	10.3	49,294	3,032	6.2	81.7
1981	61,019	6,851	11.2	49,630	3,394	6.8	81.3
1982	61,393	7,512	12.2	49,908	3,789	7.6	81.3
1984	62,706	7,277	11.6	50,350	3,488	6.9	80.3
1985	63,558	7,223	11.4	50,933	3,438	6.7	80.1
1985	62,015	7,647	12.3	50,081	3,815	7.6	80.8
1986	64,491	7,023	10.9	51,537	3,123	6.1	79.9
1987	65,204	7,005	10.7	51,675	3,011	5.8	79.3
1988	65,837	6,874	10.4	52,100	2,897	5.6	79.1
1989	66,090	6,784	10.3	52,137	2,931	5.6	78.9
1990	66,322	7,098	10.7	52,147	2,981	5.7	78.6
1991	67,175	7,712	11.5	52,457	3,158	6.0	78.1
1992	68,216	8,144	11.9	53,090	3,385	6.4	77.8
1993	68,506	8,393	12.3	53,181	3,481	6.5	77.6
1994	69,313	8,053	11.6	53,865	3,272	6.1	77.7
1995	69,597	7,532	10.8	53,570	2,982	5.6	77.0
1996	70,241	7,708	11.0	53,604	3,010	5.6	76.3
1997	70,884	7,324	10.3	54,321	2,821	5.2	76.6
1998	71,551	7,186	10.0	54,778	2,879	5.3	76.6

[Continued]

Poverty Rate of All Families and Married-Couple Families, 1973-2000

[Continued]

	All Families			Married-Couple Families			Couples as % of Total
	Total	Below Poverty Level		Total	Below Poverty Level		
		Number	Percent		Number	Percent	
1999	72,031	6,676	9.3	55,315	2,673	4.8	76.8
2000	72,388	6,222	8.6	55,611	2,638	4.7	76.8

Source: U.S. Bureau of the Census, March *Current Population Survey.*"Poverty Status: Status of Families, by Type of Family, Presence of Children, Race, and Hispanic Origin: 1959-2000," February 13, 2002, accessed at http://www.w3.org/TR/REC-html40/loose.dtd.

The Minimum Wage in Actual and Constant 2000 Dollars, 1938 to 2000

Constant dollars were calculated using the Consumer Price Index "All Items" deflator.

	Current Dollars	2000 Dollars
1938	0.25	3.05
1939	0.30	3.72
1940	0.30	3.69
1941	0.30	3.51
1942	0.30	3.17
1943	0.30	2.99
1944	0.30	2.94
1945	0.40	3.83
1946	0.40	3.53
1947	0.40	3.09
1948	0.40	2.86
1949	0.40	2.89
1950	0.75	5.36
1951	0.75	4.97
1952	0.75	4.87
1953	0.75	4.84
1954	0.75	4.80
1955	0.75	4.82
1956	1.00	6.33
1957	1.00	6.13
1958	1.00	5.96
1959	1.00	5.92
1960	1.00	5.82
1961	1.15	6.62
1962	1.25	6.56
1963	1.25	7.03
1964	1.25	6.94
1965	1.25	6.83
1966	1.25	6.64

[Continued]

The Minimum Wage in Actual and Constant 2000 Dollars, 1938 to 2000

[Continued]

	Current Dollars	2000 Dollars
1967	1.40	7.22
1968	1.60	7.72
1969	1.60	7.92
1970	1.60	7.51
1971	1.60	7.10
1972	1.60	6.80
1973	1.60	6.59
1973	1.60	6.21
1974	2.00	6.99
1975	2.10	6.72
1976	2.30	6.96
1977	2.30	6.54
1978	2.65	7.00
1979	2.90	6.88
1980	3.10	6.48
1981	3.35	6.35
1982	3.35	5.98
1983	3.35	5.79
1984	3.35	5.79
1985	3.35	5.55
1986	3.35	5.26
1987	3.35	5.08
1988	3.35	4.88
1989	3.35	4.65
1990	3.35	5.01
1991	4.25	5.37
1992	4.25	5.22
1993	4.25	5.06
1994	4.25	4.94
1995	4.25	4.80
1996	4.75	5.21
1997	5.15	5.53
1998	5.15	5.44
1999	5.15	5.32
2000	5.15	5.15

Source: U.S. Department of Labor, "Value of the Federal Minimum Wage, 1938- 2000," retrieved December 6, 2001 from http://www.dol.gov.

Poverty Rates of Different Categories of Families in 1999

The Poverty Rate is the percentage of families in a category of total families in the category.

Family Category	Poverty Rate (%)
All families	6.2
All families without children	2.1
All families with related children under 18	9.3
All families with one member in the labor force	12.8
Families headed by men with related children under 18	10.7
Families headed by women with related children under 18	23.9
Families headed by men without related children under 18	3.5
Families headed by women without related children under 18	5.7
Married couples without children	1.5
Married couples with related children under 18	5.2
Married couples with one member in the labor force	7.9

Source: Beers, Thomas M. U.S. Department of Labor, Bureau of Labor Statistics, "A Profile of The Working Poor," U.S. Government Printing Office, Washington D.C.

Educational Attainment: Workers 25 Years Old and Over by Mean Earnings and Sex: 1991 to 2000

Workers 25 years old and over as of March of the following year. Earnings in current and 2000 inflation-adjusted dollars.

Educational Attainment and Year	Male Number with Earnings (000)	Male Mean Earnings Current Dollars	Male Mean Earnings 2000 Dollars	Female Number with Earnings (000)	Female Mean Earnings Current Dollars	Female Mean Earnings 2000 Dollars	Women's Earnings as % of Men's
TOTAL							
1991	60,048	30,469	37,738	50,774	17,825	22,078	58.5
1992	60,423	31,382	37,866	51,148	18,701	22,565	59.6
1993	60,743	34,046	40,046	52,317	19,663	23,128	57.8
1994	61,760	35,717	41,110	53,368	20,461	23,551	57.3
1995	62,407	36,818	41,340	54,249	21,252	23,862	57.7
1996	63,666	38,459	42,042	55,244	22,521	24,619	58.6
1997	64,293	40,392	43,218	56,134	23,538	25,185	58.3
1998	64,628	42,066	44,388	56,950	24,992	26,372	59.4
1999	65,412	44,730	46,233	58,225	25,818	26,685	57.7
2000	66,186	47,536	47,536	58,462	27,350	27,350	57.5
Less than 9th Grade							
1991	3,343	14,464	17,915	1,728	8,389	10,390	58.0
1992	3,316	14,775	17,828	1,686	8,915	10,757	60.3
1993	3,120	14,411	16,951	1,669	8,721	10,258	60.5
1994	3,056	18,427	21,210	1,641	9,163	10,547	49.7
1995	3,134	16,119	18,099	1,643	10,021	11,252	62.2

[Continued]

Educational Attainment: Workers 25 Years Old and Over by Mean Earnings and Sex: 1991 to 2000

[Continued]

Educational Attainment and Year	Male			Female			Women's Earnings as % of Men's
	Number with Earnings (000)	Mean Earnings		Number with Earnings (000)	Mean Earnings		
		Current Dollars	2000 Dollars		Current Dollars	2000 Dollars	
1996	3,163	17,179	18,779	1,566	10,727	11,726	62.4
1997	2,993	19,230	20,576	1,624	10,655	11,401	55.4
1998	2,798	19,096	20,150	1,571	13,461	14,204	70.5
1999	2,833	19,507	20,162	1,673	12,561	12,983	64.4
2000	2,844	21,691	21,691	1,738	12,997	12,997	59.9
9th to 12th Grade (No Diploma)							
1991	5,307	18,419	22,814	3,844	10,305	12,764	55.9
1992	5,030	18,297	22,077	3,519	10,834	13,072	59.2
1993	4,955	18,585	21,860	3,446	11,697	13,758	62.9
1994	4,732	19,701	22,676	3,511	10,968	12,624	55.7
1995	4,996	21,019	23,601	3,616	11,469	12,878	54.6
1996	5,145	22,602	24,707	3,545	12,263	13,405	54.3
1997	5,103	24,331	26,034	3,574	12,897	13,799	53.0
1998	4,918	23,307	24,594	3,536	12,802	13,509	54.9
1999	4,608	23,354	24,139	3,489	14,349	14,831	61.4
2000	4,674	27,229	27,229	3,449	15,094	15,094	55.4
High School Graduate							
1991	20,571	24,531	30,384	19,271	14,269	17,673	58.2
1992	20,273	24,744	29,856	18,810	14,878	17,952	60.1
1993	19,814	26,182	30,796	18,462	15,347	18,052	58.6
1994	19,754	27,376	31,510	18,395	15,888	18,287	58.0
1995	19,966	28,624	32,140	18,357	17,016	19,106	59.4
1996	20,528	30,073	32,874	18,918	17,297	18,908	57.5
1997	20,615	30,798	32,953	18,794	18,033	19,295	58.6
1998	20,463	30,949	32,658	18,760	19,049	20,101	61.6
1999	20,656	33,084	34,195	18,756	19,306	19,955	58.4
2000	20,806	34,568	34,568	18,374	20,516	20,516	59.3
Some College, No Degree							
1991	10,629	29,233	36,208	9,380	17,241	21,354	59.0
1992	10,843	29,275	35,323	9,903	17,742	21,407	60.6
1993	11,098	30,590	35,981	10,441	18,104	21,294	59.2
1994	11,409	30,878	35,541	10,799	18,269	21,028	59.2
1995	11,470	33,726	37,869	10,601	19,223	21,584	57.0
1996	11,634	36,058	39,417	10,609	20,674	22,600	57.3
1997	11,540	37,079	39,674	10,702	21,431	22,931	57.8
1998	11,577	38,147	40,253	11,170	22,719	23,973	59.6
1999	11,908	40,282	41,635	11,483	23,955	24,760	59.5
2000	11,906	42,682	42,682	11,314	24,751	24,751	58.0

[Continued]

Educational Attainment: Workers 25 Years Old and Over by Mean Earnings and Sex: 1991 to 2000

[Continued]

Educational Attainment and Year	Male			Female			Women's Earnings as % of Men's
	Number with Earnings (000)	Mean Earnings		Number with Earnings (000)	Mean Earnings		
		Current Dollars	2000 Dollars		Current Dollars	2000 Dollars	
Associate Degree							
1991	3,662	31,432	38,931	4,100	20,185	25,001	64.2
1992	4,066	31,615	38,147	4,381	20,404	24,619	64.5
1993	4,453	31,888	37,507	5,061	20,865	24,542	65.4
1994	4,561	34,826	40,085	5,181	21,391	24,621	61.4
1995	4,698	35,579	39,949	5,352	23,287	26,147	65.5
1996	4,693	37,120	40,578	5,444	23,307	25,478	62.8
1997	5,003	38,081	40,746	5,502	24,977	26,725	65.6
1998	5,099	41,474	43,764	5,431	26,527	27,991	64.0
1999	5,175	42,006	43,417	5,844	25,978	26,851	61.8
2000	5,453	44,705	44,705	6,180	26,631	26,631	59.6
Bachelor's Degree or More							
1991	16,536	45,539	56,404	12,451	26,622	32,974	58.5
1992	16,894	47,800	57,675	12,850	27,895	33,658	58.4
1993	17,304	53,791	63,270	13,238	29,905	35,175	55.6
1994	18,248	55,046	63,358	13,842	31,646	36,425	57.5
1995	18,142	56,038	62,921	14,679	30,941	34,741	55.2
1996	18,503	57,661	63,032	15,161	33,666	36,802	58.4
1997	19,039	61,028	65,298	15,938	34,646	37,070	56.8
1998	19,773	63,936	67,466	16,481	36,506	38,521	57.1
1999	20,232	68,335	70,631	16,980	37,880	39,152	55.4
2000	20,503	72,481	72,481	17,407	40,371	40,371	55.7
Bachelor's Degree							
1991	10,416	40,170	49,754	8,537	23,647	29,289	58.9
1992	10,621	41,509	50,085	8,799	25,039	30,212	60.3
1993	11,022	45,472	53,485	9,072	26,432	31,090	58.1
1994	11,609	48,095	55,358	9,389	27,636	31,809	57.5
1995	11,486	48,101	54,009	10,144	27,786	31,199	57.8
1996	11,900	48,234	52,727	10,550	29,701	32,468	61.6
1997	12,338	51,656	55,271	11,108	31,071	33,245	60.1
1998	12,869	56,658	59,786	11,367	32,632	34,434	57.6
1999	13,057	59,490	61,488	11,548	33,779	34,914	56.8
2000	13,316	65,124	65,124	11,844	36,500	36,500	56.0
Master's Degree							
1991	3,899	47,311	58,599	3,141	30,781	38,125	65.1
1992	3,865	48,539	58,567	3,229	31,258	37,716	64.4
1993	3,810	53,809	63,291	3,295	34,595	40,691	64.3
1994	4,066	55,500	63,881	3,435	35,928	41,353	64.7
1995	4,199	58,434	65,611	3,519	35,078	39,387	60.0

[Continued]

Educational Attainment: Workers 25 Years Old and Over by Mean Earnings and Sex: 1991 to 2000

[Continued]

Educational Attainment and Year	Male			Female			Women's Earnings as % of Men's
	Number with Earnings (000)	Mean Earnings		Number with Earnings (000)	Mean Earnings		
		Current Dollars	2000 Dollars		Current Dollars	2000 Dollars	
1996	4,058	62,416	68,230	3,548	36,575	39,982	58.6
1997	3,996	63,393	67,829	3,726	38,463	41,154	60.7
1998	4,186	64,815	68,393	3,984	40,483	42,718	62.5
1999	4,462	68,622	70,927	4,238	42,552	43,981	62.0
2000	4,445	76,552	76,552	4,348	45,698	45,698	59.7
Professional Degree							
1991	1,394	72,590	89,909	472	45,134	55,902	62.2
1992	1,495	83,107	100,277	497	48,750	58,822	58.7
1993	1,486	100,594	118,321	491	50,714	59,651	50.4
1994	1,526	92,504	106,472	614	58,514	67,350	63.3
1995	1,433	101,947	114,469	626	48,182	54,100	47.3
1996	1,495	103,055	112,655	604	72,015	78,724	69.9
1997	1,547	109,830	117,515	663	62,113	66,459	56.6
1998	1,470	109,289	115,323	651	65,850	69,485	60.3
1999	1,480	121,105	125,173	687	60,856	62,900	50.3
2000	1,484	111,190	111,190	721	62,156	62,156	55.9
Doctorate Degree							
1991	827	59,224	73,354	301	38,564	47,765	65.1
1992	913	60,041	72,445	326	39,917	48,164	66.5
1993	986	76,168	89,591	380	45,242	53,215	59.4
1994	1,048	75,735	87,171	404	47,598	54,785	62.8
1995	1,024	71,016	79,739	391	47,968	53,860	67.5
1996	1,049	81,492	89,083	460	51,865	56,696	63.6
1997	1,158	87,520	93,644	441	51,189	54,771	58.5
1998	1,248	82,619	87,180	480	55,431	58,491	67.1
1999	1,233	97,605	100,884	507	61,136	63,190	62.6
2000	1,258	90,327	90,327	494	54,477	54,477	60.3

Source: U.S. Bureau of the Census, March *Current Population Survey*, created March 21, 2002, retrieved from http://www.w3.org/TR/REC- html40/ loose.dtd.

Educational Attainment of Householder - Families with Householder 25 Years Old and Over by Median and Mean Income: 1991 to 2000

Families as of March of the following year. Income in current and 2000 inflation adjusted dollars. Current dollar medians above 100,000 are plugged at 100,000.

Educational Attainment and Income Year	Number (000)	Median Income		Mean Income	
		Current Dollars	2000 Dollars	Current Dollars	2000 Dollars
TOTAL					
1991	64,531	36,904	45,709	44,197	54,742
1992	65,319	37,671	45,454	45,319	54,682
1993	65,506	38,231	44,968	48,425	56,959
1994	66,234	40,159	46,223	50,626	58,271
1995	66,578	41,771	46,902	52,642	59,108
1996	67,277	43,603	47,665	54,964	60,084
1997	67,866	45,874	49,084	58,242	62,317
1998	68,309	48,194	50,855	60,988	64,355
1999	68,678	50,571	52,270	64,232	66,390
2000	68,899	52,166	52,166	67,038	67,038
Less than 9th grade					
1991	6,048	17,709	21,934	22,370	27,707
1992	5,941	18,040	21,767	22,686	27,373
1993	5,614	18,573	21,846	23,211	27,301
1994	5,223	19,397	22,326	24,433	28,122
1995	5,063	20,550	23,074	25,833	29,006
1996	4,767	20,781	22,717	26,762	29,255
1997	4,667	21,208	22,692	28,818	30,835
1998	4,464	22,328	23,561	29,547	31,178
1999	4,385	23,668	24,463	30,176	31,190
2000	4,178	24,964	24,964	32,730	32,730
9th to 12th grade (no diploma)					
1991	7,045	22,402	27,747	26,912	33,333
1992	6,741	22,054	26,610	26,369	31,817
1993	6,756	22,224	26,140	28,013	32,950
1994	6,618	22,484	25,879	27,952	32,173
1995	6,477	23,331	26,197	29,815	33,477
1996	6,771	24,575	26,864	32,199	35,198
1997	6,604	25,465	27,247	32,948	35,254
1998	6,227	26,707	28,181	33,356	35,197
1999	5,989	27,050	27,959	33,182	34,297
2000	6,026	28,878	28,878	36,706	36,706
High School Graduate					
1991	22,160	33,255	41,189	37,398	46,321
1992	22,153	33,953	40,968	37,868	45,692
1993	21,340	33,674	39,608	39,242	46,157
1994	21,358	35,275	40,602	41,078	47,281

[Continued]

Educational Attainment of Householder - Families with Householder 25 Years Old and Over by Median and Mean Income: 1991 to 2000

[Continued]

Educational Attainment and Income Year	Number (000)	Median Income		Mean Income	
		Current Dollars	2000 Dollars	Current Dollars	2000 Dollars
1995	21,468	36,751	41,265	43,182	48,486
1996	21,870	38,563	42,155	45,146	49,352
1997	21,991	40,040	42,842	46,523	49,778
1998	21,689	41,302	43,582	48,434	51,108
1999	21,702	42,995	44,439	50,892	52,602
2000	21,502	44,248	44,248	52,255	52,255
Some College, No Degree					
1991	10,726	40,288	49,900	45,219	56,008
1992	11,252	40,604	48,993	45,216	54,558
1993	11,815	40,736	47,915	46,526	54,725
1994	12,136	41,595	47,876	47,703	54,906
1995	12,166	43,448	48,785	50,679	56,904
1996	12,092	44,814	48,989	53,539	58,526
1997	12,107	46,936	50,220	55,596	59,486
1998	12,612	48,495	51,172	57,315	60,479
1999	12,747	50,967	52,679	61,419	63,482
2000	12,593	51,642	51,642	63,275	63,275
Associate Degree					
1991	3,715	44,186	54,728	48,245	59,756
1992	3,984	43,028	51,918	48,317	58,299
1993	4,408	45,054	52,994	49,457	58,172
1994	4,669	46,742	53,800	53,515	61,596
1995	4,786	48,700	54,682	54,354	61,030
1996	4,955	51,176	55,943	56,153	61,384
1997	5,226	52,393	56,059	63,063	67,476
1998	5,420	54,719	57,740	63,524	67,031
1999	5,560	56,602	58,503	64,482	66,648
2000	5,869	57,814	57,814	67,517	67,517
Bachelor's Degree or More					
1991	14,837	60,670	75,145	69,706	86,337
1992	15,249	61,902	74,691	72,633	87,639
1993	15,574	64,941	76,385	80,098	94,213
1994	16,230	66,529	76,575	82,216	94,631
1995	16,618	67,529	75,824	82,874	93,053
1996	16,823	69,688	76,180	85,557	93,527
1997	17,272	73,578	78,727	91,180	97,560
1998	17,896	76,999	81,250	95,481	100,752
1999	18,295	81,140	83,866	100,267	103,635
2000	18,732	84,172	84,172	103,794	103,794

[Continued]

Educational Attainment of Householder - Families with Householder 25 Years Old and Over by Median and Mean Income: 1991 to 2000

[Continued]

Educational Attainment and Income Year	Number (000)	Median Income		Mean Income	
		Current Dollars	2000 Dollars	Current Dollars	2000 Dollars
Bachelor's Degree					
1991	9,288	56,052	69,425	63,155	78,223
1992	9,421	56,821	68,560	65,021	78,454
1993	9,673	59,703	70,224	70,209	82,581
1994	10,101	61,918	71,268	73,365	84,443
1995	10,421	61,780	69,368	73,334	82,342
1996	10,753	64,293	70,282	75,311	82,327
1997	11,201	67,230	71,934	81,026	86,696
1998	11,593	71,680	75,637	85,423	90,139
1999	11,743	76,059	78,614	91,075	94,134
2000	12,016	77,245	77,245	96,012	96,012
Master's Degree					
1991	3,579	65,552	81,192	72,548	89,857
1992	3,705	66,216	79,896	75,423	91,005
1993	3,687	68,365	80,413	81,298	95,625
1994	3,864	70,651	81,320	83,887	96,554
1995	4,091	73,926	83,006	88,198	99,031
1996	4,009	76,065	83,151	90,956	99,429
1997	3,903	81,734	87,453	96,519	103,273
1998	4,093	83,052	87,637	101,670	107,283
1999	4,395	85,632	88,509	104,403	107,910
2000	4,518	91,126	91,126	110,924	110,924
Professional Degree					
1991	1,247	85,919	106,418	99,068	122,704
1992	1,324	92,396	111,485	110,326	133,119
1993	1,297	99,943	117,555	132,918	156,341
1994	1,302	92,509	106,478	122,956	141,523
1995	1,193	96,935	108,842	129,959	145,922
1996	1,189	100,000	109,315	138,118	150,984
1997	1,249	100,000	106,997	144,709	154,835
1998	1,228	100,000	105,521	147,170	155,295
1999	1,174	100,000	103,359	147,894	152,862
2000	1,161	100,000	100,000	138,933	138,933
Doctorate Degree					
1991	723	78,928	97,759	89,146	110,415
1992	799	75,657	91,288	86,980	104,950
1993	918	82,480	97,015	104,839	123,314
1994	964	86,912	100,036	113,238	130,337
1995	913	90,463	101,575	106,375	119,441
1996	872	92,316	100,916	115,415	126,166

[Continued]

Educational Attainment of Householder - Families with Householder 25 Years Old and Over by Median and Mean Income: 1991 to 2000

[Continued]

Educational Attainment and Income Year	Number (000)	Median Income		Mean Income	
		Current Dollars	2000 Dollars	Current Dollars	2000 Dollars
1997	919	100,000	106,997	119,550	127,915
1998	982	96,945	102,297	123,796	130,630
1999	982	100,000	103,359	134,713	139,238
2000	1,036	100,000	100,000	123,561	123,561

Source: U.S. Bureau of the Cencus, March *Current Population Survey,* created March 21, 2002, retrieved from http://www.w3.org/TR/REC-html40/loose.dtd.

Chapter 5
PEOPLE, TECHNOLOGY, AND PRODUCTIVITY

Indexes of Productivity - Manufacturing

The Index base is 1992 = 100.

	Output	Output per Hour	Compen-sation	Hours Worked
1992	100.0	100.0	100.0	100.0
1993	103.3	101.9	104.2	101.4
1994	108.7	105.0	109.4	103.6
1995	113.4	109.0	112.2	104.0
1996	117.0	112.8	113.4	103.6
1997	124.1	117.6	117.5	105.5
1998	130.4	124.0	123.5	105.2
1999	135.2	129.6	127.4	104.3
2000	142.9	138.3	134.5	103.4

Source: Bureau of Labor Statistics, U.S. Department of Labor, http://www.bls.gov/lpc/.

Business Productivity - All Sectors

The Index base is 1992 = 100.

	Hours Worked in Business	Business Output	Output per Hour in Business
1947	65.0	20.7	31.8
1948	65.5	21.8	33.3
1949	63.3	21.6	34.0
1950	64.1	23.7	36.9
1951	66.1	25.2	38.0
1952	66.2	26.0	39.2
1953	67.0	27.2	40.7
1954	64.6	26.9	41.6
1955	67.0	29.0	43.3
1956	68.0	29.5	43.4
1957	67.0	30.0	44.7
1958	63.9	29.4	46.0
1959	66.6	31.9	47.9

[Continued]

Business Productivity - All Sectors
[Continued]

	Hours Worked in Business	Business Output	Output per Hour in Business
1960	66.6	32.5	48.8
1961	65.5	33.1	50.6
1962	66.6	35.2	52.9
1963	67.0	36.8	55.0
1964	68.1	39.2	57.5
1965	70.4	41.9	59.6
1966	72.3	44.8	62.0
1967	72.0	45.6	63.4
1968	73.4	47.9	65.4
1969	75.2	49.4	65.7
1970	73.7	49.4	67.0
1971	73.3	51.3	69.9
1972	75.7	54.7	72.2
1973	78.5	58.5	74.5
1974	78.6	57.6	73.2
1975	75.2	57.0	75.8
1976	77.6	60.9	78.5
1977	80.6	64.3	79.8
1978	84.7	68.3	80.7
1979	87.5	70.6	80.7
1980	86.8	69.8	80.4
1981	87.4	71.7	82.0
1982	85.2	69.6	81.7
1983	86.6	73.3	84.6
1984	91.6	79.7	87.0
1985	93.6	83.1	88.7
1986	94.2	86.1	91.4
1987	97.0	89.2	91.9
1988	100.0	92.9	93.0
1989	102.4	96.2	93.9
1990	102.6	97.6	95.2
1991	100.2	96.5	96.3
1992	100.0	100.0	100.0
1993	102.6	103.1	100.5
1994	106.2	108.1	101.9
1995	108.7	111.5	102.6
1996	110.4	116.4	105.4
1997	113.6	122.5	107.8
1998	116.1	128.5	110.7
1999	118.5	134.4	113.4
2000	120.3	140.6	116.9

Source: Bureau of Labor Statistics, U.S. Department of Labor, http://www.bls.gov/lpc/.

Gross Domestic Product and Components

All data are in billions of Chained 1996 Dollars. Chained dollars are constant dollars.

	Gross Domestic Product	Services	Non-durable Goods	Equipment and Software	Durable Goods
1987	6,113.3	2,379.3	1,274.5	360.0	455.2
1988	6,368.4	2,477.2	1,315.1	386.9	481.5
1989	6,591.8	2,546.0	1,351.0	414.0	491.7
1990	6,707.9	2,616.2	1,369.6	415.7	487.1
1991	6,676.4	2,651.8	1,364.0	407.2	454.9
1992	6,880.0	2,729.7	1,389.7	437.5	479.0
1993	7,062.6	2,802.5	1,430.3	487.1	518.3
1994	7,347.7	2,886.2	1,485.1	544.9	557.7
1995	7,543.8	2,963.4	1,529.0	607.6	583.5
1996	7,813.2	3,047.0	1,574.1	674.4	616.5
1997	8,159.5	3,147.0	1,619.9	764.2	657.3
1998	8,508.9	3,273.4	1,686.4	875.4	726.7
1999	8,856.5	3,393.2	1,766.4	978.3	817.8
2000	9,224.0	3,527.7	1,849.9	1,087.4	895.5

Source: U.S. Department of Commerce, Bureau of Economic Analysis, and Survey of Current Business, September 2001, published by the same agency.

Number of Employees Required to Generate $1 mil. in Output in 1997

	1997 Output ($ mil.)	1997 Employment (000)	Employees Required to produce $1 mil. Output
Wholesale Trade	4,059,658	5,796.6	1.4
Utilities	411,713	702.7	1.7
Finance and Insurance	2,197,771	5,835.2	2.7
Mining	173,989	509.0	2.9
Manufacturing	3,842,061	16,888.0	4.4
Information	623,214	3,066.2	4.9
Educational Services	65,439	321.1	4.9
Retail Trade	2,460,886	13,991.1	5.7
Construction	858,581	5,664.8	6.6
Real Estate, Rental, Leasing	240,918	1,702.4	7.1
Profession, Scientific, Technical Services	579,542	5,212.7	9.0
Transportation and Warehousing	318,245	2,920.8	9.2
Arts and Entertainment	170,176	1,587.7	9.3
Health Care	885,054	13,561.6	15.3

[Continued]

Number of Employees Required to Generate $1 mil. in Output in 1997

[Continued]

	1997 Output ($ mil.)	1997 Employment (000)	Employees Required to produce $1 mil. Output
Admin Suport and Waste Management	295,936	7,347.4	24.8
Accommodations and Food Services	350,389	9,451.1	27.0

Source: U.S. Department of the Census, 1997 Economic Census.

Employees Required to Produce $1 Million in Manufacturing Shipments or in Construction Put Into Place

Data normalized to 1996 dollars.

	Manufacturing			Construction		
	Value of Shipments (mil. 1996)	Employment (000)	Employees per $1 mil. in Shipments	Construction Put in Place (mil. 1996)	Employment (000)	Employees per $1 mil. in Constr.
1958	1,535,796.148	15,945	10.38	-	-	-
1959	1,680,245.030	16,675	9.92	-	-	-
1960	1,684,250.000	16,796	9.97	-	-	-
1961	1,669,217.274	16,326	9.78	-	-	-
1962	1,779,875.500	16,853	9.47	-	-	-
1963	1,849,186.813	16,995	9.19	-	-	-
1964	1,941,777.200	17,274	8.90	405,864	3,097	7.63
1965	2,101,401.111	18,062	8.60	428,899	3,232	7.54
1966	2,242,548.938	19,214	8.57	430,631	3,317	7.70
1967	2,265,783.916	19,447	8.58	424,218	3,248	7.66
1968	2,356,309.617	19,781	8.39	446,145	3,350	7.51
1969	2,400,946.148	20,167	8.40	452,092	3,575	7.91
1970	2,263,082.143	19,367	8.56	429,041	3,588	8.36
1971	2,297,523.973	18,623	8.11	465,633	3,704	7.95
1972	2,502,716.744	19,151	7.65	498,463	3,889	7.80
1973	2,746,933.459	20,154	7.34	506,572	4,097	8.09
1974	2,896,319.385	20,077	6.93	449,424	4,020	8.94
1975	2,733,662.194	18,323	6.70	404,132	3,525	8.72
1976	2,957,991.517	18,997	6.42	435,292	3,576	8.22
1977	3,179,068.570	19,682	6.19	470,439	3,851	8.19
1978	3,326,470.074	20,505	6.16	505,446	4,229	8.37
1979	3,466,253.261	21,040	6.07	513,753	4,463	8.69
1980	3,355,712.733	20,285	6.04	464,144	4,346	9.36
1981	3,358,095.872	20,170	6.01	455,260	4,188	9.20
1982	3,087,923.756	18,780	6.08	423,729	3,904	9.21
1983	3,128,212.721	18,432	5.89	465,073	3,946	8.48

[Continued]

Employees Required to Produce $1 Million in Manufacturing Shipments or in Construction Put Into Place

[Continued]

	Manufacturing			Construction		
	Value of Shipments (mil. 1996)	Employment (000)	Employees per $1 mil. in Shipments	Construc-tion Put in Place (mil. 1996)	Employment (000)	Employees per $1 mil. in Constr.
1984	3,334,087.134	19,372	5.81	534,557	4,380	8.19
1985	3,288,429.356	19,248	5.85	567,689	4,668	8.22
1986	3,212,157.591	18,947	5.90	588,804	4,810	8.17
1987	3,279,780.103	18,999	5.79	585,103	4,958	8.47
1988	3,436,735.943	19,314	5.62	583,396	5,098	8.74
1989	3,469,795.993	19,391	5.59	579,583	5,171	8.92
1990	3,400,943.595	19,076	5.61	560,802	5,120	9.13
1991	3,237,169.047	18,406	5.69	503,711	4,650	9.23
1992	3,279,553.591	18,104	5.52	533,322	4,492	8.42
1993	3,333,999.574	18,075	5.42	544,285	4,668	8.58
1994	3,498,452.456	18,321	5.24	574,256	4,986	8.68
1995	3,671,770.174	18,524	5.04	570,188	5,160	9.05
1996	3,715,460.000	18,495	4.98	615,797	5,418	8.80
1997	3,854,639.003	18,675	4.84	632,680	5,691	9.00
1998	3,933,075.803	18,805	4.78	664,244	6,020	9.06
1999	4,067,543.927	18,552	4.56	692,281	6,415	9.27
2000	4,198,935.082	18,469	4.40	706,899	6,698	9.48

Source: U.S. Bureau of the Census, U.S. Department of Commerce (shipments and construction put in place) and Bureau of Labor Statistics, U.S. Department of Labor (employment data).

Labor and Multi-Factor Productivity in Manufacturing, 1949 to 2000

Index - 1996 = 100. For a discussion of these indexes, please see text.

	Milti-factor Productivity Index	Labor Productivity Output per Hour Index
1949	59.7	29.7
1950	62.7	30.1
1951	62.9	30.0
1952	63.8	31.2
1953	65.0	32.3
1954	64.9	33.1
1955	66.9	34.4
1956	66.0	34.2
1957	66.4	34.9
1958	65.2	35.5
1959	68.1	36.3

[Continued]

Labor and Multi-Factor Productivity in Manufacturing, 1949 to 2000

[Continued]

	Milti-factor Productivity Index	Labor Productivity Output per Hour Index
1960	68.3	37.1
1961	68.9	37.9
1962	71.6	39.2
1963	73.6	40.5
1964	75.7	42.0
1965	77.7	43.0
1966	78.0	43.5
1967	77.5	45.1
1968	79.9	46.7
1969	80.5	47.4
1970	79.2	48.0
1971	81.4	51.2
1972	84.4	53.5
1973	85.9	54.4
1974	81.3	54.3
1975	78.9	57.0
1976	81.7	59.4
1977	82.9	61.8
1978	83.6	62.4
1979	82.7	61.9
1980	81.3	62.1
1981	81.9	62.7
1982	83.3	65.8
1983	85.2	68.0
1984	87.8	70.5
1985	89.2	73.0
1986	90.7	76.2
1987	93.5	78.3
1988	95.2	80.0
1989	93.4	80.1
1990	93.3	82.4
1991	92.4	84.2
1992	94.0	88.7
1993	94.9	90.3
1994	97.3	93.1
1995	99.2	96.6
1996	100.0	100.0
1997	103.5	104.3
1998	106.3	109.9
1999	109.4	114.9
2000	-	122.6

Source: Bureau of Labor Statistics, U.S. Department of Labor, http://www.bls.gov/mprhome.htm.

Educational Attainment of Adults, 25 Years and Older

Population and percent of age group total. Persons with High School or Higher include those with College degrees.

	Total Population 25-years or Older (000)	Population with High School or Higher (000)	Population with Less Than High School (000)	Population with 4 Years of College (000)	High School or Higher, Percent of Total	Less than High School, Percent of Total	4 years of College, Percent of Total
1940	74,776	18,034	55,700	3,407	24.1	74.5	4.6
1947	82,578	26,883	54,406	4,424	32.6	65.9	5.4
1950	87,484	29,143	55,925	5,272	33.3	63.9	6.0
1952	88,358	33,906	53,506	6,118	38.4	60.6	6.9
1957	95,630	38,989	54,828	7,172	40.8	57.3	7.5
1959	97,478	41,841	53,826	7,734	42.9	55.2	7.9
1960	99,465	40,804	58,661	7,617	41.0	59.0	7.7
1962	100,664	46,649	54,015	9,002	46.3	53.7	8.9
1964	102,421	49,158	53,265	9,345	48.0	52.0	9.1
1965	103,245	50,584	52,662	9,742	49.0	51.0	9.4
1966	103,876	51,838	52,042	10,212	49.9	50.1	9.8
1967	104,864	53,637	51,225	10,550	51.1	48.8	10.1
1968	106,469	56,028	50,439	11,171	52.6	47.4	10.5
1969	107,750	58,232	49,517	11,535	54.0	46.0	10.7
1970	109,310	60,360	48,948	12,062	55.2	44.8	11.0
1971	110,627	62,423	48,204	12,612	56.4	43.6	11.4
1972	111,133	64,652	46,482	13,364	58.2	41.8	12.0
1973	112,866	67,507	45,358	14,228	59.8	40.2	12.6
1974	115,005	70,425	44,580	15,300	61.2	38.8	13.3
1975	116,897	73,115	43,782	16,244	62.5	37.5	13.9
1976	118,848	76,130	42,717	17,496	64.1	35.9	14.7
1977	120,870	78,476	42,394	18,627	64.9	35.1	15.4
1978	123,019	81,092	41,929	19,332	65.9	34.1	15.7
1979	125,295	84,887	40,407	20,579	67.7	32.2	16.4
1980	130,409	89,506	40,902	22,193	68.6	31.4	17.0
1981	132,899	92,631	40,267	22,674	69.7	30.3	17.1
1982	135,526	96,168	39,357	24,050	71.0	29.0	17.7
1983	138,020	99,506	38,514	25,915	72.1	27.9	18.8
1984	140,794	103,216	37,575	26,862	73.3	26.7	19.1
1985	143,524	106,079	37,446	27,808	73.9	26.1	19.4
1986	146,606	109,556	37,050	28,489	74.7	25.3	19.4
1987	149,144	112,785	36,358	29,637	75.6	24.4	19.9
1988	151,635	115,526	36,111	30,787	76.2	23.8	20.3
1989	154,155	118,515	35,641	32,565	76.9	23.1	21.1
1990	156,538	121,485	35,052	33,291	77.6	22.4	21.3
1991	158,694	124,468	34,228	34,026	78.4	21.6	21.4
1992	160,827	127,717	33,110	34,337	79.4	20.6	21.4
1993	162,826	130,630	32,194	35,590	80.2	19.8	21.9
1994	164,512	133,073	31,440	36,544	80.9	19.1	22.2
1995	166,438	135,925	30,513	38,226	81.7	18.3	23.0
1996	168,323	137,599	30,724	39,668	81.7	18.3	23.6

[Continued]

Educational Attainment of Adults, 25 Years and Older

[Continued]

	Total Population 25-years or Older (000)	Population with High School or Higher (000)	Population with Less Than High School (000)	Population with 4 Years of College (000)	High School or Higher, Percent of Total	Less than High School, Percent of Total	4 years of College, Percent of Total
1997	170,581	140,057	30,523	40,697	82.1	17.9	23.9
1998	172,211	142,653	29,558	41,973	82.8	17.2	24.4
1999	173,754	144,914	28,071	43,803	83.4	16.2	25.2
2000	175,230	147,376	27,854	44,845	84.1	15.9	25.6

Source: U.S. Census Bureau, U.S. Department of Commerce, Current Population Survey, March 2000.

Educational Attainment by Race - High School or Higher, Population Aged 25 or Older

Data are shown as percent of total age group.

	All Races			Whites			Blacks			Hispanics		
	Total	Male	Female	Total	Male	Female	Total	Male	Female	Total	Male	Female
1940	24.5	22.7	26.3	26.1	24.2	28.1	7.7	6.9	8.4	NA	NA	NA
1950	34.3	32.6	36.0	NA	NA	NA	13.7	12.5	14.7	NA	NA	NA
1962	46.3	45.0	47.5	48.7	47.4	49.9	24.8	23.2	26.2	NA	NA	NA
1970	55.2	55.0	55.4	57.4	57.2	57.6	33.7	32.4	34.8	NA	NA	NA
1980	68.6	69.2	68.1	70.5	71.0	70.1	51.2	51.1	51.3	45.3	46.4	44.1
1990	77.6	77.7	77.5	79.1	79.1	79.0	66.2	65.8	66.5	50.8	50.3	51.3
2000	84.1	84.2	84.0	84.9	84.8	85.0	78.5	78.7	78.3	57.0	56.6	57.5

Source: U.S, Bureau of the Census, U.S. Department of Commerce, Current Population Survey, March 2000.

Average Earnings by Educational Attainment and Growth in Productivity - 1975-1999

Earnings data are shown in year 2000 constant dollars.

	Average Earnings			Index, 1975=100			
	High School and Higher	Less than High School	College and Higher	High School and Higher	Less than High School	College and Higher	Output per Hour - Business
1975	29,946	19,838	45,069	100.0	100.0	100.0	100.0
1976	30,251	20,337	45,467	101.0	102.5	100.9	103.6
1977	30,643	20,079	46,096	102.3	101.2	102.3	105.3
1978	30,876	20,492	45,821	103.1	103.3	101.7	106.5
1979	30,162	19,971	44,550	100.7	100.7	98.8	106.5
1980	28,537	18,484	42,280	95.3	93.2	93.8	106.1
1981	27,788	17,726	41,069	92.8	89.4	91.1	108.2
1982	27,596	16,751	41,250	92.1	84.4	91.5	107.8
1983	28,094	17,035	42,247	93.8	85.9	93.7	111.6

[Continued]

Average Earnings by Educational Attainment and Growth in Productivity - 1975-1999

[Continued]

	Average Earnings			Index, 1975=100			
	High School and Higher	Less than High School	College and Higher	High School and Higher	Less than High School	College and Higher	Output per Hour - Business
1984	28,603	17,210	43,140	95.5	86.8	95.7	114.8
1985	29,512	17,166	45,032	98.5	86.5	99.9	117.0
1986	30,597	17,602	47,017	102.2	88.7	104.3	120.6
1987	30,874	17,923	46,414	103.1	90.3	103.0	121.2
1988	31,363	17,306	46,878	104.7	87.2	104.0	122.7
1989	31,954	17,001	48,515	106.7	85.7	107.6	123.9
1990	30,749	16,577	46,497	102.7	83.6	103.2	125.6
1991	30,147	15,947	45,750	100.7	80.4	101.5	127.0
1992	30,367	15,721	46,576	101.4	79.2	103.3	131.9
1993	31,413	15,278	49,867	104.9	77.0	110.6	132.6
1994	32,000	15,915	50,478	106.9	80.2	112.0	134.4
1995	32,331	15,834	49,034	108.0	79.8	108.8	135.4
1996	32,865	16,475	49,965	109.7	83.0	110.9	139.1
1997	33,641	17,299	51,154	112.3	87.2	113.5	142.2
1998	34,773	16,959	52,890	116.1	85.5	117.4	146.0
1999	35,639	16,663	54,660	119.0	84.0	121.3	149.6

Source: Data on earnings from *Current Population Survey*, March 2000. Productivity data are from Bureau of Labor Statistics. The Consumer Price Index, published by the BLS, was used to deflate current dollar earnings estimates.

Earnings by Educational Attainment in Actual and Year 2000 Dollars

	Average Annual Earnings						Difference Between High Only and College	
	High School Only		High School and Higher		College and Higher			
	Actual $	2000 $	Actual $	2000 $	Actual $	2000 $	Actual $	2000 $
1975	7,843	25,103	9,356	29,946	14,081	45,069	6,238	19,965
1976	8,393	25,400	9,996	30,251	15,024	45,467	6,631	20,067
1977	9,013	25,611	10,784	30,643	16,222	46,096	7,209	20,485
1978	9,834	25,973	11,691	30,876	17,349	45,821	7,515	19,848
1979	10,624	25,199	12,717	30,162	18,782	44,550	8,158	19,351
1980	11,314	23,644	13,655	28,537	20,232	42,280	8,918	18,636
1981	12,109	22,939	14,669	27,788	21,679	41,069	9,570	18,130
1982	12,560	22,413	15,464	27,596	23,116	41,250	10,556	18,837
1983	13,044	22,552	16,249	28,094	24,436	42,247	11,392	19,695
1984	13,893	23,026	17,258	28,603	26,029	43,140	12,136	20,114
1985	14,457	23,137	18,441	29,512	28,138	45,032	13,681	21,895
1986	15,120	23,756	19,474	30,597	29,925	47,017	14,805	23,261
1987	15,939	24,161	20,367	30,874	30,619	46,414	14,680	22,253
1988	16,750	24,382	21,546	31,363	32,205	46,878	15,455	22,497
1989	17,594	24,433	23,010	31,954	34,936	48,515	17,342	24,082
1990	17,820	23,478	23,339	30,749	35,291	46,497	17,471	23,019
1991	18,261	23,088	23,844	30,147	36,185	45,750	17,924	22,662
1992	18,737	22,997	24,741	30,367	37,947	46,576	19,210	23,578

[Continued]

Earnings by Educational Attainment in Actual and Year 2000 Dollars

[Continued]

	Average Annual Earnings						Difference Between	
	High School Only		High School and Higher		College and Higher		High Only and College	
	Actual $	2000 $	Actual $	2000 $	Actual $	2000 $	Actual $	2000 $
1993	19,422	23,145	26,360	31,413	41,846	49,867	22,424	26,722
1994	20,248	23,527	27,540	32,000	43,443	50,478	23,195	26,951
1995	21,431	24,215	28,613	32,331	43,396	49,034	21,965	24,819
1996	22,154	24,314	29,945	32,865	45,526	49,965	23,372	25,651
1997	22,895	24,564	31,355	33,641	47,678	51,154	24,783	26,590
1998	23,594	24,926	32,915	34,773	50,064	52,890	26,470	27,964
1999	24,572	25,398	34,480	35,639	52,883	54,660	28,311	29,262

Source: Data on earnings from *Current Population Survey*, March 2000. The Consumer Price Index, published by the Bureau of Labor Statistics, was used to deflate current dollar earnings estimates.

Educational Attainment Boundaries - % of Adults 25 or Older with High School or Higher Education

The first column shows the educational attainment achieved if each ethnic group grows at rates experienced between 1990 and 2000. The second column shows the result if there is no further growth in attainment and each ethnic group continues to have the rates achieved in 2000. The second scenario reflects the growth in the population of ethnic groups with lower achievements in 2000.

	1990 to 2000 rate extended	2000 rate extended	Population 25 or Older Older (000)	Percent of Age Group			
				Nonhispanic White %	Nonhispanic Black %	Asian %	Hispanic %
2000	84.1	84.1	181,984	73.6	10.7	3.6	9.4
2001	84.5	83.7	198,909	73.5	11.2	3.9	10.7
2002	85.1	83.6	200,767	73.1	11.3	4.0	11.0
2003	85.7	83.6	202,668	72.6	11.4	4.1	11.3
2004	86.4	83.5	204,670	72.2	11.4	4.2	11.5
2005	87.0	83.4	206,812	71.8	11.5	4.2	11.8
2006	87.7	83.3	208,961	71.4	11.6	4.3	12.0
2007	88.4	83.2	211,169	71.0	11.6	4.4	12.2
2008	89.0	83.1	213,363	70.7	11.7	4.5	12.5
2009	89.7	83.1	215,481	70.3	11.7	4.6	12.7
2010	90.4	83.0	217,697	69.9	11.8	4.7	12.9
Change 2000-2010	6.3	-1.1	35,713	-3.7	1.1	1.1	3.5
Attainment in 2000				88.4	78.9	84.7	57.0

Source: For educational attainment, *Current Population Survey*, March 2000. Population projections from the Middle Series, U.S. Bureau of the Census. Projections made by the authors using these two sources. For a sophisticated analysis of this subject, see Jennifer Cheeseman Day and Kurt J. Bauman, *Have We Reached the Top? Educational Attainment Projections of the U.S. Population*, May 2000, Working Paper No. 43, Population Division, U.S. Census Bureau.

Relationship Between Wages/Salaries in Manufacturing and Output per Hour (Productivity)

	Constant 2000 Dollars		Output per Hour in Manu- facturing 1992=100
	Manufacturing Wages & Salaries ($ bil.)	Wages & Salaries per Empl. ($)	
1950	359.4	23,581	34.0
1951	393.4	23,999	33.8
1952	417.2	25,083	35.2
1953	459.8	26,203	36.4
1954	432.7	26,526	37.3
1955	474.8	28,127	38.8
1956	503.3	29,189	38.6
1957	505.6	29,435	39.4
1958	468.9	29,409	40.0
1959	514.2	30,839	40.9
1960	522.4	31,104	41.8
1961	517.8	31,713	42.8
1962	552.0	32,751	44.2
1963	566.7	33,344	45.7
1964	596.0	34,505	47.4
1965	632.5	35,018	48.5
1966	681.4	35,462	49.1
1967	692.4	35,605	50.9
1968	722.4	36,522	52.7
1969	739.9	36,691	53.5
1970	703.0	36,299	54.2
1971	682.4	36,644	57.8
1972	723.4	37,774	60.3
1973	762.5	37,833	61.4
1974	739.8	36,848	61.2
1975	677.3	36,963	64.3
1976	720.3	37,915	67.0
1977	757.9	38,505	69.7
1978	792.6	38,654	70.4
1979	795.1	37,788	69.8
1980	744.4	36,697	70.1
1981	734.3	36,404	70.7
1982	688.3	36,649	74.2
1983	692.8	37,586	76.7
1984	738.2	38,106	79.5
1985	749.8	38,953	82.3
1986	755.3	39,862	85.9
1987	753.2	39,645	88.3
1988	771.3	39,937	90.2
1989	760.9	39,239	90.3
1990	739.7	38,774	92.9
1991	711.2	38,638	95.0

[Continued]

Relationship Between Wages/Salaries in Manufacturing and Output per Hour (Productivity)
[Continued]

| | Constant 2000 Dollars | | Output per Hour in Manu- facturing 1992=100 |
	Manufacturing Wages & Salaries ($ bil.)	Wages & Salaries per Empl. ($)	
1992	716.2	39,559	100.0
1993	706.0	39,057	101.9
1994	720.8	39,340	105.0
1995	731.6	39,496	109.0
1996	739.4	39,978	112.8
1997	770.8	41,273	117.6
1998	799.3	42,505	124.0
1999	808.3	43,569	129.6
2000	830.1	44,946	138.3
% Change, 1950-2000	131.0	90.6	306.8

Source: Productivity data from Bureau of Labor Statistics, U.S. Department of Labor; wage and salary disbursement are from the National Income and Product Accounts maintained by the Bureau of Economic Analysis, U.S. Department of Commerce; manufacturing employment is from the Bureau of Labor Statistics.

Relationship Between Wages/Salaries, Corporate Profits, and Productivity, All Business

Data are in constant 2000 dollars or in index values.

	Corporate Profits ($ bil.)	All Business Aggregate Wages/Salaries ($ bil.)	Wages/ Salaries per Empl. ($)	Index of Produc- tivity 1992=100
1950	-	890.3	22,729	36.9
1951	-	942.5	22,748	38.0
1952	-	989.7	23,460	39.2
1953	-	1,062.2	24,388	40.7
1954	-	1,039.6	24,613	41.6
1955	-	1,128.3	25,803	43.3
1956	-	1,204.1	26,705	43.4
1957	-	1,218.9	26,943	44.7
1958	118.7	1,175.0	27,022	46.0
1959	146.8	1,265.2	27,999	47.9
1960	138.9	1,301.4	28,392	48.8
1961	136.9	1,313.1	28,920	50.6
1962	154.9	1,385.6	29,695	52.9
1963	166.1	1,433.9	30,232	55.0
1964	187.6	1,515.9	31,137	57.5
1965	221.0	1,606.1	31,686	59.6
1966	231.1	1,710.8	32,209	62.0

[Continued]

Relationship Between Wages/Salaries, Corporate Profits, and Productivity, All Business

[Continued]

	Corporate Profits ($ bil.)	All Business Aggregate Wages/Salaries ($ bil.)	Wages/ Salaries per Empl. ($)	Index of Productivity 1992=100
1967	214.8	1,765.8	32,452	63.4
1968	214.9	1,857.1	33,128	65.4
1969	199.4	1,936.4	33,278	65.7
1970	170.2	1,927.5	33,047	67.0
1971	191.8	1,944.8	33,341	69.9
1972	220.3	2,064.8	34,218	72.2
1973	270.5	2,171.9	34,443	74.5
1974	277.7	2,137.0	33,340	73.2
1975	251.1	2,044.0	32,831	75.8
1976	289.5	2,151.1	33,345	78.5
1977	323.4	2,249.4	33,402	79.8
1978	358.2	2,380.2	33,511	80.7
1979	373.1	2,416.3	32,707	80.7
1980	312.6	2,332.6	31,452	80.4
1981	274.3	2,333.3	31,061	82.0
1982	213.9	2,295.0	31,137	81.7
1983	239.5	2,351.0	31,649	84.6
1984	257.7	2,497.6	31,864	87.0
1985	230.5	2,595.3	32,044	88.7
1986	194.6	2,699.0	32,655	91.4
1987	258.7	2,801.3	32,976	91.9
1988	326.7	2,913.9	33,179	93.0
1989	302.5	2,940.0	32,629	93.9
1990	322.8	2,948.5	32,366	95.2
1991	337.4	2,880.9	32,064	96.3
1992	359.4	2,964.0	32,949	100.0
1993	392.7	2,979.6	32,432	100.5
1994	431.1	3,059.2	32,190	101.9
1995	499.2	3,166.0	32,344	102.6
1996	538.1	3,276.6	32,704	105.4
1997	582.9	3,459.8	33,547	107.8
1998	500.2	3,697.7	34,870	110.7
1999	535.3	3,873.9	35,635	113.4
2000	573.9	4,068.8	36,630	116.9
Change, 1958-2000, %	383.4	246.3	35.6	154.1

Source: Productivity data from Bureau of Labor Statistics, U.S. Department of Labor; wage and salary disbursement data and data on corporate profits are from the National Income and Product Accounts maintained by the Bureau of Economic Analysis, U.S. Department of Commerce; profits are normalized using the GDP deflator.

Corporate Profits After Tax and their Distribution

Table shows that undistributed profits, available for investment, have decreased as a percent of total after tax profits.

	Profits After Tax (Bil. $)	Dividends (Bil. $)	Undistributed Profits (Bil. $)	Undistributed as % of A.T. Profits
1950	25.3	8.8	16.5	65.2
1951	22.2	8.6	13.7	61.7
1952	20.8	8.6	12.3	59.1
1953	21.4	8.9	12.5	58.4
1954	21.7	9.3	12.4	57.1
1955	27.8	10.5	17.4	62.6
1956	28.5	11.3	17.2	60.4
1957	27.7	11.7	15.9	57.4
1958	24.0	11.6	12.4	51.7
1959	30.0	12.6	17.5	58.3
1960	28.8	13.4	15.5	53.8
1961	28.7	13.9	14.8	51.6
1962	32.9	15.0	17.9	54.4
1963	35.7	16.2	19.5	54.6
1964	40.9	18.2	22.7	55.5
1965	49.1	20.2	28.9	58.9
1966	52.8	20.7	32.1	60.8
1967	50.6	21.5	29.1	57.5
1968	52.8	23.5	29.3	55.5
1969	51.4	24.2	27.2	52.9
1970	46.2	24.3	21.9	47.4
1971	54.7	25.0	29.7	54.3
1972	65.5	26.8	38.6	58.9
1973	84.9	29.9	55.0	64.8
1974	95.0	33.2	61.8	65.1
1975	93.9	33.0	60.9	64.9
1976	114.4	39.0	75.4	65.9
1977	136.0	44.8	91.2	67.1
1978	161.4	50.8	110.6	68.5
1979	182.1	57.5	124.6	68.4
1980	166.6	64.1	102.6	61.6
1981	159.8	73.8	86.0	53.8
1982	132.4	76.2	56.2	42.4
1983	154.1	83.6	70.5	45.7
1984	172.0	91.0	81.0	47.1
1985	158.7	97.7	61.0	38.4
1986	136.9	106.3	30.6	22.4
1987	187.5	112.2	75.3	40.2
1988	244.8	129.6	115.2	47.1
1989	235.3	155.0	80.2	34.1
1990	260.9	165.6	95.3	36.5
1991	282.6	178.4	104.1	36.8

[Continued]

Corporate Profits After Tax and their Distribution

[Continued]

	Profits After Tax (Bil. $)	Divi-dends (Bil. $)	Undistri-buted Profits (Bil. $)	Undistri-buted as % of A.T. Profits
1992	308.4	185.5	122.9	39.9
1993	345.0	203.1	141.9	41.1
1994	386.7	234.9	151.8	39.3
1995	457.5	254.2	203.3	44.4
1996	502.7	297.7	205.0	40.8
1997	555.2	335.2	220.0	39.6
1998	482.3	348.7	133.6	27.7
1999	523.3	343.5	179.8	34.4
2000	573.9	379.6	194.3	33.9

Source: National Income and Product Accounts, Bureau of Economic Analysis, U.S. Department of Commerce.

Chapter 6
BENEFITS

Civilian Labor Force: Wages and Salaries and Employment Benefits, 1986-1999

	Wages & Salaries as % of Total Compensation	Total Benefits as % of Total Compensation	Average Weekly Wages in 2000 Dollars	Average Weekly Benefits in 2000 Dollars
1986	73	27	479	129
1987	73	27	474	127
1988	73	27	469	128
1989	73	27	464	127
1990	72	28	455	126
1991	72	28	448	124
1992	72	28	446	126
1993	71	29	445	128
1994	71	29	448	130
1995	72	28	446	127
1996	72	28	446	125
1997	73	28	456	125
1998	73	27	467	127
1999	73	27	472	127

Source: U.S. Department of Labor, Bureau of Labor Statistics, "Civilian employment by demographic characteristic, 1955-2000," and "Hours and earnings in private nonagricultural industries, 1959-2000." Both reports are available online at http://w3.access.gpo.gov/usbudget/fy2002/erp.html#erp2.

Civilian Work Force, Earnings, and National Health Care Expenditures, 1960-1999

Figures are dollars, normalized to the base year 2000, unless otherwise specified.

	All Civilian Workers (000 workers)	Average Hourly Earnings	Average Weeky Earnings	National per Capita Health Care Expenditures	Private Sector per Capita Health Care Expenditures
1960	65,778	12.16	469.30	1,726.90	1,299.33
1965	71,088	13.45	521.79	2,184.41	1,641.28
1966	72,895	13.61	525.21	2,276.68	1,592.86
1967	74,372	13.82	525.06	2,365.60	1,485.26
1968	75,920	14.10	533.08	2,497.14	1,554.42
1969	77,902	14.26	537.76	2,605.29	1,621.61
1970	78,678	14.34	531.82	2,732.88	1,701.34
1971	79,367	14.67	541.30	2,816.36	1,729.30
1972	82,153	15.24	563.98	3,020.54	1,854.28
1973	85,064	15.28	563.88	3,189.06	1,941.60
1974	86,794	14.81	540.56	3,271.05	1,937.47
1975	85,846	14.50	523.42	3,300.83	1,903.78
1976	88,752	14.71	530.98	3,423.41	1,991.41
1977	92,017	14.92	537.06	3,519.40	2,062.86
1978	96,048	15.03	537.99	3,591.26	2,083.84
1979	98,824	14.61	521.60	3,672.91	2,126.00
1980	99,303	13.92	491.31	3,757.77	2,155.43
1981	100,397	13.73	483.45	3,900.19	2,242.50
1982	99,526	13.70	476.91	3,898.07	2,267.81
1983	100,834	13.87	485.31	3,911.54	2,280.61
1984	105,005	13.79	485.38	4,018.02	2,357.12
1985	107,150	13.72	478.66	4,109.89	2,428.04
1986	109,597	13.76	478.97	4,059.86	2,369.23
1987	112,440	13.61	473.70	4,107.31	2,384.33
1988	114,968	13.51	468.74	4,281.45	2,543.76
1989	117,342	13.41	464.16	4,393.31	2,615.89
1990	118,793	13.19	455.01	4,457.85	2,648.22
1991	117,718	13.05	447.54	4,440.61	2,571.67
1992	118,492	12.97	446.28	4,441.46	2,516.02
1993	120,259	12.91	445.27	4,452.82	2,494.70
1994	123,060	12.92	448.35	4,442.06	2,415.76
1995	124,900	12.92	445.57	4,437.43	2,377.29
1996	126,708	12.97	446.26	4,468.21	2,383.04
1997	129,558	13.18	455.86	4,536.73	2,438.84
1998	131,463	13.50	467.15	4,563.90	2,481.74
1999	133,488	13.69	472.13	4,616.05	2,524.51

Source: U.S. Department of Labor, Bureau of Labor Statistics, three reports: "Employer Costs for Employee Compensation, 1986-1999," "Civilian employment by demographic characteristic, 1955-2000," and "Hours and earnings in private nonagricultural industries, 1959- 2000." All three tables are available online at http://w3.access.gpo.gov/usbudget/fy2002/erp.html#erp2.

Rates of Participation of Full-time Private Sector Employees in Various Employment Benefit Packages by Size of Employer, 1996 & 1997

Participation rates are in percentages. Medium to large firms have 100 or more employees. Small firms have 99 or fewer employees.

Benefits	Medium and Large Private Estab. 1997	Small Private Estab-lishments 1996	Percentage Covered in Private Estab.
Primary Benefits			
Retirement income	79.0	46.0	62.2
Prescription drug	73.0	57.0	64.9
Vision care	26.0	12.0	18.9
Dental care	59.0	31.0	44.7
Medical care	76.0	64.0	69.9
Life Insurance	87.0	62.0	74.3
Paid sick leave	56.0	50.0	52.9
Personal leave	20.0	14.0	16.9
Vacations	95.0	86.0	90.4
Holidays	89.0	80.0	84.4
Other Non-Core Benefits			
Cafeteria plans	52.0	23.0	37.2
Educational assistance	67.0	38.0	52.2
Subsidized commuting *	6.0	1.0	3.5
Fitness center	21.0	4.0	12.3
Employee assistance	61.0	14.0	37.1
Wellness programs	36.0	8.0	21.7
Flexible workplace *	2.0	1.0	1.5
Long-term care insurance *	7.0	1.0	3.9
Adoption assistance *	10.0	1.0	5.4
Child care assistance *	10.0	2.0	5.9
Severance pay	36.0	15.0	25.3
Family leave *	2.0	2.0	2.0

Source: U.S. Department of Labor, Bureau of Labor Statistics, "Employee Benefits in Small Private Establishments," 1996, Tables 1 & 2. "Employee Benefits in Medium and Large Private Establishments, 1997," Tables 1 & 3. Note: Categories marked with an * (asterisk) do not include teachers. The data on teachers is calculated differently due to the academic work year.

Share of Private-Sector Employees with Family Leave Coverage by Size of Employer, 1991-97

Percentages. Medium to large firms have 100 or more employees. Small firms have 99 or fewer employees.

	1991	1993	1995	1997
Full-time medium/large firms:				
Maternity leave coverage	39	63	86	95
Paternity leave coverage	27	54	86	95
Part-time medium/large firms:				
Maternity leave coverage	20	37	42	54
Paternity leave coverage	14	33	42	54
Full-time small firms:				
Maternity leave coverage	19	20	49	50
Paternity leave coverage	8	9	49	50

Source: U.S. Depart of Commerce, Bureau of Labor Statistics, "Family Leave Coverage in the 1990s," *Monthly Labor Review,* October 1999, page 4.

Retirement Age Population and Median Age at Retirement by Gender, 1950-2005

Data for 1990 and later are projections.

	Popuulation in (000)				Percent of Population Aged 65 Years +	Median Age at Retirement	
	Total	Male	Female	65 Years and Over		Men	Women
1950-55	151,326	75,187	76,139	12,362	8.17	67	68
1955-60	165,325	81,759	83,566	14,489	8.76	66	66
1960-65	179,323	88,331	90,992	16,675	9.30	65	65
1965-70	191,268	93,622	97,646	18,451	9.65	64	64
1970-75	203,212	98,912	104,300	20,085	9.88	63	63
1975-80	214,879	104,483	110,397	22,793	10.61	63	63
1980-85	226,546	110,053	116,493	25,500	11.26	63	63
1985-90	237,669	115,669	122,000	28,415	11.96	63	63
1990-95	248,791	121,284	127,507	31,084	12.49	63	63
1995-00	262,049	127,919	134,130	33,620	12.83	62	62
2000-05	275,306	134,554	140,752	34,837	12.65	62	61

Source: U.S. Census Bureau, Decennial Censuses, *Statistical Abstract of the United States 2000*, page 12. U.S. Bureau of Labor, *Monthly Labor Review,* July 1992, page 27.

Population Figures by Selected Age Groups, 1900-2030

In thousands. Data for years after 2000 are projections.

	Population Aged		Total Dependent Population	Population Aged 20 to 64
	19 Years and under	65 Years and over		
1900	33,681	3,080	36,761	39,234
1910	38,563	3,950	42,513	49,459
1920	43,043	4,933	47,976	57,735
1930	47,609	6,634	54,243	68,532
1940	45,307	9,019	54,326	77,343
1950	51,100	12,270	63,370	87,327
1960	68,635	16,525	85,160	93,304
1970	76,969	20,066	97,035	106,177
1980	72,458	25,550	98,008	128,538
1990	71,768	31,084	102,852	145,939
2000	78,451	34,837	113,288	162,018
2010	81,113	39,715	120,828	179,034
2020	85,724 ·	53,733	139,457	185,470
2030	92,643	70,319	162,962	188,108

Source: U.S. Department of Commerce, U.S. Census Bureau, *Historical Statistics of the United States, Colonial Times to 1970,* September 1975, page 15. *Statistical Abstract of the United States, 2000,* 120th edition, page 15.

Projections of Social Security Income and Outlays, 2000-2050

Rates are percentages of taxable payroll.

	Income Rate	Cost Rate	Balance
2000	12.65	10.34	2.31
2001	12.67	10.36	2.31
2002	12.67	10.42	2.25
2003	12.67	10.51	2.16
2004	12.68	10.62	2.06
2005	12.68	10.74	1.95
2006	12.69	10.87	1.82
2007	12.70	11.02	1.69
2008	12.71	11.17	1.54
2009	12.73	11.35	1.37
2010	12.74	11.55	1.18
2011	12.75	11.77	0.98
2012	12.76	12.02	0.75
2013	12.78	12.29	0.48
2014	12.79	12.59	0.20
2015	12.81	12.91	(0.10)

[Continued]

Projections of Social Security Income and Outlays, 2000-2050

[Continued]

	Income Rate	Cost Rate	Balance
2016	12.83	13.24	(0.41)
2017	12.85	13.59	(0.74)
2018	12.87	13.94	(1.07)
2019	12.89	14.30	(1.41)
2020	12.91	14.66	(1.75)
2021	12.93	15.00	(2.08)
2022	12.95	15.33	(2.38)
2023	12.97	15.64	(2.68)
2024	12.98	15.95	(2.96)
2025	13.00	16.24	(3.24)
2026	13.02	16.51	(3.49)
2027	13.04	16.76	(3.72)
2028	13.05	16.98	(3.93)
2029	13.07	17.18	(4.11)
2030	13.08	17.35	(4.26)
2031	13.10	17.49	(4.40)
2032	13.11	17.63	(4.52)
2033	13.12	17.74	(4.62)
2034	13.13	17.81	(4.68)
2035	13.14	17.86	(4.72)
2036	13.14	17.88	(4.74)
2037	13.15	17.89	(4.74)
2038	13.16	17.89	(4.74)
2039	13.16	17.88	(4.72)
2040	13.16	17.87	(4.71)
2041	13.17	17.86	(4.69)
2042	13.17	17.85	(4.68)
2043	13.17	17.85	(4.67)
2044	13.18	17.85	(4.67)
2045	13.18	17.85	(4.67)
2046	13.19	17.86	(4.68)
2047	13.19	17.88	(4.69)
2048	13.20	17.90	(4.71)
2049	13.20	17.93	(4.73)
2050	13.21	17.96	(4.76)

Source: U.S. Social Security Administration, Office of the Chief Actuary, Table II.F13, "Comparison of Estimated Income Rates and Cost Rates by Trust Fund, Calendar Years 2000-2075," Intermediate Assumptions, March 31, 2000, available online at http://www.ssa.gov/OACT/TR00/lrIndex.html.

Consumer Household Expenditures for the U.S. Population Over 65, 1985-1999

Figures are in 2000 dollars.

	1985	1990	1995	1999
Income before tax	16,315	18,854	22,138	26,562
Income after tax	14,958	17,716	21,059	25,307
Average Annual Expenditures	15,998	18,523	22,243	26,555
Food	2,482	2,913	3,385	3,527
Alcoholic Beverages	149	125	171	173
Housing	5,134	6,021	7,586	8,951
Apparel	836	761	874	1,077
Transportation	2,687	2,882	3,374	4,385
Health Care	1,652	2,208	2,647	3,020
Entertainment	576	700	926	1,238
Personal Care products	231	267	326	334
Reading	123	137	160	164
Education	65	54	154	139
Tobacco products	127	158	139	148
Miscellaneous	308	553	603	798
Cash Contributions	1,028	1,026	1,099	1,627
Personal insurance & pensions	602	718	799	980

Source: U.S. Department of Labor, Bureau of Labor Statistics, "Consumer Expenditure Survey 1985 - 1999," available online at ftp://ftp.bls.gov/pub/special.requests/ce/standard/1990/age.txt. Note: All dollar amounts have been normalized to the year 2000 using the Bureau of Labor Statistic Consumer Price Index.

Disposable Income and Savings, 1960-2000

	Per Capita Disposable Personal Income 2000 Dollars	Savings Rate as a % of Disposable Personal Income
1960	13,761	7.2
1961	13,959	8.3
1962	14,196	8.3
1963	14,404	7.8
1964	14,958	8.8
1965	15,188	8.6
1966	15,373	8.3
1967	15,716	9.4
1968	15,366	8.4
1969	15,309	7.8
1970	15,252	9.4
1971	15,478	10.0
1972	15,805	8.9
1973	16,476	10.5
1974	16,246	10.7

[Continued]

Disposable Income and Savings, 1960-2000

[Continued]

	Per Capita Disposable Personal Income 2000 Dollars	Savings Rate as a % of Disposable Personal Income
1975	16,465	10.6
1976	15,834	9.4
1977	16,051	8.7
1978	16,681	9.0
1979	16,807	9.2
1980	17,171	10.2
1981	17,403	10.8
1982	17,460	10.9
1983	18,218	8.8
1984	19,658	10.6
1985	20,212	9.2
1986	20,720	8.2
1987	21,350	7.3
1988	22,216	7.8
1989	22,928	7.5
1990	23,658	7.8
1991	23,027	8.3
1992	23,389	8.7
1993	23,360	7.1
1994	23,706	6.1
1995	23,748	5.6
1996	23,884	4.8
1997	24,183	4.2
1998	24,761	4.7
1999	24,770	2.4
2000	24,889	1.0

Source: U.S. Department of Commerce, Bureau of Economic Analysis, "Personal Income and Its Disposition," November 30, 2001, available online at http://www.bea.doc.gov/.

Chapter 7
WORKPLACE ISSUES

Fatal Occupational Injuries by Gender and Top Three Categories of Injury, 1993-2000

| | Number of Fatal Injuries | | | Leading Causes of Death as % of All Workplace Fatalities by Category | | |
				Assault	Transpor-tation	Contact w/ Object
	Total	Males	Females			
1993	6,271	5,790	481	20.9	39.6	16.6
1994	6,588	6,067	521	19.9	41.6	15.4
1995	6,210	5,676	534	20.3	41.2	14.7
1996	6,112	5,605	507	18.7	41.8	16.4
1997	6,218	5,743	475	17.7	41.8	16.6
1998	6,026	5,544	482	15.9	43.6	15.6
1999	6,023	5,582	441	14.8	43.4	17.1
2000	5,915	5,467	448	15.7	43.5	17.0

Source: U.S. Department of Labor, Bureau of Labor Statistics, "Fatal Occupational Injuries by Event or Exposure and Major Private Industry Division 2000," avaliable online at http://www.bls.gov/iif/oshcfoi1.htm.

Workplace Injury and Illness Rates, by Severity of Injury/Illness, 1973-2000

Figures are rates—number of injuries and/or illnesses per 100 full-time workers over a one year period.

	Rate of Injury and Illness	Rate of Lost Work Day Injuries (Serious)	Rate of Non-Lost Work Day Injuries (Minor)
1973	11.0	3.4	7.6
1974	10.4	3.5	6.9
1975	9.1	3.3	5.8
1976	9.2	3.5	5.7
1977	9.3	3.8	5.5
1978	9.4	4.1	5.3
1979	9.5	4.3	5.2
1980	8.7	4.0	4.7
1981	8.3	3.8	4.5
1982	7.7	3.5	4.2
1983	7.6	3.4	4.2

[Continued]

Workplace Injury and Illness Rates, by Severity of Injury/Illness, 1973-2000

[Continued]

	Rate of Injury and Illness	Rate of Lost Work Day Injuries (Serious)	Rate of Non-Lost Work Day Injuries (Minor)
1984	8.0	3.7	4.3
1985	7.9	3.6	4.3
1986	7.9	3.6	4.3
1987	8.3	3.8	4.5
1988	8.6	4.0	4.6
1989	8.6	4.0	4.6
1990	8.8	4.1	4.7
1991	8.4	3.9	4.5
1992	8.9	3.9	5.0
1993	8.5	3.8	4.7
1994	8.4	3.8	4.6
1995	8.1	3.6	4.5
1996	7.4	3.4	4.0
1997	7.1	3.3	3.8
1998	6.7	3.1	3.6
1999	6.3	3.0	3.3
2000	6.1	3.0	3.1
%Change 1973 to 2000	-45.0	-12.0	-59.0

Source: U.S. Department of Labor, Bureau of Labor Statistics, "Incidence rate of occupational injuries and illness for private industry by selected case types, 1973- 2000," available online at: http://www/bls.gov/news.release/ osha.t06.htm.

Number of Work-related Injuries and Illnesses Involving Days Away from Work in 1999

Nature of Injury/Illness	All Cases	Women	Men
Sprain, strain	739,742	262,315	470,536
Fracture	113,734	30,355	82,460
Cuts, lacerations, punctures	153,762	29,815	122,937
Bruises, contusions	155,965	56,300	97,899
Heat burns	27,108	9,031	18,012
Chemical burns	11,614	1,949	9,624
Amputations	9,985	1,228	8,679
Carpal tunnel syndrome	27,922	18,651	9,185
Tendonitis	16,582	10,127	6,406
Multiple injuries	59,343	19,710	39,966
Soreness, pain	109,257	38,233	70,374

[Continued]

Number of Work-related Injuries and Illnesses Involving Days Away from Work in 1999
[Continued]

Nature of Injury/Illness	All Cases	Women	Men
All Others	277,456	80,953	193,165
Total	1,702,470	558,667	1,129,243

Source: U.S. Department of Labor, Bureau of Labor Statistics, "Case and Demographic Characteristics of Work- related Injuries and Illnesses Involving Days Away From Work - 1999," available online at http://www.bls.gov/iif/oshcdnew.html. Note: The figures for women and men do not add to the totals for every category. This is the result of rounding and of cases in which an injury or illness reported made no reference to the gender of the injured party.

Fatal and Non-fatal Workplace Injuries and Illnesses by Private Industrial Sector, 1999

Sector	Fatal Injury Rate (per 1,000 employed in sector)	Non-Fatal Injury Rate (per 100 full-time in sector)	Percent of Workforce		Employment by Sector (000)	Total Fatalities by Sector
			Female	Male		
Overall Private Sector	0.041	6.3	46.5	53.5	133,488	5,461
Agriculture	0.246	7.3	25.9	74.1	3,281	807
Mining	0.214	4.4	12.3	87.7	565	121
Construction	0.132	8.6	9.9	90.1	8,987	1,190
Manufacturing	0.036	9.2	32.0	68.0	20,070	719
Transportation	0.105	7.3	28.7	71.3	9,554	1,006
Wholesale & Retail	0.027	6.1	47.6	52.4	27,572	744
FIRE[1]	0.012	1.8	58.0	42.0	8,815	105
Services	0.015	4.9	62.0	38.0	48,687	732

Source: U.S. Department of Commerce, Bureau of the Census, *Statistical Abstract of the United States: 2001,* Tables 409, 596, 633 and 635.
Note: 1. FIRE stands for Finance, Insurance, and Real Estate.

Rate of Violent Victimization in the Workplace, by Occupational Field, 1993-99

Rate of victimization per 1,000 employees in the field.

	Medical	Mental Health	Teaching	Law Enforcement	Retail Sales	Transportation
1993	20.3	64.4	25.8	163.1	21.9	20.6
1994	16.7	63.7	19.3	156.4	22.8	24.1
1995	16.0	56.7	15.4	157.2	22.2	13.8
1996	11.9	63.9	16.6	125.9	20.4	12.6
1997	8.4	39.7	14.9	122.0	20.5	15.4
1998	9.2	49.3	18.9	88.5	16.2	18.3
1999	10.0	46.1	12.4	74.1	14.1	8.4

[Continued]

Rate of Violent Victimization in the Workplace, by Occupational Field, 1993-99

[Continued]

	Medical	Mental Health	Teaching	Law Enforcement	Retail Sales	Transpor- tation
Percentage change 1993 - 1999	-51.0	-28.0	-52.0	-55.0	-36.0	-59.0

Source: U.S. Department of Justice, Bureau of Justice Statistics, *National Crime Victimization Survey,* "Violence in the Workplace, 1993-99," December 2001, p. 5.

Equal Employment Opportunity Commission Discrimination Charges and Case Outcomes by Category, 1992-2001

	1992	1993	1994	1995	1996	1997	1998	1999	2000	2001
Disability:										
Charges Filed	1,048	15,274	18,859	19,798	18,046	18,108	17,806	17,007	15,864	16,470
Charges Resolved	88	4,502	12,523	18,900	23,451	24,200	23,324	22,152	20,475	19,084
Monetary Benefits Paid ($ mil.)	0.2	15.9	32.6	38.7	38.7	36.1	49.1	49.9	47.9	42.2
Age:										
Charges Filed	19,573	19,809	19,618	17,416	15,719	15,785	15,191	14,141	16,008	17,405
Charges Resolved	19,975	19,761	13,942	17,033	17,699	18,279	15,995	15,448	14,672	15,155
Monetary Benefits Paid ($ mil.)	57.3	40.7	42.3	29.4	31.5	44.3	34.7	38.6	45.2	53.7
National Origin:										
Charges Filed	7,434	7,454	7,414	7,035	6,687	6,712	6,778	7,108	7,792	8,025
Charges Resolved	7,196	6,788	6,453	7,619	9,047	8,795	8,482	8,750	8,691	8,899
Monetary Benefits Paid ($ mil.)	9.5	8.8	15.5	10.5	10.5	9.1	11.2	19.7	15.7	48.1
Race:										
Charges Filed	29,548	31,695	31,656	29,986	26,287	29,199	28,820	28,819	28,945	28,912
Charges Resolved	28,497	27,440	25,253	31,674	35,127	36,419	35,716	35,094	33,188	32,077
Monetary Benefits Paid ($ mil.)	31.9	33.3	39.7	30.1	37.2	41.8	32.2	53.2	61.7	86.5
Sex:										
Charges Filed	21,796	23,919	25,860	26,181	23,813	24,728	24,454	23,907	25,194	25,140
Charges Resolved	20,102	21,606	21,545	26,726	30,965	32,836	31,818	30,643	29,631	28,602
Monetary Benefits Paid ($ mil.)	30.7	44.0	44.1	23.6	47.1	72.5	58.7	81.7	109.0	94.4
Sexual Harassment:										
Charges Filed	10,532	11,908	14,420	15,549	15,342	15,889	15,618	15,222	15,836	15,475
Charges Resolved	7,484	9,971	11,478	13,802	15,861	17,333	17,115	16,524	16,726	16,383
Monetary Benefits Paid ($ mil.)	12.7	25.1	22.5	24.3	27.8	49.5	34.3	50.3	54.6	53.0
Pregnancy:										
Charges Filed	3,385	3,577	4,170	4,191	3,743	3,977	4,219	4,166	4,160	4,287
Charges Resolved	3,045	3,145	3,181	3,908	4,186	4,595	4,467	4,343	4,480	4,280
Monetary Benefits Paid ($ mil.)	3.7	3.9	4.0	4.7	4.1	5.6	5.3	6.7	20.6	7.5
Religion:										
Charges Filed	1,388	1,449	1,546	1,581	1,564	1,709	1,786	1,811	1,939	2,127
Charges Resolved	1,297	1,286	1,274	1,606	1,911	2,137	2,247	2,187	2,230	2,217
Monetary Benefits Paid ($ mil.)	1.4	2.1	1.5	1.5	1.8	2.2	2.6	3.1	5.5	14.1

Source: U.S. Equal Employment Opportunity Commission, "Charge Statistics Fiscal Year (FY) 1992 through FY 2001," available online at http://www.eeoc.gov/stats/charges.html.

Annual Discrimination and Harassment Charge Filings and Case Outcomes at the Equal Employment Opportunity Commission, 1992-2001

Charges filed are not always resolved within the same year they are filed.

	1992	1993	1994	1995	1996	1997	1998	1999	2000	2001
Total Charges Filed	72,302	87,942	91,189	87,529	77,990	80,680	79,591	77,444	79,896	80,840
Charges Resolved	68,366	71,716	71,563	91,774	103,467	106,312	101,470	97,846	93,672	90,106
Resolved with a Finding of *No Cause*	41,736	40,183	34,451	46,700	63,216	64,567	61,794	58,174	54,578	51,562
All Other Resolutions	26,630	31,533	37,112	45,074	40,251	41,745	39,676	39,672	39,094	38,544
Resolved in the Plaintiff's Favor	10,627	11,248	11,100	10,921	9,430	11,668	12,558	16,102	19,938	19,908
Charges Litigated	626	427	469	338	296	231	312	317	434	354
Monetary Benefits in millions of dollars										
Administrative	117.7	126.8	146.3	136.0	145.2	176.7	169.2	210.5	245.7	247.8
Established through litigation	71.1	36.4	39.6	18.9	50.8	112.3	92.2	96.9	46.0	50.6
Total Monetary Benefits Paid Out	188.8	163.2	185.9	154.9	196.0	289.0	261.4	307.4	291.7	298.4

Source: U.S. Equal Employment Opportunity Commission, "Charge Statistics Fiscal Year (FY) 1992 through FY 2001," available online at http:// www.eeoc.gov/stats/charges.html.

Number of Discrimination or Harassment Charges, by Category, Resolved with Any Finding Other Than No Cause 1992-2001

These are all charges filed with the U.S. Equal Empoyment Opportunity Commission.

Discrimination based on:	1992	1993	1994	1995	1996	1997	1998	1999	2000	2001
Sex	9,287	11,127	12,755	14,886	14,244	15,006	14,318	13,943	13,660	12,957
Race	9,717	10,345	11,187	12,321	10,924	11,436	11,215	11,932	11,881	11,772
Sexual Harassment	5,029	6,641	7,954	9,606	9,707	10,157	9,875	9,253	9,350	9,076
Disability	81	3,061	7,789	10,508	10,436	10,285	9,866	9,392	9,050	8,760
Age	7,890	8,280	7,069	8,721	6,619	7,111	6,126	6,272	6,162	6,774
National Origin	2,583	2,559	2,917	3,101	3,203	3,087	3,045	3,264	3,190	3,435
Pregnancy	1,547	1,595	1,746	2,056	1,909	2,164	1,934	1,954	2,029	1,909
Religion	590	656	710	827	776	872	883	919	888	869

Source: U.S. Equal Employment Opportunity Commission, "Charge Statistics Fiscal Year (FY) 1992 through FY 2001," available online at http://www.eeoc.gov/stats/charges.html.

Percentage Change, by Category, in Discrimination Filings and Outcomes, 1993 to 2001

These are all charges filed with the U.S. Equal Employment Opportunity Commission (EEOC).

Charge Categories	Percentage Change from 1993 to 2001 in:			
	Number of Charges Filed	Number of Charges Resolved	Benefits Paid Out	Number of Charges Found to be "With Cause"
Disabilities	7.8	323.9	165.4	186.1
Age-based	-12.1	-23.3	31.9	-18.2
National Origin	7.7	31.1	446.6	34.2
Race-based	-8.8	16.9	159.8	13.8
Sex-based	5.1	32.4	114.5	16.4
Sexual Harassment	30.0	64.3	111.2	36.7

[Continued]

Percentage Change, by Category, in Discrimination Filings and Outcomes, 1993 to 2001

[Continued]

Charge Categories	Percentage Change from 1993 to 2001 in:			
	Number of Charges Filed	Number of Charges Resolved	Benefits Paid Out	Number of Charges Found to be "With Cause"
Pregnancy	19.8	36.1	92.3	19.7
Religion	46.8	72.4	571.4	32.5

Source: U.S. Equal Employment Opportunity Commission, "Charge Statistics Fiscal Year (FY) 1992 through FY 2001," available online at http://www.eeoc.gov/stats/charges.html.

Annual Data on Sexual Harassment Charges Filed with the Equal Employment Opportunity Commission, 1992-2001

	1992	1993	1994	1995	1996	1997	1998	1999	2000	2001
Charges Filed	10,532	11,908	14,420	15,549	15,342	15,889	15,618	15,222	15,836	15,475
Charges Resolved	7,484	9,971	11,478	13,802	15,861	17,333	17,115	16,524	16,726	16,383
Found to have *no cause*	2,455	3,330	3,524	4,196	6,154	7,176	7,240	7,271	7,376	7,307
Found to have some cause	5,029	6,641	7,954	9,606	9,707	10,157	9,875	9,253	9,350	9,076
Resolved in Plaintiff's Favor	2,019	2,524	2,713	2,709	2,882	3,253	3,576	3,840	4,724	4,768
Monetary Benefits Paid ($000)	13,000	25,000	23,000	24,000	28,000	50,000	34,000	50,000	55,000	53,000

Source: U.S. Equal Employment Opportunity Commission, "Charge Statistics FY 1992 through FY 2001," available online at http://www.eeoc.gov/stats/charges.html.

Chapter 8
THE FAMILY AND FREE TIME

Average Work Week, 1969-1999

Data are shown in hours.

	Average Weekly Hours	Men	Women
1969	37.7	43.7	34.3
1970	37.1	-	-
1971	36.9	-	-
1972	37.0	-	-
1973	36.9	-	-
1974	36.5	-	-
1975	36.1	-	-
1976	36.1	-	-
1977	36.0	-	-
1978	35.8	-	-
1979	35.7	43.0	34.3
1980	35.3	-	-
1981	35.2	-	-
1982	34.8	-	-
1983	35.0	-	-
1984	35.2	-	-
1985	34.9	-	-
1986	34.8	-	-
1987	34.8	-	-
1988	34.7	-	-
1989	34.6	43.1	35.6
1990	34.5	-	-
1991	34.3	-	-
1992	34.4	-	-
1993	34.5	-	-
1994	34.7	-	-
1995	34.5	-	-
1996	34.4	-	-
1997	34.6	-	-
1998	34.6	43.2	36.1

Source: "Are Managers and Professionals Really Working More?" *Issues in Labor Statistics*, May 12, 2000; "Overwork Overstated." Retrieved online March 8, 2002 from http://www.ncpa.org; Elaine L. Chao, U.S. Department of Labor, *Report on the American Workforce.*

Time Spent Per Week on Work and Leisure

Figures are based on a Gallup Poll.

	Work Hours	Leisure Hours
1973	41	26
1975	43	24
1980	47	19
1984	47	18
1987	47	17
1989	49	19
1993	50	19
1994	51	20
1995	51	19
1997	51	20
1998	50	19
1999	50	20
2000	50	20
2001	50	20

Source: "Reading, TV, Spending Time With Family, Gardening and Fishing Top List of Favorite Leisure-Time Activities." *PR Newswire*, August 8, 2001.

Where Are We Happier - At Home or Work?

Figures are based on a Gallup survey. The question asked: "Which do you enjoy more: the hours when you are on the job or the hours when you are not on the job?

	On the Job	Not the Job
Jun-55	39	48
Sep-88	20	68
Sep-90	18	60
Sep-91	18	68
May-93	22	70
Oct-98	23	69
Aug-99	16	77

Source: Bowman, Karlyn. "Attitudes About Work and Leisure in America," Retrieved online September 28, 2001 from http://www.aei.org.

Types of Meals Consumed

Average meals per person

	Home-cooked meals	Restaurant meals
1990	933	122
1999	917	139

Source: "NPD Sees Focus On Cost, Convenience Reshaping Eating Patterns in America." Retrieved online March 19, 2002 from: http://www.npd.com.

Time Spent on Household Chores - Hours a Week

	1965	1975	1985
All women	40.2	32.9	30.9
Women, employed	26.1	23.7	25.6
All men	11.5	12.2	15.7
Men, employed	11.1	10.7	14.5

Source: Chao, Elaine L. U.S. Department of Labor, *Report on the American Workforce*, 2001, p. 123.

Children's Time with Mom and Dad

Data are in hours per week.

	1981	1997
With Mothers	25.05	30.89
With Working Mothers	22.52	26.54
With Nonworking Mothers	26.06	32.05
With Fathers	18.51	22.73

Source: "Children Spend More Time With Parents Than They Used To." Retrieved online November 16, 2001 from: http://www.umich.edu.

Selected Spending on Recreational Products and Services

	Millions of Dollars						
	1990	1994	1995	1996	1997	1998	1999
Video/audio/computer products	52.9	71.0	77.0	80.0	83.7	90.7	99.1
Commercial participant amusements	24.6	38.6	43.9	48.3	52.8	56.4	63.1
Nondurable toys and sports supplies	32.8	43.4	47.2	50.6	53.2	57.3	63.1
Books and maps	16.2	20.8	23.1	24.9	26.3	27.8	29.8
Admissions to movies, theater, opera	14.8	18.2	19.2	20.7	22.1	23.6	25.8

[Continued]

Selected Spending on Recreational Products and Services

[Continued]

	Millions of Dollars						
	1990	1994	1995	1996	1997	1998	1999
Flowers, seeds, potted plants	10.9	13.2	13.8	14.9	15.3	16.3	17.5
Clubs and fraternal organizations	8.7	11.8	12.7	14.0	14.6	15.0	15.8

Source: U.S. Bureau of the Census, *Statistical Abstract of the United States*, 2001, Washington D.C.

Selected Data on U.S. and Other Countries: Work and Leisure Activities

	Working Hours per Week	Eating out per Month	Hosting Meals per Month	Renting Movies per Month
South Korea	55.1	4.5	1.2	2.7
Hong Kong	52.2	8.7	1.0	4.7
Russia	46.9	0.3	2.4	21.1
Japan	46.5	2.7	0.9	2.8
United States	42.4	4.5	1.8	7.0
Great Britain	41.9	1.8	0.9	6.0
France	40.3	2.2	2.9	9.9

Source: "No Work, All Play?" *U.S. News & World Report*, June 18, 2001, p. 10; "Hong Kong Eats Out Most, New Roper 32-Country Study Shows." Retrieved online March 8, 2002 from: http://www.roperasw.com.

Chapter 9
VACATIONS AND TRAVEL

Millions of Trips Taken in the United States

	Business Travel	Pleasure Travel
1980	97.1	342.8
1985	156.6	301.2
1990	182.2	361.1
1991	176.9	364.3
1992	210.8	411.7
1993	210.4	413.4
1994	158.3	316.5
1995	164.0	319.7
1996	157.4	323.7
1997	156.1	329.5
1998	163.0	334.0
1999	165.0	330.5

Source: "TIA Releases Travel Forecast Through 2003." Retrieved January 9, 2002 from the World Wide Web: http://www.tia.org.

Millions of Leisure Trips Taken in the United States

Trips	Weekend Trips	Nonweekend
1986	356.8	484.0
1996	604.0	557.0

Source: "Popularity of Weekend Travel Grows." Retrieved January 9, 2002 from the World Wide Web: http://www.tia.org.

Sales of Homes and Second Homes

	All homes	Second homes
1989	97,700	99,200
1991	102,400	85,500
1993	108,200	110,000
1995	116,100	115,000

[Continued]

Sales of Homes and Second Homes
[Continued]

	All homes	Second homes
1997	126,200	124,800
1999	138,800	127,800

Source: "Second Homes/Recreational Property." Retrieved January 16, 2002 from the World Wide Web: http://www.realtor.org.

U.S. Travel Industry

Sales are in billions of dollars.

	Online Travel Spending ($ bil.)	% of Travel Spending	% Travel Agency Commission
1996	0.3	0.2	10.0
1997	0.9	0.7	8.0
1998	2.2	1.6	8.0
1999	6.5	4.5	5.0
2000	11.0	7.2	6.2

Source: Dixon, Pam. "Fare Game: Airlines, Travel Agents Duke It Out Over the Web." *San Diego Union-Tribune*, January 9, 2000, P. F1.; Erin Allday, "Travel Agents Tough It Out." *Press Democrat*, December 26, 2001; "Jupiter: Triple Digit Growth Rates to Fade in Internet Travel Market." Retrieved April 17, 2000 from the World Wide Web: http://www.businesswire.com; Tricia A. Holly; "Welcome to the Outside." *Travel Agent*, April 23, 2001, p. 18; "PhoCusWright Survey Reveals 21 Million Americans Bought Travel Online in 2000." Retrieved January 29, 2002 from the World Wide Web: http://www.phocuswright.com; "Internet Usage by Travelers Continues to Soar." Retrieved January 29, 2002 from the World Wide Web: http://www.tia.org.

Chapter 10
PEOPLE AND SPORTS

Fastest Growing Sports - 1987 to 2000 - Percent Increase in Participation

	Percent Increase
Snowshoeing	14.5
Fast-pitch softball	15.4
Golf	15.6
Paintball	20.2
Yoga/Tai chi	29.6
Artificial wall climbing	30.3
Surfing	49.4
Wakeboarding	58.9
Weight/resistance machines	65.0
Elliptical motion trainers	159.9
Snowboarding	237.9
Treadmill exercise	828.5

Source: "Extreme Sports Participation Surges Ahead While Old Favorites Falter." *Research Alert*, June 1, 2001, p. 1; "The Scope of the Health Club Industry."

Popular Sports For 12-17 Year Olds - Participation per 100 Teens

To be counted in this survey, individual had to have participated in the sport at least once during the past year.

	Participants per 100 Teens			Change 1987-1993	Change 1993-2000
	1987	1993	2000		
Basketball	54.8	57.4	45.5	2.6	-11.9
Running/jogging	42.6	37.9	31.2	-4.7	-6.7
In-line skating	-	16.9	30.3	16.9	13.4
Free weights	25.1	28.5	27.1	3.4	-1.4
Volleyball	48.9	46.3	26.0	-2.6	-20.3
Touch football	35.5	33.4	22.6	-2.1	-10.8
Soccer	29.4	25.1	20.7	-4.3	-4.4
Skateboarding	21.3	8.4	16.8	-12.9	8.4
Softball	36.6	33.1	16.1	-3.5	-17.0
Tennis	23.7	20.7	13.3	-3.0	-7.4
Weight/resistance machines	9.6	6.9	13.1	-2.7	6.2

[Continued]

Popular Sports For 12-17 Year Olds - Participation per 100 Teens

[Continued]

	Participants per 100 Teens			Change	Change
	1987	1993	2000	1987-1993	1993-2000
Baseball	26.5	22.7	11.5	-3.8	-11.2
Snowboarding	-	4.5	9.1	4.5	4.6

Source: "Older Americans Exercise More While Teenagers Take It Easy." *Research Alert*, August 3, 2001.

High School Enrollment and Athletes

	Total Enrolled 14 to 17	Total Athletes	Athletes as % of Total	Male Athletes - %	Female Athletes - %	% of Athletes on Teams
1972-73	13,848,000	4,587,694	33.1	82.2	17.8	33.1
1973-74	14,044,000	5,370,294	38.2	75.8	24.2	38.0
1975-76	14,304,000	5,754,060	40.2	71.4	28.6	40.0
1977-78	14,203,000	6,450,482	45.4	67.7	32.3	45.0
1978-79	14,088,000	5,563,912	39.5	66.7	33.3	39.0
1979-80	13,616,000	5,268,093	38.7	66.8	33.2	39.0
1980-81	13,231,000	5,356,913	40.5	65.4	34.6	40.0
1981-82	12,764,000	5,219,752	40.9	65.3	34.7	41.0
1982-83	12,405,000	5,135,530	41.4	65.3	34.7	41.0
1983-84	12,271,000	5,050,945	41.2	65.4	34.6	41.0
1984-85	12,304,000	5,112,168	41.5	65.6	34.4	41.5
1985-86	12,388,000	5,151,396	41.6	64.9	35.1	41.5
1986-87	12,333,000	5,200,438	42.2	64.7	35.3	42.0
1987-88	12,076,000	5,275,461	43.7	64.9	35.1	43.6
1988-89	11,687,000	5,256,196	45.0	65.0	35.0	44.9
1989-90	11,390,000	5,256,851	46.2	64.6	35.4	46.0
1990-91	11,338,000	5,298,671	46.7	64.3	35.7	46.7
1991-92	11,541,000	5,370,654	46.5	63.9	36.1	46.5
1992-93	11,735,000	5,413,878	46.1	63.1	36.9	46.1
1993-94	11,961,000	5,603,282	46.8	62.0	38.0	46.8
1994-95	12,213,000	5,776,820	47.3	61.2	38.8	47.3
1995-96	12,500,000	6,001,988	48.0	60.5	39.5	48.0
1996-97	12,847,000	6,180,268	48.1	60.0	40.0	48.1
1997-98	13,054,000	6,333,453	48.5	59.4	40.6	48.5
1998-99	13,191,000	6,485,078	49.2	59.1	40.9	49.0

Source: U.S. Bureau of the Census, *Statistical Abstract of the United States*, Washington D.C.; U.S. Department of Education, National Center for Education Statistics, Statistics of State School Systems: Statistics of Public Elementary and Secondary School Systems; Statistics of Nonpublic Elementary and Secondary Schools: Projections of Education Statistics to 2010.

Average Spending per NCAA Institution

Values are in dollars per institution. NCAA stands for National Collegiate Athletic Association.

	1997-98	1995-96
Scholarships, men's	1,320,688	1,052,540
Scholarships, women's	906,176	634,689
Operating expenses, men's	808,093	1,165,100
Operating expenses, women's	406,265	338,600
Head coach salaries, men's	404,478	330,456
Head coach salaries, women's	271,024	216,419
Recruiting expenses, men's	171,098	133,303
Recruiting expenses, women's	72,346	49,176

Source: "Suit Unfairly Attacks Effort to Boost Women's Sports." *USA TODAY,* January 21, 2002.

Women Participating in College Level Athletic Activities

Data are from National Collegiate Athletic Association (NCAA) and show actual number of participants.

	1996-97	1998-99
Rowing	3,951	5,628
Tennis	8,223	8,492
Swimming/diving	8,745	10,012
Cross country	10,141	12,042
Volleyball	12,284	13,194
Basketball	13,392	14,365
Softball	13,167	14,943
Track, indoor	13,061	15,460
Soccer	14,829	17,520
Track, outdoor	15,578	18,220

Source: U.S. Census Bureau, *Statistical Abstract of the United States,* Washington D.C. 2000.

Professional Sports Attendance, 1990 to 2000

MLB is Major League Baseball, NBA is National Basketball Association, NFL is National Football League, and NHL is National Hockey League.

	MLB	NBA	NFL	NHL
1990	54,823,768	17,368,659	14,807,439	13,935,244
1991	56,813,760	16,876,125	14,654,706	13,786,100
1992	55,872,271	17,367,240	14,644,797	14,097,596
1993	70,256,459	17,778,295	14,781,450	15,204,211
1994	50,010,016	17,984,014	14,810,173	17,545,699
1995	50,469,236	18,516,484	15,834,468	10,563,014
1996	60,097,381	20,513,218	15,381,727	18,581,754

[Continued]

Professional Sports Attendance, 1990 to 2000
[Continued]

	MLB	NBA	NFL	NHL
1997	63,196,222	20,304,629	15,769,193	19,135,407
1998	70,372,221	20,373,079	16,187,758	18,772,094
1999	70,139,380	12,134,906	16,208,640	19,511,152
2000	72,748,970	20,057,419	20,953,652	18,779,845

Source: Doyle, Tom. "The Baseball & Softball Participation Paradox." *Sporting Goods Dealer*, November-December 2001, p. 42; Tom Powell. "Big Four Sports Draw A Billion In A Decade." *Amusement Business*, December 27, 1999, p. 26; John Morrell, "New Stadiums Pay Off For Professional Teams." *Amusement Business*, December 25, 2000, p. 44.

Average Growth in Player Salaries and Ticket Prices, 1991 to 2000

	Increase 1991 to 2000
National Hockey League	
Growth in Player Salaries - %	380.0
Growth in Ticket Prices - %	90.7
National Basketball Association	
Growth in Player Salaries - %	289.0
Growth in Ticket Prices - %	108.0
Major League Baseball	
Growth in Player Salaries - %	237.0
Growth in Ticket Prices - %	92.7
National Football League	
Growth in Player Salaries - %	164.0
Growth in Ticket Prices - %	81.0

Source: Swift, E.M. "Hey, Fans, Sit On It!" *Sports Illustrated*, May 15, 2000, p. 70. "High Cost of Pro-Sports Fandom May Ease." *Christian Science Monitor*, November 19, 2001, p. 16.

Chapter 11
ARTS AND CULTURE

Cultural Activities Pursued by People - 1985, 1992, and 1997

Percent of people 18 or older who participated in the activity.

	1985	1992	1997
Reading literature	56	54	63
Historic park	35	35	47
Art museums	22	27	35
Musical play	17	17	25
Non-musical play	14	14	16
Classical music concert	13	13	16
Jazz concert	10	11	12
Ballet	4	5	6
Opera	3	3	3

Source: U.S. Bureau of the Census, *Statistical Abstract of the United States*, Washington D.C. and the U.S. National Endowment for the Arts, Survey of Public Participation in the Arts Research Division.

Percent of People 18 and Over Who Participated in Arts Activities, 1992 and 1997

	1992	1997
Buying art	22	35
Weaving	25	28
Photography	12	17
Painting/drawing	10	16
Pottery	8	15
Modern dancing	8	13
Creative writing	7	12
Playing classical music	4	1

Source: U.S. Bureau of the Census, *Statistical Abstract of the United States*, Washington D.C. and the U.S. National Endowment for the Arts, Survey of Public Participation in the Arts Research Division.

Who Buys Books - By Age Group - 1999

	Percent of Book buyers	Percent of Population
18-24	6	13
25-29	6	9
30-34	9	10
35-39	11	11
40-44	15	11
45-49	14	9
50-54	11	8
55-64	13	11
65-up	15	17

Source: "The Age of Book Buyers." *USA TODAY*, March 24, 1999, p. D1.

Profiling Movies: Attendance, Box Office Grosses, and Video Sales and Rentals, 1990-2000

	Movie Admissions (bil.)	Box Office Grosses ($ bil.)	Home Video Sales/Rentals ($ bil.)
1990	1.19	5.02	9.80
1991	1.14	4.80	10.10
1992	1.17	4.87	11.00
1993	1.24	5.15	12.50
1994	1.29	5.40	15.50
1995	1.26	5.49	16.00
1996	1.34	5.91	15.18
1997	1.39	6.37	16.26
1998	1.48	6.95	17.47
1999	1.47	7.45	18.97
2000	1.42	7.67	20.66

Source: "Media Forecast: Strong Spending." *USA TODAY*, July 25, 1997, p. 2B; Jim McCullaugh. "Special Interest Looks for Retail Respect." *Billboard*, October 31, 1992, data from the Motion Picture Industry of America; some home video figures are estimated.

Attendance at Performing Arts Events - 1985, 1989-1997

Attendance is in millions.

	Opera	Broadway Shows	Nonprofit Theaters	Broadway Tours	Symphony Orchestras
1985	6.7	7.3	14.2	8.2	24.0
1989	7.4	8.0	18.7	8.3	25.8
1990	7.5	8.0	15.2	11.1	24.7
1991	7.6	7.3	16.9	13.0	26.7
1992	7.3	7.4	16.0	13.0	26.3
1993	5.5	7.9	16.5	15.0	24.0
1994	6.0	8.1	20.7	16.0	24.4
1995	6.5	9.0	18.6	16.0	30.9
1996	6.5	9.5	17.1	18.1	31.1
1997	6.9	10.6	17.2	18.0	31.9

Source: U.S. Census Bureau, *Statistical Abstract of the United States*, Washington D.C., 1999; "Who Goes to Broadway." Retrieved November 16, 2001 from the World Wide Web: http://www.livebroadway.com.

Electronics in the Typical Home - Selected Years, 1975-2000

	Percent of Households With -				
	TV	Cable	VCR	Personal Computer	Internet Access
1975	97.1	12.6	-	-	-
1980	97.9	19.9	1.1	-	-
1985	98.1	42.8	20.9	-	-
1990	98.2	56.4	68.6	-	-
1994	98.3	63.4	81.0	24.1	-
1995	98.3	63.4	81.0	27.0	-
1996	98.3	65.3	82.2	36.0	-
1997	98.4	66.5	84.2	43.0	-
1998	98.3	67.2	84.6	50.0	26.2
1999	98.2	67.5	84.6	50.0	31.0
2000	98.2	68.0	85.1	51.0	41.5

Source: Snider, Mike. "Safe at Home and All Plugged In." *USA TODAY*, January 8, 2002, p. D1. Broadcasting data from Television Bureau of Advertising; Computer and Internet data from Dataquest and U.S. Department of Commerce, using U.S. Bureau of the Census *Current Population Survey* supplements.

Number of Museums Established, by Decade, 1900 to 1980

Figures are estimated.

	Number
1900	150
1910	135
1920	375
1930	500
1940	470
1950	900
1960	2,000
1970	2,400
1980	950

Source: Mihm, Stephen. "Museums: Firsts, Facts and Figures." *New York Times*, April 19, 2000, p. 20.

Changes in the Rating of Films Between 1980 and 1998

Rating	Percent Change in Films Released 1980 to 1998
G	-31.2
PG/PG13	-7.6
R	14.1
X/Not Rated	140.7

Source: Sterritt, David. "Movie Ratings from G to X: Are They Out of Focus?" *Christian Science Monitor*, September 16, 1982; video game ratings retrieved January 16, 2002 from the World Wide Web: http://www.esrb.org; Kaiser Foundation report *Sex On TV* retrieved from the World Wide Web: http://www.kaiser.org; "How Many and How Much." *Christian Science Monitor*, December 24, 1998, p. B10.

Chapter 12
LEISURE TIME IN OUR COMMUNITY

Volunteering and Contributing to Charity, 1987-2000

	% of House-holds That Contribute to Charity	% of Population That Volunteer
1987	71.1	45.3
1989	75.1	54.4
1991	72.2	51.1
1993	73.4	47.7
1995	68.5	48.8
1998	70.1	55.5
2000	89.0	44.0

Source: Giving and Volunteering in the United States 1999. Retrieved October 3, 2001 from http://www.indepsec.org/GandV/. Giving and Volunteering in the United States 2001: Key Findings. Retrieved February 6, 2002 from http://www.independentsector.org/PDFs/GV01keyfind.pdf.

Percentage of Volunteers, 1974-2000

Numbers in percent.

	Total	Men	Women	% Difference Women vs. Men
1974	NA	41.0	59.0	18.0
1981	52.0	47.0	56.0	9.0
1985	48.0	45.0	51.0	6.0
1987	45.0	44.0	47.0	3.0
1989	NA	43.8	56.2	12.4
1991	51.1	49.2	52.9	3.7
1993	47.7	43.9	51.2	7.3
1995	48.8	45.1	52.2	7.1
1998	55.5	49.4	61.7	12.3
2000	44.0	42.0	46.0	4.0

Source: U.S. Census Bureau. Statistical Abstract of the United States: 1980, 1991, 1994, 1996, 1999, and 2001. 2000 data: Giving and Volunteering in the United States 2001: Key Findings, Washington D.C.:INDEPENDENT SECTOR, 2002. Notes: NA stands for data not available.

Educational Attainment of Adult Volunteers, 1981-1998

Numbers in percent. 1981 and 1985 include those 14 years old and over. All other years include those 18 years old and over.

	1981	1985	1987	1991	1993	1995	1998
Total	52.0	48.0	45.0	51.1	47.7	48.8	55.5
College graduate	75.0	65.0	64.0	76.6	67.2	70.7	67.7
Some college	65.0	61.0	58.0	66.1	56.9	56.3	67.2
Technical, trade, or business school	NA	NA	NA	51.5	49.2	51.2	53.5
High school graduate	54.0	46.0	41.0	44.7	40.4	43.1	43.2
Some high school	31.0	38.0	25.0	22.1	29.9	26.1	43.0
Elementary school	26.0	29.0	23.0	25.0	31.8	18.7	29.4

Source: U.S. Census Bureau. *Statistical Abstract of the United States, 1991, 1994, 1996, 1999,* and *2001. Note:* NA stands for not available.

Adult Volunteers, by Age, 1987-1998

Numbers in percent.

	Total	18-24	25-34	35-44	45-54	55-64	65-74	75 and over
1985	48.0	43.0	53.0	NA	NA	NA	43.0	26.0
1987	45.0	42.0	45.0	54.0	47.0	47.0	40.0	29.0
1991	51.1	48.3	52.9	60.8	55.9	49.4	42.0	26.6
1993	47.7	45.3	46.1	54.5	53.8	46.6	42.9	34.6
1995	48.8	38.4	50.8	55.0	55.3	47.9	44.7	33.7
1998	55.5	45.8	54.9	67.3	62.7	50.3	46.6	43.0

Source: U.S. Census Bureau. *Statistical Abstract of the United States: 1991, 1994, 1996, 1999,* and *2001. Note:* NA stands for data not available.

Adult Volunteers, by Race, 1991-1998

Numbers in percent.

	Total	White	Black	Hispanic
1991	51.1	52.6	43.3	37.6
1993	47.7	51.1	29.1	32.4
1995	48.8	51.9	35.3	40.4
1998	55.5	58.6	46.6	46.4

Source: U.S. Census Bureau. *Statistical Abstract of the United States: 1994, 1996, 1999,* and *2001.*

Where We Contribute, 1987-1998

Numbers in percent.

	1987	1989	1991	1993	1995	1998
Arts, culture, humanities	8.0	9.6	9.4	8.1	9.4	11.5
Education	15.1	19.1	21.1	17.5	20.3	12.6
Environment	10.8	13.4	16.3	11.6	11.5	12.4
Health	23.9	32.4	32.9	25.7	27.3	20.8
Human services	23.9	23.0	27.5	26.7	25.1	27.3
International	4.2	4.2	3.5	2.8	6.1	4.5
Private, community foundations	4.8	6.4	6.0	5.3	6.1	4.8
Public, societal benefit	6.5	11.2	11.2	11.2	10.3	11.1
Recreation — adults	NA	6.2	6.3	4.6	7.0	5.0
Religion	52.5	53.2	51.3	49.2	48.0	45.2
Youth development	18.5	21.6	22.1	17.9	20.9	21.4

Source: U.S. Census Bureau. *Statistical Abstract of the United States: 1994, 1996, 1999*, and *2001*.
Note: NA stands for not available.

Where We Volunteer, 1991-1998

Numbers in percent.

	1991	1993	1995	1998
Arts, culture, humanities	6.2	4.4	6.2	8.6
Education	15.4	15.7	17.5	17.3
Environment	8.6	6.2	7.1	9.2
Health	12.9	10.8	13.2	11.4
Human services	12.1	9.8	12.7	15.9
International	2.3	1.3	1.6	2.5
Private, community foundations	2.3	2.2	2.7	3.4
Public and societal benefit	6.4	5.4	6.7	7.9
Recreation — adults	6.7	5.4	7.3	8.6
Religion	26.8	24.1	25.8	22.8
Youth development	14.7	11.7	15.4	17.6
Informal	23.4	17.2	20.3	24.4
Work-related organizations	7.1	6.9	7.9	10.3
Political organizations	4.7	3.7	3.8	4.6

Source: U.S. Census Bureau. *Statistical Abstract of the United States: 1994, 1996, 1999*, and *2001*.

Membership in Religious Bodies, 1890-2001

	Membership (000)	Membership (% of pop.)
1890	21,699	34
1906	35,068	41
1916	41,927	41
1926	54,576	47

[Continued]

Membership in Religious Bodies, 1890-2001
[Continued]

	Membership (000)	Membership (% of pop.)
1931	59,798	48
1935	62,678	49
1940	64,502	49
1945	71,700	54
1950	86,830	57
1955	100,163	61
1960	114,449	64
1965	124,682	64
1970	131,046	63
1975	131,012	61
1980	134,817	59
1985	142,926	60
1989	147,607	60
2001	153,790	54

Source: U.S. Census Bureau. *Statistical Abstract of the United States: 1980* and *1992.* U.S. Census Bureau. *Historical Statistics of the United States: Colonial Times to 1970.* 2001 data: U.S. Census Bureau. "National Population Estimates." Retrieved February 15, 2002 from http://eire.census.gov/popest/data/national.php. Barry A. Kosmin, et. al. *American Religious Identification Survey 2001*, December 19, 2001. Retrieved February 15, 2002 from http://www.gc.cuny.edu/studies/aris.pdf.

Adult Religious Membership vs. Attendance, 1957-2000

Percent of the adult population.

	Membership	Attendance
1957	73	47
1967	73	43
1975	71	41
1980	69	40
1985	71	42
1987	69	40
1988	65	42
1989	69	43
1990	65	40
1991	68	42
1992-93	69	40
1993	68	40
1994	68	42
1995	69	43
1996	65	38
1997	67	40
1998	70	40

[Continued]

Adult Religious Membership vs. Attendance, 1957-2000

[Continued]

	Membership	Attendance
1999	70	43
2000	68	44

Source: U.S. Census Bureau. *Statistical Abstract of the United States,1990, 1991, 1995, 1996, and 2001.*

Religious Attitudes and Attendance: 12th Graders

Numbers in percent.

	Weekly Attendance	Religion Plays an "Important" Role in Their Lives
1976	41	29
1981	40	31
1986	34	26
1991	31	28
1992	32	29
1993	32	29
1994	32	30
1995	32	30

Source: Office of the Assistant Secretary for Planning and Evaluation. U.S. Department of Health and Human Services. *Trends in the Well-Being of America's Children and Youth*, 1997 Edition. Retrieved February 11, 2002 from http://aspe.hhs.gov/hsp/97trends/sd1-3.htm.

Top 15 Growing Religions, 1990-2000

Data include those who identify with the religion.

	% Change 1990-2000
Deity (Deism)	717
Sikhism	338
New Age	240
Hinduism	237
Baha'i	200
Buddhism	170
Native American religion	119
Nonreligious/secular	110
Islam	109
Taoism	74
Humanism	69
Eckankar	44

[Continued]

Top 15 Growing Religions, 1990-2000

[Continued]

	% Change 1990-2000
Unitarian Universalism	25
Scientology	22
Christianity	5

Source: "Largest Religious Groups in the United States of America." Retrieved February 7, 2002 from http://www.adherents.com/rel_USA.html.

Public Libraries and Bookmobiles, 1993-1999

	Total Library Outlets	Central Libraries	Branch Libraries	Bookmobiles	Public Libraries
1993	15,904	8,887	7,017	1,035	8,929
1994	15,904	8,879	7,025	997	8,921
1995	15,994	8,937	7,057	978	8,981
1996	16,047	8,923	7,124	966	8,946
1997	16,090	8,943	7,147	947	8,967
1998	16,180	8,887	7,293	933	8,964
1999	16,220	8,883	7,337	907	9,046

Source: National Center for Education Statistics. U.S. Department of Education. *Public Libraries in the United States: 1993, 1994, 1995, 1996, 1997, 1998,* and *1999,* various publication dates. Retrieved February 18, 2002 from http://nces.ed.gov.

Public Library Funding, 1993-1999

Total income in constant 2000 dollars. All other data in percent.

	Total Income ($ mil.)	Distribution of Income (%)			
		Local	State	Other	Federal
1993	6,040.7	78.0	12.5	8.4	1.1
1994	6,111.9	78.2	12.3	8.4	1.1
1995	6,320.8	78.3	12.0	8.7	1.0
1996	6,480.7	78.1	12.2	8.7	1.0
1997	6,724.1	77.6	12.1	9.3	0.9
1998	7,118.1	77.6	12.6	9.0	0.8
1999	7,383.1	77.7	12.7	9.0	0.6

Source: National Center for Education Statistics. U.S. Department of Education. *Public Libraries in the United States: 1993, 1994, 1995, 1996, 1997, 1998,* and *1999,* various publication dates. Retrieved February 18, 2002 from http://nces.ed.gov. Total income data were converted to constant 2000 dollars using using CPI data from U.S. Bureau of Labor Statistics and U.S. Bureau of Economic Analysis.

Library Usage, in Millions, 1993-1999

	Visits	Circulation, Total	Circulation, Children's	Children's Program Attendance
1993	810.8	1,586.0	462.9	35.6
1994	821.7	1,570.0	491.7	38.4
1995	981.6	1,609.9	559.9	41.0
1996	1,013.8	1,642.6	571.0	42.4
1997	1,057.8	1,690.2	596.4	43.4
1998	1,088.0	1,701.2	612.1	45.9
1999	1,119.7	1,693.4	612.4	47.7

Source: National Center for Education Statistics. U.S. Department of Education. *Public Libraries in the United States: 1993, 1994, 1995, 1996, 1997, 1998,* and *1999,* various publication dates. Retrieved February 18, 2002 from http://nces.ed.gov.

Participation in Adult Education, 1978-1999

Data in percent. 1978 "% of adult population" data are rounded.

Reasons for Taking Adult Education Classes	1978	1991	1995	1999
Complete degree or diploma	NA	13	10	11
Train for a new job	NA	9	11	12
Personal/social	NA	30	44	43
Advance on the job	NA	60	54	54
% of adult population	12	32	40	46

Source: U.S. Census Bureau. *Statistical Abstract of the United States, 1980, 1994, 1996,* and *2001.* Note: NA stands for data not available.

Gender Differences in Adult Education, 1991 and 1999

Data in percent.

Reasons for taking adult education classes	1991		1999	
	Men	Women	Men	Women
Advance on the job	67	54	59	50
Personal/social	24	35	34	50
Train for new job	8	10	11	12
Complete degree or diploma	11	14	13	9

Source: U.S. Census Bureau. *Statistical Abstract of the United States: 1994* and *2001.*

Reasons for Participating in Adult Education, by Educational Attainment, 1999

Data in percent.

	% of Adult Population	Advance on the Job	Personal/ Social	Train for a New Job	Complete Degree or Diploma
Up to 8th grade	14	39	41	3	21
9th to 12th grade	26	28	35	15	21
High school diploma or GED	37	52	39	12	7
Vocational school after high school	42	57	44	11	5
Some college	52	46	48	14	15
Associate's degree	59	60	38	15	14
Bachelor's degree or higher	62	63	45	9	8

Source: U.S. Census Bureau. *Statistical Abstract of the United States: 2001.*

Chapter 13
PEOPLE AND THE INTERNET

Our Time Spent on Selected Entertainment

Hours per year.

	1995	1996	1997	1998	1999
Recorded music	288	292	270	283	290
Internet	5	10	34	61	99
Daily newspapers	166	161	159	156	154
Home video games	22	25	36	43	61
Consumer books	100	99	95	96	91
Television	1,580	1,559	1,544	1,551	1,588
Radio	970	973	964	936	967

Source: U.S. Census Bureau, *Statistical Abstract of the United States: 2001*, Washington D.C. 2001.

Internet Population by Race

In percent.

	Oct-97	Dec-98	Aug-00	Sep-01
Whites	25.3	37.6	50.3	59.9
Blacks	13.2	19.0	29.3	39.8
Asians/Pacific Islanders	26.4	35.8	49.4	60.4
Hispanics	11.0	16.6	23.7	31.6
Percent of Total Population	22.2	32.7	44.4	53.9

Source: U.S. Department of Commerce, Economics and Statistics Administration, National Telecommunications and Information Administration, *A Nation Online: How Americans Are Expanding Their Use of the Internet*, February 2002.

Internet Population by Age Group

In percent.

	Oct-97	Dec-98	Aug-00	Sep-01
Age 3-8	7.2	11	15.3	27.9
Age 9-17	33.2	43	53.4	68.6
Age 18-24	31.6	44.3	56.8	65.0
Age 25-49	27.1	40.9	55.4	63.9
Age 50 and over	11.2	19.3	29.6	37.1

Source: U.S. Department of Commerce, Economics and Statistics Administration, National Tele-communications and Information Administration, *A Nation Online: How Americans Are Expanding Their Use of the Internet,* February 2002.

Internet Households by Income

In percent.

	Oct-97	Dec-98	Aug-00	Sep-01
Less than $15,000	9.2	13.7	18.9	25
$15,000-$24,999	11.6	18.4	25.5	33.4
$25,000-$34,999	17.1	25.3	35.7	44.1
$35,000-$49,999	22.8	34.7	46.5	57.1
$50,000-$74,999	32.3	45.5	57.7	67.3
$75,000 and above	44.5	58.9	70.1	78.9

Source: U.S. Department of Commerce, Economics and Statistics Administration, National Telecom-munications and Information Administration, *A Nation Online: How Americans Are Expanding Their Use of the Internet,* February 2002.

Online Population by Gender

In percent.

	1997	1998	1999	2000	2001
Women	45.0	48.0	49.0	50.0	52.0
Men	55.0	52.0	51.0	50.0	48.0
Online Population	56.7	84.5	104.5	116.4	142.8

Source: U.S. Department of Commerce, Economics and Statistics Administration, National Telecommu-nications and Information Administration, *A Nation Online: How Americans Are Expanding Their Use of the Internet,* February 2002.

Kids and Teens Take to the Web

Internet use in percent.

	Oct-97	Dec-98	Aug-00	Sep-01
Ages 3-8	7.2	11.0	15.3	27.9
Ages 9-17	33.2	43.0	53.4	68.6

Source: U.S. Department of Commerce, Economics and Statistics Administration, National Telecommunications and Information Administration, *A Nation Online: How Americans Are Expanding Their Use of the Internet,* February 2002.

The Internet Grows, So Do Computer Attacks

Number of domain hosts are in millions.

	1997	1998	1999	2000	2001
No. of computer attacks	2,134.0	3,734.0	9,858.0	21,756.0	52,658.0
Internet domain hosts	16.1	29.6	43.2	72.3	109.5

Source: U.S. Department of Commerce, Economics and Statistics Administration, National Telecommunications and Information Administration, *A Nation Online: How Americans Are Expanding Their Use of the Internet,* February 2002.

Top Search Terms, March 1999-January 2001

Term	Percent
Games	6.59
AOL	7.31
Ebay	7.31
Horoscopes	8.00
MP3	9.35
Chat/chatrooms	12.33
Porn/porno/pornography	14.02
Yahoo	20.44
Hotmail	21.21
Sex	32.89

Source: U.S. Department of Commerce, Economics and Statistics Administration, National Telecommunications and Information Administration, *A Nation Online: How Americans Are Expanding Their Use of the Internet,* February 2002.

Visitors to Relationship Web Sites, January 2000 and January 2001

In millions.

	Jan-00	Jan-01
Personal Web sites	3.9	5.6
Gift, flower, greeting card e-tailers	12.3	17.9

Source: Mullins, Robert. "Love Silicon Valley Style." *Silicon Valley/San Jose Business Journal,* June 22, 2001; "Valentine's Day Lights E-Commerce Fire." Retrieved February 27, 2002 from the World Wide Web: http://www.ecommercetimes.com; "Online Love in the Time of Calamity." *Knight- Ridder/Tribune News Service,* December 31, 2001

What Do We Buy on eBay?

In $ millions.

	Total sales
Computers	7.7
Toys	8.2
Jewelry	9.4
Music, movies, books	9.8
Electronics	9.8
Antiques	11.2
Sports	18.3
Automobiles	23.7
Collectibles	25.4

Source: Brown, Eryn. "How Can a Dot-Com Be This Hot?" *Fortune,* January 21, 2002.

KEYWORD INDEX

This index allows users to access all subjects, issues, government agencies, companies, programs, books, reports, titles, personal names, associations, schools, educational institutions, and locations cited in the panels of *Social Trends & Indicators USA: Work & Leisure*. Page reference numbers follows each citation. Page references do not necessarily identify the page on which a panel begins. In cases in which panels span two or more pages, references point to the page on which the index term appears-which may be the second or subsequent page of a panel. Cross-references have been added to index citations for ease in locating related topics and panels.

Employee benefits continued:
— supplemental pay, p. 129
— vacation time, pp. 128, 133
— vision care, p. 133
Employee contributions, p. 132
Employees
— benefits, pp. 127, 341*t*
— occupation, p. 296*t*
— productivity, pp. 328*t*-329*t*
Employer costs
— employee benefits, p. 127
— health insurance, p. 131
— salaries, p. 128
— wages, p. 128
Employer-provided benefits, pp. 133, 135, 137
Employment, pp. 1, 16
— administrative support occupations (including clerical), pp. 20, 296*t*
— African-Americans, p. 16
— agriculture, pp. 3-4, 291*t*
— amusement industries, p. 7
— automotive repair, p. 7
— Baby Boomers, p. 16
— business services, p. 7
— construction, p. 34
— Defense Department, p. 13
— economic sectors, pp. 3, 291*t*
— education, p. 1
— elementary education, p. 11
— engineering services, p. 7
— executive, administrative, and managerial occupations, pp. 20, 296*t*
— farming, forestry, and fishing occupations, pp. 20, 296*t*
— finance and real estate, p. 292*t*
— finance, insurance, and real estate, p. 6
— for-profit health care, p. 7
— for-profit social services, gender, p. 7
— goods-producing industries, p. 291*t*
— government, pp. 1, 3, 5, 9-11, 13, 291*t*-293*t*
— handlers, equipment cleaners, and laborers, pp. 20, 296*t*
— health care, p. 34
— high school education, pp. 11-12
— Hispanics, p. 16
— hotels and lodging, p. 7
— household service occupations, p. 20
— household service occupations (private), p. 296*t*
— legal services, p. 7
— machine operators, assemblers, and inspectors, pp. 20, 296*t*
— manufacturing, p. 34
— membership organizations, p. 7
— men, p. 16
— municipal government, p. 9
— museums, p. 7
— nonprofit health care, p. 7
— nonprofit social services, p. 7
— personal services, p. 7
— Postal Service, pp. 1, 13, 293*t*
— precision, production, craft and repair occupations, pp. 20, 296*t*
— private household service occupations, pp. 20, 296*t*

Employment continued:
— professional specialties, pp. 20, 296*t*
— public education, pp. 10, 12
— public schools, p. 34
— real estate, p. 292*t*
— retail trade, pp. 6, 292*t*
— sales occupations, pp. 20, 296*t*
— secondary education, p. 11
— service occupations, pp. 291*t*-292*t*
— services, pp. 1, 3-4, 6
— social services, p. 34
— teachers and support staff, p. 11
— technical and related support occupations, pp. 20, 296*t*
— transportation and material moving occupations, pp. 20, 296*t*
— transportation and public utilities, pp. 6, 292*t*
— unions, pp. 1, 14
— whites, p. 16
— wholesale trade, pp. 6, 292*t*
— women, p. 16
— zoological gardens, p. 7
Employment-practice liability cases, p. 170
Engineering services, p. 7
Engineers, p. 32
— *See also:* computer engineers
Engineers (industrial), pp. 22-25, 296*t*
Enrollment
— elementary education, p. 292*t*
— high school sports, pp. 204-205
Entertainment, p. 268
— *See also:* arts and entertainment
Environment
— charitable giving, pp. 242-244
— volunteering, pp. 245-246
Equal Employment Opportunity Commission, pp. 159, 163
— *See also:* EEOC
Equipment and software, p. 102
Equipment cleaners and laborers
— *See:* handlers, equipment cleaners, and laborers
Europe, p. 41
Executive, administrative, managerial occupations
— employment, pp. 20, 296*t*
— independent contractors, pp. 69-70
Executives, top
— *See:* general managers and top executives
Exercise, p. 203
Expenditures
— health insurance, p. 130
— worker's compensation claims, p. 153
Fabricators and laborers
— *See:* Operators, fabricators, and laborers
Fair Labor Standards Act, p. 43
Families
— dining at home, p. 180
— income, p. 92
— leisure time, p. 173
— mealtimes, p. 180
— poverty rates, pp. 92-93, 315*t*, 318*t*
— restaurant dining, p. 180
Family and Medical Leave Act, pp. 137, 344*t*

Museums continued:
— art, as percentage of all museums, p. 229
Music, pp. 218, 268, 286
Musical plays, p. 216
Napster, p. 283
NASCAR, pp. 211, 283
A Nation Online, pp. 273, 278
National Association for Stock Car Auto Racing
— *See:* NASCAR
National Association of Realtors, p. 194
National Basketball Association, p. 210
— *See also:* NBA
National Collegiate Athletic Association
— *See:* NCAA
National Education Association, p. 221
National Electronic Injury Surveillance System, p. 205
National Endowment for the Arts, p. 218
National Football League, p. 210
— *See also:* NFL
National health care expenditures, p. 342t
National Hockey League, p. 210
— *See also:* NHL
National origin-based discrimination
— case resolutions for, pp. 163, 167
— charges filed with the EEOC, p. 161
Native American, p. 252
Native Americans, p. 253
Natural history museums, p. 229
Navigators, p. 296t
Navigators (airline), p. 22
NBA, pp. 211-212
— *See also:* National Basketball Association
NC-17, p. 231
NCAA, p. 363t
Network and computer systems administrators, p. 52
New Age, pp. 252-253
New York, p. 190
New York Knicks, p. 213
Newspapers, p. 268
NFL, pp. 211-212
— *See also:* National Football League
NHL, pp. 211-212
— *See also:* National Hockey League
Nicaragua, p. 47
Nielsen ratings, p. 211
Nondurable goods, p. 102
Nonworking mothers, p. 183
Nostradamus, p. 283
Nurses, pp. 24-25, 58-59, 61-62
— registered, p. 22
— retirement, p. 23
— worker shortages, p. 59
Nursing aides, orderlies, and attendants, pp. 61-62
Nursing home care, p. 131
Obesity in children, p. 203
Occupational fatalities, pp. 149, 151, 156, 349t
Occupational Safety and Health Administration, pp. 153-154
Occupational therapy aides, p. 53

Occupations
— degrees conferred, pp. 296t, 305t
— growth rate, p. 303t
— illegal labor, p. 43
— independent contractors, pp. 69, 307t
— job declines, p. 303t
— job openings, pp. 296t, 298t, 305t
— retirement, p. 296t
— workplace violence, pp. 351t-352t
Occupations in decline, pp. 51, 54-55, 303t
Offbearers
— *See also:* machine feeders and offbearers p. 54
Office clerks (general), pp. 61-62
Office machine operators, p. 55
Office machine operators (except computer), p. 54
Oklahoma City, p. 229
Oneandonly.com, p. 284
Online auctions, p. 286
Online banking, p. 273
Online dating, pp. 284, 380t
Online dating services, p. 284
Online search terms, pp. 282-283, 379t
Online shopping, pp. 273, 277, 279
Online travel spending, pp. 196-197, 360t
Opera, pp. 185, 216, 224-225
Operation Child Watch, p. 45
Operators, p. 54
Operators, fabricators, and laborers, pp. 31-32, 43, 69-70
Order Clerks, pp. 54-55
Orderlies and attendants
— *See:* nursing aides, orderlies, and attendants
Osama bin Laden, p. 283
Outdoor track, p. 208
Pacific Islanders
— income, pp. 75, 82
— Internet use, pp. 270-271
— salaries, p. 38
Packagers
— *See:* hand packers and packagers
Paid leave, p. 129
Paid sick time, p. 133
Pain
— injuries in the workplace, p. 155
Paintball, pp. 200-201
Painting, p. 218
Parents, pp. 183-184
Parks, p. 216
Part-time employment, pp. 65-66, 306t
— independent contractors, p. 68
— marital status, pp. 65-66
Paternity leave, p. 137
PCs, pp. 226-227
Pensions, p. 145
Performing arts, pp. 216-217
— attendance figures, pp. 224, 367t
— Baby Boomers, p. 224
Personal computers
— *See:* PCs
Personal home care aides, p. 52

CUMULATIVE KEYWORD INDEX

This index allows users to locate all subjects, issues, government agencies, companies, programs, associations, schools, educational institutions, books, reports, personal names, and locations cited in *Social Trends & Indicators USA: Work & Leisure*; *Social Trends & Indicators USA: Community & Education*; *Social Trends & Indicators USA: Health & Sickness*; and *Social Trends & Indicators USA: Crime & Justice*. Page references do not necessarily identify the page on which a topic begins. In cases where the topic spans two or more pages, page numbers point to where the index term appears-which may be the second or subsequent page on the topic. Cross-references have been added to index citations for ease in locating related topics.

419 Fraud
— *See:* Nigerian Letter Fraud Scheme
AARP
— *See:* Association for the Advancement of Retired Persons
Abandonment of elders, p. III:199
Abortions, pp. II:321*t*
— by age group, pp. III:306-307
— by race/ethnicity, pp. II:10-13
— Catholic hospitals, pp. III:367-368
Abstention, pp. II:15, III:304-305
Acambis, Inc., p. III:393
Accidents, pp. II:21, III:430*t*
— by race/ethnicity, p. III:8
— by race/ethnicity and sex, pp. III:32-33
— causes of death, p. III:4
— causes of disability, p. III:228
— infant mortality, p. III:10
— research funding, p. III:401
Accommodations and food services, pp. I:104-105
Accountability in education, p. II:166
Acquired immunodeficiency syndrome
— *See:* AIDS
ACT scores, pp. II:173, II:369*t*
ACT UP, p. III:287
Active Community Environments, pp. III:405-406
Active physicians, p. III:522*t*
Activities of daily living, pp. III:203-204, III:225
Acupuncture, pp. III:78, III:82, III:162-163
AD
— *See:* Alzheimer's Disease
ADD
— *See:* Attention Deficit Disorder
Adderall, pp. II:303, III:129
Adelphia, p. IV:85
ADHD
— *See:* Attention Deficit/Hyperactivity Disorder

Adidas, p. IV:100
Administration on Aging, pp. III:204, III:206, IV:240
Administrative and managerial occupations
— *See:* Executive, administrative, managerial occupations
Administrative support occupations, pp. I:20, I:69-70, I:104-105, I:296*t*
Adoption assistance, p. I:134
Adrenal gland surgery, p. III:151
Adult education, p. I:233
— attainment levels, pp. I:264-265, I:332*t*
— by sex, pp. I:262, I:375*t*
— job advancement, pp. I:260-261
Adult immunizations, p. III:98
Adult leisure activities, pp. I:221, I:234, I:242, I:245-246
Adult literacy, p. II:156
Adult Protective Services, p. III:199
Adult religious affiliation, pp. II:131, II:135
Adult smoking, pp. III:121, III:135, III:138
Adult substance use, pp. III:121-122
Advance directives
— *See:* Living wills
Advanced classes, pp. II:259, II:392*t*
Advanced degree recipients, p. II:295
Advanced Fee Fraud
— *See:* Nigerian Letter Fraud Scheme
Advanced mathematics classes, pp. II:259-260
Advanced practice nurses, pp. III:351-352
— *See also:* Nurse practitioners
Advanced sciences classes, p. II:260
Advertising and public relations managers
— *See:* marketing, advertising, public relations managers
Advertising expenditures, pp. III:177-178, III:483*t*
Aerobics instructors
— *See:* fitness trainers and aerobics instructors
Afghanistan, p. III:332
African-Americans, p. IV:205

African-Americans continued:
— *See also:* Blacks
— arrests, p. IV:53
— births, pp. II:6, II:321*t*
— causes of death, pp. III:8, III:31, III:33, III:35-36, III:43
— diseases, pp. III:14, III:97
— employment, p. I:16
— families, pp. II:53, II:62
— homicides, pp. IV:217-218
— hospital closings, p. III:370
— income, p. II:21
— infant mortality, pp. II:21, III:313
— law enforcement personnel, p. IV:204
— life expectancy, p. II:20
— population, pp. II:24, II:70-71, II:345*t*
— population mobility, p. II:39
— risk behaviors, p. III:17
— single-parent households, p. II:61
— specialized museums, p. I:229
— Total Fertility Rates, p. II:8
African wastewater treatment, p. III:326
Age-based discrimination, pp. I:161, I:163, I:167
Age groups
— abortion rates, p. III:307
— book purchases, p. I:220
— death rates, 1917-1918, p. II:17
— depression, p. III:64
— disabled population, p. III:226
— employment, pp. I:20, III:296
— first marriages, p. II:338*t*
— high-school completion rates, p. I:39
— illegal labor, pp. I:43, I:301*t*
— Internet use, pp. I:272-273, I:378*t*
— mathematics proficiency, p. II:161
— population, p. I:345*t*
— psychiatric treatment, p. III:262
— reading proficiency, p. II:159
— retirement, pp. I:139, I:344*t*
— sexual activity, p. III:270
— suicides, p. III:261
— volunteering, pp. I:239-240, I:370*t*
— voter turnout, p. II:104
— work hours, p. I:44
Agency for Healthcare Research and Quality, p. III:361
Aggravated assaults, p. IV:135
— by sex, pp. IV:36, IV:38
— juveniles arrested, pp. IV:133, IV:137-138
— recidivism, p. IV:260
— reported, p. IV:5
— victimization, p. IV:31
Aging population, p. III:485*t*
— *See also:* Elderly population
— *See also:* Senior citizens
— causes of disability, p. III:228
— health problems, pp. III:203-204
— living arrangements, pp. III:191-192
— Medicaid, p. III:386
— perceptions of quality of life, pp. III:205-206
Agoraphobia, pp. III:252-253

Agriculture, pp. II:256-257, II:262
— child labor, p. I:46
— employment, pp. I:3-4, I:291*t*
— workplace injuries, p. I:156
The AGS Foundation for Health in Aging, p. III:344
Aides
— *See:* personal home care aides
AIDS
— attendant diseases, pp. III:3, III:61, III:333
— by race/ethnicity, pp. III:52, III:54
— causes of death, pp. III:53, III:131, III:440*t*
— Centers for Disease Control and Prevention (CDC), p. III:287
— cyclical patterns, p. III:51
— disability benefits, p. III:243
— funding, pp. III:400-402
— new cases, p. III:506*t*
— origins, pp. III:62, III:95
— total occurrences reported, pp. III:444*t*
— treatment, p. III:286
AIDS Coalition to Unleash Power
— *See:* ACT UP
Air pollution, pp. III:316-320, III:518*t*
Air Rage: Crisis in the Skies, p. III:140
Aircraft hijacking, p. IV:245
Aircraft pilots and flight engineers, pp. I:27-28
— *See also:* airline pilots
Airline passenger screening, pp. IV:232-234, IV:367*t*
Airline pilots, pp. I:22, I:296*t*
— *See also:* aircraft pilots and flight engineers
Airplane crashes, p. III:4
al-Rahman, Abd, p. IV:184
Alabama, pp. II:246, IV:284, III:370
Alaska, pp. IV:121, II:217, III:409
Alaska Natives, pp. IV:159-160
— diseases, pp. III:288-289
— educational attainment, pp. II:258-259, II:287-290
— low birth weight, p. III:40
— physicians, p. III:337
— population, pp. II:70-72
— risk behaviors, p. III:136
Albuterol, p. III:167
Alcohol
— adults, p. III:121
— cirrhosis, pp. III:6, III:108
— mouth cancer, p. III:161
— North America, p. III:64
— teenagers, pp. III:117-118
Alcohol consumption, pp. III:108, IV:173, IV:352*t*
Alcohol-related arrests, pp. IV:112, IV:334*t*
Alcohol-related crimes, p. IV:334*t*
— crime rate, p. IV:10
— Prohibition era, p. IV:29
— public-order crimes, pp. IV:101, IV:104, IV:111-112
— rate fluctuation, p. IV:174
Alcohol-related deaths, pp. IV:115-116, III:125, III:131, IV:174, IV:335*t*
Aleuts, p. II:24
All Handicapped Children Act, p. II:299
Allegra, p. III:178

Allergies, p. III:229

Alliance for Aging Research, p. III:341

Allopaths, p. III:336

Alternative medicine practitioners
— by specialization, pp. III:78-82, III:450t
— clinical trials, pp. III:162-163
— herbal medicines, p. III:75

Altruistic suicides, p. III:35

Alzheimer's Disease (AD), p. III:5
— aging population, p. III:204
— causes of death, pp. III:4, III:7-8, III:71-72, III:449t
— disabled population, pp. III:225, III:243
— fluoride, p. III:328
— hormone replacement therapy, p. III:168
— hospice care, p. III:376
— mental illnesses, pp. III:248-249

Amber, pp. IV:142-143

American Academy of Arts and Sciences, p. II:293

American Academy of Dermatology, p. III:147

American Academy of Family Physicians, p. III:339

American Academy of Pediatrics, pp. III:46, III:96

American Association of Colleges of Nursing, p. III:347

American Association of Law Libraries, p. IV:96

American Attitudes Toward Physical Activity & Fitness, p. III:93

American Bar Association, p. IV:284

American Booksellers Association, p. I:220

American Civil Liberties Union (ACLU)
— hate crimes, p. IV:287
— hospital closings, p. III:363
— prison population, p. IV:247
— single-sex education, p. II:308
— use of force by police, p. IV:214
— women's reproductive health care, p. III:366

American College Testing program
— See: ACT

American Dietetic Association, p. III:84

American Federation of Teachers, pp. II:231-232, II:240

American Front Skinheads, p. IV:181

American Hospital Association, p. III:82

American Housing Survey, p. III:191

American Indians, p. II:343t
— abortions, pp. II:12-13
— births, pp. II:10, II:321t
— causes of death, pp. III:8, III:27
— drug arrests, p. IV:161
— drug use, pp. IV:159-160
— educational attainment, pp. II:151, II:258-259, II:287-290
— health problems, pp. III:40, III:288-289
— juveniles arrested, p. IV:137
— law enforcement personnel, p. IV:203
— population, pp. II:24, II:70-72, II:347t
— risk behaviors, p. III:136
— Total Fertility Rates, p. II:8

American Medical Association, pp. III:75, III:79, III:82, II:250, IV:276
— community health centers, p. III:101
— elder abuse, p. III:197
— emergency medical technicians, p. III:357

American Medical Association continued:
— medical malpractice jury awards, p. III:416
— physician-assisted suicide, p. III:216

American Medical Student Association, p. III:395

American Nurses Association, p. III:350

American Psychiatric Association, pp. III:170, III:251, II:302

American Psychological Association, p. IV:290

American Society of Criminology, p. IV:243

American Society of Health-System Pharmacists, p. III:390

American Society of Plastic Surgeons, p. III:277

Americans with Disabilities Act, pp. III:223, III:245

America's Missing: Broadcast Emergency Response, p. IV:141

America's Most Wanted, p. IV:142

Amharic, p. II:76

Amino acid dietary supplements, p. III:75

Amnesty International, p. IV:248

Amoxil, pp. III:166-167

Amphetamines, p. III:125

Amputations, p. I:155

Amusement industries, p. I:7

Amyl nitrite, p. III:120

Anabolic steroids, p. IV:153

Analgesics, p. III:128

Analytic geometry, p. II:259

Androstenedione, p. III:130

Anemia, pp. III:39-40

Anesthesiology, p. III:341

Angiocardiography, p. III:152

Angioplasty, balloon, pp. III:25, III:151

Anglicans, pp. II:130-133, II:135

Animal Liberation Front, p. IV:181

Annual Report on Eating Patterns in America, p. I:180

Anomic suicides, p. III:35

Anorexia nervosa, pp. III:115, III:248-249, III:256-257

Anthrax, p. III:392

Anti-Defamation League, p. IV:287

Anti-inflammatory steroid injections, p. III:390

Antibiotics, pp. III:166, III:329-331, III:390-392

Antidepressants, pp. III:63-64, III:165, III:169-170, III:445t

Antiques, p. I:286

Antitrust violations sentencing, p. IV:108

Anxiety disorders, pp. III:247-248, III:250, III:252, III:262

AOL, p. I:282

Apache Indian tribe, pp. II:72-73

Apples, p. III:87

Aquariums, p. I:229

Arabic, p. II:76

Arabs, p. IV:184

Archer, Dennis, p. IV:288

Architecture-related occupations, p. II:296

Arizona, pp. II:63-64, IV:121, IV:277

Arizona State University, p. IV:118

Armed Forces of Puerto Rican Liberation, p. IV:181

Armed robbery, pp. IV:36, IV:38

Armenia, p. II:163

Arrests, pp. IV:294t
— alcohol-related crimes, pp. IV:112-113
— Border Patrol, pp. I:49, I:302t
— by race/ethnicity, p. IV:53

Arrests continued:
— crime index, pp. IV:330*t*
— crimes cleared, pp. IV:268-269
— homicides, p. IV:39
— justice system employment, p. IV:266
— larceny, p. IV:322*t*
— lesser offenses, pp. IV:102-103
— not included in crime rate, p. IV:9
— property crime, pp. IV:67-68
Arsenic, pp. III:315, III:327
Arsinger v Hamlin, p. IV:282
Arson, pp. IV:63, IV:68, IV:79-81
Art museums, p. I:229
Art purchases, pp. I:218-219
Arteriography, p. III:152
Arthritis, pp. III:227-228
Arthur Andersen, p. IV:85
Arthur Ashe Academy for Boys, p. II:309
Artificial-wall climbing, pp. I:200-201
Arts and entertainment, pp. I:104-105
Arts, culture, and humanities, pp. I:242, I:244-246
Aryan Nation, p. IV:181
Asian-Americans
— *See:* Asians
Asian Indians
— *See:* Asians
Asians
— births, pp. II:10, II:12-13, I:40, II:321*t*
— causes of death, pp. III:8, III:27, III:43
— diseases, pp. III:52, III:289
— drug arrests, p. IV:161
— drug use, pp. IV:159-160
— educational attainment - college, pp. II:151-153, II:287-290
— educational attainment - high school and above, pp. I:118-119
— educational attainment - vocational education, pp. II:258-259
— employment, pp. I:35, I:37
— income, pp. I:75, I:82
— Internet use, pp. I:270-271
— interracial marriages, p. II:55
— juveniles arrested, p. IV:137
— law enforcement personnel, p. IV:203
— low birth weight, p. III:40
— percentage of total population, pp. II:24, II:70-71, II:74-75, II:344*t*
— percentage of workforce population, p. I:41
— physicians, p. III:337
— population mobility, p. II:38
— salaries, p. I:38
— single-parent households, p. II:61
— Total Fertility Rates, pp. II:6-8
Asians and Pacific Islanders
— *See:* Asians
Asperger's Disorder, pp. III:258-259
Aspirin, p. III:130
Assaults
— alcohol-related crimes, p. IV:104
— domestic violence, pp. IV:25-26
— household income, p. IV:31
— *National Crime Victimization Survey*, pp. IV:4, IV:10

Assaults continued:
— perpetrators, pp. IV:36, IV:38
— population density, p. IV:58
— workplace, pp. I:151, I:157
Assemblers and inspectors
— *See:* machine operators, assemblers, and inspectors
Assemblies of God, pp. II:132-138
Assigned counsel, p. IV:281
Assisted living facilities, p. III:194
Assisted Living Federation of America, p. III:194
Assisted reproductive technology, pp. III:291, III:299-300
Assisted-suicide movement, p. III:213
Associated Press, p. I:45
Associate's degrees, pp. I:57, I:61, I:94, I:264-265, II:283
Association for the Advancement of Retired Persons (AARP), p. IV:83, III:192, III:194, III:220
Asthma, pp. III:3, III:229, III:231, III:315, III:319-320
Atelectasis, p. III:10
Atherosclerosis, p. III:2
Athletes, p. I:204
Atkins, Dr., p. III:90
Atomic bombs, p. III:105
Attendance at entertainment events, pp. I:210, I:222, I:224-225, I:363*t*
Attendance at religious services, pp. I:249, I:372*t*
Attendants
— *See:* nursing aides, orderlies, and attendants
Attention Deficit Disorder (ADD), p. III:446*t*
— National Health Interview Survey, pp. III:65-66
— Ritalin, p. II:302
Attention Deficit/Hyperactivity Disorder (ADHD), p. III:483*t*
— National Health Interview Survey, pp. III:65-66
— Ritalin, pp. III:165, III:171-174, II:302
Attitudes About Work and Leisure in America, p. I:178
Attitudes toward religion, pp. I:250-251, I:373*t*
Auctions, p. I:286
Audio products, p. I:185
Audiologists, p. I:52
Auditing clerks
— *See:* bookkeeping, accounting, and auditing clerks
Austin (TX), p. I:50
Australia, pp. II:163-165
Austria, pp. II:163, II:165
Autism, pp. III:247, III:255, III:259, III:500*t*
— California Department of Mental Health services, p. III:258
— home schooling, p. III:234
— mental illnesses, pp. III:248-249
— school performance, pp. III:229, III:231
— special education, p. II:298
Automated Data Processing Inc., p. I:172
Automated Data Processing Inc. (ADP), p. I:171
Automated Meter Reading (AMR), p. I:55
Automobiles, pp. I:7, IV:71-72, I:286, IV:324*t*
Azerbaijan, p. II:163
AZT, p. III:286
Baby Boom generation, pp. IV:29-30, IV:43, III:187
— age at first marriage, p. II:51
— attendance at performing arts, p. I:224
— breastfeeding, p. III:41

Blacks continued:
III:32, III:34, IV:53
— mathematics proficiency, pp. II:161-162
— Medicare, p. III:380
— murders, pp. III:37-38
— physicians, p. III:337
— political-party affiliation, p. II:108
— Population Replacement Rate, p. II:6
— poverty, p. IV:53
— racial profiling, p. IV:222
— risk behaviors, pp. III:16, III:135-137
— risk factors, p. III:20
— single-parent households, p. II:61
— suicides, pp. III:260, III:434*t*
— Total Fertility Rates, pp. II:6-7
— unemployment, p. IV:53
— volunteering, p. I:241
— voter turnout, p. II:106
Bladder cancer, p. III:156
Blindness, pp. III:227, III:229, III:231, III:386
Blood-alcohol concentration (BAC), p. IV:115
Blood clots, p. III:168
Body Mass Index (BMI), p. III:16
Bok, Sissela, p. IV:145
Bombs, p. II:245
Bones, broken, p. III:227
Bookkeeping, accounting, and auditing clerks, pp. I:61-62
Bookmobiles, pp. I:254, I:374*t*
Books, pp. I:185, I:220-221, I:268, I:286, I:366*t*
Border Patrol, pp. IV:24, I:49
Born Again Christians, pp. II:132-133
Boston College, p. II:294
The Boston Globe, p. II:293
Boston Public Schools, p. IV:131
Boston University, p. II:294
Botanicals, p. III:75
Botox, p. III:279
Botulinum toxoids, p. III:392
Bowling, p. I:200
Bowling Alone, p. III:93
Box-office revenues, pp. I:222, I:366*t*
Boy Scouts, p. I:205
Brady Handgun Violence Prevention Act, pp. IV:46-47
Brady, James, p. IV:46
Branch libraries, p. I:254
Brand-name prescription drugs, pp. III:175-176, III:179
Breakfast, pp. III:139-140
Breast cancer
— causes of death, pp. III:3, III:12-13, III:18, III:67-68
— Fred Hutchinson Cancer Research Center, p. III:144
— hormone replacement therapy, p. III:168
— survival rates, pp. III:19, III:158, III:426*t*
— work-related stress, p. III:144
Breastfeeding, pp. III:41-42, III:435*t*
Bribery sentencing, p. IV:108
Britney Spears, p. I:283
Broadway shows, pp. I:224-225
Broken bones, p. III:227
Bronchial cancer, pp. III:67, III:156, III:158

Bronchitis, p. III:3
Broward County (FL), p. IV:267
Brown University, p. II:294
Bruises, p. I:155
BuddhaNet, p. II:145
Buddhism, pp. II:132-135, I:252-253
— Internet, p. II:145
— non-Christian houses of worship, pp. II:140-141
Bulgaria, pp. II:5, II:163-164
Bulimia nervosa, pp. III:115, III:248-249, III:256-257
Bullying, pp. II:249-250
Bureau of Alcohol, Tobacco, and Firearms, pp. IV:24, IV:227
Bureau of Diplomatic Security, p. IV:227
Bureau of Education of the Handicapped, p. III:232
Bureau of Health Professions, pp. III:338, III:349, III:355
Bureau of Justice Assistance, p. IV:266
Bureau of Justice Statistics, pp. IV:243, IV:272, IV:283
Bureau of Labor Statistics, pp. I:54, III:141, III:146, III:351
Bureau of Prisons, p. IV:227
Bureau of the Census, p. IV:159
Burglaries
— arrests, p. IV:67
— by location, pp. IV:73-74
— by time of day, p. IV:325*t*
— corrections expenditures, p. IV:249
— decrease in rates, p. IV:65
— reported to police, pp. IV:4, IV:7-8, IV:77, IV:373*t*
Burns, p. I:155
Bush administration (President George W.), pp. III:106, II:242, III:416
Business
— education, pp. II:256-257, II:262
— productivity, pp. I:122, I:326*t*
— profits, p. I:122
— salaries and wages, pp. I:122, II:296
Business management and administrative services, p. II:284-285
Business services, p. I:7
Business trips, pp. I:190-191, I:359*t*
Businesses
— *See:* Home-based businesses
— home-based,
Butchers and meat cutters, p. I:54
Bypass, coronary
— *See:* Coronary bypass
Cable television, p. I:226
Cadmium, p. III:324
Cafeteria plans, p. I:135
Calculus, p. II:259
California
— Asian population, p. II:75
— cigarette smoking, p. III:409
— class size reduction programs, p. II:196
— community hospital beds, p. III:369
— distribution of elderly population, p. III:190
— expulsions from school, p. II:246
— gay-couple households, pp. II:63-64
— hate crimes, p. IV:290
— law enforcement deaths, p. IV:211

Central Intelligence Agency (CIA) continued:
IV:227
Central libraries, p. I:254
Central nervous system defects, p. III:310
Ceramics, p. I:218
Cereals, p. III:83
Cerebral palsy, pp. III:229, III:231
Cerebrovascular disease, pp. III:2, III:4
— *See also:* Stroke
Certification of teachers
— *See:* Teacher certification
Certifications of nurses, p. III:351
Cervical cancer, pp. III:19, III:68, III:158, III:168
Cesarean sections, pp. III:151, III:301-302
Character education, pp. II:206-207
Charismatics, pp. II:130-131, II:134-135
Charitable giving, pp. I:233-235, I:242-244, I:369*t*
Charter schools, pp. II:231-232
Chat, p. I:282
Chat rooms, p. I:282
Cheese, p. III:83
Chemical burns, p. I:155
Chemical peels, pp. III:277-279
Chemistry, p. II:194
Chemists, pp. I:22, I:24-25
Chemotherapy, pp. III:152, III:159
Cherokee Indian tribe, pp. II:70, II:72
Chicago (IL) law enforcement personnel, p. IV:203
Chicken pox, p. III:96
Child abuse, pp. IV:10, IV:139-140, IV:206
Child Abuse Prevention and Treatment Act, p. IV:107
Child care, pp. II:66-67, I:135, II:262, II:341*t*
Child Care Bureau, p. II:227
Child labor, pp. I:45-46
Child rape, p. IV:245
Childbirth
— by age of mother, pp. III:297-298
— by method of delivery, pp. III:513*t*
— Cesarean sections, pp. III:301-302
— oxytocin, p. III:23
— surgical procedures, p. III:154
Childhood diseases, pp. III:55-57, III:441*t*
Childhood Immunization Act, p. III:97
Children, p. IV:127
— *See also:* Infants
— *See also:* Juveniles
— *See also:* Teenagers
— Attention Deficit/Hyperactivity Disorder (ADHD), pp. III:65, III:483*t*
— attitudes toward religion, p. I:251
— autism, p. III:258
— breastfeeding, p. III:41
— disabilities, pp. III:229-231, III:494*t*
— eating habits, p. II:211
— emotional problems, p. III:230
— employment, p. II:149
— family households, pp. II:44, II:333*t*
— homicides, p. II:243

Children continued:
— illegal labor, p. I:45
— Internet use, pp. I:278-279, I:379*t*
— learning disabilities, pp. III:65, III:229-231
— living arrangements, pp. II:46, II:58-59, II:61, II:334*t*
— low birth weight, p. III:39
— married-couple households, p. II:46
— Medicaid, p. III:386
— multiple disabilities, p. II:298
— museums, p. I:229
— participation in sports, p. I:204
— poverty, p. I:92
— programs, p. I:258
— Ritalin, p. III:483*t*
— single-parent households, pp. II:46, II:340*t*
— soda consumption, p. II:311
— suicides, p. II:243
— time spent with parents, pp. I:183-184, I:357
— two-parent households, p. II:46
— video games, p. IV:144
Children Now, p. III:221
Chin augmentation, pp. III:277-279
Chin, Vincent, pp. IV:286, IV:288
China, pp. II:5, II:30
Chinese (language), pp. II:76-77
Chinese population, pp. III:40, III:42-43, II:74
Chippewa Indian tribe, pp. II:72-73
Chiropractic medicine, pp. III:78-79, III:82, III:162, II:286, II:290
Chlamydia, pp. III:51-52, III:95
Chloroform, p. III:120
Choctaw Indian tribe, pp. II:72-73
Cholera, pp. III:58-59, III:326, III:442*t*
Cholesterol levels, pp. III:12, III:14, II:18, III:20, III:83, III:210, III:426*t*
Christian houses of worship, pp. II:136-138
Christianity, pp. I:252-253
Christians, pp. II:132-135
Christiansen/Cummings Associates, p. IV:117
Chromosomal defects, pp. III:310, III:312
Chronic illnesses, p. III:204
Church Arsons Prevention Act, p. IV:287
Church of God, pp. II:132-133
Church of Jesus Christ of the Latter-Day Saints, pp. II:136-138
Churches, p. II:360*t*
Churches of Christ, pp. II:130-138
Cigarette smoking, pp. III:64, III:107, IV:173, III:479*t*
— adults, pp. III:121, III:135
— brands, pp. III:136, III:138
— causes of death, p. III:125
— diseases, pp. III:68, III:160
— low birth weight, p. III:40
— prevalence, p. III:409
— school-based health centers, p. III:104
— teenagers, pp. III:117-118
Cincinnati (OH), pp. IV:204, IV:215
Cipro, p. III:392
Circulatory system diseases, pp. III:10, III:152, III:235-238
Cirrhosis, p. III:6
— *See also:* Liver disease

Contraceptive practices, pp. II:14-15, III:161, III:304-305, II:323*t*

Contracts, p. I:14

Contusions, p. I:155

Convict labor, pp. IV:254-255

Conyers, Jr., John, p. IV:287

Cook County (IL), pp. IV:266-267

Copyright infringement, pp. IV:95-97, IV:328*t*

Cornell University, pp. III:195, II:294

Coronary bypass, p. III:25

Corporate profits, pp. I:122, I:124, I:339*t*

Correctional population, pp. IV:19-20, IV:299*t*

Corrections Corporation of America (CCA), pp. IV:251-252

Corrections system employment, pp. IV:21-22

Corrections system expenditures, pp. IV:249-250, IV:373*t*

Cosmetic surgery, pp. III:179, III:277-279, III:504*t*

Cough syrup, p. III:130

Coughlin, Lt. Paula, p. I:166

Council on Graduate Medical Education, p. III:344

Counterfeiting, pp. IV:88-89, IV:99-100, IV:105, IV:108, IV:327*t*

County mental hospitals, p. III:264

Court trials, pp. IV:273-274

Crack cocaine, pp. IV:151, IV:162

Cream products, p. III:83

Creatine, p. III:130

Creative writing, pp. I:218-219

Creditcards.com, p. IV:91

Creek Indian tribe, pp. II:72-73

Creole, French
— *See:* French Creole

Crib death, pp. III:45-46
— *See also:* Sudden Infant Death Syndrome (SIDS)

Crime Act, p. IV:206

Crime and Punishment: Women in Prison, p. IV:243

Crime control costs, pp. IV:23-24

Crime Index, pp. IV:3, IV:6, IV:14

Crime prevention, p. IV:206

Crime rate
— arrests, pp. IV:102, IV:149, IV:175-176, IV:354*t*
— history, p. IV:15
— justice system employment, p. IV:21

Crimes Against Children, p. IV:139

Crimes against the family, p. IV:136

Crimes cleared by arrest, p. IV:379*t*

Crimes in schools, pp. II:245, II:387*t*

Croatia, p. II:163

Crocheting, p. I:218

Cross-country sports, pp. I:208-209

Cruises, p. I:196

Crystal Cathedral, p. II:145

Cuba, p. II:163

Culture and humanities
— *See also:* arts, culture, and humanities p. I:242

Curfew violations, pp. IV:106-107, IV:136

Curriculum specialization, p. II:261

Cuts, p. I:155

Cyberchurches, p. II:145

Cyberstalking, p. IV:120

Czech Republic, pp. II:163-165, I:187

Dance, pp. I:218-219

Danish, pp. II:76-77

D.A.R.E.
— *See:* Drug Abuse Resistance Education

Database administrators, p. I:52

Date-rape drugs, pp. IV:56, IV:154
— *See also:* Rohypnol

Dating online, pp. I:284-285

DAWN
— *See:* Drug Abuse Warning Network

DCBE
— *See:* Double-Contrast Barium Enema
— *See:* Double-contrast barium enema (DCBE)

DDT, p. III:323

Deaconess-Waltham Hospital (MA), p. III:370

Dead Rabbits, p. IV:43

Deafness, pp. III:227, III:229, II:298

Death penalty, pp. IV:245-246

Death row inmates, pp. IV:244, IV:246, IV:371*t*

Death With Dignity Law, p. III:216

Deaths
— by cause, pp. III:1-2
— by race/ethnicity, p. II:21
— diseases, pp. III:15, III:18, III:423*t*
— influenza epidemic, p. II:17
— life expectancy, pp. II:324*t*
— police officers, pp. IV:210-212, IV:217-218, IV:361*t*
— schools, p. II:243
— terrorism, pp. IV:190-191, IV:358*t*

Defense Department, pp. I:13, I:293*t*

Defense research and development, p. III:398

Degree completion, pp. I:260-262, I:265

Degrees conferred, pp. I:58, II:283, I:296*t* II:399*t*

Degrees conferred, professional
— *See:* professional degrees conferred

Deism, pp. II:134-135, I:252-253

Delaware, pp. II:64, II:187, II:217

Dementia, pp. III:71, III:198, III:204, III:243

Democratic Republic of the Congo, pp. III:332, III:334

Democrats, p. II:98

Denmark, p. IV:125

Dental care benefits, pp. III:103, I:131, I:133, III:210

Dentists, pp. III:79, IV:93, II:286, II:290

Department of Education, pp. IV:290, II:304

Department of Health and Human Services, p. III:63

Department of Justice, pp. IV:203, IV:207, IV:270, IV:290

Department of Labor, p. I:45

Dependency ratio, pp. II:22, I:141

Depressants, p. IV:153

Depression, pp. III:445*t*
— age groups, p. III:262
— cases, pp. III:247-248
— senior citizens, p. III:204
— treatment, pp. III:63-64, III:169
— treatments, pp. III:75-76

Dermabrasion, pp. III:277-278

Desktop publishers, p. I:52

Drug-related arrests continued:
— trafficking, p. IV:245
Drug-related crimes, pp. IV:101-104
— Baby Boom generation, p. IV:29
— firearms-related crimes, p. IV:40
— not included in crime rate, p. IV:10
— possession and trafficking, p. IV:109
— recidivism, p. IV:260
— state prisons population, pp. IV:236-237
Drug-resistant bacteria, p. III:329
Drug shortages, pp. III:389-391, III:530*t*
Drug treatment programs, p. IV:263
Drug use, pp. IV:157-158, IV:345*t*
— by race/ethnicity, pp. IV:159, IV:162
— by type of drug, pp. IV:169-170
DrugFreeTeenagers.com, p. III:133
Drugs distributed, pp. IV:349*t*
Drunk driving, pp. IV:101, IV:104, IV:206
— *See also:* Driving under the influence
DTP, p. III:96
— *See:* Diphtheria, Tetanus, and Pertussis (DTP)
DUI
— *See:* Driving under the influence
— *See:* Driving under the influence (DUI)
DUKE NUKEM, p. IV:145
Duke University, pp. III:81, I:171, III:237, II:294, III:345
Durable goods, p. I:102
Durex [company], pp. III:271, III:273
Durham versus United States, p. IV:276
Durkheim, Emile, p. III:35
Dutch, p. II:77
DVD players, p. I:227
Dyslexia, p. III:243
E-learning, p. II:292
E-mail, pp. I:273, I:278
E-tailers, p. I:284
Ear infections, p. III:229
Ear surgery, pp. III:150, III:277-279
Earnhardt, Dale, p. I:211
Earnings, p. III:498*t*
— by educational attainment and sex, p. II:295
— by race/ethnicity and sex, p. I:71
— by sex, p. I:318*t*
— college degrees, pp. I:114-116
— disabilities, pp. III:244-245
— doctoral degrees, p. II:404*t*
— householders, pp. I:322*t*
— independent contractors, pp. I:71, I:307*t*
— workforce, p. I:342*t*
Earth First!, pp. IV:177, IV:181
Earth Liberation Front, p. IV:181
Eastern equine encephalitis, p. III:392
Eating habits, pp. II:211, III:466*t*
— disease prevention, p. III:90
— eating disorders, pp. III:256-257
— mental health, p. III:247
— stress, pp. III:139-140
— U.S. Surgeon General's recommendations, p. III:83
— weight, pp. III:89, III:115-116

eBay, pp. IV:100, I:282, I:380*t*
Ebola virus, pp. III:62, III:95
Echinacea, p. III:75
Eckankar, pp. II:134-135, I:252-253
Economic Growth and Tax Relief Reconciliation Act of 2001, p. II:278
Economic sectors, pp. I:3, I:104, I:291*t*
Ecstasy, pp. III:119-120, III:124, IV:147, IV:153
Ectopic pregnancy, p. III:23
Edison project, p. II:233
Education
— accountability, p. II:166
— adults, p. I:233
— attainment, pp. II:284-285
— charitable giving, pp. I:242-244
— college preparatory, p. II:262
— costs of universities, p. II:281
— elementary and secondary, pp. II:189-190
— employment, pp. I:1, I:10-12
— enrollment, p. I:292*t*
— expenditures, p. II:399*t*
— funding, pp. II:377*t*
— grants, p. II:273
— job advancement, pp. I:260-262
— volunteering, pp. I:245-246
Education administrators, pp. I:22, I:24-25, I:58-59
Education assistance, p. I:135
Education budget, p. II:384*t*
Education for All Handicapped Children Act, p. III:232
Education of the Handicapped Act, p. III:232
Education revenues, pp. II:212, II:279, II:397*t*
Educational achievements, pp. II:293, II:369*t*
Educational attainment, pp. IV:53, I:56, IV:264, I:335*t*
— adults, pp. I:264-265, I:332*t*
— Asians, pp. I:118-119
— blacks, pp. I:112, I:118-119
— breastfeeding mothers, p. III:42
— disabled population, p. III:497*t*
— earnings, pp. I:114-116, II:295, I:318*t* 405*t*
— exercise habits, p. III:92
— Hispanics, pp. I:112, I:118-119
— householders, p. I:322*t*
— income, pp. I:94-95, II:177
— labor force, p. I:304*t*
— literacy, p. II:155
— men, p. I:94
— productivity, pp. I:110-111
— race/ethnicity, pp. II:152-153
— smoking, p. III:136
— teachers, pp. II:184-185
— volunteering, pp. I:238, I:370*t*
— whites, pp. I:112, I:118-119
— women, p. I:94
— workforce, p. I:56
Educational services, pp. I:104-105
EEOC
— *See:* Equal Employment Opportunity Commission (EEOC)
Eggs, p. III:83

Egoistic suicides, p. III:35

Eight-ball chicks, p. IV:134

El Salvador, p. I:47

E.L.A., p. II:169

Elder abuse, pp. IV:10, III:198, III:486*t*
— Adult Protective Services, p. III:199
— American Medical Association, p. III:197
— nursing homes, pp. III:201-202
— perpetrators, p. III:200

Elderly population, pp. II:22, II:35, IV:83, III:189, III:196, IV:241
— causes of death, p. III:448*t*
— diseases, p. III:210
— geographic distribution, pp. III:189-190
— health care, p. III:379
— health problems, pp. III:210-211
— immunizations, p. III:463*t*
— living arrangements, p. III:195
— living wills, p. III:211
— Medicare benefits, p. III:207
— prisoners, pp. I:141, IV:240

Elders, Jocelyn, p. III:107

Electrical and electronics engineers, p. I:58

Electronic commerce, pp. I:196, I:280

Electronic Communications Privacy Act, p. IV:229

Electronic fetal monitoring, p. III:302

Electronic surveillance
— *See:* wiretapping

Electronics, pp. I:286, I:367*t*

Electronics engineers
— *See:* electrical and electronics engineers

Electronics purchases, p. I:227

Elementary and Secondary Education Act, p. II:199

Elementary education, pp. I:11, II:189-190, I:292*t*

Elementary school principals, p. II:308

Elementary school teachers
— job openings, pp. I:24-25, I:58, I:61-62
— retirement, pp. I:22-23
— worker shortages, p. I:59

Eli Lilly & Co., p. III:170

Eligibility clerks, p. I:27

Elliptical motion trainers, p. I:200

Embezzlement, pp. IV:105, IV:108, IV:136

Eme Edict, p. IV:40

Emergency medical technicians (EMTs), pp. III:357-358

Emergency medicine physicians, p. III:341

Emergency room visits, pp. III:124-125, III:130, III:471*t*

Emory University, p. II:280

Emotional abuse of elderly, p. III:199

Emotional problems, pp. III:227, III:229-231, III:264

Emotionally disturbed children, pp. II:298-299

Emphysema, pp. III:3, III:5-6

Employee benefits, pp. I:127-130, I:133, I:135-138

Employee contributions, p. I:132

Employees, pp. I:127, I:296*t*

Employer costs, pp. I:127-128, I:131

Employment, pp. I:1, I:16, IV:22
— administrative support occupations (including clerical), pp. I:20, I:296*t*
— by industry, pp. I:1, I:3-7, I:9-14, I:20, I:34, III:141-143, III:234,

Employment continued:
   III:244-245, I:291*t*
— by race/ethnicity and sex, p. I:16
— disabled workers, p. III:233
— Fair Labor Standards Act, p. II:146
— high school diplomas, p. II:177
— high school education, pp. I:11-12
— justice system, p. IV:21
— literacy, pp. II:157-158

Employment-practice liability cases, p. I:170

EMTs
— *See:* Emergency medical technicians
— *See:* Emergency medical technicians (EMTs)

End-stage renal disease, p. III:380

Endocrine system, pp. III:150-151, III:236

Endometrial cancer
— *See:* Uterine cancer

Endoscopy, p. III:151

Endotracheal tube insertion, p. III:152

Endowments, p. II:279

Engineering occupations, pp. II:284-285, II:296

Engineering services, p. I:7

Engineers, p. I:32
— *See also:* computer engineers

Engineers (industrial), pp. I:22-25, I:296*t*

England, pp. IV:125, II:165

English language, p. II:284

English Language Arts test
— *See:* E.L.A.

English literature, p. II:284

English, honors
— *See:* Honors English

Enrollment, pp. II:222-223, II:231
— elementary education, p. I:292*t*
— high school sports, pp. I:204-205
— Medicaid, p. III:386
— Medicare, pp. III:490*t*

Enron Corp., pp. IV:85, IV:109

Entertainment, p. I:268
— *See also:* arts and entertainment

Environment, pp. I:242-246, III:315

Environmental crimes and sentencing, p. IV:108

Environmental interest organizations, p. IV:181

Environmental Protection Agency, pp. III:322, III:327

Epidemic-related deaths, p. III:463*t*

Epilepsy, pp. III:229, III:231

Episcopalians, pp. II:130-133, II:135-138

Episiotomy, p. III:151

Equal Employment Opportunity Commission (EEOC), p. I:159, I:163, I:165, I:167, I:169, I:353*t*

Equipment and software, p. I:102

Equipment cleaners and laborers
— *See:* handlers, equipment cleaners, and laborers

Erectile dysfunction treatments, pp. III:275-276

Escherichia coli infections, p. III:111

Eskimos, p. II:24

Esophageal cancer, pp. III:156, III:161

Estonia, p. II:163

Estrogen, p. II:18

Females continued:
— violent crimes, pp. IV:135-136
— vocational education, pp. II:258-259
Fertility rates
— birth rate, pp. III:507*t*
— by decade, pp. II:2, II:4
— by race/ethnicity, p. I:40
— European community, p. II:5
— live births, pp. II:315*t*
— population replacement rates, p. II:4
— reproductive patterns, pp. III:292-295
Fibril injections, pp. III:277-278
Fiction, p. I:220
Filipinos, pp. III:40, II:74
Finance, insurance, and real estate, pp. I:6, I:104-105, I:292*t*
Financial aid, p. II:273
Financial Executives International, pp. IV:84, I:171
Financial exploitation of elderly, p. III:199
Financial managers, pp. I:22, I:24-25, I:58
Financial restatements, p. IV:84
Finland, p. II:163
Finnish, p. II:76
Firearms, p. II:245
Firearms-related crimes, pp. IV:45, IV:47-48, IV:314*t*
Fires, p. III:4
First Church of Cyberspace, p. II:145
First-line supervisors and managers, pp. I:61-62
First marriages, p. II:338*t*
Fishing occupations
— *See:* farming, forestry, and fishing occupations
Fitness centers, p. I:135
Fitness trainers and aerobics instructors, p. I:52
Five Point Gang, p. IV:43
The Fix, p. IV:30
Flexible spending accounts, p. I:136
Flexible workplace, p. I:135
Flight engineers
— *See:* aircraft pilots and flight engineers
Florida
— gay-couple households, pp. II:63-64
— geographic distribution of elderly population, p. III:190
— hate crimes, p. IV:289
— hospital beds, p. III:369
— malpractice litigation, pp. III:415, III:417
— sex offender registries, pp. IV:121-122
— smoking prevalence, p. III:409
— vacation travel, p. I:190
— youth gangs, p. IV:138
Florida State Department of Health, p. III:392
Flour, p. III:83
Flowers, pp. I:185, I:284
FLSA
— *See:* Fair Labor Standards Act
— *See:* Fair Labor Standards Act (FLSA)
Flu epidemic
— *See:* influenza epidemic
Fluid cream products, p. III:83
Fluoride, pp. III:315, III:327-328

FOBT
— *See:* Fecal occult blood test
— *See:* Fecal occult blood test (FOBT)
Food and Drug Administration, pp. III:176, III:330, III:389-391
Food Guide Pyramid, p. III:83
Food poisoning, pp. III:111-112
Food preparation workers, pp. I:61-62
Food services, p. II:262
— *See:* accommodations and food services
FoodNet, p. III:111
Foods, pp. II:66-67
— bioterrorism, p. III:88
— consumption of major commodities, pp. III:451*t*
— nutrient levels, pp. III:459*t*
— pesticide use, pp. III:87-88
— phytochemicals, p. III:90
Foods, organic
— *See:* organic foods
Fools Gold: A Critical Look at Computers in Childhood, p. II:265
Football, p. I:209
Foreign-born physicians, p. III:337
Foreign-born population, pp. I:301*t*
Foreign-educated physicians
— *See:* IMGs
Foreign Intelligence Surveillance Act (FISA), p. IV:230
Foreign languages used in the United States, pp. II:76-77, II:344*t*
Forensic pathology physicians, p. III:341
Forestry and fishing occupation
— *See:* farming, forestry, and fishing occupations
Forestry and fishing occupations
— *See:* farming, forestry, and fishing occupations
Forgery, pp. IV:105, IV:108
Fortune 500 firms, p. II:120
Foundations, pp. I:242, I:245-246
Fourth graders, p. II:200
Fractures, p. I:155
France
— breastfeeding, p. III:42
— duration of school year, p. II:254
— entertainment, p. I:187
— literacy, pp. II:163-165
— prostitution, p. IV:125
— terrorism, p. IV:184
— tuberculosis, p. III:334
— vacation time, p. I:192
Franklin W. Olin College of Engineering, p. II:280
Fraternal organizations, p. I:185
Fraud, pp. IV:64, IV:82, IV:85, IV:101, IV:104-105, III:376
Fred Hutchinson Cancer Research Center, p. III:144
Free weights, p. I:202
French, p. II:76
French (language), p. II:77
French Creole, p. II:77
Fresno (CA), p. IV:72
Friends Don't Let Friends Drive Drunk, p. IV:113
Frost & Sullivan, p. IV:117
Fruits, p. III:83
Funding, pp. II:211, II:224-225, I:256, II:377*t*

Fuqua School of Business, p. I:171

G-ratings, p. I:230

GAAP
— *See:* Generally Accepted Accounting Principles (GAAP)

GAD
— *See:* Generalized Anxiety Disorder

Gallbladder cancer, p. III:161

Gambling, pp. IV:10, IV:101, IV:105, IV:108

Games, p. I:282

Gangs, pp. IV:39, IV:43, IV:206, IV:313t
— *See also:* Street gangs
— *See also:* Youth gangs

Garlic, p. III:75

Gasoline, p. III:120

Gastroesophageal Reflux Disease (GERD), p. III:167

Gays, pp. III:54, II:63-64, II:122, I:191, II:342t
— *See also:* Homosexuals
— *See also:* Lesbians

GDP
— *See:* Gross Domestic Product

GEDs
— *See:* General equivalency diplomas (GEDs)

General equivalency diploma
— *See:* GED

General Equivalency Diplomas (GEDs), p. I:264

General managers and top executives, pp. I:58, I:61-62

General office clerks, pp. I:61-62

The General Social Survey, p. II:295

General surgeons' medical malpractice premiums, p. III:415

Generalized Anxiety Disorder (GAD), p. III:252

Generally Accepted Accounting Principles (GAAP), p. IV:85

Generic prescription drug prices, p. III:175

Genetic engineering, pp. III:105-106

Genital cancer, p. III:3

Genital herpes, p. III:95

Genital surgery, pp. III:150-151

Genitourinary system diseases, pp. III:236, III:310

Genome research centers, p. III:105

Geographic distribution of population, pp. III:189-190

Geographic maldistribution of physicians, p. III:344

Geometry, analytic
— *See:* Analytic geometry

Georgia, pp. I:50, II:63-64, II:163, II:246, IV:248, IV:284

German (language), p. II:76

German measles, p. III:57
— *See also:* Rubella

Germany, pp. II:163, I:187, II:254, III:334

Getting America's Students Ready for the 21st Century, p. II:263

Ghettos, p. IV:162

GI Bill, pp. II:273-274
— *See also:* Serviceman's Readjustment Act

Gideon v Wainwright, p. IV:281

Gift shopping, p. I:284

Gifted children, pp. II:304-305, II:406t

Ginkgo Biloba, p. III:75

Ginseng, p. III:75

Girl Scouts, p. I:205

Giuliani, Mayor Rudy, p. IV:216

Glandular surgery, p. III:151

Global Tuberculosis Control: WHO Report 2002, p. III:332

Glucophage, p. III:167

Golf, pp. I:200, I:211

Gonorrhea, pp. III:51-52

Goods-producing industries, p. I:291t

Government, p. II:193

Government drug-control budget, pp. IV:350t

Government expenditures on crime control, p. IV:24

Government funding, p. I:256
— Human Genome Project, pp. III:464t
— National Institutes of Health, pp. III:400-401, III:535t
— research and development, pp. III:397-399, III:532t

Grade inflation, p. II:293

Grandtravel, p. I:191

Grants, pp. III:100, II:273

Grapes, p. III:87

Great Britain, pp. III:42, I:187, I:192

Great Lakes water pollution, p. III:321

Greek (language), p. II:76

Greeting cards, p. I:284

Grenades, p. II:245

Griffin v Illinois, p. IV:282

Grocery expenditures, pp. III:85-86, III:457t

Gross Domestic Product (GDP), pp. I:102, I:143, I:328t

Grossman, Lt. Colonel David, p. IV:145

Groundskeeping laborers
— *See also:* landscaping and groundskeeping laborers p. I:61

Guards and watch guards, pp. I:61-62

Guatemala, p. I:47

Gun Control Act, p. IV:46

Gun-Free Schools Act, pp. IV:129-132, II:245-246

Gun-related homicide arrests, pp. IV:311t

Gun-related violent crime, pp. IV:39, IV:45, IV:47

Guyana, p. II:163

Gym classes
— *See:* physical education classes

Gynecologists, pp. III:341, III:415

H-1B visas, p. I:59

Hacking, p. I:208

Hair salons, p. I:54

Hair transplantation for men, pp. III:277-278

Haiti, p. I:47

Hallucinogens, pp. IV:151-153

Hamm, Mia, p. I:209

Hand packers and packagers, pp. I:61-62

Handguns, pp. IV:40, II:245

Handlers, equipment cleaners, and laborers, pp. I:20, I:296t

Hanta virus, pp. III:62, III:95

Happy Meals, p. III:110

Harassment, pp. I:19, I:149, I:159, I:161, I:163, I:169, I:353t

Hard Pack, p. III:138

Harrison Act, p. IV:12

Harry Potter and the Sorcerer's Stone, pp. I:221, I:283

Harvard Mental Health Letter, p. III:135

Harvard School of Public Health Department of Nutrition, p. III:109

Harvard University, pp. III:75, II:293

Harvest Christian Fellowship, p. II:144

Hashish, pp. III:118, III:121, III:124, IV:152
— illicit substance use, teenagers, p. III:117
Hate crimes, pp. IV:286-290, IV:382*t*
— *See also:* Bias-related crimes
Hawaii, p. II:64
Hawaiian Natives, p. II:72
Hay fever, p. III:229
Hayflick Limit, p. III:48
Hazelden Foundation, p. III:123
HBV immunizations, p. III:97
HDL
— *See:* High-Denisty Lipoprotein (HDL)
Head injuries, pp. III:227, III:243
Head Start, pp. II:222-225, II:383*t*
Heaemophilus influenzae type b
— *See:* Hib
Health assessments, pp. III:488*t*
Health care, pp. I:242-244, III:484*t*
— costs for children, pp. II:66-67
— employment, pp. I:7, I:34
— expenditures, p. I:342*t*
— fraud, pp. IV:93-94, IV:328*t*
— Medicare enrollment, p. III:379
— productivity, pp. I:104-105
— vocational education, pp. II:256-257, II:262
— volunteering, pp. I:245-246
Health Care Financing Administration, p. III:374
Health clubs, pp. I:200-201
Health information technicians
— *See:* medical records and health information technicians
Health insurance, p. I:131
— employee benefits, pp. I:128-130, I:132
— independent contractors, p. I:72
— same-sex partners, p. I:136
Health Maintenance Organizations (HMOs), pp. III:345, III:382-383
Health Professional Shortage Areas, p. III:338
Health professions, p. II:284
Health sciences, p. II:284
Health services, pp. III:394-395, III:531*t*
Health violations in community water systems, p. III:326
Healthy Eating Index, p. III:84
Healthy People, pp. III:73, III:303, III:403-404, III:408
Hearing impairments, pp. III:203, III:227, III:229, II:298, III:487*t*
Hearing screenings, p. III:103
Heart attacks, pp. III:3, III:275-276
Heart disease, pp. III:5, III:14, II:18
— *See also:* Cardiovascular disease
— aging population, p. III:203
— Baby Boom generation, p. III:69
— causes of death, pp. III:4, III:6, III:8-9, III:12, III:24-25, III:69, III:401
— causes of disability, p. III:227
— funding, pp. III:400-401
— risk behaviors, p. III:136
— risk factors, pp. III:12, III:328
— treatments, pp. III:25, III:155
Heat burns, p. I:155

Hebrew, p. II:77
Helpers and laborers, p. I:43
Hemic system surgical procedures, pp. III:150-151
Hemorrhages in maternal mortality, p. III:23
Henderson, Charles, p. II:145
Hepatitis, pp. III:6, III:61, III:96, III:148, III:444*t*
Herbal therapies, pp. III:75, III:77, III:82, III:450*t*
Herbs, medicinal
— *See:* medicinal herbs
Hero Syndrome, p. IV:81
Heroin, p. IV:147
— control legislation, p. IV:11
— description, pp. IV:151-152
— emergency room visits, pp. III:124-125
— trafficking, pp. IV:12, IV:167-168
Herpes, genital
— *See:* Genital herpes
Heterosexuals, pp. III:53, III:289
Hib vaccinations for children, pp. III:96-97
High blood pressure
— *See also:* Hypertension
— causes of disability, pp. III:227-228
— obesity, p. III:405
High-Density Lipoprotein (HDL), pp. III:20-21
High school
— diplomas, pp. I:39, II:148, II:177, I:300*t*
— dropouts, pp. II:148-149
— sports, pp. I:199, I:204-205, I:362
— students, pp. I:250-251
— vocational education, pp. II:256-257, II:260-262, II:363*t*
High school education
— adults, p. I:264
— earnings, pp. I:114-116
— employment, pp. I:11-12
— enrollment, p. I:292*t*
— income, p. I:94
— staff, p. I:292*t*
— workforce, p. I:57
High-speed pursuits, pp. IV:219, IV:364*t*
Highly Active Anti-Retroviral Therapy, p. III:54
Hill, Anita, pp. I:162, I:165
Hinckley, John, pp. IV:277, IV:280
Hindi (language), p. II:76
Hinduism, pp. II:134-135, II:140-141, I:252-253
Hispanics, p. I:47
— abortions, pp. II:12-13
— births, pp. II:10, I:40, II:321*t*
— breastfeeding, p. III:41
— causes of infant mortality, pp. III:44, III:313
— computer learning opportunities, p. II:263
— deaths, pp. III:8-9, III:15
— diseases, pp. III:97, III:289
— drug use, pp. IV:159-160
— earnings, p. I:71
— education, pp. II:161-162, II:259
— educational attainment, pp. I:39, I:112, I:118-119, II:151-153, II:258, II:287-290
— employment, pp. I:16, I:30, I:37, I:67-68
— families, p. I:38

Hispanics continued:
— federal law enforcement officers, p. IV:227
— housing, p. II:35
— immunizations, p. III:99
— income, pp. I:82-83
— Internet use, pp. I:270-271
— law enforcement personnel, pp. IV:203-204
— learning disabilities, p. III:66
— literacy, p. II:159
— low birth weight, p. III:309
— Medicare, p. III:380
— physicians, p. III:337
— population, pp. II:24-25, II:39, II:70-71, II:346*t*
— risk behaviors, p. III:137
— single-parent households, p. II:61
— Total Fertility Rates, pp. II:6-8
— volunteering, p. I:241
— voter turnout, p. II:106
— youth gangs, p. IV:43
Historical diseases, pp. III:442*t*
History museums, p. I:229
HIV, pp. III:51, III:286, III:288-290
— attendant diseases, pp. III:3, III:333
— by race/ethnicity and sex, p. III:54
— Centers for Disease Control, p. III:288
— deaths, pp. III:8, III:53, III:289
— number of cases, p. III:506*t*
Hmong population, p. II:74
Hobson, Senator Cal, p. IV:253
Holidays, p. I:133
Holland, p. III:215
Holy Anorexia, p. III:115
Home-based businesses, pp. I:51, I:73-74, I:308*t*
Home care aides, p. I:53
— *See also:* personal home care aides
Home-cooked meals, p. I:357*t*
Home-entertainment products, p. I:226
Home health agencies, pp. III:207-209, III:393
Home health aides, p. I:52
Home health care, p. I:131
Home ownership, pp. II:35, III:191-192, I:194-195, II:331*t*
Home School Legal Defense Association, p. II:235
Home security, p. I:171
Home theatre in a box, p. I:227
Homeland Defense, p. IV:357*t*
Homeland Security Council, p. IV:187
Homelessness, p. IV:7
Homeopathy, pp. III:78, III:80, III:82
Homes, p. I:194
Homeschooling, p. II:234
Homework, pp. II:252-253, I:278, II:390*t*
Homicides, p. IV:41
— *See also:* Murders
— by age, pp. IV:308*t*
— by location, p. IV:319*t*
— by race/ethnicity, pp. IV:52-53, IV:217-218
— by sex, pp. II:18, IV:35, IV:310*t*
— children, p. II:243
— Columbine High School, p. II:24

Homicides continued:
— deaths, pp. III:4, III:8-9, II:21, III:131, III:432*t*
— domestic, pp. IV:48-49
— firearms-related, pp. IV:45, IV:311*t*
— incarcerations, pp. IV:306*t*
— population density, pp. IV:57-58
— rate fluctuation, pp. IV:28-30
— recidivism, p. IV:260
— reported to the police, pp. IV:4, IV:6
— students at school, p. II:243
— terrorism, pp. IV:190-191
— victims, pp. IV:34, IV:315*t*
Homosexuals, pp. III:53, III:287
— *See also:* Gays
— *See also:* Lesbians
— *See also:* Same-sex partners
Honda Accord, p. IV:71
Honduras, p. I:47
Honest Cannabis Information Foundation, p. III:134
Hong Kong, pp. II:5, II:31, II:163-165, I:187
Honolulu, p. II:75
Honor graduates, pp. II:293-294
Honors English, p. II:259
Hormone replacement therapy (HRT), pp. III:161, III:168
Horoscopes, p. I:282
Hospice care, pp. III:213, III:363, III:373, III:375
— diseases, p. III:376
— Hospice Home Care movement, p. III:373
— Kubler-Ross, Elisabeth, pp. III:212, III:374
— Medicare, pp. III:214, III:374, III:377-378
— pain control, pp. III:213-214
— patients, pp. III:525*t*
— Saunders, Dr. Cicely, pp. III:376, III:378
— United Government Services, pp. III:377-378
Hospitality, p. II:262
Hospitals, pp. I:131, III:212, III:264, III:364-365, III:525*t*
— *See also:* Catholic hospitals
— admissions, pp. III:369-370
— closings, pp. III:363, III:367, III:369-372
— expenditures, p. III:395
— medical procedures, pp. III:477*t*
— mergers, pp. III:366, III:525*t*
Hosting meals, pp. I:187, I:358*t*
Hot Network, p. III:280
Hotels and lodging, pp. I:7, I:196
Hotmail, p. I:282
House Select Committee on Aging, p. III:198
Household activities, pp. I:181-182, I:357
Household expenditures, pp. I:145, I:347*t*
Household income, pp. I:309*t*
— benefits, p. I:145
— college tuition, pp. II:271-272
— infant mortality, p. III:313
— Internet use, pp. I:270, I:378*t*
— life expectancy, p. II:21
— victimization rates, pp. IV:31-32
— weekend travel, p. I:192
Household service occupations, pp. I:20, I:32, I:296*t*
Households, pp. II:42-43, II:45, II:333*t*

Households continued:
— charitable giving, p. I:234
— earnings, pp. I:322*t*
Houses of worship, p. II:361*t*
Housing, pp. II:66-67
Housing stock, pp. II:32-34, II:330*t*
Houston (TX), p. II:30
Howard, Dennis, p. I:213
HRT
— *See:* Hormone replacement therapy
Human Genome Project, pp. III:105-106, III:464*t*
Human immunodeficiency virus
— *See:* HIV
Human resources occupations, pp. I:22, I:296*t*
Human Rights Campaign Foundation, p. II:65
Human Rights Watch, p. IV:248
Human services, pp. I:242, I:244-246
Human services assistants
— *See also:* social and human services assistants p. I:52
Humanism, pp. II:134-135, I:252-253
Humanities, p. II:285
— *See also:* arts, culture, and humanities p. I:242
Hungarian, p. II:76
Hungary, pp. II:163, II:165, III:334
Hydrocodone/APAP, p. III:167
Hyperkinetic Disorder of Children, p. II:302
Hypertension, p. III:14
— *See also:* High blood pressure
— aging population, p. III:203
— causes of death, p. III:2
— causes of disability, p. III:227
— low birth weight, pp. III:11, III:40
— maternal mortality, p. III:23
Hyperthyroidism and Synthroid, p. III:168
Hypothalamus gland surgery, p. III:151
Iceland, pp. II:163-164
Idaho, pp. II:187, IV:276, III:349
Identity theft, pp. IV:82, IV:90-92, IV:328*t*
Identity Theft and Assumption Deterrence Act, p. IV:92
IHD
— *See:* Ischemic heart disease
Illegal aliens, pp. I:49, IV:251
Illegal drug consumption, pp. IV:148, IV:167-168, IV:346*t*
Illegal gambling profits, p. IV:117
Illegal labor, p. II:349*t*
— age group, p. I:301*t*
— arrests, pp. I:49, I:302*t*
— country of origin, p. I:302*t*
— foreign countries, p. I:47
— minors, p. I:302*t*
— *Operation Child Watch*, p. I:45
— teenagers, p. I:43
Illicit substance use, pp. IV:350*t*
— Baby Boom generation, p. III:134
— by race/ethnicity, p. III:126
— emergency room visits, p. III:124
— inhalants, pp. III:119-120
— public health concerns, pp. III:411-412
— youth, pp. III:117-120

Illinois, pp. IV:248, IV:290, III:415, III:417
— gay-couple households, p. II:63
— geographic distribution of elderly population, p. III:190
— hospital beds, p. III:369
— teacher certification, p. II:187
— vacation time, p. I:190
— youth gangs, p. IV:138
IMGs, pp. III:342-343
Immigrants, pp. I:41, I:47, II:349*t*
Immigration and Naturalization Service, pp. I:47, I:49, IV:188, IV:226-227, IV:251
Immigration crimes and sentencing, p. IV:108
Immunizations, pp. III:94, III:99, III:103, III:462*t*
— adults, p. III:98
— diseases, p. III:96
— elderly population, p. III:463*t*
— HBV, p. III:97
Implants, p. II:15
Improving Teacher Quality State Grants, p. II:225
In-line skating, p. I:202
Incarceration rates, p. IV:30
Income
— Baby Boomers, pp. I:75-78
— charitable giving, pp. I:234-235
— educational attainment, pp. I:94-95
— exercise habits, p. III:92
— families, p. I:92
— grocery expenditures, p. III:86
— household, pp. I:80-81, I:85-87, II:177, II:370*t*
— Internet use, pp. I:274-275
— Medicare, p. III:528*t*
— minimum wage, p. I:90
— productivity, p. I:120
— race/ethnicity, pp. I:38, I:75, I:82-83, I:211*t*
— sex, pp. I:84, I:94, I:312*t*
Income, supplemental
— *See:* supplemental income
Independent contractors
— characteristics, p. I:307*t*
— earnings, p. I:71
— educational attainment, p. I:67
— health insurance, p. I:72
— marital status, p. I:68
— occupations, pp. I:69-70, I:307*t*
— part-time employment, p. I:68
Independents, p. II:98
India, pp. II:5, III:42, I:187
Indiana, pp. II:63, III:409
Indians, p. III:52
Indigent defendants, pp. IV:283-285, IV:381*t*
Individuals with Disabilities Education Act, pp. III:232, III:258, II:299-300
Indonesia, pp. I:187, III:332
Indoor track, p. I:208
Industrial engineers, pp. I:22-25, I:296*t*
Industry, pp. II:256-257, II:262
Infant mortality, p. II:21
— birth defects, pp. III:310-311
— causes, pp. III:10-11, III:423*t*

Jewish gangs, p. IV:43
Jews, pp. II:110, II:145
Jobs, pp. I:52-53
— advancement, pp. I:260-262, I:265
— college education, pp. I:51, I:58, I:61-62
— entrants, p. I:37
— gains, pp. I:32-33, I:299*t*
— leavers, p. I:37
— losses, pp. I:33, I:299*t*
— openings, pp. II:189-190, I:296*t*
— satisfaction, p. II:295
— training, pp. I:260-262
— worker supply, pp. I:24-25, I:27-28
Joe Camel, p. III:138
Jogging, p. I:202
Johns Hopkins University, p. II:294
Joint Legislative Task Force on Government Oversight, p. IV:223
Jones, Paula, p. I:166
Jonesboro (AR), p. IV:129
Jordan, Michael, p. I:211
Journal of the American Medical Association, pp. III:81, III:168, III:273-274, III:405
Judaism, pp. II:130-133, II:135, II:140-141
Judges, p. I:32
Jupiter Communications, p. I:196
Jury awards, p. I:170
Justice Policy Institute, pp. IV:129, IV:134, IV:237
Justice system employment
— arrests, pp. IV:266, IV:378*t*
— by government level, p. IV:302*t*
— crime rate, pp. IV:21-23
Justice system expenditures, pp. IV:303*t*
Justifiable homicides, pp. IV:217, IV:363*t*
Juveniles, pp. IV:39-40, IV:70, IV:101, I:221
— *See also:* Children
— *See also:* Infants
— *See also:* Teenagers
— *See also:* Youth
— arrests by race/ethnicity, pp. IV:133-137
— by sex, pp. IV:340*t*
— drugs, p. IV:149
— poverty, p. IV:134
— special units of police departments, p. IV:206
— violent crimes, pp. IV:340*t*
Kaczynski, Theodore, p. IV:181
Kaiser Family Foundation, p. I:231
Kanner, Leo, p. III:259
Kansas, p. IV:276
Kanzai, Amil, p. IV:182
Kazakhstan, p. II:163
Kennedy School of Government, p. III:75
Kennedy, President John F., p. IV:46
Kennedy, Robert F., p. IV:46
Kentucky, pp. II:187, III:409
Kenya, p. III:332
Kerr-Mills Act, p. III:384
Ketamine, p. IV:154
Kevorkian, Dr. Jack, p. III:216

Kidnapping, pp. IV:142, IV:245, IV:260
Kidney diseases, pp. III:8, III:40, III:161
— *See also:* Nephritis, nephrosis, and nephrotic syndrome
Kids Walk-to-School Program, p. III:406
Kilpatrick, William Heard, p. II:204
King, Jr., Dr. Martin Luther, p. IV:46
King, Rodney, pp. IV:204, IV:288
KKK
— *See:* Ku Klux Klan
Klaas, Polly, p. IV:142
Koppel, Ted, p. IV:243
Korea, pp. II:164-165, II:195, II:254
Korean population, pp. II:74, II:76-77
Kozol, Jonathan, p. II:221
Kru, p. II:77
Ku Klux Klan (KKK), pp. IV:181, IV:286
Kubler-Ross, Elisabeth, pp. III:212, III:374
Kurdistan Workers Party, p. IV:183
Kyrgyzstan, p. II:163
Labor force distribution, pp. I:299*t*
Labor law violations, p. I:45
Labor relations managers
— *See:* personnel and labor relations managers
Laboratory animal caretakers
— *See:* veterinary assistants and laboratory animal caretakers
Laboratory technologists
— *See:* Clinical laboratory technologists
Lacerations, p. I:155
Lakes and water pollution, pp. III:323, III:325
Landscaping and groundskeeping laborers, pp. I:61-62
Language-impaired children, pp. II:298-299
Lanoxin, p. III:167
Laotian population, p. II:74
Larcenies
— arrests, pp. IV:68-69
— by type, pp. IV:322*t*
— corrections system expenditures, p. IV:249
— females, p. IV:136
— property crime, pp. IV:7-8
— reported to police, p. IV:373*t*
Larsen, Elena, p. II:142
Las Vegas (NV), p. IV:124
Laser skin resurfacing, pp. III:277-279
Last Tango in Paris, p. I:231
Latin America, pp. II:25, I:47, III:326
Latinos, pp. I:41, II:70-71
Latter-Day Saints, pp. II:130-131
Latvia, pp. II:5, II:163-164
Law, pp. II:286, II:290
Law enforcement, pp. IV:30, I:157-158, IV:201-202, IV:205
— by race/ethnicity and sex, pp. IV:203-204, IV:360*t*
— deaths, pp. IV:361*t*
— departments, p. IV:199
— employment, p. IV:359*t*
— salaries, p. IV:209
— timeline, pp. IV:197-198
Lawyers, pp. I:22-25, I:32, I:58
LDP
— *See:* Low-Density Lipoprotein

Medicare

— Baby Boom generation, pp. III:380, III:382
— benefits, pp. III:207-209, III:214, III:489*t*
— elderly population, p. III:219
— enrollment, pp. III:380, III:527*t*
— expenditures, p. III:528*t*
— fraud, pp. IV:93-94
— hospice care, pp. III:374, III:376-379, III:526*t*
— income, p. III:381
— legislation, p. III:341
— medical infrastructure, p. III:363
— per-capita expenditures, p. I:131
— risk behaviors, pp. III:490*t*
— solvency, pp. III:381-382

Medicare+Choice program, pp. III:382-383

Medications, pp. III:102, II:301-302

Medicine, pp. III:75, II:286, II:290

Medicine, alternative
— *See:* Alternative medicine

Medicine, chiropractic
— *See:* Chiropractic medicine

Medicine, veterinary
— *See:* Veterinary medicine

Meditation, pp. III:162-163

Megan's Law, p. IV:121

Melanomas, pp. III:147-148, III:476*t*
— *See also:* Cancer
— *See also:* Skin cancer

Melissa, p. I:280

Membership organizations, pp. I:7, I:205, I:247-249, I:371*t*

Men
— *See also:* Males
— accidents, p. II:18
— activities of daily living, p. III:204
— age at first marriage, p. II:50
— art purchases, p. I:219
— athletic programs, p. I:206
— cancer survival rates, p. III:158
— causes of death, pp. III:6-7, III:12, II:18, II:21, III:24-26, III:30, III:32, III:34, III:37-38, III:53, III:422*t*
— coaches' salaries, pp. I:206-207
— cosmetic surgery, pp. III:277-278, III:504*t*
— creative writing, p. I:219
— disabled, pp. III:225, III:236
— diseases, pp. III:13, II:18, III:28, III:54, III:116, III:147, I:155, III:160, III:247, III:249, III:262, III:288
— domestic homicides, pp. IV:48-49
— earnings, p. I:71
— education, pp. II:259, I:262
— educational attainment, pp. I:94, II:258, II:283, II:285
— employment, pp. I:16, I:29-30, I:33, I:65-67, I:69, I:174-175
— homicides, p. II:18
— household activities, pp. I:181-182
— income, pp. I:84, I:94
— injuries at work, pp. I:155-156
— Internet use, p. I:276
— job training, p. I:262
— life expectancy, pp. II:18-19, III:47
— living arrangements, p. III:192

Men continued:
— Medicare, p. III:380
— modern dance, p. I:219
— occupational fatalities, p. I:156
— occupations, pp. I:31-32, I:156
— online shopping, p. I:277
— police officers, p. IV:200
— political-party affiliation, pp. II:100-101
— pottery, p. I:219
— prisoners, pp. IV:18, IV:238-239
— risk behaviors, pp. III:16-17, III:135-136
— risk factors, pp. II:18, III:20
— sexual activity, pp. III:269-270
— Social Security benefits, p. I:29
— sports scholarships, p. I:206
— suicides, pp. II:18, III:260, III:432*t*
— teachers, p. II:182
— violent crime, pp. IV:35-38
— volunteering, pp. I:236-237
— writing, p. I:219

Mental health, pp. III:103, III:107, III:247
— facilities, pp. III:264-265, III:501*t*
— professionals, pp. I:157-158
— services, p. I:131

Mental Health Systems Act, p. III:251

Mental illness, p. III:499*t*
— disabilities, pp. III:227, III:235, III:248-251, III:265-266
— educational attainment, p. III:241
— workforce disabilities, pp. III:238-239

Mental retardation, pp. III:229-231, III:243

Mental Retardation Facilities and Community Mental Health Centers Construction Act, p. III:265

Mercury, p. III:324

MergerWatch, p. III:366

Merit resolutions, pp. I:167-168

Message distributing occupations
— *See:* Mail and message distributing occupations

Metals, pp. III:323-325

Metalworking, p. I:218

Meter readers, pp. I:54-55

Meth Tour, p. IV:156

Methadone Control Act, p. IV:12

Methamphetamines, pp. III:124-125, III:129
— drug-related arrests, pp. IV:11, IV:147
— drug trafficking, pp. IV:167-168
— laboratories, pp. IV:155-156
— lifetime use reported, pp. IV:151-153

Methodists, pp. II:130-133, II:135

Methylphenidate, p. II:302

Metropolitan areas, pp. II:27-28, II:30, II:330*t*

Metropolitan Statistical Areas (MSAs), p. II:29

Mexican Mafia, p. IV:40

Mexico, pp. I:47, III:334

Miami (FL), p. IV:72

Miao, p. II:77

Michigan
— gay-couple households, p. II:63
— geographic distribution of elderly population, p. III:190
— insanity defense, p. IV:277

Michigan continued:
— litigation for school funding, pp. II:220-221
— medical liability insurance premiums, pp. III:415-417
— NAEP rankings, p. II:217
— physician-assisted suicide, p. III:216
— prison population, p. IV:248
— sex offender registries, p. IV:121
— uncertified teachers, p. II:187
Michigan Department of Community Health, p. III:407
Michigan Educational Assessment Program test, p. II:169
Microsoft Corporation, p. I:59
MIDCAB
— *See:* Minimally Invasive Direct Coronary Artery Bypass
Midwestern United States, p. III:189
Migrant workers, p. I:46
Military, pp. II:122, II:357*t*
Militia, p. IV:181
Milk, low-fat, p. III:83
Milk, Mayor Harvey, p. IV:276
Milk, whole, p. III:83
Million Man March, p. II:61
**Minimally Invasive Direct Coronary Artery Bypass
  (MIDCAB)**, p. III:25
Minimum wage, pp. I:90-91, I:316*t*
Mining, pp. I:104-106, I:156
Minnesota, pp. II:187, II:218
Missing children, pp. IV:141-143, IV:206, IV:342*t*
Mississippi, pp. IV:286, III:369-370, III:418
Missouri, pp. II:63, II:246, III:387, III:409
MMR, pp. III:57, III:96
— *See:* Measles, Mumps, and Rubella vaccine
M'Naghten, Daniel, p. IV:275
Moderates, p. II:114
Modern dance, pp. I:218-219
Moldova, p. II:163
Mon-Khmer (language), p. II:77
Monaco, p. II:30
Monetary damages, pp. I:165-166, I:169
Money-related crimes, pp. IV:10, IV:105, IV:108
Mongolia, p. II:30
Monitoring the Future, pp. III:118-119, III:132, III:137
Monk Eastman Gang, p. IV:43
Monoamine oxidase inhibitors, p. III:64
Montana, pp. II:75, II:218, IV:276, IV:290, III:369, III:387
Montana v Cowan, p. IV:276
Mood disorders, pp. III:251-252, III:499*t*
Morehouse College, pp. II:53, II:61
Mormons, pp. IV:12, II:130-133
Morning-after pill, p. II:15
Morphine, p. III:124
Mortality, maternal
— *See:* maternal mortality
Mothers, p. I:183
Mothers Against Drunk Driving (MADD), pp. IV:113, IV:207
Motor vehicle accidents, pp. III:4, II:21, III:32, III:131
Motor vehicle thefts, pp. IV:7, IV:65, IV:67, IV:76-77
Mouth cancer, pp. III:150, III:161
Movie admissions, pp. I:185, I:222
Movie ratings, pp. I:230-231, I:368*t*

Movie releases, p. I:230
Movie rentals, pp. I:187-188, I:358*t*
Movies, pp. I:222, I:286, I:366*t*
Mozambique, p. III:332
MP3, pp. I:227, I:282
MSAs, p. II:29
Multifactor Productivity, pp. I:108-109
Multinational Monitor, p. III:138
Multiple births, pp. III:39, III:299-300, III:512*t*
Multiple jobs, pp. I:63-64, I:306*t*
Multiple sclerosis, p. III:225
Multipurpose Arcade Combat Simulator (MACS), p. IV:145
Mumps, pp. III:55-56, III:94-95
Municipal government, p. I:9
Murders, pp. III:36-38
— *See also:* Homicides p. IV:5
— by age group, p. IV:33
— by race/ethnicity, p. IV:52
— by race/ethnicity, sex, and marital status, pp. IV:50-51
— crime index, p. IV:6
— death penalty, p. IV:245
— firearms-related, pp. IV:39, IV:312*t*
— juveniles, pp. IV:33, IV:133, IV:135, IV:137-138
— rate fluctuation, pp. IV:25-26
— victimization, p. IV:38
Murphy Brown, p. II:62
Murray, John, p. IV:144
Musculoskeletal system diseases, pp. III:150, III:155, III:235, III:238, III:310
Museums, pp. I:7, I:216, I:228-229, I:368*t*
Music, pp. I:218, I:268, I:286
Musical plays, p. I:216
Muslims, pp. II:132-135, II:145, IV:224
NAACP Legal Defense Fund, p. IV:244
Najim, Eyad Mahmoud Ismail, p. IV:184
Nandrolone, p. IV:153
Napster, pp. IV:95, I:283
Narcotics, pp. IV:12, IV:153
NASCAR, pp. I:211, I:283
— *See:* National Association for Stock Car Auto Racing
A Nation At Risk, pp. II:162, II:167, III:174, II:176, II:199, II:204
A Nation Online, pp. I:273, I:278
National Academy of Science, pp. III:21, III:327
National Adult Literacy Survey, pp. II:156-157
National Alliance for the Mentally Ill, p. III:251
National Ambulatory Medical Care Survey, p. III:63
National Assembly on School-Based Health Care, p. III:102
National Assessment of Educational Progress (NAEP), p. II:159, II:162, II:203, II:235-236
National Assessment of Educational Progress (NAEP) rankings, pp. II:217-218, II:376*t*
National Association for Stock Car Auto Racing (NASCAR), p. I:211, I:283
National Association of Anorexia Nervosa and Associated Disorders, p. III:257
National Association of Bilingual Education, p. II:307
National Association of Gifted Children, p. II:304
National Association of Police Organizations, p. IV:224**

National Association of Realtors, p. I:194

National Association of School Nurses, p. II:303

National Basketball Association (NBA), p. I:210

National Burglar and Fire Alarm Association, p. IV:73

National Cancer Institute, pp. III:31, III:400-401

National Center for Chronic Disease Prevention & Health Promotion, p. III:90

National Center for Complementary and Alternative Medicine, pp. III:76, III:80-81, III:162-163, III:451t

National Center for Education Statistics, pp. II:234-235, II:269

National Center for Missing and Exploited Children, p. IV:141

National Center for Policy Analysis, p. IV:250

National Center for State Courts, p. IV:273

National Center on Addiction and Substance Abuse (CASA), p. IV:155

National Center on Institutions and Alternatives, p. IV:248

National Child Abuse and Neglect Data System, p. IV:139

National Cholesterol Education Program, p. III:167

National Coalition for Parent Involvement in Education, p. II:198

National Collegiate Athletic Association (NCAA), p. IV:118

National Commission on Excellence in Education, p. II:257

National Conference of Catholic Bishops, p. III:367

National Consumer League, p. IV:83

National Council of Teachers of Mathematics, p. II:205

National Crime Victimization Survey
— actual crimes reported, pp. IV:4, IV:6-9
— crimes reported, p. IV:294t
— gangs in schools, p. IV:42
— property crime, p. IV:65
— rate fluctuation, p. IV:26
— victimization of children, p. IV:139

National Data Collection - Police Use of Force, p. IV:214

National Defense Act, p. II:204

National Education Association, p. I:221

National Elder Abuse Incidence Study, pp. III:199-200

National Electronic Injury Surveillance System, p. I:205

National Endowment for the Arts, p. I:218

National Firearms Act, p. IV:46

National Football League (NFL), pp. I:210-212

National Fraud Information Center, p. IV:83

National Gambling Impact Study Commission, p. IV:117

National Governors Association, p. III:387

National Health and Nutrition Examination Survey, p. III:16

National Health Care Anti-Fraud Association, p. IV:93

National health care expenditures, p. I:342t

National Health Service Corps, p. II:278

National Heart, Lung, and Blood Institute, pp. III:400-401

National Highway Traffic Safety Administration, pp. IV:115, IV:219

National Hockey League (NHL), p. I:210

National Home Builders Association, p. IV:63

National Hospital Discharge Survey, p. III:152

National Instant Criminal Background Check System, p. IV:46-47

National Institute for Occupational Safety and Health, p. III:141-142

National Institute of Allergies and Infectious Diseases
— *See:* NIAID

National Institute of Child Health and Human Development, p. III:45, II:201

National Institute of Diabetes & Digestive & Kidney Diseases
— *See:* NIDDK

National Institute of General Medical Sciences, pp. III:400-401

National Institute of Justice, pp. IV:132, IV:220

National Institute of Mental Health, pp. III:116, III:172, III:248, III:255-256, II:302

National Institute on Aging, pp. III:148, III:204

National Institute on Drug Abuse, p. III:128

National Institutes of Health, pp. III:3, III:28, III:76, III:105, III:143, III:163, III:167, III:400-402, III:535t

National Insurance Crime Bureau, p. IV:71

National Literacy Act, p. II:191

National Long-Term Care Surveys, p. III:204

National Longitudinal Study on Adolescent Health, p. IV:136

National Longitudinal Survey of Youth, p. IV:134

National Medical Care [company], p. IV:94

National Office of Drug Policy, p. IV:168

National origin-based discrimination, pp. I:161, I:163, I:167

National Park Service, p. IV:227

National Pharmaceutical Stockpike, p. III:392

National Prosecutors Survey, p. IV:282

National Public Radio, p. III:75

National Reading Panel, pp. II:201-202

National Registry of Emergency Medical Technicians, p. III:357

National School Lunch Program, pp. III:113-114, III:468t

National School Safety Center, pp. II:247-248

National Sleep Foundation, pp. III:140, III:143

National Survey on Drug Abuse, p. IV:157

National Tactical Officers Association, p. IV:211

National Vaccine Injury Compensation Program, p. III:97

National Water Quality Inventory, p. III:322

Native American religion, pp. II:134-135

Native Americans, pp. II:55, I:252-253, III:337

Native Hawaiians, pp. II:70-71

Native North Americans, pp. II:6-7, II:24

Natural history museums, p. I:229

Naturopathy, pp. III:78, III:80

Navajo Indian tribe, pp. II:72-73

Navigators, pp. I:22, I:296t

NBA, pp. I:211-212
— *See also:* National Basketball Association
— *See:* National Basketball Association (NBA)

NC-17, p. I:231

NCAA, p. I:363t
— *See:* National Collegiate Athletic Association (NCAA)

NCCAM
— *See:* National Center for Complementary and Alternative

Nebraska, pp. II:218, III:369

Needle use, pp. III:54, III:101

Neglect of elderly, p. III:199

Neonatal deaths, pp. III:10, III:312

Neoplasms, pp. III:3-4, III:235-236, III:238
— *See also:* Cancer
— *See also:* Malignancies

Nephritis, nephrosis, and nephrotic syndrome, pp. III:4-5
— *See also:* Kidney diseases

Obesity continued:
— eating habits, p. III:90
— elderly population, p. III:210
— *Journal of the American Medical Association*, p. III:405
— prevention programs, p. III:407
— risky behaviors, pp. III:20-21, III:107, III:109, III:115, III:425*t*
— women's health, pp. III:16-17, III:21
Obsessive-compulsive disorder, pp. III:247, III:250, III:252-253
Obstetricians, pp. III:150, III:303, III:341, III:415
Occupational fatalities, pp. I:149, I:151, I:156, I:349*t*
Occupational Safety and Health Administration, pp. I:153-154
Occupational therapy aides, p. I:53
Occupations, p. II:296
— decline, pp. I:51, I:54-55, I:303*t*
— degrees conferred, pp. I:296*t*
— growth rate, p. I:303*t*
— illegal labor, p. I:43
— independent contractors, pp. I:69, I:307*t*
— job declines, p. I:303*t*
— job openings, pp. I:296*t*
— retirement, p. I:296*t*
— workplace violence, pp. IV:60-61, I:351*t*
O'Connor, Justice Sandra Day, pp. IV:96, IV:246
Offbearers
— *See also:* machine feeders and offbearers p. I:54
Office clerks (general), pp. I:61-62
Office machine operators, pp. I:54-55
Office of Alternative Medicine, p. III:81
Office of Homeland Security, pp. IV:187-189
Office of Juvenile Justice and Delinquency Prevention, p. IV:136, IV:142
Office of National Drug Control Policy, pp. IV:174, IV:263
Ohio, pp. II:63, IV:138, III:190, III:367, III:409, III:417
Oils, p. III:83
Oklahoma City, pp. I:229, IV:285
Older Americans Act, p. IV:107
On Death and Dying, pp. III:212, III:374
On Killing: The Psychological Cost of Learning to Kill in War and Society, p. IV:145
Oneandonly.com, p. I:284
Online auctions, p. I:286
Online banking, p. I:273
Online churches, pp. II:144, II:362*t*
Online dating services, pp. I:284, I:380*t*
Online gambling, p. IV:335*t*
Online search terms, pp. I:282-283, I:379*t*
Online shopping, pp. I:273, I:277, I:279
Online travel spending, pp. I:196-197, I:360*t*
Opera, pp. I:185, I:216, I:224-225
Operation Child Watch, p. I:45
Operation Pipeline, pp. IV:223-224
Operators, p. I:54
Operators, fabricators, and laborers, pp. I:31-32, I:43, I:69-70
Ophthalmologists, p. III:341
Opium Poppy Control Act, p. IV:12
Optometry degrees conferred, pp. II:286, II:290
Oral cavity cancers, p. III:156
Oral contraceptives, p. III:161
Order Clerks, pp. I:54-55

Orderlies and attendants
— *See:* nursing aides, orderlies, and attendants
Oregon, pp. II:64, III:216, IV:277
Organic foods, pp. III:87-88, III:458*t*
Oriental medicine (traditional), pp. III:78, III:80
Orthopedic surgeons, p. III:341
Osama bin Laden, p. I:283
Osteopaths, pp. III:78-79, II:286, II:290, III:336
Osteoporosis, pp. III:168, III:328
Out of Control: Seattle's Flawed Response to Protests Against the World Trade Organization
— 214,
Outdoor track, p. I:208
Ovarian cancer, pp. III:19, III:67-68, III:158
Ovarian surgeries, p. III:151
Over-the-counter medications, pp. III:128, III:474*t*
Overweight, pp. III:17, III:90, III:107, III:210
Oxycodone, p. III:130
Oxycontin, pp. III:129-130
Oxygen-depleting substances, pp. III:323-325
Oxymetholone, p. IV:153
Oxytocin, p. III:23
P-notes, p. IV:88
Pacific Islanders
— *See also:* Asians and Pacific Islanders
— abortions, pp. II:10, II:12-13
— advanced classes, p. II:259
— Bachelor's Degrees conferred, pp. II:287-288
— causes of death, pp. III:8, III:43
— doctoral degrees conferred, pp. II:289-290
— drug arrests, p. IV:161
— drug use, pp. IV:159-160
— educational attainment, pp. II:152-153
— fertility rates, p. II:321*t*
— HIV, p. III:289
— income, pp. I:75, I:82
— Internet use, pp. I:270-271
— interracial marriages, p. II:55
— law enforcement personnel, p. IV:203
— live births, pp. II:10, II:321*t*
— low birth weight, p. III:40
— population, pp. II:24, II:71, II:347*t*
— population mobility, p. II:38
— salaries, p. I:38
— single-parent households, p. II:61
— Total Fertility Rates, pp. II:6, II:8
— vocational education credits accumulated, p. II:258
Packagers
— *See:* hand packers and packagers
Paid leave, pp. I:129, I:133
Pain, p. I:155
Pain control, pp. III:213-214
Paintball, pp. I:200-201
Painting, p. I:218
Pakistani population, p. II:74
Palliative care
— *See:* Hospice care
Palm Beach County Health Department (FL), p. III:392
Pancreas surgeries, p. III:151

Phytochemicals, p. III:90

Piaget, Jean, p. II:203

The Pill, pp. II:15, III:304-305

Pineal gland surgeries, p. III:151

Pipefitters and steamfitters
— *See:* plumbers, pipefitters, and steamfitters

Pistols, p. II:245

Pituitary gland surgeries, p. III:151

Placebos, p. III:76

Plague, pp. III:58, III:60, III:392, III:442*t*

Planes, p. I:190

Plants, p. I:185

Plastic surgery
— *See:* Cosmetic surgery

The Playboy Channel, p. III:280

Plays (nonmusical), p. I:216

Playstation 2, p. I:283

Plug Uglies, p. IV:43

Plumbers, pipefitters, and steamfitters, pp. I:22, I:27-28

PM-10
— *See:* Particulate matter
— *See:* Particulate matter (PM-10)

PMDD
— *See:* Premenstrual dysphoric disorder

Pneumonia, pp. III:5, II:22
— Baby Boom generation, pp. III:69-70
— by century, p. III:2
— by race/ethnicity, pp. III:8-9
— childhood immunizations, pp. III:96, III:98
— funding, p. III:401
— immunizations, p. III:99
— leading diseases, p. III:4

Pocket-picking, p. IV:69

Podiatry degrees conferred, pp. II:286, II:290

Pokemon, p. I:283

Poland, pp. I:47, II:163, I:187

Police and detective supervisors, pp. I:22-23, I:27

Police department technology, pp. IV:208-209

Police forces, pp. IV:23, IV:43-44
— by sex, p. IV:200
— deaths, pp. IV:210-212, IV:217-218
— employment, pp. IV:21-22
— excessive force, pp. IV:213-214

Police pursuits, pp. IV:220-221

Police shootings, pp. IV:363*t*

Policy processing clerks
— *See:* insurance claims and policy processing clerks

Polio, pp. III:55-56, III:94-96

Polish, p. II:76

Political organizations, pp. I:245-246

Political-party affiliation, pp. II:99, II:350*t*
— by party, pp. II:98, II:114
— by race/ethnicity, p. II:108
— by sex, pp. II:100-101

Pollution, pp. III:315-316, III:326-328

Ponds, pp. III:323, III:325

Population, pp. II:70-72, II:343*t*
— births, p. II:4
— by sex, p. II:323*t*

Population continued:
— central cities, pp. II:27-28
— dependency ratio, p. II:22
— foreign-born, pp. II:348*t*
— geographic distribution, pp. II:24-25, II:30, II:36, II:331*t*
— growth rates, pp. II:37, I:302*t*
— households, pp. II:333*t*
— metropolitan areas, pp. II:27-28, II:330*t*
— Metropolitan Statistical Areas (MSAs), p. II:29
— MSAs, p. II:29
— never-married adults, p. II:339*t*
— nonmetropolitan areas, pp. II:27, II:330*t*
— over age 65, p. I:347*t*
— rural areas, p. II:329*t*
— suburban areas, pp. II:27-28, II:329*t*
— Total Fertility Rates, p. II:4
— urban areas, p. II:329*t*
— youth, pp. II:327*t*

Population changes in geographic areas, p. II:39

Population density, pp. II:30-31, IV:57-58, II:330*t*

Population mobility, pp. II:38-39, II:331*t*

Population Replacement Rate, pp. II:4, II:6, II:8

Pornography, pp. IV:108, III:280-281, I:282

Portland (OR), p. IV:124

Portuguese (language), p. II:76

Posse Comitatus Act of 1878, p. IV:24

Post-traumatic stress disorder, pp. III:247, III:252-253

Postal Inspection Service, p. IV:227

Postal Service clerks, pp. I:1, I:13, I:22-23, I:27-28, I:293*t*

Postneonatal deaths, p. III:312

Pottery, p. I:218

Poultry, p. III:83

Poverty rate
— by race/ethnicity, p. IV:53
— children, p. II:335*t*
— family demographics, pp. I:315*t*
— juveniles arrested, p. IV:134
— living arrangements, p. II:47
— minimum wage, p. I:91
— single-parent households, p. II:60
— U.S. Government definition, pp. I:88-89
— working families, pp. I:92-93

Powdered cocaine, p. IV:162

Powell v Alabama, p. IV:281

Precision, production, craft, repair occupations, pp. I:20, I:31, I:43, I:69-70, I:296*t*

Pregnancy-based discrimination, pp. I:161, I:164, I:167

Pregnancy, ectopic
— *See:* Ectopic pregnancy

Premarin, p. III:167

Premarital sex, pp. III:267-268, III:502*t*

Premenstrual dysphoric disorder (PMDD), p. III:170

Prepress technicians and workers, p. I:54

Preprimary schools, pp. II:222-223, II:382*t*

Presbyterian Church (U.S.A.), pp. II:136-138

Presbyterians, pp. II:130-133, II:135

Preschool teachers, pp. I:58-59

Prescription drug plans, p. I:133

Prescription drugs, p. III:75

Public schools continued:
— college enrollment, p. II:150
— funding, pp. II:211, II:213
— graduates, p. II:148
— mathematics proficiency, p. II:237
Public universities, pp. II:269, II:279, II:281
Public utilities
— *See:* transportation and public utilities
Publishers (desktop), p. I:52
Pueblo Indian tribe, pp. II:72-73
Pulmonary diseases, pp. III:69-70
Punctures, p. I:155
Pupil-teacher ratio, pp. II:180, II:371*t*
Purse-snatching, pp. IV:69-70
Q fever, p. III:392
Quadruplets, p. III:39
Quayle, Dan, p. II:62
Quilting, p. I:218
Quinlan, Karen Ann, p. III:188
R-rated movies, p. I:230
Race-based discrimination, pp. I:161, I:167
Race/ethnicity
— abortions, pp. II:12-13, II:321*t*
— births, pp. II:10, I:40, II:319*t*
— cancer survival rates, pp. III:156, III:158
— causes of death, pp. III:8, II:21, III:28, III:30, III:32, III:34, III:43, III:422*t*
— computer learning opportunities, p. II:263
— correctional population, pp. IV:19-20
— crib death, p. III:45
— death row inmates, p. IV:244
— deaths, pp. III:15, II:21
— diseases, pp. III:26, III:52
— domestic homicides, pp. IV:48-49
— drug arrests, pp. IV:161-162
— drug use, p. IV:162
— earnings, p. I:71
— educational attainment, pp. I:39, I:112, I:118, II:151-152, II:258-259, II:287-290, I:300*t*
— employment, pp. I:35, I:37, I:299*t*
— exercise habits, p. III:92
— federal law enforcement officers, p. IV:227
— hate crimes, p. IV:290
— health problems, p. III:20
— housing, p. II:35
— illicit substance use, p. III:126
— income, pp. I:82, I:311*t*
— infant mortality, pp. III:313, III:517*t*
— Internet use, pp. I:270-272, I:377*t*
— law enforcement, pp. IV:203, IV:360*t*
— life expectancy, pp. II:20, III:47
— literacy, pp. II:154, II:159
— live births, pp. II:10, II:321*t*
— low birth weight, pp. III:308-309, III:516*t*
— mammograms, p. III:18
— marriage, pp. II:52-53
— maternal mortality, p. III:22
— mathematics proficiency, p. II:161
— mobility, p. II:38

Race/ethnicity continued:
— murder, p. IV:52
— physicians, p. III:337
— political-party affiliation, p. II:108
— population, pp. II:24, II:70, II:343*t*
— Population Replacement Rate, pp. II:6, II:8
— poverty, p. IV:53
— prisoners, pp. IV:238-239, IV:242
— single-parent households, p. II:61
— Total Fertility Rates, pp. II:6, II:8
— volunteering, pp. I:241, I:370*t*
— voter turnout, p. II:106
— youth gangs, pp. IV:43-44
Racial discrimination, p. IV:162
Racial profiling, pp. IV:222-225, IV:365*t*
Racketeering and sentencing, p. IV:108
Radiation, pp. III:105, III:159
Radioisotope scans, p. III:152
Radiologic technologists, p. III:355
Railroad brake, signal, and switch operators, pp. I:54-55
Railroad conductors and yardmasters, p. I:54
Ranchers
— *See:* farmers and ranchers
Rape, pp. IV:55-56, IV:58, IV:318*t*
— actual crimes reported, p. IV:5
— household income, pp. IV:31, IV:38
— juveniles arrested, pp. IV:133, IV:135, IV:137-138
— rate fluctuation, pp. IV:25-26
— recidivism, p. IV:260
Reading proficiency, pp. II:159-160, II:163, II:200-202, II:366*t*
Reagan, President Ronald, pp. IV:46, IV:277
Real estate, p. I:292*t*
Real estate, rental, and leasing services, pp. I:104-105
Reality Check, pp. II:170, II:177
Receptionists and information clerks, pp. I:61-62
Recidivism
— by race, p. IV:166
— by type of crime committed, pp. IV:260-261, IV:263
— prison industries, pp. IV:256-259
— state prisoners, pp. IV:374*t*
Recommended Energy Allowance, p. III:89
Recreation, pp. I:185, I:242, I:244-246, I:357*t*
Recreational time
— *See:* leisure time
Recreational vehicles (RVs), p. I:190
Rectal cancers, pp. III:156, III:161
Red meat, p. III:83
Registered nurses, p. III:523*t*
— growing occupations, p. I:58
— job openings, pp. I:24-25, I:61-62
— nursing school graduates, pp. III:347-348
— retirement, pp. I:22-23
— supply, p. III:349
— worker shortages, p. I:59
Rehabilitation Act, p. III:232
Rehabilitation programs, p. IV:263
Relationship Web sites, pp. I:284, I:380*t*
Religion-based discrimination, pp. I:161, I:167
Religion surfers, pp. II:142, II:361*t*

Religions, pp. II:358t
— attendance at services, pp. I:233, I:249-250, I:343t
— Christian churches, p. II:134
— gains/losses in membership, pp. II:359t
— membership, pp. I:252-253, II:358t
— traditional denominations, pp. II:130-133
— volunteering, pp. I:242, I:244-246
— voting preferences, p. II:110
Religious activities, p. II:142
Religious diversity, p. I:164
Religious organizations, pp. I:247-249, I:371t
Renal disease, pp. III:2, III:380
Reno, Janet, p. I:50
Rensselaer Polytechnic Institute, p. II:280
Rental households, pp. II:35, III:195, II:331t
Repair occupations
— *See:* precision, production, craft, repair occupations
Repeat offenders, p. IV:206
Repetitive-strain injuries, p. III:236
Report on Smoking and Health, pp. III:107, III:136
Reproduction, p. III:291
Republicans, p. II:98
Research grants, p. III:81
Reservoirs, pp. III:323, III:325
Residency, pp. II:287-290
Residential treatment centers, p. III:264
Resistance machines, pp. I:200, I:202
Respiratory diseases, p. III:5
— birth defects, p. III:310
— causes of death, pp. III:3-4, III:8-10
— causes of disability, pp. III:227-228, III:235-236, III:238
— children, p. III:229
— surgical procedures, p. III:150
— therapeutic procedures, p. III:152
Restaurant dining, pp. I:180, I:357t
Restaurant expenditures, pp. III:109-110
Retail buyers
— *See:* wholesale and retail buyers
Retail trade, pp. I:6, I:61, I:104-105, I:157-158, I:292t
Retirement, pp. I:23, I:344t
— age group, pp. I:22, I:24, I:27, I:127, I:139, I:344t
— dependency ratio, p. I:142
— employee benefits, p. I:136
— household expenses, p. I:145
— income, pp. I:128-129, I:133
— occupations, pp. I:22-23, I:296t
Rett's Syndrome, p. III:258
Rheumatism, pp. III:227-228
Rhode Island, pp. II:64, II:217, IV:224, III:338
Ridge, Tom, p. IV:188
Rifles, p. II:245
Riley, Richard, p. II:263
Risk behaviors, pp. III:489t
Ritalin, pp. III:129, III:165, III:171-174, II:302-303, II:407t
    III:483t
River water pollution, pp. III:323, III:325
R.J. Reynolds, p. III:138
Road rage, p. III:140
Robbery, p. IV:373t

Robbery continued:
— corrections expenditures, p. IV:249
— household income, pp. IV:31, IV:38
— juveniles arrested, pp. IV:133, IV:135, IV:137-138
— murders, p. IV:58
— rate fluctuation, pp. IV:25-26
— recidivism, p. IV:260
Robert Wood Johnson Medical School, p. III:167
Rockets, p. II:245
Rocky Mountain Spotted Fever, p. III:95
Roe v. Wade, p. III:306
Rohypnol, pp. III:120, IV:154
Roman Catholic Church, pp. II:136-138, II:242
Romania, p. II:163
Room and board, pp. II:271, II:277
Roosevelt, President Franklin D., p. IV:230
Roper Starch Worldwide, p. I:187
Rose, Mike, p. II:155
Rowing, p. I:208
Rubella, pp. III:55-56, III:94-95
— *See also:* German measles
Rubeola, p. III:56
Rudolph, Eric Robert, p. IV:181
Runaways, pp. IV:101, IV:136
Running, p. I:202
Running on Ritalin, p. II:303
Rural population, pp. II:27, II:329t
Russia, pp. II:5, I:187
Russian (language), pp. II:76-77
Russian Federation, pp. II:163-165, III:334
RVs, p. I:190
— *See:* Recreational vehicles (RVs)
Sacramento (CA), p. IV:72
SAD
— *See:* Social anxiety disorders
Safety in schools, pp. II:247-248
Safety issues, pp. I:171-172
Sailer, Steven, p. II:55
St. John's Wort, pp. III:75-76, III:81, III:87, III:162-163
Salaries
— athletes, pp. I:212, I:364t
— baggage screeners, p. IV:233
— law enforcement personnel, p. IV:209
— medical school graduates, p. III:414
— net worth, p. I:38
— productivity, p. I:120
— teachers, pp. II:182, II:193-194
— weekly, p. I:128
Sales occupations, pp. I:20, I:32, I:61-62, I:69-70, I:296t
Sales of educational services, p. II:279
Salk, Dr. Jonas, p. III:95
Sally Ride Academy for Girls, p. II:309
Salmonella infections, p. III:111
Salts, pp. III:20-21
Same-sex partners, pp. II:64, I:136
— *See also:* Gays
— *See also:* Homosexuals
— *See also:* Lesbians
Sarafem, p. III:170

Satellite television receivers, p. I:227

SATs, pp. II:166, II:171, II:217, II:293, II:368t

Saudi Arabia, p. IV:184

Saum, William, p. IV:118

Saunders, Dr. Cicely, pp. III:376, III:378

Savage Inequalities: Children in America's Schools, p. II:221

Savings, pp. I:347t

Savings & loans fraud, p. IV:109

Saw palmetto, p. III:75

Schistosomiasis, p. III:326

Schizophrenia, pp. III:247-249

Schlafly, Phyllis, p. II:223

Schlosser, Eric, p. III:110

Scholastic Aptitude Test
— *See:* SATs

Scholastic Assessment Test
— *See:* SATs

School-based health centers, pp. III:102-104, III:464t

School choice, pp. II:239-240

School finances, pp. II:220-221, II:379t

School performance, p. II:385t

School-to-Work Opportunities Act, p. II:262

School vending machines, p. II:310

School vouchers, pp. II:241-242

School-year duration, p. II:254

Schools, p. I:34
— bullying, pp. II:249-250
— by type, pp. II:211, II:222-223, II:231, II:233, II:237
— crime, pp. IV:128, IV:130, II:245
— expulsions, pp. IV:131-132
— problems perceived by teachers, p. II:198
— problems perceived by the general public, p. II:199
— youth gangs, pp. IV:42-43

Schools and Staffing Survey, pp. II:191, II:198

Science museums, p. I:229

Sciences, advanced
— *See:* Advanced sciences

Scientific and technical services
— *See:* professional, scientific, and technical services

Scientology, pp. II:134-135, I:252-253

Scofflaws, p. IV:266

Search engines, p. I:278

Seasonal workers, p. I:46

Seconal, p. III:129

Second homes, p. I:194

Secondary education, pp. I:11, II:189-190

Secondary school teachers, pp. I:58-59, I:61-62

Secret Service, p. IV:228

Secretaries, stenographers, and typists, pp. I:32, I:61-62

Secularism, pp. I:252-253

Securities and Exchange Commission, pp. IV:84-85, IV:109

Security measures, p. I:281

Sedatives, pp. III:119, III:128

Seeds, p. I:185

Segregation, p. II:345t

Seizure disorders, pp. III:229, III:231

Self-employment income, p. I:145

Senior citizens, pp. III:187-188

Senior citizens continued:
— *See also:* Aging population
— *See also:* Elderly population
— living arrangements, pp. III:193-194
— media images, pp. III:221-222
— Medicaid expenditures, p. III:220
— Medicare expenditures, p. III:219
— quality of life, p. III:210
— risk behaviors, pp. III:489t
— suicides, p. III:260

Sentencing, pp. IV:108-110, IV:333t

SEOG, p. II:273

Sepsis, bacterial
— *See:* Bacterial sepsis

September 11, 2001
— airline passenger screening, p. IV:232
— corporate responses, p. I:171
— deaths, p. IV:190
— food-borne terrorism, p. III:112
— genetic engineering, p. III:106
— Immigration and Naturalization Service, p. IV:227
— racial profiling, p. IV:224
— terrorism, pp. IV:177, IV:182
— timeline, pp. IV:192-194
— workplace safety, p. I:150

Septicemia, pp. III:4-5, III:7-8

Service occupations
— employment, pp. I:31-32, I:291t
— independent contractors, pp. I:69-70
— injuries in the workplace, p. I:156

Serviceman's Readjustment Act, pp. II:150, II:273
— *See also:* GI Bill

Services industry, pp. II:256-257, II:262
— employment, pp. I:1, I:3-4, I:6
— productivity, p. I:102

Seventh Day Adventists, p. II:132

Severance pay, p. I:134

Sewing, p. I:218

Sewing machine operators, p. I:54

Sex-based crimes, pp. IV:10, IV:101

Sex-based discrimination
— case resolutions, pp. I:163, I:167
— charges filed with the EEOC, p. I:161

Sex education, p. III:103

Sex information, pp. III:282-283, III:505t

Sex offenders, pp. IV:121, IV:336t

Sex on TV, p. I:231

Sexes
— *See also:* Females
— *See also:* Males
— *See also:* Men
— *See also:* Women
— deaths, pp. II:17, II:21
— earnings, pp. I:71, II:295
— educational attainment, pp. II:258-259, I:262, II:283, II:285, I:318t
— employment, pp. I:65-67, I:69, I:174, I:298t I:355t
— high school athletes, p. I:362t

Special education programs continued:
  407*t*
Special education teachers, pp. I:22, I:24-25, I:58
Special units of police departments, pp. IV:206-207
Special weapons and tactics (SWAT), p. IV:211
Specialized museums, p. I:229
Specialty hospitals, p. III:365
Speech impairments, pp. III:229-231, II:298-299
Speed, p. III:124
Spending on sports, p. I:206
The Spice Channel, p. III:280
Spinal problems, pp. III:227-228
Sponges, p. II:15
Sports, pp. I:199-200
—high school athletes, p. I:204
—injuries, p. I:205
—marketing, p. I:213
—online auctions, p. I:286
—professional, p. I:210
—scholarships, p. I:206
—supplies, p. I:185
—teenagers, pp. I:201-202, I:361*t*
—television, p. I:211
Sports Illustrated, p. I:213
Spouse abuse, p. IV:10
Sprains, p. I:155
Springfield (OR), p. IV:129
Stalking, pp. IV:119-120, IV:336*t*
Standardized tests, pp. II:168, II:170, II:218, II:367*t*
Stanford Sleep Disorders Clinic, p. III:144
Stanford University, pp. II:268, II:280, II:294
Starter pistols, p. II:245
State and local grants, p. II:279
State Department, p. IV:183
State government, pp. I:1, I:9-10, II:211, I:256, I:292*t*
State mental hospitals, p. III:264
State prisoners, pp. IV:236, IV:369*t*
State University of New York at Buffalo, p. II:292
STDs
—*See:* Sexually transmitted diseases
Steamfitters
—*See:* plumbers, pipefitters, and steamfitters
Stenographers and typists
—*See:* Secretaries, stenographers, and typists
Stents, pp. III:25, III:151
Sterility, p. II:14
Sterilization, pp. III:304-305
Steroid use, p. III:104
Stimulants, pp. IV:11, III:119, III:128, IV:151-152, III:173
Stock performance, p. I:103
Stomach cancer, pp. III:67-68, III:156
Streams, pp. III:323, III:325
Street gangs, p. IV:44
Street, Picabo, p. I:209
Stress
—cancer, p. III:161
—morning habits, pp. III:139-140
—nighttime habits, pp. III:143-144
—noonday habits, pp. III:141-142

Stress continued:
—risk behaviors, p. III:108
—vacations, p. III:145
Strikes, p. I:210
Strokes, p. II:18
—*See also:* Cerebrovascular disease
—Baby Boom generation, p. III:69
—causes of death, pp. III:2-5, III:8-9
—disabilities, pp. III:227, III:243, III:401
—women, pp. III:12-13
Students
—*See also:* Children
—*See also:* Juveniles
—*See also:* Teenagers
—*See also:* Youth
—deaths in school, pp. II:243-244
—disabilities, p. II:258
—financial assistance, pp. II:395*t*
—indebtedness, pp. II:275, II:277-278, III:414
—LEP, pp. II:306-307
—limited English proficiency, p. II:306
Students Against Drunk Driving, p. IV:113
Subsidized commuting, p. I:135
Substance abuse, pp. IV:53, III:102, III:411, III:471*t*
Substance Abuse and Mental Health Services Administration (SAMHSA), pp. IV:157, IV:159, III:412
Substance use, pp. III:121-123
Suburbs, pp. II:27-28, II:30, II:329*t*
Sudden Infant Death Syndrome, pp. III:10, III:437*t*
—*See also:* Crib death
—*See also:* SIDS
Sudden Sniffing Death Syndrome, p. III:120
Sugars, pp. III:20-21
Suicide, p. III:35
Suicides, pp. III:431*t*
—aging population, pp. III:204, III:261
—causes of death, pp. III:4, III:8, II:21, III:131
—Columbine High School, p. II:243
—firearms-related, p. IV:39
—men, pp. II:18, III:34-36, III:260
—mental health, pp. III:248-249
—school-based health centers, p. III:103
—terrorists, p. IV:190
Suicides, altruistic
—*See:* Altruistic suicides
Suicides, anomic
—*See:* Anomic suicides
Suicides, egoistic
—*See:* Egoistic suicides
Suicides, fatalistic
—*See:* Fatalistic suicides
Sulfa drugs, pp. III:2, II:22
Sulfur dioxide, pp. III:316-317
Sunbeam Corp., p. IV:84
Super Nintendo, p. IV:145
Supplemental Educational Opportunity Grants
—*See:* SEOG
Supplemental income, p. II:183
Supplemental pay, p. I:129

Support staff
— *See:* teachers and support staff
Suppositories, p. II:15
Supreme Court, pp. IV:24, IV:277, IV:281-282
Surfing, p. I:200
Surgeon General of the United States, pp. III:83, III:403
Surgeons
— *See:* Physicians and Surgeons
— *See:* physicians and surgeons
Surgical hospitals, pp. III:364-365
Surgical procedures, pp. III:150-151, III:154-155
Survival rates for cancers, pp. III:13, III:19, III:447*t*
    III:478*t*
Sweden, pp. III:42, II:163-164, III:334
Swedish (language), p. II:77
Swimming, pp. I:200, I:208-209
Switch operators
— *See:* railroad brake, signal, and switch operators
Switchboard operators (including answering service)
— occupations in decline, p. I:54
Switzerland, pp. II:163-165
Symbionese Liberation Army, p. IV:181
Symphonies, pp. I:224-225
Synthroid, pp. III:167-168
Syphilis, pp. III:51-52, III:58, III:442*t*
Systematic phonics, pp. II:200-202
Systems analysts, pp. I:58-59, I:61-62
— *See also:* computer systems analysts
Tagalog, pp. II:76-77
T'ai chi, pp. I:200-201
Tailhook, pp. I:162, I:166
Taiwanese population, p. II:74
Tajikistan, p. II:163
Talking Back to Prozac, p. III:64
Tanning, p. III:147
Taoism, pp. II:134-135, II:140-141, I:252-253
Task Force on Antimicrobial Resistance, p. III:330
Tattoos, pp. III:148, I:283
Tax evasion and sentencing, p. IV:108
Taxes, pp. II:211, II:213
TB
— *See:* Tuberculosis
Teacher Followup Survey, p. II:191
Teacher-pupil ratio, pp. II:180, II:371*t*
Teachers, p. II:371*t*
— by sex, pp. II:182, II:372*t*
— certification, pp. II:186, II:373*t*
— dissatisfaction, p. II:374*t*
— educational attainment, pp. II:184-185, II:373*t*
— elementary schools, pp. I:24-25, I:58, I:61-62
— preschool, pp. I:58-59
— problems perceived in schools, p. II:198
— retirement, pp. I:22-23
— salaries, pp. II:182, II:193-194, II:374*t*
— secondary schools, pp. I:58-59, I:61-62
— shortages, p. II:189
— Singapore, p. II:188
— special education, pp. I:22, I:24-25, I:58, I:296*t*
— supplemental income, p. II:183

Teachers continued:
— turnover, pp. II:191-192
— uncertified, p. II:187
— worker shortages, p. I:59
— workplace assaults, pp. I:157-158
Teachers' aides, pp. I:22-23, I:296*t*
Teachers and support staff, p. I:11
Team Marketing Report, p. I:212
Technical and related support occupations, pp. I:20, I:296*t*
Technical services
— *See:* professional, scientific, and technical services
Technical, sales, and administrative support occupations, p. I:31-32
Technicians and related support occupations, pp. I:32, I:69
Technology and communications, pp. II:256-257, II:262
Teenagers, pp. IV:33, IV:75, IV:106, IV:325*t*
— *See also:* Children
— *See also:* Juveniles
— *See also:* Students
— *See also:* Youth
— illegal labor, p. I:43
— illicit substance use, pp. III:117-120, III:132, III:134
— Internet use, pp. I:278-279, I:379
— physical education classes, p. I:203
— reading habits, p. I:221
— religious services attendance, p. I:373*t*
— sedatives, p. III:119
— sexual activity, pp. III:282-285, III:505*t*
— smoking, pp. III:137-138
— sports, pp. I:199, I:201-202, I:204
Telemarketing, p. IV:82
Telemedicine, pp. III:361-362, III:524*t*
Telephone operators, p. I:54
Television, pp. III:221-222, I:226-227, I:231, I:268, III:280, III:491*t*
Tellers, p. I:54
Tendinitis, p. I:155
Tennessee, pp. II:63, II:196, II:246
Tennis, pp. I:202, I:208-209
Terrorism
— civil liberty, p. IV:185
— deaths, pp. IV:183, IV:190-191, IV:356*t*
— domestic, pp. IV:180, IV:182
— global, p. IV:177
— timeline, pp. IV:178-179
Terrorism Information and Prevention System (TIPS), p. IV:186
Test scores, pp. II:171-175
Testosterone levels, pp. III:6, III:29, III:151, IV:153
Tests, standardized
— *See:* standardized tests
Tetanus, pp. III:94-95
Texas, pp. IV:122, IV:284, III:415, III:417
— Asian population, p. II:75
— education for gifted children, p. II:305
— expulsions from school, p. II:246
— gay-couple households, pp. II:63-64
— geographic distribution of elderly population, p. III:190
— hospital beds, p. III:369

Texas continued:
— standardized tests, p. II:218
— vacation spending, p. I:190
— youth gangs, p. IV:138
Thai population, p. II:74
Thailand, p. III:42
Theatres, pp. I:185, I:217, I:224-225
Theft, p. II:245
— arrests, pp. IV:68-70
— by property stolen, p. IV:76
— correction expenditures, p. IV:249
— crimes reported to the police, p. IV:373*t*
— juveniles, p. IV:136
— property crime, pp. IV:4, IV:7-8
Theology degrees conferred, pp. II:286, II:290
Therapeutic procedures, pp. III:152-154
They Say You're Crazy, p. III:170
Third International Mathematics and Science Study
— *See:* TIMSS
Third National Incidence Study of Child Abuse and Neglect, p. IV:107
Thomas, Clarence, pp. I:162, I:165
Thomas, Timothy, p. IV:204
Thompson, Tommy, pp. III:73, III:112
Thyroid gland surgeries, p. III:151
Ticket prices, pp. I:212-213, I:222, I:364*t*
Time for Kids, p. II:249
Time for Life: Surprising Ways Americans Use Their Time, p. I:181
Timelines
— drug-control legislation, p. IV:12
— hate crimes, p. IV:286
— law enforcement, pp. IV:197-198
— September 11, 2001, pp. IV:192-194
— terrorism, pp. IV:178-179
TIMSS, pp. II:188, II:195, II:253-254
Title IX, pp. I:204, II:308
Tobacco advertising, p. III:138
Tobacco consumption, pp. IV:12, IV:148, IV:352*t*
Tobacco control programs, pp. III:102, III:408-409
Tomatoes, p. III:87
Tonsillitis, p. III:229
Tort reform, p. III:417
Total Fertility Rate, p. III:295
Total Fertility Rates, pp. II:5-8
Touch football, p. I:202
Toxemia, p. III:23
Toxic Shock Syndrome, pp. III:61-62, III:444*t*
Toyota Camry, p. IV:71
Toys, pp. II:66, I:286
Toys and sports supplies, p. I:185
Tracheal cancer, p. III:67
Track and field, p. I:209
Trade, pp. I:6, II:256-257, II:262
Traditional workers, pp. I:71-72
Traffic deaths, pp. II:18, IV:115-116
Train robbery, p. IV:245
Tranquilizers, pp. III:119, III:128, IV:151
Trans fat, p. III:109

Transportation
— assaults in the workplace, pp. I:157-158
— child rearing costs, pp. II:66-67
— college costs, p. II:271
— injuries in the workplace, p. I:156
— occupational fatalities, p. I:151
Transportation and material moving occupations, pp. I:20, I:43, I:296*t*
— *See also:* material moving occupations
Transportation and public utilities, pp. I:6, I:292*t*
Transportation and warehousing, pp. I:104-105
Transportation Security Administration, p. IV:233
Traumatic brain injury, p. II:298
Travel, pp. I:190-192
Travel agencies, pp. I:194, I:196-197, I:360*t*
Treadmill exercise, p. I:200
Treason, p. IV:245
Tricyclic antidepressants, p. III:64
Trigonometry, p. II:259
Trimox, pp. III:166-167
Trinidad and Tobago, p. II:163
Triplets, pp. III:39, III:299-300
Truancy, p. IV:101
The Truly Disadvantaged, p. II:53
Trust fund assets of Medicare, p. III:528*t*
Tuberculosis, pp. III:2-3, III:58-59
— cases and rates, pp. III:442*t*
— foreign countries, pp. III:332-334
Tufts University, pp. III:175, II:294
Tuition and fees, pp. II:151, II:269-270, II:272, II:394*t* III:539*t*
— Consumer Price Index, p. II:268
— medical school, p. II:277
— public universities, p. II:279
Tularemia, p. III:392
Turkey, p. I:187
Turkmenistan, p. II:163
Turning the Corner on Father Absence in Black America, p. II:53
Twinkie Defense, p. IV:276
Twins, pp. III:39, III:299-300
Two-parent households, pp. II:46, II:67
Typhoid fever, pp. III:58-59, III:442*t*
Typists
— *See also:* word processors and typists p. I:54
U. S. Customs Service, p. IV:329*t*
Uganda, p. III:332
Ukraine, p. II:163
Ultrasound, p. III:152
Umbilical cord complications, p. III:10
Uncertified teachers, p. II:187
Underemployment, p. I:57
Unemployment, pp. IV:53, I:145
UNESCO, p. II:250
UNICOR, p. IV:255
Uniform Crime Report, pp. IV:3-5, IV:7, IV:9, IV:14, IV:139
Uninsured population, pp. III:384-385
Unions, pp. I:1, I:14, I:16, I:294*t*
Unitarian Universalism, pp. II:134-135, I:252-253

Whites continued:
— voter turnout, p. II:106
Whole language movement, p. II:201
Whole Math Movement, p. II:205
Whole milk, p. III:83
Wholesale and retail buyers (except farm products), p. I:54
Wholesale trade, pp. I:6, I:104-105, I:156, I:292*t*
Whooping Cough, p. III:56
Whyos, p. IV:43
Wiccan, pp. II:134-135
Widowed parents, p. II:59
Willett, Dr. Walter C., pp. III:90, III:109-110
Wilson, Dr. James Q., pp. IV:52, IV:137-138
Wilson, Dr. William Julius, p. II:53
Wiretapping, pp. IV:229-231, IV:366*t*
Wisconsin, pp. IV:122, II:218
Women, p. I:298*t*
— *See also:* Females
— activities of daily living, p. III:204
— age at first marriage, p. II:50
— art purchases, p. I:219
— births, p. III:295
— cancer survival rates, p. III:158
— causes of death, pp. III:6-7, III:12, III:24, III:26, III:30, III:32, III:34, III:36, III:53, III:422*t*
— contraceptive practices, pp. II:14-15, III:514*t*
— cosmetic surgery, pp. III:277, III:279
— creative writing, p. I:219
— deaths, pp. III:15, III:424*t*
— disabled population, pp. III:225, III:236
— diseases, pp. III:13-14, III:18, III:54, III:64, III:116, III:147, III:154, III:160, III:247, III:249, III:262, III:289-290, III:366
— domestic homicides, pp. IV:48-49
— earnings, p. I:71
— educational attainment, pp. I:94, I:262, II:283, II:285
— elderly population, p. III:196
— employment, pp. I:16, I:29-33, I:36, I:65-67, I:69, I:156, I:174-175, II:182, I:262, III:296, III:509*t*
— estrogen, p. II:18
— federal law enforcement personnel, p. IV:226
— household activities, pp. I:181-182
— housing, p. III:195
— income, pp. I:84, I:94
— injuries in the workplace, pp. I:155-156
— Internet use, p. I:276
— life expectancy, pp. II:18-19, III:47
— living arrangements, p. III:192
— mammograms, p. III:18
— Medicare, p. III:380
— modern dance, p. I:219
— occupational fatalities, p. I:156
— online shopping, p. I:277
— physicians, p. III:337
— police officers, p. IV:200
— political-party affiliation, pp. II:100-101
— poverty, pp. I:92-93
— prisoners, pp. IV:18, IV:242
— risk behaviors, pp. III:16-17, III:135-136

Women continued:
— risk factors, p. III:20
— sexual activity, pp. III:269-270
— single-parent households, pp. II:46-47
— specialized museums, p. I:229
— sports, pp. I:206-209, I:363*t*
— state prisons, p. IV:371*t*
— sterility, p. II:14
— suicides, pp. III:260, III:434*t*
— Total Fertility Rate, p. III:295
— violent crime, pp. IV:35-38
— volunteering, pp. I:236-237
— voting in presidential elections, pp. II:102-103
— weaving, p. I:219
Women's Rights Movement, p. I:30
Women's Sports Foundation, p. I:207
Woods, Tiger, p. I:211
Word processors and typists, pp. I:54-55
Work activities, p. I:358*t*
Work hours, pp. I:176-177, I:356*t*
— age groups, p. I:43
— by sex, pp. I:174-175, I:355*t*
— foreign countries, p. I:187
— illegal labor, p. I:43
Work-related injuries and illnesses, p. I:350*t*
Work-related organizations, pp. I:245-246
Work-study programs, p. II:273
Worker shortages, p. I:59
Worker's compensation, pp. I:145, I:153
Workforce participation, pp. III:295-296, I:298*t*
Workforce population
— age groups, p. I:20
— Baby Boomers, p. I:21
— by sex, pp. I:29-30
— earnings, p. I:342*t*
— educational attainment, p. I:56
— fertility rates, p. I:40
— foreign-born, p. I:41
— high school education, p. I:57
— national health care expenditures, p. I:342*t*
— race/ethnicity, pp. I:29-30, I:35, I:41
— unions, p. I:294
Working for Children and Families, p. II:226
Working parents, p. I:183
Workplace assaults, pp. I:157-158
Workplace discrimination, pp. I:158-159
Workplace harassment, p. I:159
Workplace illnesses, pp. I:153, I:349*t*
Workplace injuries, pp. I:153, I:155-156, I:349*t*
Workplace issues, pp. I:164-165, I:351*t*
Workplace safety, pp. I:151-152, I:351*t*
World Church of the Creator, p. IV:288
World Health Organization, pp. III:316, III:332
World Sports Exchange, p. IV:118
World Trade Center, pp. IV:179, IV:183-184, IV:195, I:283
World Trade Organization, p. I:192
WorldCom, p. IV:85
Worldwide Web, pp. I:97, I:233, I:280
Worms, p. I:280